Hawaii The Big Island Revealed
The Ultimate Guidebook; 7th Edition

Published by Wizard Publications, Inc.
Post Office Box 991
Lihuʻe, Hawaiʻi 96766–0991

ISBN: 978–0–9838887–4–1   4075
Library of Congress Control Number 2013943438
Printed in China

Cataloging-in-Publication Data

Doughty, Andrew
    Hawaii the Big Island revealed : the ultimate guidebook / Andrew Doughty. – 7th ed.
Lihue, HI : Wizard Publications, Inc., 2015
    312 p.: col. illus., col. photos, col. maps; 21 cm.
    Includes index.
    Summary : a complete traveler's reference to the island of Hawaii, with full color
photos, maps, directions, and candid advice by an author who resides in Hawaii.
    ISBN 978-0-9838887-4-1
    LCCN 2013943438
 	
    1. Hawaii Island (Hawaii) – Guidebooks. 2. Hawaii Island (Hawaii) – Description
and travel. I. Title.
 	
DU 622   919.69__dc21

All photographs (except cover & page 16) taken by Andrew Doughty and Leona Boyd.
Cover space imagery courtesy of Earthstar Geographics (www.earth-imagery.com).
Cartography by Andrew Doughty.
All artwork and illustrations by Andrew Doughty and Lisa Pollak.

Past and present lava flow information for maps was graciously provided by an over-worked and under-appreciated United States Geological Survey, the silent partner to all mapmakers. Keep up the good work!

Pages 2–3: Kilauea's Puʻu ʻOʻo vent.

We welcome any comments, questions, criticisms or contributions you may have, and have incorporated some of your suggestions into this edition. Please send to the address above, or e-mail us at **aloha@wizardpub.com**.

Check out our website at **www.hawaiirevealed.com** for up-to-the-minute changes. Find us on **Facebook**, **YouTube** and **Twitter** (@hawaiirevealed).

7TH EDITION **HAWAII**
THE BIG ISLAND
REVEALED
THE ULTIMATE GUIDEBOOK

ANDREW DOUGHTY

PHOTOGRAPHS BY ANDREW DOUGHTY & LEONA BOYD

WIZARD
PUBLICATIONS
INC

To Harry and Mary—
Their love of travel lives on...

CONTENTS

VOLCANO SIGHTS
85

SADDLE ROAD SIGHTS
138

HILO & PUNA SIGHTS
106

BEACHES
147

HAMAKUA & WAIMEA SIGHTS
123

ACTIVITIES
176

ACTIVITIES
(Continued)
176

ISLAND DINING
244

ADVENTURES
229

WHERE TO STAY
282

INDEX
306

The Big Island has it all. Nowhere else in the world will you find the diversity available here. Pristine rain forests, lava deserts, world-class beaches, snow-covered mountains, an active volcano, dazzling sunsets and just about every activity you can think of. The island is huge—about the size of Connecticut. Navigating your way through this maze of opportunity can be daunting.

Most travel publishers send a writer or writers to a given location for a few weeks to become "experts" and to compile information for guidebooks. To our knowledge, we at Wizard Publications are the only ones who actually *live* our books.

We hike the trails, ride the boats, eat in the restaurants, explore the reefs and do the things we write about. It takes us two *years*, full time, to do a first edition book, and we visit places *anonymously*. We marvel at writers who can do it all in a couple of weeks staying in a hotel. Wow, they must be *really* fast. Our method, though it takes much longer, gives us the ability to tell it like it is in a way no one else can. We put in many long hours, and doing all these activities is a burdensome grind. But we do it all for you—only for you. (Feel free to gag at this point.)

We produce brand new editions of our books every two years or so, but in the intervening time we constantly incorporate changes into the text nearly every time we do a new printing. We also post these changes on our website. This allows us to make some modifications throughout the life of each edition.

We have found many special places that people born and raised here didn't even know about because that's *all we do*—explore the island.

In this day of easy-to-access online reviews from countless sources, you can get "ratings" for nearly every company out there. What you get from our reviews is a single source, *beholden to*

none, and with a comprehensive exposure to all of the companies. There are two critical shortcomings to online reviews. One is that you don't know the source or agenda of the reviewer. Nearly every company that offers a service to the public *thinks* they are doing a good job. (But as you know, not everyone does.) So who can blame a company for trying to rig the system by seeding good reviews of their company at every opportunity or having friends write good reviews? Many also encourage *satisfied* customers to write favorable online reviews (obviously *not* encouraging *unhappy* customers to do so). But maybe their enemies or competitors retaliate with bad reviews. The point is, you never *really know* where those reviews come from, and it's almost impossible to reconcile terrible reviews right next to glowing ones for the same company. Which do you believe?

The other problem is a lack of a frame of reference. A visitor to Hawai'i goes on a snorkel boat and has a great time. (Hey, he snorkeled in Hawai'i, swam with a turtle—*cool!*) When he goes back home, he posts good reviews all around. That's great. But the problem is, he only went on *one* snorkel boat. We do 'em all. If only he'd known that another company *he didn't even know about* did a much better job, had way better food, and a much nicer boat for the same price.

We are also blessed with hundreds of thousands of readers—from our books as well as our smartphone apps—who alert us to issues with companies and places. *Every single message* from our readers is received, placed in a special database that we constantly have available while we're out and about, and we personally follow up on every observation made by our readers. So when we walk into a business or restaurant, we check to see what our readers say and tips they send us, and we use them to our advantage. (Thanks for the head's up about that incredible coconut cake at so-and-so restaurant—I know what *I'll* be ordering for dessert today.) With such a resource, and after two decades reviewing companies in Hawai'i full-time, there ain't much that's gonna get past us.

A quick look at this book will reveal features never before used in other guidebooks. Let's start with the maps. They are more detailed than any other maps you'll find, and yet they omit extraneous information that can sometimes make map reading a chore. We know that people in unfamiliar territory sometimes have a hard time determining where they are on a map, so we include landmarks. Most notable among these are mile markers. At every mile on main roads, the government has erected numbered markers to tell you where you are. Where needed, we've drawn legal public beach access in yellow, so you'll *know* when you're legally entitled to cross someone's land. Most guidebooks have the infuriating habit of mentioning a particular place or sight but then fail to mention how to get there! You won't find that in our book. We tell you exactly how to find the hidden gems and use our own special maps to guide you.

As you read this book, you will also notice that we are very candid in assessing businesses. Unlike some other guidebooks that send out questionnaires asking a business if they are any good (gee, they *all* say they're good), we've had personal contact with the businesses listed in this book. One of the dirty little secrets about guidebook writers is that they sometimes make cozy little deals for good reviews. Well, you won't find that here. We accept no payment for our reviews, we make no deals with businesses for saying nice things, and there are no advertisements in our book. What we've seen and experienced is what you get. If we gush over a certain company, it comes from personal experience. If we rail against a business, it is for the same reason. All businesses mentioned in this book are here by *our* choosing. None has had any input into what we say, and we have not received *a single cent* from any of them for their inclusion. (In fact, there are some who would probably pay to be left out, given our comments.) We always review businesses as anonymous visitors and only later as guidebook writers if we need more information. This ensures that we are treated the same as you. (Amazingly, most travel writers *announce* themselves.) What you get is our opinion on how they operate. Nothing more, nothing less.

Sometimes our candor gets us into trouble. More than once we've had our books pulled from shelves because our comments hit a little too close to home. That's OK, because we don't work for the people who *sell* the book; we work for the people who *read* the book. It's also true that a handful of local residents have become upset because we've told readers about places that they'd rather keep for themselves. Ironically, it's usually not people born and raised here who have this selfish attitude, but rather the newcomers who have read about these places *in our book* (of all things), then adopted the *I'm here now— close the door* mentality.

This book is intended to bring you independence in exploring the Big Island. We don't want to waste any of your precious time by giving you bad advice or bad directions. We want you to experience the best that the island has to offer. Our objective in writing this book is to give you the tools and information necessary to have the greatest Hawaiian experience possible.

We hope we succeeded.

Andrew Doughty
Kailua-Kona, Hawai'i

Brand new liquid land flows in a scene as primordial as the island's birth.

As with people, volcanic islands have a life cycle. They emerge from their sea floor womb to be greeted by the warmth of the sun. They grow, mature and eventually die before sinking forever beneath the sea.

HOW IT BEGAN

Sometime around 70 million years ago a cataclysmic rupture occurred in the Earth's mantle, deep below the crust. A hot spot of liquid rock blasted through the Pacific plate like a giant cutting torch, forcing magma to the surface off the coast of Russia, forming the Emperor Seamounts. As the tectonic plate moved slowly over this hot spot, this torch cut a long scar along the plate, piling up mountains of rock, producing island after island. The oldest of these islands to have survived is Kure. Once a massive island with its own unique ecosystem, only its ghost remains in the form of a fringing coral reef, called an atoll.

As soon as the islands were born, a conspiracy of elements proceeded to dismantle them. Ocean waves unmercifully battered the fragile and fractured rock. Abundant rain, especially on the northeastern sides of the mountains, easily carved up the rock surface, seeking faults in the rock and forming rivers and streams. In forming these channels, the water carried away the rock and soil, robbing the islands of their very essence. Additionally, the weight of the islands ensured their doom. Lava flows on top of other lava, and the union of these flows is always weak. This lava also contains countless air pockets and is criss-crossed with hollow lava tubes, making it inherently unstable. As these massive amounts of rock accumulated, their bases were crushed under the weight of subsequent lava flows, causing their summits to sink back into the sea.

What we call the Hawaiian Islands are simply the latest creations from this island-making machine. Someday they will disappear, existing as nothing more than footnotes in the Earth's turbulent geologic history.

Kaua'i and Ni'ihau are the oldest of the eight major islands. Lush and deeply eroded, the last of Kaua'i's fires died with its volcano a million years ago. O'ahu, Moloka'i, Lana'i, Kaho'olawe— their growing days are over, as well. Maui is in its twilight days as a growing island. After growing vigorously, Hawaiian volca-

noes usually go to sleep for a million years or so before sputtering back to life for one last fling. Maui's volcano Haleakala has entered its final stage and last erupted around 1790.

The latest and newest star in this island chain is Hawai'i. Born less than a million years ago, this youngster is still vigorously growing. Though none of its five volcano mountains is considered truly dead, these days Mauna Loa and Kilauea are doing most of the work of making the Big Island bigger. Mauna Loa, the most massive mountain on Earth, consists of 10,000 *cubic miles* of rock. Quieter of the two active volcanoes, it last erupted in 1984. Kilauea is the most boisterous of the volcanoes and is the most active volcano on the planet. Kilauea's most recent eruption began in 1983 and was still going strong as we went to press. Up and coming onto the world stage is Lo'ihi. This new volcano is still 3,200 feet below the ocean's surface, 20 miles off the southeastern

The wonder of creation can still be seen at night at Kilauea Volcano.

In regions of the island blessed with abundant rains, verdant growth carpets the landscape.

coast of the island. Yet in a geologic heartbeat, the Hawaiian islands will be richer with its ascension, sometime in the next 100,000 years.

These virgin islands were barren at birth. Consisting only of volcanic rock, the first life forms to appreciate these new islands were marine creatures. Fish, mammals and microscopic animals discovered this new underwater haven and made homes for themselves. Coral polyps attached themselves to the lava rock and succeeding generations built upon these, creating what would become a coral reef.

Meanwhile, on land, seeds carried by the winds were struggling to colonize the rocky land, eking out a living and breaking down the lava rock. Storms brought the occasional bird, hopelessly blown off course. The lucky ones found the islands. The even luckier ones arrived with mates or had fertilized eggs when they got here. Other animals, stranded on a piece of floating debris, washed ashore against all odds and went on to colonize the islands. These introductions of new species were rare events. It took an extraordinary set of circumstances for a new species to actually make it to the islands. Single specimens were destined to live out their lives in lonely solitude. On average, a new species was successfully deposited here only once every 20,000 years.

When a volcanic island is old, it is a sandy sliver, devoid of mountains. When it's middle-aged, it can be a lush wonderland, a haven for anything green, like Kaua'i. And when it is young, it is dynamic and unpredictable, like the Big Island of Hawai'i. Of all the Hawaiian Islands, none offers a larger range of climates and landscapes than the Big Island. The first people to discover Hawai'i's treasures must have been humbled at their good fortune.

THE FIRST SETTLERS

Sometime around the fifth century AD a large, double-hulled voyaging canoe, held together with flexible sennit lashings and propelled by sails made of woven pandanus, slid onto the sand on the Big Island of Hawai'i. These first intrepid adventurers, only a few dozen or so, encountered an island chain of unimaginable beauty.

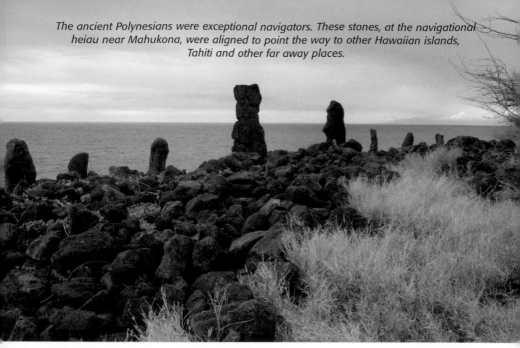
The ancient Polynesians were exceptional navigators. These stones, at the navigational heiau near Mahukona, were aligned to point the way to other Hawaiian islands, Tahiti and other far away places.

They had left their home in the Marquesas Islands, 2,500 miles away, for reasons we will never know. Some say it was because of war, overpopulation, drought, or just a sense of adventure. Whatever their reasons, these initial settlers took a big chance and surely must have been highly motivated. They left their homes and searched for a new world to colonize. Doubtless, most of the first groups perished at sea. The Hawaiian Islands are the most isolated island chain in the world, and there was no way for them to know that there were islands in these waters. (Though some speculate that they were led here by the golden plover—see box on facing page.)

Those settlers who did arrive brought with them food staples from home: taro, breadfruit, pigs, dogs and several types of fowl. This was a pivotal decision. These first settlers found a land that contained almost no edible plants. With no land mammals other than the Hawaiian bat, the first settlers subsisted on fish until their crops matured. From then on, they lived on fish and taro. Although many associate throw-net fishing with Hawai'i, this practice was introduced by Japanese immigrants much later. The ancient Hawaiians used fishhooks and spears, for the most part, or drove fish into a net already placed in the water. They also had domesticated animals, which were used as ritual foods or reserved for chiefs.

Little is known about the initial culture. Archaeologists believe that a second wave of colonists, probably from Tahiti, may have subdued these initial inhabitants around 1000 AD. Some may have resisted and fled into the forest, creating the legend of the Menehune.

Today, Menehune are always referred to as being small in stature. Initially referring to their social stature, the legend evolved to mean that they were physically short and lived in the woods away from the Hawaiians. (The Hawaiians avoided the woods when possible, fearing that they held evil spirits, and instead stayed on the coastal plains.) The Menehune were purported to build fabulous structures, always in one night. Their numbers were said to be vast, as many as

500,000. It is interesting to note that in a census taken of Kaua'i in around 1800, 65 people from a remote valley identified themselves as Menehune.

The second wave probably swept over the island from the south, pushing the first inhabitants ever-north. On a tiny island north of Kaua'i, archeologists have found carvings, clearly not Hawaiian, that closely resemble Marquesan carvings, probably left by the doomed exiles.

This second culture was far more aggressive and developed into a highly class-conscious society. The culture was governed by chiefs, called Ali'i, who established a long list of taboos called kapu. These kapu were designed to keep order, and the penalty for breaking one was usually death by strangulation, club or fire. If the violation was serious enough, the guilty party's entire family might also be killed. It was kapu, for instance, for your shadow to fall across the shadow of the Ali'i. It was kapu to interrupt the chief if he was speaking. It was kapu to prepare men's food in the same container used for women's food. It was kapu for women to eat pork or bananas. It was kapu for men and women to eat together. It was kapu not to observe the days designated to the gods. Certain areas were kapu for fishing if they became depleted, allowing the area to replenish itself.

While harsh by our standards today, this system kept the order. Most Ali'i were sensitive to the disturbance their presence caused and often ventured outside only at night, or a scout was sent ahead to warn people that an Ali'i was on his way. All commoners were required to pay tribute to the Ali'i in the form of food and other items. Human sacrifices were common, and war among rival chiefs the norm.

By the 1700s, the Hawaiians had lost all contact with Tahiti, and the Tahitians had lost all memory of Hawai'i. Hawaiian canoes had evolved into fishing, and interisland canoes and were no longer capable of long ocean voyages. The Hawaiians had forgotten how to explore the world.

Hawai'i's First Tour Guide?

Given the remoteness of the Hawaiian Islands relative to the rest of Polynesia (or anywhere else for that matter), you'll be forgiven for wondering how the first settlers found these islands in the first place. Many *scientists think it might have been this little guy here. Called the kolea, or golden plover, this tiny bird flies over 2,500 miles nonstop to Alaska every year for the summer, returning to Hawai'i after mating. Some of these birds continue past Hawai'i and fly another 2,500 miles to Samoa and other South Pacific islands. The early Polynesians surely must have noticed this commute and concluded that there must be land in the direction that the bird was heading. They never would have dreamed that the birds leaving the South Pacific were heading to a land 5,000 miles away, and that Hawai'i was merely a stop in between, where the lazier birds wintered.*

OUTSIDE WORLD DISCOVERS HAWAI'I

In January 1778 an event occurred that would forever change Hawai'i. Captain James Cook, who usually had a genius for predicting where to find islands, stumbled upon Hawai'i. He had not expected the islands to be here. He was on his way to Alaska on his third great voyage of discovery, this time to search for the Northwest Passage linking the Atlantic and Pacific oceans. Cook approached the shores of Waimea, Kaua'i, at night on January 19, 1778. The next morning Kaua'i's inhabitants awoke to a wondrous sight and thought they were being visited by gods. Rushing out to greet their visitors, the Kauaians were fascinated by what they saw: pointy-headed beings (the British wore tri-cornered hats) breathing fire (smoking pipes) and possessing a death-dealing instrument identified as a water squirter (guns). The amount of iron on the ship was incredible. (They had seen iron before in the form of nails on driftwood but never knew where it originated.)

It's hard to believe that the Big Island will eventually look like this oldest Hawaiian island, Kure Atoll. One day its last ghostly remains will sink forever beneath the sea.

Cook left Kaua'i and briefly explored Ni'ihau before heading north for his mission on February 2, 1778. When Cook returned to the islands in November after failing to find the Northwest Passage, he visited the Big Island of Hawai'i.

The Hawaiians had probably seen white men before. Local legend indicates that strange white people washed ashore at Ke'ei Beach sometime around the 1520s and integrated into society. This coincides with Spanish records of two ships lost in this part of the world in 1528. But a few weird-looking stragglers couldn't compare to the arrival of Cook's great ships and instruments.

Despite some recent rewriting of history, all evidence indicates that Cook, unlike some other exploring sea captains of his era, was a thoroughly decent man. Individuals need to be evaluated in the context of their time. Cook knew that his mere presence would have a profound impact on the cultures he encountered, but he also knew that change for these cultures was inevitable, with or without him. He tried, unsuccessfully, to keep the men known to be infected with venereal diseases from mixing with local women, and he frequently flogged infected men who tried to sneak ashore at night. He was greatly distressed when a party he sent to Ni'ihau was forced to stay overnight due to high surf, knowing that his men might transmit diseases to the women (which they did).

Cook arrived on the Big Island at a time of much upheaval. The mo'i, or king, of the Big Island had been badly spanked during an earlier attempt to invade Maui and was now looting and raising hell throughout the islands as retribution. Cook's arrival and his physical appearance (he was 6 feet, 4 inches) assured that the Hawaiians would assume him to be

The Day the Gods Cried...

At the south end of Alii Drive in Kona, when you've past the last resort, there is a lava road leading toward the ocean. This field of lava and an area around the point called Kuamo'o have an extraordinary past. Here occurred an event that forever changed a people. For it was here that the Hawaiians abolished their ancient religion one day in 1820.

The Hawaiian religion was based on the kapu system. A myriad of laws were maintained, with death being the usual punishment for violation. The Hawaiians believed that rigid enforcement for a single violation was necessary, or else the gods would punish the whole community in the form of earthquakes, tsunamis, lava flows and famine. When Captain Cook came, he and his men were unaware of the many laws and inadvertently violated many of them. When natural punishments failed to materialize, many Hawaiians concluded that the gods would not enforce the laws. Since many found the kapu laws burdensome and oppressive, there was pressure to abolish them. While King Kamehameha I was alive, however, none dared challenge the kapu system. Almost as soon as he died, King Kamehameha II, pressured by his stepmother Ka'ahumanu, decided to put an end to the kapu system and destroy the temples around the island. This was before any missionaries ever came to these islands.

It was decided that the action would be consecrated by the simple act of having the king eat with women in public in November 1819. This had heretofore been kapu, and the penalty for breaking this law was death. In breaking this kapu in public, Kamehameha II declared an end to the old ways. One of his cousins, Kekuaokalani, was to be king of the spiritual world and challenged him. The ferocious battle took place near here in early 1820. His cousin was hit by Kamehameha II's forces, and the man's grieving wife ran to his side as he fell. She cried out, begging that her wounded husband's life be spared. Instead she and her husband were summarily executed on the spot, with her body falling on top of his. The Hawaiian religion, as a dominant force, died with them on that bloody day. If you look to the south, you can see what look like terraces cut into the side of the mountain. These are the graves of the many hundreds who died in that very battle.

Today there is a resurgence of the Hawaiian religion. Hawaiians are grappling with their role in the world and are reaching back to their roots. The religion that seemingly died on that raw lava field is being reborn in the hearts of some contemporary Hawaiians.

the god Lono, who was responsible for fertility of the land. Every year the ruling chiefs and their war god Ku went into abeyance, removing their power so that Lono could return to the land and make it fertile again, bringing back the spring rains. During this time all public works stopped and the land was left alone. At the end of this *Makahiki* season, people would again seize the land from Lono to grow crops and otherwise make a living upon it. Cook arrived at the beginning of the Makahiki, and the Hawaiians naturally thought *he* was the god Lono, coming to make the land fertile. Cook even sailed into Kealakekua Bay, *exactly* where legend said Lono would arrive.

The Hawaiians went to great lengths to please their "god." All manner of supplies were made available. Eventually, they became suspicious of the visitors. If they were gods, why did they accept Hawaiian women? And if they were gods, why did one of them die?

Cook left at the right time. The British had used up the Hawaiians' hospitality (not to mention their supplies). But shortly after leaving the Big Island, the ship broke a mast, making it necessary to return to Kealakekua Bay for repairs. As they sailed back into the bay, the Hawaiians were nowhere to be seen. A chief had declared the area kapu to help replenish it. When Cook finally found the Hawaiians, they were polite but wary. *Why are you back? Didn't we please you enough already? What do you want now?*

As repair of the mast went along, things began to get tense. Eventually the Hawaiians stole a British rowboat (for the nails), and the normally calm Cook blew his cork. On the morning of February 14, 1779, he went ashore to trick the chief into coming aboard his ship where he would detain him until the rowboat was returned. As Cook and the chief were heading to the water, the chief's wife begged the chief not to go. By now tens of thousands of Hawaiians were crowding around Cook, and he ordered a retreat. A shot was heard from the other side of the bay, and someone shouted that the Englishmen had killed an important chief. A shielded warrior with a dagger came at Cook, who fired his pistol (loaded with non-lethal small shot). The shield stopped the small shot,

and the Hawaiians were emboldened. Other shots were fired. Standing in knee-deep water, Cook turned to call for a cease-fire and was struck in the head from behind with a club, then stabbed. Dozens of other Hawaiians pounced on him, stabbing his body repeatedly. The greatest explorer the world had ever known was dead at age 50 in a petty skirmish over a stolen rowboat.

When things calmed down, the Hawaiians were horrified that they had killed a man they had earlier presumed to be a god. See page 71 to see what finally happened to Cook's body.

KAMEHAMEHA THE GREAT

The most powerful and influential king in Hawaiian history lived during the time of Captain Cook and was born on this island sometime around 1758. Until his rule, the Hawaiian chain had never been ruled by a single person. He was the first to "unite" (i.e., conquer) all the islands.

Kamehameha was an extraordinary man by any standard. He possessed herculean strength, a brilliant mind and boundless ambition. He was marked for death before he was even born. When Kamehameha's mother was pregnant with him, she developed a strange and overpowering craving—she wanted to *eat* the eyeball of a chief. The king of the Big Island, mindful of the rumor that the unborn child's real father was his bitter enemy, the king of Maui, asked his advisors to interpret. Their conclusion was unanimous: The child would grow to be a rebel, a killer of chiefs. The king decided that the child must die as soon as he was born, but the baby was instead whisked away to a remote part of Waipi'o Valley to be raised.

In ancient Hawaiian society, your role in life was governed by the class you were

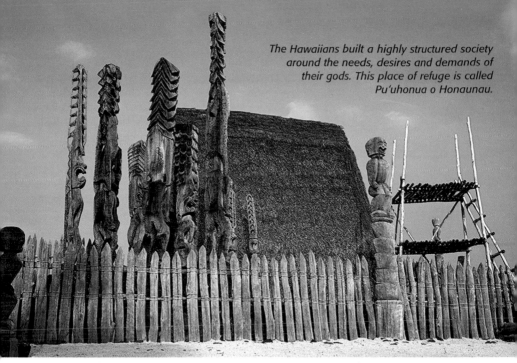

The Hawaiians built a highly structured society around the needs, desires and demands of their gods. This place of refuge is called Pu'uhonua o Honaunau.

born into. The Hawaiians believed that breeding among family members produced superior offspring (except for the genetic misfortunates who were killed at birth), and the highest chiefs came from brother/sister combinations. Kamehameha was not of the highest class (his parents were merely cousins), so his future as a chief would not come easily.

As a young man, Kamehameha was impressed by his experience with Captain Cook. He was among the small group that stayed overnight on Cook's ship during Cook's first pass of Maui. (Kamehameha was on Maui valiantly fighting a battle in which his side was getting badly whooped.) Kamehameha recognized that his world had forever changed, and he shrewdly used the knowledge and technology of westerners to his own advantage.

Kamehameha participated in numerous battles. Many of them were lost (by his side), but he learned from his mistakes and developed into a cunning tactician. When he finally consolidated his rule over the Big Island (by luring his enemy to be the inaugural sacrifice at the Pu'ukohola Heiau near Kawaihae), he fixed his sights on the entire chain. In 1795 his large company of troops, armed with some western armaments and advisors, swept across Maui, Moloka'i, Lana'i and O'ahu. After some delays with the last of the holdouts, Kaua'i, their king finally acquiesced to the inevitable, and Kamehameha became the first ruler of all the islands. He spent his final years governing the islands peacefully from his capital at Kailua Bay and died in 1819.

MODERN HAWAI'I

During the 19th century, Hawai'i's character changed dramatically. Businessmen from all over the world came here to exploit Hawai'i's sandalwood, whales, land and people. Hawai'i's leaders, for their part, actively participated in these ventures and took a piece of much of the action for themselves. Workers were brought in from many parts of the world, changing the racial makeup of the islands. Government corruption became the order of the day, and everyone seemed to be profiting, except the Hawaiian commoner. By the time Queen Lili'uokalani lost her throne to a group of American businessmen in 1893, Hawai'i had become directionless, barely resembling the Hawai'i Captain Cook had encountered the previous century. The kapu system had been abolished by the Hawaiians shortly after the death of Kamehameha the Great. The "Great Mahele," begun in 1848, had changed the relationship Hawaiians had with the land. Large tracts of land were sold by the Hawaiian government to royalty, government officials, commoners and foreigners, effectively stripping many Hawaiians of the land they had lived on for generations.

The United States recognized the Republic of Hawai'i in 1894 with Sanford Dole as its president. It was later annexed and became an official territory in 1900. During the 19th and 20th centuries, sugar established itself as king. Pineapple was also a major crop in the islands, with the island of Lana'i purchased in its entirety for the purpose of growing pineapples. As the 20th century rolled on, Hawaiian sugar and pineapple workers found themselves in a lofty position—they became the highest paid workers for these crops in the world. As land prices rose and competition from other parts of the world increased, sugar and pineapple became less and less profitable. Today, these crops no longer hold the position they once had. The "pineapple island" of Lana'i has shifted away from pineapple growing and focuses on luxury tourism, with software mogul Larry Ellison buying the island in 2012. The sugar industry is now dead on the Big Island, and sugar lands are being converted to other purposes while the workers move into other vocations, often tourist-related.

The story of Hawai'i is not a story of good versus evil. Nearly everyone shares in the blame for what happened to the Hawaiian people and their culture. Westerners certainly saw Hawai'i as a potential bonanza and easily exploitable. They knew what buttons to push and pushed them well. But the Hawaiians, for their part, were in a state of flux. The mere appearance of westerners seemed to reveal a discontent, or at least a weakness, in their system that had been lingering just below the surface. In fact, in 1794, a mere 16 years after first encountering westerners and under no military duress from the West, Kamehameha the Great *volunteered* to cede his island over to Great Britain. He was hungry for western arms so he could defeat his neighbor island opponents. He even declared that, as of that day, they were no longer people of Hawai'i, but rather people of Britain. (Britain declined the offer.) And in 1819, immediately after the death of the strong-willed Kamehameha, the Hawaiians, of their own accord, overthrew their own religion, dumped the kapu system and denied their gods. This was *before* any western missionaries ever came to Hawai'i.

Nonetheless, Hawai'i today is once again seeking guidance from her heritage. The echoes of the past seem to be getting louder with time, rather than diminishing. Interest in the Hawaiian language and culture is at a level not seen in many decades. All who live here are very aware of the issues and the complexities involved, but there is little agreement about where it will lead. As a result, you will be exposed to a more "Hawaiian" Hawai'i than those who might have visited the state a generation ago. This is an interesting time in Hawai'i. Enjoy it as observers, and savor the flavor of Hawai'i.

Going with the flow—Big Island style.

In order to get to the islands, you've got to fly here. While this may sound painfully obvious, many people contemplate cruises to the islands. Here's a tip—there isn't a single spec of land between the west coast and Hawai'i. And 2,500 miles of open water is a pretty monotonous stretch to cover.

GETTING HERE

When planning your trip, a travel agent can be helpful. Their commission has been paid directly by the travel industry, though that may change in the future. The Internet has dot.com sites such as Orbitz, Expedia, Cheaptickets, Cheapair, Panda-online, Priceline, Travelocity, etc. If you don't want to or can't go through these sources, there are large wholesalers that can get you airfare, hotel and a rental car, often cheaper than you can get airfare on your own. **Pleasant Holidays** (800–742–9244) is one of the more well-known providers of complete package tours. They are renowned for their impossibly low rates. We've always been amazed that you can sometimes get round trip airfare from the mainland, a hotel, and car for a week for as low as $850 per person, depending on where you fly from and where you stay. That's a small price to pay for your little piece of paradise.

If you arrange airline tickets and hotel reservations yourself, you can often count on paying top dollar for each facet of your trip. The prices listed in the WHERE TO STAY chapter reflect the RACK rates, meaning the published rates before any discounts. Rates can be significantly lower if you go through a wholesaler.

When you pick your travel source, shop around—the differences can be dramatic. A good source can make the difference between affording a *one-week* vacation and a *two-week* vacation. It's not always a straightforward process; there is an art to it. Look in the Sunday travel section of your local newspaper—the bigger the paper, the better, or check online versions of major papers.

Flight schedules change all the time, but United and others often have *direct* flights to Kona from the mainland. Not having to cool your heels while changing planes on O'ahu is a *big* plus because interisland flights aren't quite as simple and painless as they used to be. Flight attendants zip up and down the aisles hurling juice at you for the short, interisland flight. If you fly to Kona from Honolulu, sit on the left side (seats with an "A") coming in (right side going out) for superb views of several other islands. If you fly into Hilo, sit on the right side coming in. When flying to O'ahu from the mainland, seats on the left side have the best views. Interisland flights are done by **Hawaiian** (800–367–5320), **Island Air** (800–652–6541) and **Mokulele** (866–260–7070). We prefer Mokulele when possible because their smaller planes leave out of the commuter terminal in Kona, avoiding TSA and the rest of the airport system. Arrive 10 minutes early instead of 90.

WHAT TO BRING

This list may assist you in planning what to bring. Obviously you won't bring everything on the list, but it might make you think of a few things you may otherwise overlook:

- Water-resistant sunscreen (SPF 30 or higher) or use a rashguard
- Two bathing suits
- Light rain jacket
- Hat or cap for sun protection
- Shorts and other cool clothing
- Warm clothes (for Mauna Kea or other high-altitude activities) and junk clothes for bikes, etc.
- Shoes—flip-flops, trashable sneakers, water shoes, hiking shoes
- Flashlight, if you like caves or for the lava field at night if there's a surface flow
- Digital camera with extra batteries
- Mosquito repellent for some hikes *(Lotions*—not liquids—with DEET seem to work the longest)
- Cheap, simple backpack or mesh gearbag—you don't need to go backpacking to use one; a 10-minute trek to a secluded beach is much easier if you bring a simple pack

GETTING AROUND
Rental Cars

Rental car prices in Hawai'i *can be* (but aren't always) cheaper than almost anywhere else in the country, and the competition is ferocious. Nearly every visitor to the Big Island gets around in a rental car, and for good reason—it's a *big* island. Fortunately, none have mileage charges.

At Kona Airport, rental cars are a shuttle bus ride away. It's a good idea to reserve your car in advance since companies can run out of cars during peak times.

Many hotels, condos and rental agents offer excellent room/car packages. Find out from your hotel or travel agent if one is available. You can rent a car in Hilo and return it to Kona (or vice versa). There's usually an extra fee of about $50–$100 (depending on the company and car). And prices overall are usually *much* higher in Hilo than in Kona.

Below is a list of rental car companies. The local area code is 808. Some have desks at various hotels.

Alamo	**(877) 222–9075**
	Kona: 329–8896
	Hilo: 961–3343
Avis	**(800) 321–3712**
	Kona: 327–3000
	Hilo: 935–1290
Budget	**(800) 527–0700**
	Kona: 329–8511
	Hilo: 935–6878
Dollar	**(800) 800–4000**
	Kona & Hilo:
	(866) 434–2226

The tasty waters of Makalawena Beach make it worth the walk.

Enterprise	**(800) 261–7331**
	Kona: 334–1810
	Hilo: 933–9683
Harper	**(800) 852–9993**
	Kona & Hilo: 969–1478
Hertz	**(800) 654–3131**
	Kona: 329–3566
	Hilo: 935–2896
National	**(877) 222–9058**
	Kona: 329–1674 *(answer!)*
	Hilo: 935–0891
Thrifty	**(800) 367–5238**
	Kona & Hilo:
	(877) 283–0898

If you're 21–24 years old, most of the companies will rent to you, but you'll pay about $25 extra *per day* for the crime of being young and reckless. If you're under 21—rent a bike or moped or take the bus.

4-Wheel Drive

We *strongly* believe that the best vehicle for the island is a 4-wheel drive vehicle. They come closed (like an Explorer or a Trailblazer) or open (like a Wran-gler). They are more expensive, but there are several roads, beaches and sights that you can't visit without 4WD. Even the short paved road into Waipi'o Valley requires the low gear offered in 4WD. Unpaved roads are contractually off limits with most of the rental car companies. That means that if you drive one, the insurance you take out with the rental company is void, so you or your insurance company back home would have to eat it. Different companies have different restrictions, but from a *practical* standpoint, 4WD is the way to go. The drawbacks to *open* JEEPS are more wind and heat and no trunk. Closed 4WDs are best. Expect to pay up to $60–$100 per day for the privilege of cheating the road builders. For some reason, they usually cost much more in Kona than Hilo.

Motorcycles & Scooters

If you really want to ham it up, you can try renting a HOG. *(Disclaimer*—Wizard Publications will not be held liable for bad puns.)* **Big Island Harley-Davidson**

(329–4464) rents Harleys starting at $180 per day plus taxes and junk fees. Cheaper prices at **Big Island Motorcycle** (886–2011) in Waikoloa with insurance included. Both include helmets, which are *not* required by law in Hawai'i. **Scooter Brothers** (327–1080) in Kona has scooters for $60 for 24 hours. (These are only useful around Kailua town.)

Motor Homes

The Big Island is the only Hawaiian island where staying in an RV is a viable alternative to hotels. (Ironically, in New Zealand the biggest RV brand is *Maui* brand.) With so much territory to cover and good roads leading to so many places, the RV life might be for you, especially if you're traveling with kids.

Some things to consider:

Motor homes are a relatively strange concept here, and you won't find any RV parks or facilities that you might be used to on the mainland.

Beach parks and campgrounds are your best bet for parking. Technically you're supposed to get camping permits to stay at most of them. The best place is Kapa'a Beach Park in North Kohala (though bees are sometimes a problem there). Spencer Beach Park is also good and Namakani Paio (866–536–7972) at Volcanoes National Park (it's $15 per day). There are no campgrounds near Kona that we can recommend, but remember, you can park anywhere. See CAMPING on page 179 for more on campsites.

These things don't carry as much waste as you may think, so finding places to empty it will be an ongoing consideration. You can only dump it in Hilo or Kona. Try to use the bathroom facilities at the campgrounds whenever possible.

Island RV (334–0464) will separate you from $357 each day. 5-day minimum.

A Few Driving Tips

Gasoline is *obscenely* expensive here. You may want to have some FedExed to you from home to save money. (OK, maybe not *that* expensive.) Kona is said to have the highest gas prices in the United States (about 15¢ higher than expensive Hilo). Whether that's true or not, prepare to get hammered at the pump. If you're in the Kohala resort area, there's a station off the road to the Waikoloa Resorts at the 76 mile marker. The cheapest gas on the east side of the island is in Hilo or Pahoa, south of Hilo. The cheapest on the *whole island* is in Kona at Costco (but you have to be a Costco member). It's marked on the map on page 164 and not far from the Kona Airport. Many companies charge a top-off fee due to the airport's distance to town, so fill it to the top. And make sure you check your bill. On *many* occasions we've topped off the tank all the way to the brim, only to find a $20 "fuel charge" tacked onto our final tab.

Seat belt and **child restraint** use is required by law, and the police will pull you over for this alone. Wide open roads and frequently changing speed limits make it easy to accidentally speed here. Police usually cruise in their own private, unmarked vehicles with a small blue light on top, so you might not see them coming. And we've noticed a *huge* increase in the number of speed traps on the island in recent years. We strongly recommend using cruise control and paying attention to changes in speed limits if you want to leave the island with the same driving score you arrived with.

Cell phone use is illegal for drivers unless you have a headset or wireless.

It's best not to leave anything valuable in your car. There are teenagers here who pass the time by breaking into cars. Hapuna Beach and several Hilo waterfalls are notorious for car break-ins. When we park at a beach or waterfall, or any other place frequented by visitors, we take all valuables with us, leave the windows up, and leave the doors unlocked. (Just in case someone is curious enough about the inside to smash a window.) There are plenty of stories about someone walking 100 feet to a waterfall in Hilo, coming back to their car, and finding that their brand new video camera has walked away. And don't be gullible enough to think that trunks are safe. Someone who sees you put something in your trunk can probably get at it faster than you can with your key.

Kailua-Kona possesses the dry town syndrome: At the first drop of rain, many Kona drivers become vehicularly uncoordinated, driving like a drunken cat on ice, so beware of this.

Traffic has increased *a lot* in the past few years and you should expect to get stuck in it, especially in Kona. Just remember that it could be worse—you could be in traffic back home *and on your way to work.*

Buses

Our main island bus is called **Hele-On** (961–8744). It was designed for local use, so it doesn't go to all the places that visitors want to go. It's $2 (If you're 60, or over, a student or disabled it's $1). However, it does go between Hilo and Kona, and they do take luggage (for an extra buck). Call them for a schedule and rates. There are also bus tours from **Roberts Hawai'i** (329–1688).

GETTING MARRIED ON THE BIG ISLAND

A beautiful beach at sunset—many couples dream of such a background for their special day. 'Anaeho'omalu Beach, pictured on page 43, is one of the more popular spots for sunset weddings. The Big Island offers an almost unlimited selection of wedding, reception and honeymoon possibilities. Although you can set everything up yourself using the Internet and e-mail, it's usually easier and *some-*

times less expensive to use a professional who can assist you.

This one's hard for us. Unlike other activities in this book, we can't exactly get married with all the companies and review them. (The flower bills alone would bankrupt us.) Almost all of the major resorts have wedding coordinators who can offer help. And there are lots of private wedding coordinators. A good resource is **www.bigislandwednet.com**, a wedding network professional exchange.

Expect to pay around $500ish for a minimal wedding package (officiant, flower leis and license assistance). Resorts generally charge a hefty fee to use their grounds whether you are a guest or not. All beaches are public, so it won't be a *private* ceremony. Consider renting a private home or an entire B&B in which to hold the ceremony and reception. See our website at **www.hawaiirevealed.com** for links and wedding license requirements.

WEATHER

The weather on the Big Island is more diverse than any island or other comparably sized chunk of land *in the world.* You name it, we got it. According to the Köppen Climate Classification System (which is probably *your* favorite system, too, right?), the Big Island has 10 of the 15 types of climatic zones in the world. (Not *climactic* zones, which we accidentally printed in a previous edition. Boy, people were *really* anxious to find one of *those!*) Only Cold Continental Climate categories are absent. Here we've got tropical, monsoonal, desert and even *periglacial* climates, among others. So no matter what kind of weather you like, we are sure to have it here. As you ascend the slopes of the volcanoes, you lose about 3 degrees for every thousand feet. Call 961–5582 for a recording of today's forecast.

Kailua-Kona *traditionally* has had weather that can best be described as

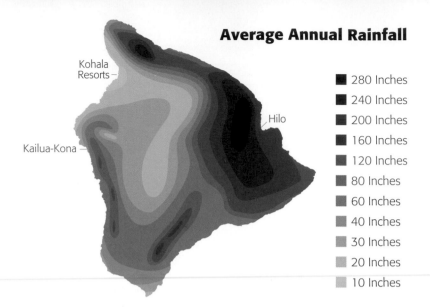

Average Annual Rainfall

Kohala Resorts

Hilo

Kailua-Kona

- 280 Inches
- 240 Inches
- 200 Inches
- 160 Inches
- 120 Inches
- 80 Inches
- 60 Inches
- 40 Inches
- 30 Inches
- 20 Inches
- 10 Inches

eternal springtime. Quite simply, it's almost always warm and wonderful. The average high and low in February (the coldest month) is 80° and 64°, whereas the high and low in August (the warmest month) is 87° and 69°. Humidity is usually between 50% and 80%. The temperature change between night and day is greater than the temperature change between winter and summer, so it could easily be said that nighttime is the winter of the Big Island. Balmy wraparound onshore breezes usually keep it comfortable. The exception is during Kona winds (so named because they come from the Kona direction, rather than out of the northeast as is usually the case). Kona winds occur about 5% of the time and bring stillness or warm air to Kona, creating uncomfortably humid conditions. Normal conditions in Kona and Kohala mean clear mornings with afternoon clouds created by thermal heating, so morning is usually better for activities such as air tours. During the summer, evening showers often occur as warm moist air is cooled, squeezing rain out of the humidity. Because it is totally protected from the trade winds by Hualalai, Kona is the only place in the state that gets most of its rainfall in the summer afternoons and evenings. The

higher up the mountain, the more rain you get. *However*, since Halema'uma'u began belching exhaust in 2008, the air quality has worsened and the air is much voggier. We're looking forward to the day Halema'uma'u stops its tantrum and allows the air to return to its former glory.

Hilo's weather is almost always described with one word—*rain*. Hilo is the wettest city in the United States. Annual rainfall is rarely less than 100 inches, usually much more. But rain is not a constant here. Hilo has times of drought like anywhere else. (Like when rainfall was a *mere* 70 inches one year, triggering *rationing*.) Most of the rain falls at night. When daytime showers do occur, they are often intense but short-lived. That said, rain or cloudiness *will* be a factor here. One of the reasons that Kailua-Kona is so much more popular than Hilo is that visitors like sunny weather, and Hilo can't compete in that area. Also, all that rain has to go somewhere, which is why the ocean off Hilo is not nearly as clear as Kona's runoff-free waters.

The Kohala resort area is the driest part of the island, with rainfall usually around 10 inches per year. Sunshine is almost assured (which is why it is so popular). The weather penalty here is the wind. As the lava fields heat up during the day, the air heats and rises. Air from the ocean rushes in to fill the void, creating strong afternoon convective breezes. The hotter, drier and sunnier it is that day, the breezier it may be that afternoon.

The general rule of thumb is that in wet areas like Hilo, most of the rain falls at night and early morning. Dry areas like Kona and Kohala get their rains in the late afternoon and early evenings.

Water temperatures range from 75° at its coldest in February to 82° at its warmest in September/October. It's colder in some areas where freshwater springs percolate from the ocean's floor and float to the top, forming a boundary called a *Ghyben-Herzberg lens*.

PLANNING YOUR TRIP

Visitors are usually unprepared for the sheer size and diversity of the Big Island. The island is over 4,000 square miles, and a circular trip around, on Highways 19 and 11, is a hefty 222 miles. During that drive you pass through dozens of different terrains and climates. (And that doesn't even include Saddle Road, Lower Puna, any of North Kohala or scores of other places.) Put simply, this island is too big and too diverse to try to see in a few days. The graphic on page 29 will put it in perspective.

If you are on the island for three days or less, we recommend that you don't try to see the whole island; you'll only end up touring Hawai'i's exotic blacktop. Pick a side. Since one of your days should be spent at the volcano, that leaves you with a scant two days to experience either Hilo's and Puna's beauty or the Kona side's diversity and activities.

Deciding which side of the island to spend the most time on is a difficult decision, but the numbers are definitely skewed. Most visitors spend most of their time on the western, or Kona, side. There are several reasons for this:

Kona Side

The Kona side has the sunshine. The climate in Kona is as perfect as weather gets when the vog isn't too thick, and the Kohala resort area has the highest number of sunny days of anywhere in the state. The Kona side also has *far* more activities available. This leads to another reason— the ocean. Since it's on the leeward side of the island, and because there are no permanent streams on the entire west side of the island (except for the one from Kona to Hilo that's filled with tax money), Kona has the calmest, clearest water in the state. Water sports such as swimming, snorkeling, SCUBA, fishing—you name it—are usually unmatched on the Kona side. This side also has the best beaches on the island, with some, such as Hapuna, consistently rated in the top five in the United States. (With a few notable exceptions, the

Only on the Big Island can you experience both conditions on the same day a few dozen miles apart.

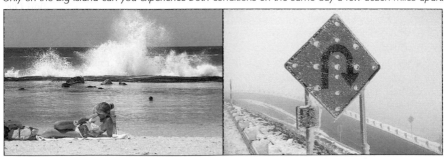

Hilo side has poor beaches.) All this adds up to a traveler's delight, one of the reasons that the Kona side has such a high visitor repeat ratio.

But stand by for a shock when you fly into Kona Airport for the first time. Kona makes a *rotten* first impression on the uninitiated airborne visitor. Part of the airport sits atop a lava flow from 1801, and the first thing you think when you fly in over all that jet black lava is, "I came all this way for *this?*" Don't worry; it gets much better.

Hilo Side

On the other hand, the Kona side is short of what Hilo has in abundance— green. Whereas much of the Kona side is dominated by lava, Hilo is plant heaven. The weather usually comes from the northeast, so Hilo gets around 140 inches of rain per year. This is paradise for anything that grows. Hilo also has breathtaking waterfalls. You won't find *one* on the Kona side unless it's in the lobby of your hotel. Hilo's weather has created beautiful folds and buckles in the terrain. The unweathered Kona side lacks angles—it's mostly gentle slopes. Lastly, Hilo is *much* more convenient for exploring Kilauea volcano.

The Two Sides

The schism between the two sides of the island is wide and deep. Because the two sides are so different and the distances so large (for Hawai'i, that is), most people who live on the west side haven't been to Hilo or Kilauea volcano in years. Most Hilo residents haven't been to Kona in years. Both sides tend to playfully badmouth the other. The Kona side creates the tax base, and the Hilo side, the center of county government, spends it (often on Hilo-oriented infrastructure). Hilo has lots of roads that few drive, while Kona drivers curse the traffic on their limited roads.

Suggested Itinerary

If you have a week on the Big Island, you might want to spend four to five days on the Kona side and two to three days in Hilo or Puna. The volcano itself can take one to two days, and you're better off exploring it from Hilo or Puna than from Kona. Hilo all but closes down on Sundays, with most business, even the few tourist-related ones, taking the day off.

GEOGRAPHY

The Big Island is made up of five volcanoes. (See map on the foldout back cover.) Kohala in the north is the oldest. Next came Mauna Kea, Hualalai, Mauna Loa, and finally Kilauea. None of them are truly dead, but only Mauna Loa and Kilauea make regular appearances, with an occasional walk-on by Hualalai. Nearly the size of Connecticut, all the other Hawaiian Islands could easily fit inside the Big Island's 4,000 square miles. And it's the only state in the union that gets bigger every year (thanks to Kilauea's land-making machine).

Gentle slopes are the trademark of this young island. It hasn't had time to develop the dramatic, razor-sharp ridges that older islands, such as Kaua'i, possess. The exception is the windward side of Kohala Mountain where erosion and fault collapses have created a series of dramatic valleys. Two of our mountains rise to over 13,000 feet. Mauna Kea, at 13,796 feet, is the tallest mountain in the world when measured from its base, eclipsing such also-rans as Mount Everest and K-2. Mauna Loa, though slightly shorter, is much broader, earning it the moniker as the *largest* mountain in the world. It contains a mind-numbing 10,000 cubic *miles* of rock.

Another of our mountains is not really a mountain at all. Kilauea, looking more like a gaping wound on Mauna Loa, is the undisputed volcano show-off of the planet. Hundreds of thousands of cubic yards of lava per day issue from its current outlet, Pu'u 'O'o, creating and repaving land on a daily basis.

All this adds up to an exciting and dynamic geographic location. Things change faster here than any place you will ever visit. There have been lots of times that we have gone to a certain beach or area only to find that it has changed beyond recognition. A new black sand beach shifts to another location. Trails become absorbed by a restless and vigorous Mother Nature. Whole roads get covered with lava. Island hopping in this state is like traveling through time. This is an exciting time in the life cycle of this particular island. Enjoy the island in its youth, for like all youths, this, too, shall pass.

SO IS HAWAI'I AN ISLAND OR A STATE?

Both. This island, more than any other in this state, is a bit schizophrenic when it comes to names. This is the biggest island in the state, so it is commonly referred to as (brace yourself) *the Big Island*. Its Hawaiian name is *Hawai'i*. So far, so good. But the whole *state* is called Hawai'i. So you figure the capital must be here, right? Nope, Honolulu is on O'ahu. This must be where most of the people live, right? Uh-uh. O'ahu has 80% of the population. Well, this must be where Pearl Harbor is, correct? Wrong answer—it's on O'ahu, too. So why is the state named after *this* island? Because it's the *biggest* island, and this is where King Kamehameha the Great was from. It was he who brought all the islands under one rule for the first time. His first capital was here at Kailua (another naming headache—see below). When you do all that, you have some historical influence. In this book we will refer to this island as *the Big Island*. When we say Hawai'i, we mean the whole state. (Even my brother, when he came to visit the Big Island, called from Honolulu to have me pick him up, assuming it must be on the "main" is-

land.) In short, *in Hawai'i* could be anywhere—*on Hawai'i* is on the Big Island.

I won't even get into the name confusion for the town of Waimea. (Or is it Kamuela? See page 133.) Let's tackle a more annoying naming problem. The main town on the west side is called **Kailua-Kona**, **Kona**, **Kailua** or sometimes **Kailua Town**. In the old days it was simply Kailua. Though there are also towns named Kailua on O'ahu and Maui, it didn't present much of a problem to anyone until the Post Office discovered these islands. In order to keep from messing up the mail *(don't say it!)*, they decided to rename the town. (Technically, they renamed their post office, but the subtlety is lost on those who have to address mail.) Since this is the *kona* side of the island (*kona* being the name of the less common wind that comes from this direction), they cleverly named the Post Office *Kailua-Kona*. To complicate matters further, the builders of the airport here named it the *Kona Airport*, so people began to refer to a trip here as "going to Kona." All this leaves you with a quandary. What do you call this place? Well, in keeping with our

How Big is The Big Island of Hawai'i?

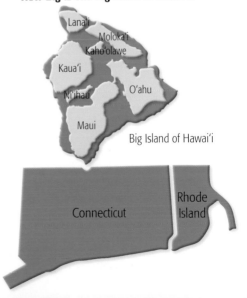

editorial policy of taking gutsy stands, we'll call it Kailua-Kona...except when we call it Kona or Kailua Town. In fairness, that's because most who live here do the same.

HAZARDS
The Sun

The hazard that affects by far the most people (excluding the accommodations tax) is the sun. The Big Island, at 19°–20° latitude, receives sunlight more directly than anywhere on the mainland. (The more overhead the sunlight is, the less atmosphere it filters through.) If you want to enjoy your *entire* vacation, make sure that you wear a strong sunscreen or cover up, even while snorkeling. We recommend a water-resistant sunscreen with at least an SPF of 30. Gels work best in the water, lotions on land. Try to avoid the sun between 11 a.m. and 2 p.m. when the sun's rays are particularly strong. If you are fair-skinned or unaccustomed to the sun and want to lay out, 15–20 minutes per side is all you should consider the first day. You can increase it a bit each day. *Beware of the fact that our ever-constant breezes will hide the symptoms of a burn until it's too late.* You might find that trying to get your tan as golden as possible isn't worth it. Tropical suntans are notoriously short lived, whereas you are sure to remember a burned vacation far longer. If, after all of our warnings, you *still* get burned, aloe vera gel works well to relieve the pain. Some come with lidocaine in them. Ask your hotel front desk if they have any aloe plants on the grounds. Peel the skin off a section and make several crisscross cuts in the meat, then rub the plant on your skin. *Oooo,* it'll feel so good!

Water Hazards

The most serious water hazard is the surf. Though more calm in the summer and on the west side, high surf can be found anywhere on the island at any time of the year. The sad fact is that more peo-

ple drown in Hawai'i each year than anywhere else in the country. This isn't said to keep you from enjoying the ocean, but rather to instill in you a healthy respect for Hawaiian waters. See BEACHES for more information on this. Also, water shoes are a good idea if you don't want to step on something sharp and painful.

Ocean Critters

Hawaiian marine life, for the most part, is quite friendly. There are, however, a few notable exceptions. Below is a list of some critters that you should be aware of. This is not mentioned to frighten you out of the water. The odds are overwhelming that you won't have any trouble with any of the beasties listed below. But should you encounter one, this information should be of some help.

Sharks—Hawai'i does have sharks. They are mostly white-tipped reef sharks and the occasional hammerhead or tiger shark. Contrary to what most people think, sharks live in every ocean and don't pose the level of danger people attribute to them. Shark attacks are rare on Big Island, averaging less than one per year, and fatalities are extremely uncommon. When encounters do occur, it's usually a tiger attacking surfers. Considering the number of people who swam in our waters during that time, you are more likely to choke to death on a bone at a lu'au than be attacked by a shark. If you do happen to come upon a shark, however, swim away slowly. This kind of movement doesn't interest them. *Don't* splash about rapidly. By doing this you are imitating a fish in distress, and you don't want to do that. The one kind of ocean water you want to avoid is murky water, such as that found near river mouths. These are not interesting to swim in anyway. Most shark attacks occur in murky water at dawn or dusk since sharks are basically cowards that like to sneak up on their prey. In general, don't go around worrying about sharks. *Any* animal can be threatening. (Even Jessica Alba was once rudely accosted by an overly affectionate male dolphin.)

Portuguese Man-of-War—These are related to jellyfish but are unable to swim.

They are instead propelled by a small sail and are at the mercy of the wind. Though small, they are capable of inflicting a painful sting. This occurs when the long, trailing tentacles are touched, triggering hundreds of thousands of spring-loaded stingers, called nematocysts, which inject venom. The resulting burning sensation is usually very unpleasant but not fatal. Fortunately, the Portuguese Man-of-War is very uncommon on the west shore of the island. When they *do* come ashore, they usually do so in great numbers, jostled by a strong storm offshore. If you see them on the beach, don't go in the water. If you do get stung, immediately remove the tentacles with a gloved hand, stick or whatever is handy. Rinse thoroughly with salt or fresh water to remove any adhering nematocysts. Then apply ice for pain control. If the condition worsens, see a doctor. The old treatments of vinegar or baking soda are no longer recommended. The folk cure is urine, (and it comes with a handy applicator for some of us), but you might look pretty silly applying it.

Sea Urchins—These are like living pin cushions. If you step on one or accidentally grab one, remove as much of the spine as possible with tweezers. See a physician if necessary.

Coral—Coral skeletons are very sharp and, since the skeleton is overlaid by millions of living coral polyps, a scrape can leave proteinaceous matter in the wound, causing infection. This is why coral cuts are frustratingly slow to heal. Immediate cleaning and disinfecting of coral cuts should speed up healing time. We don't have fire coral around the Big Island.

Sea Anemones—Related to the jellyfish, these also have stingers and are usually found attached to rocks or coral. It's best not to touch them with your bare hands. Treatment for a sting is similar to that for a Portuguese Man-of-War.

Bugs

Though devoid of the myriad of hideous buggies found in other parts of the world, there are a few evil critters brought here from elsewhere that you should know about. The worst are **centipedes**. They can get to be six or more inches long and are aggressive predators. They shouldn't be messed with. If you get stung, even by a baby, the pain can range from a bad bee sting to a bad gunshot wound. Some local doctors say the only cure is to stay drunk for three days. Others say to use meat tenderizer or a green papaya. **Scorpions** are present on the dry, western side of the island. Though not as nasty as the ones you see in the movies, a sting is unpleasant nonetheless. They're usually a couple inches across and mildly aggressive. **Cane spiders** are big, dark, and look horrifying, but they're not poisonous. (Though they seem to *think* they are. I've had *them* chase *me* across the room when *I* had the broom in my hand.) We *don't* have no-see-ums, those irritating sand fleas common in the South Pacific and Caribbean. A Hawaiian voyaging canoe that traveled to and from Tahiti on a cultural mission several years ago unknowingly brought some back. The crew was forced into quarantine against their will, where the tiny biting insects were discovered and exterminated. No-see-ums would have easily spread here and changed Hawai'i forever.

Mosquitoes were unknown in the islands until the first stowaways arrived on Maui on the *Wellington* in 1826. Since then they have thrived. A good mosquito repellent containing DEET will come in handy, especially if you plan to go hiking. *Lotions* (not thin liquids) with DEET seem to work and stick best. Forget the guidebooks that tell you to take vitamin B12 to keep mosquitoes away; it just gives the little critters a healthier diet. If you find one dive bombing you at night in your room, turn on your overhead fan to help keep them away. Local residents and resorts often rely on genetically engineered plants such as Citrosa, which irritates mosquitoes as much as they irritate us.

Bees and **yellow jackets** are more common on the drier west side of the island. Usually, the only way you'll get stung is if you run into one. If you rent a scooter, beware; I received my first bee sting while singing *Come Sail Away* on a motorcycle. A bee sting in the mouth can definitely ruin one of your precious vacation days.

Regarding **cockroaches**, there's good news and bad news. The bad news is that here, some are bigger than your thumb and can fly. The good news is that you probably won't see one. One of their predators is the **gecko**. This small, lizard-like creature makes a surprisingly loud chirp at night. They are cute and considered good luck in the Islands (probably because they eat mosquitoes and small roaches).

Leptospirosis is a type of bacteria found in some of Hawai'i's freshwater. It is transmitted from animal urine and can enter the body from open cuts, eyes and by drinking. Around 100 people a year in Hawai'i are diagnosed with leptospirosis, which can be treated with antibiotics if caught relatively early. You should avoid crossing streams such as Waipi'o with open cuts, and treat all water found in nature with treatment pills before drinking. (Many filters are ineffective for lepto.)

Though not a bug, one animal you are almost sure to see is the **mongoose**. Think of it as a stealth squirrel with mean-looking red eyes. Mongooses (no, not mongeese) are bold enough to take on cobras in their native India and were brought here to help control rats. Great idea, except mongooses are active during the day and rats work the night shift, so never the twain shall meet. It was a disaster for local birds since mongooses love bird eggs. Kaua'i is the only major island to avoid the mongoose (and vice versa), and the difference between its bird population and the Big Island's is dramatic.

There are no **snakes** in Hawai'i (except for some reporters). There is concern that the brown tree snake *might* have made its way

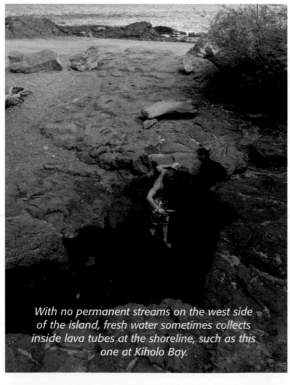

With no permanent streams on the west side of the island, fresh water sometimes collects inside lava tubes at the shoreline, such as this one at Kiholo Bay.

onto the islands from Guam. Although mostly harmless to humans, these snakes can spell extinction to native birds. Government officials aren't allowed to tell you this, but we will: If you ever see one anywhere in Hawai'i, please *kill it* and contact the **Pest Hotline** at 241–7135. At the very least, call them immediately. The entire bird population of Hawai'i will be grateful.

Pigs

We're not referring to your dining choice. We mean the wild ones you may encounter on a hiking trail. Generally, pigs will avoid you before you ever see them. If you happen to come upon any piglets and accidentally get between them and their mother, immediately bark like a big dog. Wild pigs are conditioned to run from local dogs (and their hunter masters), and Momma will leave her kids faster than you can say, "Pass the bacon."

Frogs

There are some irritating visitors that first arrived on the island a few years back and won't leave. (Well, besides the in-laws.) They're small tree frogs, called Coqui, that emit a whistle all night long. Cute at first, like a bird, but incessant and ultimately irritating. Most of the resorts do their best to deal with them, but there's a chance that some errant froggies may occasionally give you a long night. The Hilo side is froggier (I *swear* that's a real word) than Kona.

Vog

Vog is a mixture of water vapor, carbon dioxide and sulfur dioxide. Each day Kilauea belches 2,500 *tons* of sulphur dioxide. (Since the current eruption began, it has produced enough sulphur dioxide to fill a *half million* Goodyear blimps.) These gases react with sunlight, oxygen, dust particles and water in the air to form a mixture of sulfate aerosols, sulfuric acid and other oxidized sulfur compounds. Why should *you* care? Because our trade winds blow toward the southwest, carrying the vog from its source, down the coast where the winds wrap around Mauna Loa and head up the coast. Then daytime onshore breezes and nighttime offshore breezes rake it back and forth across Kona. If you have a severe lung condition or are very asthmatic, you may experience discomfort. When the volcano is *really* belching, Kona's vog bothers everyone. Those who stay in Kohala and Hilo are usually free from vog. In all, it's probably less than the smog in most mainland cities, but we wanted to alert you to one of the few negatives to living on an active volcano.

Dehydration

Bring and drink lots of water when you are out and about, especially when you are hiking. Dehydration sneaks up on people. By the time you are thirsty, you're already dehydrated. It's a good idea to take an insulated water jug with you in the car or one of those 1½ liter bottles of water. Our weather is almost certainly different than what you left behind, and you will probably find yourself thirstier than usual. Just fill it before you leave in the morning and *suck 'em up* (as we say here) all day.

Curses

Legend says that if you remove any lava from the island, bad luck will befall you. *Balderdash!* you say. Hey, we don't know if it's true or not. You don't have to be a believer, but we at Wizard Publications along with resorts and local post offices, get boxes of lava that come in all the time from visitors who brought a souvenir of lava home, only to have their house burn down, have their foot fall off or get audited by the IRS. Coincidence? Maybe. But if you decide to do it anyway, remember… you've been warned.

Also, if the curse isn't enough to dissuade you, the TSA has written us asking us to inform you that they will *confiscate* any large lava rocks, coral or sand found in your luggage.

Grocery Stores

Definitely a hazard. Though restaurants on the Big Island are expensive, don't think you'll get off cheap in grocery stores. You'll certainly save money by cooking your own food, but you'll be amazed, appalled and offended by the prices you see here. If you are staying at a condo, savvy travelers should head over to **Costco** (331–4800) just north of Kona (shown on map on page 164) to stock up. If you're not a member of this national warehouse store, you might consider a $55 membership. With one, the savings on food and everything else are incredible, especially for Hawai'i. Otherwise, ask around to see if any residents you are dealing with will let you go with them or have a member get you a Cash Card from there.

There are no large grocery stores in the Kohala resort area, just an upscale market in the **Queens' MarketPlace** in Waikoloa. You'll find a larger store 6 miles up Waikoloa Road (which is across from the 75 mile marker) in Waikoloa Village. They're easy to find in Kona and Hilo.

TRAVELING WITH CHILDREN (KEIKI)

Should we have put this section under HAZARDS, too? The Hilton Waikoloa probably has the most extensive children's activity program. Their Club Keiki (ages 5–12) is a youngster's dream. Several other Kohala resorts also try hard to cater to families. If your keiki (kid) is looking for an adventure, check out page 236 where we have a dandy adventure just for them. **All About Babies** (883–3675) has the usual assortment of keiki paraphernalia for rent, such as car seats, strollers, cribs, bathtubs, etc as does **Baby's Away** (756–5800).

For swimming, the beach in front of the King Kamehameha's Kona Beach Hotel or the tide-pools at the Natural Energy Lab in Kona, and Onekahakaha in Hilo are probably the safest on the island. (Check them out yourself to be sure.) We don't need to tell you that keiki and surf don't mix. Also check out **Keiki Beach** just north of Kailua Bay. See map on page 61 and park near the gym for the 5-minute walk to this very protected cove.

There's a great playground at **Higashi-hara Park** just south of Kona past the 115 mile marker. Another one is at the corner of Kuakini Hwy and Makala Blvd. at the north end of Kona, and **Waimea Park** in Waimea. See Waimea map. The **Na Kamalei Toddler Playground** in Kailua Park is an entertaining spot for the youngest visitors.

'Imiloa Astronomy Center (969–9700) in Hilo is a great hands on keiki experience. See page 109 for more.

Kids might enjoy the seahorse tour at **Ocean Rider** (page 57) and if they're old enough, consider SNUBA on page 223.

If you are an animal lover, the **Three Ring Ranch Animal Sanctuary** (331–8778) shouldn't be missed. A great excursion with the keiki, this exotic and native animal rehabilitation facility gives a great hands-on, educational experience. You will have to call ahead to set up a tour as time and space are limited. The genuine passion the caretakers have about the animals is contagious, and their famous albino zebra will leave you in awe. Tours last around 2 hours and a donation of $50 per person is requested.

On your way out, if you have time to kill at the Kona Airport, the **Ellison Onizuka Space Center** is a good $3 distraction for restless keiki.

Lastly, you should know that it's a big fine plus a mandatory safety class if your keiki isn't buckled up.

THE PEOPLE

There's no doubt about it, people really *are* friendlier in Hawai'i. You will

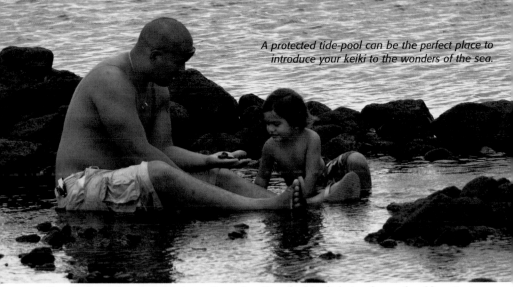

A protected tide-pool can be the perfect place to introduce your keiki to the wonders of the sea.

notice that people are quick to smile and wave at you here. (Those of us who live in Hawai'i have to remember to pack our "mainland face" when we journey there. Otherwise, we get undesired responses when we smile or wave at complete strangers.) It probably comes down to a matter of happiness. People are happy here, and happy people are friendly people. Some people compare a trip to an outer island in Hawai'i to a trip back in time, when smiles weren't rare, and politeness was the order of the day.

Ethnic Breakdown

The Big Island has an ethnic mix that is as diversified as any you will find. Here, *everyone* is a minority; there are no majorities. The last census revealed the ethnic makeup below:

White	68,110
Asian	41,791
Hispanic	21,162
Hawaiian or Other Pacific Islander	20,451
Black	1,778
American Indian or Alaska Native	1,422
Other	23,121
Total	**177,835**

SOME TERMS

A person of Hawaiian blood is Hawaiian. Only people of this race are called by this term. They are also called Kanaka Maoli, but only another Hawaiian can use this term. Anybody who was born here, regardless of race (except whites) is called a local. If you were born elsewhere but have lived here awhile, you are called a kama'aina. If you are white, you are a haole. It doesn't matter if you have been here a day or your family has been here for over a century—you will always be a haole. The term comes from the time when westerners first encountered these islands. Its precise meaning has been lost, but it is thought to refer to people with no background (since westerners could not chant the kanaenae of their ancestors).

The continental United States is called the Mainland. If you are here and are returning, you are not "going back to the states" (we *are* a state). When somebody leaves the island, they are off-island.

HAWAIIAN TIME

One aspect of Hawaiian culture you may have heard of is Hawaiian Time. The stereotype is that everyone in Hawai'i moves just a little bit slower than on the mainland. Supposedly, we are more laid-back and don't let things get to us as easily as people on the mainland. This is the stereotype... OK, it's *not* a stereotype. It's real. Hopefully, during your visit, you will notice that this feeling infects *you* as well. You may find yourself letting another driver cut in front of you in circumstances that would incur your wrath back home. You may find yourself willing to wait for a red light without feeling like you're going to explode. The whole reason for coming to Hawai'i is to experience beauty and a sense of peace, so let it happen. If someone else is moving a bit more slowly than you want, just go with it.

SHAKA

One gesture you will see often and should not be offended by is the *shaka* sign. This is done by extending the pinkie and thumb while curling the three middle fingers. Sometimes visitors think it is some kind of local gesture indicating *up yours* or some similarly unfriendly message. Actually, it is a friendly act used as a sign of greeting or just to say *Hey*. Its origin is thought to date back to the 1930s. A guard at the Kahuku Sugar Plantation on O'ahu used to patrol the plantation railroad to keep local kids from stealing cane from the slow moving trains. This guard had lost his middle fingers in an accident and his manner of waving off the youths became well known. Kids began to warn other kids that he was around by waving their hands in a way that looked like the guard's, and the custom took off.

THE HAWAIIAN LANGUAGE

The Hawaiian language is a beautiful, gentle and melodic language that flows smoothly off the tongue. Just the sounds of the words conjure up trees gently blowing in the breeze and the sound of the surf. Most Polynesian languages share the same roots, and many have common words. Today, Hawaiian is spoken *as an everyday language* only on the privately owned island of Ni'ihau. Visitors are often intimidated by Hawaiian. With a few ground rules you will come to realize that pronunciation is not as hard as you might think.

When missionaries discovered that the Hawaiians had no written language, they sat down and created an alphabet. This Hawaiian alphabet has only twelve letters. Five vowels; A, E, I, O and U, as well as seven consonants; H, K, L, M, N, P and W. The consonants are pronounced just as they are in English with the exception of W. It is often pronounced as a V if it is in the middle of a word and comes after an E or I. Vowels are pronounced as follows:

A—pronounced as in *Ah* if stressed, or *above* if not stressed.
E—pronounced as in *say* if stressed, or *dent* if not stressed.
I—pronounced as in *bee*.
O—pronounced as in *no*.
U—pronounced as in *boo*.

One thing you will notice in this book are glottal stops. These are represented by an upside-down apostrophe ' and are meant to convey a hard stop in the pronunciation. So if we are talking about the type of lava called 'a'a, it is pronounced as two separate As (AH-AH).

Another feature you will encounter are diphthongs, where two letters glide together. They are ae, ai, ao, au, ei, eu, oi, and ou. Unlike many English diphthongs, the second vowel is always pronounced. One word you will read in this book, referring to Hawaiian temples, is *heiau* (HEY-YOW). The e and i flow together as a single sound, then the a and u flow together as a single sound. The Y sound binds the two sounds, making the whole word flow together.

If you examine long Hawaiian words, you will see that most have repeating syllables, making it easier to remember and pronounce.

Let's take a word that might seem impossible to pronounce. When you see how easy this word is, the rest will seem like a snap. The Hawai'i State Fish is the humuhumunukunukuapua'a. At first glance it seems like a nightmare. But if you read the word slowly, it is pronounced just like it looks and isn't nearly as horrifying as it appears. Try it. Humu (hoo-moo) is pronounced twice. Nuku (noo-koo) is pronounced twice. A (ah) is pronounced once. Pu (poo) is pronounced once. A'a (ah-ah) is the ah sound pronounced twice, the glottal stop indicating a hard stop between sounds. Now you can try it again.

Humuhumunukunukuapua'a.

Now, wasn't that easy? OK, so it's not easy, but it's not impossible either.

Below are some words that you might hear during your visit.

'Aina (EYE-na)—Land.

Akamai (AH-ka-MY)—Wise or shrewd.

Ali'i (ah-LEE-ee)—A Hawaiian chief; a member of the chiefly class.

Aloha (ah-LO-ha)—Hello, goodbye or a feeling or the spirit of love, affection or kindness.

Hala (HA-la)—Pandanus tree.

Hale (HA-leh)—House or building.

Hana (HA-na)—Work.

Hana hou (HA-na-HO)—To do again.

Haole (HOW-leh)—Originally foreigner, now means Caucasian.

Heiau (HEY-YOW)—Hawaiian temple.

Hula (HOO-la)—The story-telling dance of Hawai'i.

Imu (EE-moo)—An underground oven.

'Iniki (ee-NEE-key)—Sharp and piercing wind (as in Hurricane 'Iniki).

Kahuna (ka-HOO-na)—A priest or minister; someone who is an expert in a profession.

Kai (kigh)—The sea.

Kalua (KA-LOO-ah)—Cooking food underground.

Kama'aina (KA-ma-EYE-na)—Long-time Hawai'i resident.

Kane (KA-neh)—Boy or man.

Kapu (KA-poo)—Forbidden, taboo; keep out.

Keiki (KAY-key)—Child or children.

Kokua (KO-KOO-ah)—Help.

Kona (KO-na)—Leeward side of the island; wind blowing from the south, southwest direction.

Kuleana (KOO-leh-AH-na)—Concern, responsibility or jurisdiction.

Lanai (LA-NIGH)—Porch, veranda, patio.

Lani (LA-nee)—Sky or heaven.

Lei (lay)—Necklace of flowers, shells or feathers. The lehua blossom lei is the lei of the Big Island.

Liliko'i (LEE-lee-KO-ee)—Passion fruit.

Limu (LEE-moo)—Edible seaweed.

Lomi (LOW-me)—To rub or massage; lomi salmon is raw salmon rubbed with salt and spices.

Lu'au (LOO-OW)—Hawaiian feast; literally means taro leaves.

Mahalo (ma-HA-low)—Thank you.

Makai (ma-KIGH)—Toward the sea.

Malihini (MA-lee-HEE-nee)—A new comer, visitor or guest.

Mauka (MOW-ka)—Toward the mountain.

Moana (mo-AH-na)—Ocean.

Mo'o (MO-oh)—Lizard.

Nani (NA-nee)—Beautiful, pretty.

Nui (NEW-ee)—Big, important, great.

'Ohana (oh-HA-na)—Family.

'Okole (OH-KO-leh)—Derrière.

'Ono (OH-no)—Delicious, the best.

Pakalolo (pa-ka-LO-LO)—Marijuana.

Pali (PA-lee)—A cliff.

Paniolo (PA-nee-OH-lo)—Hawaiian cowboy.

Pau (pow)—Finish, end; *pau hana* means quitting time from work.

Poi (poy)—Pounded kalo (taro) root that forms a paste.

Pono (PO-no)—Goodness, excellence, correct, proper.

Pua (POO-ah)—Flower.

Puka (POO-ka)—Hole.

Pupu (POO-POO)—Appetizer, snacks or finger food.

Wahine (vah-HEE-neh)—Woman.

Wai (why)—Fresh water.

Wikiwiki (WEE-kee-WEE-kee)—To hurry up, very quick.

Quick Pidgin Lesson

Hawaiian pidgin is fun to listen to. It's like ear candy. It's colorful, rhythmic and

THE BASICS

sways in the wind. Below is a list of some of the words and phrases you might hear on your visit. It's tempting to read some of these and try to use them. If you do, the odds are you will simply look foolish. These words and phrases are used in certain ways and with certain inflections. People who have spent years living in the islands still feel uncomfortable using them. Thick pidgin can be incomprehensible to the untrained ear (that's the idea). If you are someplace and hear two people engaged in a discussion in pidgin, stop and eavesdrop a bit. You won't forget it.

Pidgin Words & Phrases
An' den—And then? So?
Any kine—Anything; any kind.
Ass right—That's right.
Ass why—That's why.
Beef—Fight.
Brah—Bruddah; friend; brother.
Brok' da mouf—Delicious.
Buggah—That's the one; it is difficult.
Bus laugh—To laugh out loud.
Bus nose—How one reacts to a bad smell.
Chicken skin kine—Something that gives you goosebumps.
Choke—Plenty; a lot.
Cockaroach—Steal; rip off.
Da kine—A noun or verb used in place of whatever the speaker wishes. Heard constantly.
Fo Days—plenty; "He got hair fo days."
Geevum—Go for it! Give 'em hell!
Grind—To eat.
Grinds—Food.
Hold ass—A close call when driving your new car.
How you figga?—How do you figure that? It makes no sense.
Howzit?—How is it going? How are you? Also, Howzit o wot?
I owe you money or wot?—What to say when someone is staring at you.
Mek ass—Make a fool of yourself.
Mek house—Make yourself at home.
Mek plate—Grab some food.

Mo' bettah—This is better.
Moke—A large, tough local male. (Don't say it unless you *like beef*.)
No can—Cannot; I cannot do it.
No mek lidat—Stop doing that.
No, yeah?—No, or is "no" correct?
'Okole squeezer—Something that suddenly frightens you ('okole meaning derrière).
O wot?—Or what?
Pau hana—Quit work. (A time of daily, intense celebration in the islands.)
Poi dog—A mutt.
Shahkbait—Shark bait, meaning pale, untanned people.
Shaka—Great! All right!
Shredding—Riding a gnarly wave.
Sleepahs—Flip-flops, thongs, zoris.
Stink eye—Dirty looks; facial expression denoting displeasure.
Suck rocks—Buzz off, or pound sand.
Talk stink—Speak bad about somebody.
Talk story—Shooting the breeze; to rap.
Tanks eh?—Thank you.
Tita—A female moke. Same *beef* results.
Training brah—A haole trying (unsuccessfully) to speak pidgin.
Yeah?—Used at the end of sentences.

MUSIC

Hawaiian music is far more diverse than most people think. Many people picture Hawaiian music as someone twanging away on an 'ukulele with his voice slipping and sliding all over the place like he has an ice cube down his back. In reality, the music here can be outstanding. There is the melodic sound of the more traditional music. There are young local bands putting out modern music with a Hawaiian beat. There is even Hawaiian reggae. *Hawaiian Style Band*, the late *Israel Kamakawiwo'ole* (known locally as Bruddah Iz) and *Bruddah Waltah* are excellent examples. Even if you don't always agree with all of the messages in the songs, there's no denying the talent of these groups.

THE HULA

The hula evolved as a means of worship, later becoming a forum for telling a story with chants (called mele), hands and body movement. It can be fascinating to watch. When most people think of the hula, they picture a woman in a grass skirt swinging her hips to the beat of an 'ukulele. But in reality there are two types of hula. The modern hula, or hula 'auana, uses musical instruments and vocals to augment the dancer. It came about after westerners first encountered the islands. Missionaries found the hula distasteful, and the old style was driven underground. The modern type came about as a form of entertainment and was practiced in places where missionaries had no influence. Ancient Hawaiians didn't even use grass skirts. They were later brought by Gilbert Islanders.

The old style of hula is called hula 'olapa or hula kahiko. It consists of chants and is accompanied only by percussion and takes years of training. It can be exciting to watch as performers work together in a synchronous harmony. Both men and women participate, with women's hula being softer (though no less disciplined) and men's hula being more active. This type of hula is physically demanding, requiring strong concentration. Keiki (children's) hula can be charming to watch as well.

The world's best gather each year in Hilo for a week starting the first Thursday after Easter Sunday for the **Merrie Monarch Festival** (named after the 19th-century king credited with reviving the hula). Tickets are often hard to come by if you wait too long. Visit their website www.merriemonarch.com for ticket info. Otherwise, check it out on TV. It will utterly dazzle you.

A NOTE ABOUT ACCESS

If a lawful landowner posts a No TRESPASSING sign on their land, you need to respect their wishes. That seems simple enough. But here's where it gets tricky.

It's common in Hawai'i for someone who doesn't own or control land to erect their own No TRESPASSING, KEEP OUT and ROAD CLOSED signs. Picture a shoreline fisherman who doesn't want anyone else near his cherished spot, putting up a store-bought sign to protect his solitude. Or a neighbor on a dirt road who hates the dust from cars driving by, so he puts up a sign that he knows locals will ignore, but it might dissuade unwary visitors.

In the past we did our best to try to ferret out when No TRESPASSING signs were valid, and when they were not and we took *a lot* of heat from residents who thought we were encouraging trespassing when we weren't. But the current environment doesn't permit us to do that anymore. So if you're heading to one of the places we describe and you encounter a No TRESPASSING sign, even if you think it's not authorized by the landowner (and even if it's on *public* land), we have to advise you to turn around and heed the sign. All descriptions in our book come with the explicit assumption that you have obtained the permission of the legal landowner, and unfortunately it'll usually be up to you to determine who that is and how to get it. But please, under no circumstances are we suggesting that you trespass. Plain and clear. Don't trespass...ever...for any reason...period.

A NOTE ON PERSONAL RESPONSIBILITY

In past editions we've had the sad task of removing places that you can no longer visit. The reason, universally cited, is *liability*. Although Hawai'i has a statute indemnifying landowners, the mere threat is often enough to get something closed. Because we, more than any other publication, have exposed heretofore unknown attractions, we feel the need to pass this along.

You need to assess what kind of traveler you are. We've been accused of leaning a bit toward the adventurous side, so you should take that into account when deciding if something's right for you. To paraphrase from the movie *Top Gun*, "Don't let your ego write checks your body can't cash."

Please remember that this isn't Disneyland—it's nature. Mother Nature is hard, slippery, sharp and unpredictable. If you go exploring and get into trouble, whether it's your ego that's bruised or something more tangible, please remember that neither the state, the private land owner nor this publication *told* you to go. You *chose* to explore, which is what life, and this book, are all about. And if you complain to or threaten someone controlling land, they'll rarely fix the problem you identified. They'll simply close it... and it will be gone for good.

Sometimes even good intentions can lead to disaster. At one adventure, a trailhead led hikers to the base of a wonderful waterfall. There was only *one* trail, to the left at the parking lot, that a person could take. Neither we, other guides nor websites ever said, "stay on the trail to the left" because at the time there was only one trail to take. The state (in their zeal to protect themselves from liability at an unmaintained trail) came along and put up a DANGER KEEP OUT sign at the trailhead. Travelers encountering the sign assumed they were on the wrong trail and started to beat a path to the right instead. But that direction started sloping downward and ended abruptly at a 150-foot-high cliff. Hikers retreated and in a short time a previously non-existent trail to the right became as prominent as the correct (and heretofore *only*) path to the left. Not long after the state's well-intentioned sign went up, an unwitting pair of hikers took the new, incorrect trail to the right and fell to their deaths. They probably died because they had been dissuaded from taking the correct trail by a state sign theoretically erected to keep people safe.

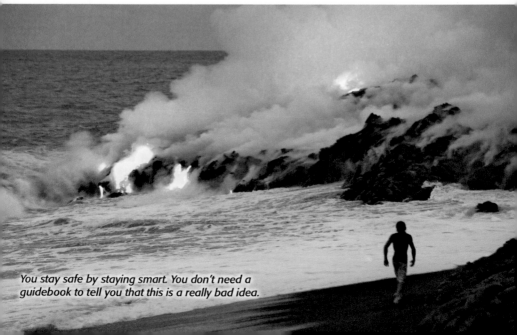

You stay safe by staying smart. You don't need a guidebook to tell you that this is a really bad idea.

Our point is that nothing is static and nothing can take the place of your own observations and good judgment. If you're doing one of the activities you read about in our book or someplace else and your instinct tells you something is wrong, *trust your judgment* and go do another activity. There are lots of wonderful things to do on the island, and we want to keep you safe and happy.

And also remember to always leave the island the same way you found it.

MISCELLANEOUS INFORMATION

It is customary here for *everyone* to remove their shoes upon entering someone's house (sometimes their office).

If you are going to spend any time at the beach, woven bamboo beach mats can be found all over the island for about $3. Some roll up, some can be folded. The sand comes off these easier than it comes off towels.

Around the island you'll see signs saying VISITOR INFORMATION, VOLCANO UPDATE or something similar. Allow me to translate. That's usually code for WE WANT TO SELL YOU SOMETHING.

The **area code** for the state is 808. **Daylight Saving** isn't observed here.

If you wear **sunglasses**, *polarized* lenses are highly recommended. Not only are our colors more vivid here, but the lower latitudes of Hawai'i make polarized lenses particularly effective.

Plastic bags are banned on the island, and rather than springing for paper bags, many stores will simply hand you your purchases, no matter how numerous. Consider bringing your own reusable bag.

If you want to arrange a lei greeting for you or your honey when you disembark the airplane, call **Greeters of Hawai'i** (800) 366–8559. In Kona, you can get a good lei for around $25. (I know where you're going with that—stop it!) Nice way to kick off a romantic trip, huh?

A WORD ABOUT DRIVING TOURS

The Big Island is, to use the scientific term, *one big bugga*. With this in mind, we have decided to describe the various parts of the island in a series of tours. You're not being pigeonholed into seeing the island in this order, but we had to organize the regions in some fashion, and this seemed the logical way to do it rather than a scattershot description. You can take these tours from any place you are staying, but we have described most of them (except the Hilo tour and the Hamakua/Waimea tour) on the assumption that you are starting from the west (Kona) side because the majority of Big Island visitors do just that. The Hamakua/Waimea section is described from the Hilo side first because it's convenient to see it that way after traveling via Saddle Road.

Nearly every guidebook divides the Big Island and its sights by districts. (See graphic on fold-out back map.) While this land division made perfect sense to the ancients who divvied up the island among themselves, it is not real helpful to the modern traveler who cruises the island by car. So we have divided the island up in a way that makes more sense to today's visitor. It takes into account where most people stay and how they drive. Look at the inside *front* cover to see how we have divided the island and on what pages we describe the sights.

Most main roads have mile markers erected every mile. Since Hawai'i is mostly void of other identification signs, these little green signs can be a big help in knowing where you are at a given time. Therefore, we have placed them on the maps represented as a number inside a small box 16. We will often describe a certain feature or unmarked road as being, "⁴/₁₀ miles past the 22 mile mark." We hope this helps.

For directions, locals usually describe things as being on the **mauka** (MOW-ka) side of the highway—toward the mountains or **makai** (ma-KIGH)—toward the ocean.

Beaches, activities and adventures are mentioned briefly, but described in detail in their own separate sections.

FARMERS' MARKETS

Kailua-Kona—The **Kailua Village Farmers' Market** (Wed.–Sun.) at the corner of Hualalai and Alii Drive is the biggest in town. There are tons of cheap, foreign-made crafts. Open 7 a.m. to 4 p.m. The **Alii Gardens Marketplace** near the 2½ mile marker on Alii Drive focuses more on crafts and local handmade items with a few decent food vendors. Open 10 a.m. to 5 p.m. Tue.–Sun. The **Keauhou Farmers' Market** (Sat.) at the Keauhou Shopping Center claims to sell only locally grown products such as coffee and mac nuts. Open 8 a.m. to noon.

Hilo—The **Hilo Farmers' Market** on the corner of Mamo Street and Kamehameha Avenue has mostly produce and flowers with a few booths of crafts and gift items. Open every day 7 a.m. *till it's gone*. Wednesdays and Saturdays have the most vendors and open at 6 a.m.

Waimea—The **Waimea Homestead Farmers' Market** is small but has a lot to offer. Among the food, flower and plant vendors, you'll find some great locally made items like goat cheese, chocolate and vanilla beans. Saturdays only, on Hwy 19 near the 55 mile marker. Open Saturdays from 7 a.m. to noon. Nearby, is the **Waimea Midweek Farmer's Market** on Wed. 9 a.m.–4 p.m. In addition to fresh foods, some opportunites to dine here. Look for the stand with the chocolate bomb bar. At Pukalani Stables.

Pahoa—The **Maku'u Farmers' Market**, on Sundays, just south of the 7 mile marker on Hwy 130 has reached flea market (or possibly bazaar) status. Open Sundays from 8 a.m. to 2 p.m.

BOOKS

There is an astonishing variety of books available about Hawai'i and the Big Island. Everything from history, legends, geology, children's stories and just plain ol' novels. **Kona Stories** (324–0350) in the Keauhou Shopping Center on Ali'i Drive has a large selection of Hawaiiana titles. Walk in and lose yourself in Hawai'i's richness. **Kona Bay Books** (326–7790) on Kaiwi Street is one of the largest *used* bookstores in the state. **Basically Books** on Kamehameha in Hilo (961–0144) also has a superb collection of Hawai'i titles. They also have the best selection of topographic maps on the island.

THE INTERNET

You will find recent changes, links to cool sites, the latest satellite weather shots and more on our website **www.hawaiirevealed.com**. We also show our own aerial photos of nearly every place to stay, so you'll know if oceanfront *really* means oceanfront. It also has links to every company listed in the book that has a site—both those we like and those we recommend against. There are no advertisements on the site. (Well...except for our own books and apps, of course.) We could have listed all of the Web addresses in the book, but it seemed pretty mean to make you type in all of those URL addresses. We also have a calendar of upcoming events.

If you're on-island and need Internet access (to check your mail, etc.), most of the big resorts have business services available for around $20 an hour. **Kona Business Center** (329–0006) in Kona has Internet access for $8 per hour. **Island Lava Java** in Kona (see ISLAND DINING) has Internet access and good cinnamon rolls—what a combo! In Kona and Hilo, Wi-Fi is easy to find.

'Anacho'omulu Beach is a sunset photographer's dream come true.

Kohala is the oldest volcano on the island, having last sputtered 60,000 years ago. It contains lush forest, dry lava desert, windswept grassy plains and outrageous beaches. Some of the most expensive resorts on the island are along the Kohala Coast.

This is a large, diverse area to cover in one section, but because of the way the island's resorts are distributed and the roads are laid out, most will see this area in a circular driving tour, so that's how we'll describe it. We're going to start as you leave Kona (see map) heading up Hwy 190. If you're staying in Kohala, you can come up Waikoloa Village Road and pick up the description on Hwy 190 heading north. If staying in Hilo, pick it up from Waimea.

UP HIGHWAY 190 FROM KAILUA-KONA

As you leave Kona, you'll take Palani Road, which becomes Mamalahoa Highway (190) heading north. (See map on page 45 or 61.) From near sea level, you will be heading up to 3,564 feet then down again into Hawi, so gas up on that cheap *(ha!)* Kona gasoline.

A Leaving Kailua-Kona, it's hard to believe that just above the town is a beautiful fern and 'ohi'a **cloud forest** steeped in fog and moss. Weather here is determined by altitude because the mountain literally creates its own rain through convection. You can see it by taking **Kaloko Drive** just south of the 34 mile marker. Follow it for 7 miles as it winds upward into another world. Just before

DIVERSION ALERT!

the end of the road, turn left and it will dead end at 5,000 feet with expansive views (clouds permitting) of Kona below. Morning is best for this drive; don't ride your brakes on the way down.

As you leave Kona, you'll get some good views down the coast. Keep an eye out for renegade peacocks (which sound like cats being tortured) from the **Makalei Golf Course** around the 32 mile marker.

The highway bisects several channels and tubes in the lava between the 28 and 26 mile markers. Rivers of molten stone coursed down the mountain here during the 1800 Hualalai lava flow. If you look down the coast, you'll get an idea of the scale of a "typical" lava flow. On your right before the 21 mile marker is the road to the Pu'u Wa'awa'a trail-head described on page 202.

By the 19 mile marker you have passed from Hualalai Mountain to the slopes of Mauna Loa. Proof is in the form of a lava flow here that ran for 30 miles in 1859 all

. . . .

Letters ($\boxed{\text{A}}$) correspond to paragraphs in text.

the way to Kiholo Bay, destroying Kame-hameha's fishpond (see BEACHES). If clouds are absent, you may see the top of Mauna Kea and its many dome-enclosed telescopes ahead and on your right.

As you continue, you'll notice cactus scattered about, and trees appear again. **Parker Ranch** starts at the 14 mile marker, part of a colossal 130,000-acre cattle ranch.

At the 11 mile marker is the road through **Waikoloa Village**, which leads down to the Kohala mega-resorts. It's marked by a giant obelisk shaped like Hawaiian sail erected by Waikoloa Land Co. in a fit of psychedelic creativity. Wai-koloa Village is a relatively stark commu-nity. Due to its location, on the leeward side of the saddle between Mauna Loa and Mauna Kea, it's usually pretty windy. *(How consistently windy? When the wind stops, the cows fall down.)* If you are staying at a mega-resort in Kohala, you'll want to know that there is a fairly large grocery store here.

Still on Hwy 190 between the 5 and 2 mile markers off to your right (up mauka), there's a large hill called **Holoholoku**. Everyone has seen the famous WWII photo and statue of the scene where Marines on Iwo Jima raised the American flag over Mt. Suribachi. Possibly the most dramatic WWII photo ever taken, it puts a lump in your throat every time you see it. What you don't know is that those very guys practiced storming the hill right there on Holoholoku because it was thought to be similar to Suribachi in size and shape.

$\boxed{\text{B}}$ As you approach the town of **Waimea** (Kamuela), you may decide to check it out now. Since this is the cross-roads between the east and west sides of the island, we could have included it here or in the section on Hamakua. After care-ful analysis of driving patterns, accommo-dation indexes and topography...we flipped a coin and put it in the HAMAKUA

South Kohala to Kona

← To Hawi

Waimea map on page 135

Kohala Mountain Rd

250

Waimea (Kamuela)

─ Holoholoku

Kawaihae Rd

190

Map continued on page 46

19

Old Saddle Road

Mamalahoa Hwy

Kawaihae

Akoni Pule Hwy

270

Crystal Cove
Detailed map on page 152

Pu'ukohola Heiau

19

Spencer Beach Park
Mau'umae Beach
Mauna Kea (Kauna'oa) Beach
Hapuna Beach
Waialea (69) Beach
Puako Bay

Puako

Detailed map on page 53

Queen Ka'ahumanu Hwy

Waikoloa Village

Gas

Waikoloa Rd

Saddle Road
200

Kohala Resort Area

Honoka'ope Beach

Gas

South Kohala District
North Kona District

'Anaeho'omalu Bay
(AKA A Bay)

Freshwater Pool
Detailed map on page 157

Ke-awa-iki Beach

Mauna Loa Flow of 1859

Big Island Country Club

Pu'u Wa'awa'a
(AKA Jello Mold)

Kiholo Bay
Detailed map on page 200

	Indicates Foot Trails
19	Roadside mile markers
	Unpaved Roads

Ka'upulehu (Hualalai) Flow of 1800

Ka'upulehu Beach
(Kona Village—Closed)

Detailed map on page 159

Kuki'o Beach

Manini'owali Beach / Kua Bay
(Part of Kekaha Kai State Park)

Hualalai Summit (8,271')

Ka'upulehu Crater

Queen Ka'ahumanu Hwy

Hu'ehu'e (Hualalai) Flow of 1801

Makalawena Beach

Mahai'ula Beach
(Kekaha Kai State Park)

Makole'a Beach

190

Mamalahoa Hwy

Makalei Golf Course

5000'

Cloud Forest

Kaloko Dr

Kona International Airport

Manta Rays

Natural Energy Lab

Wawaloli Beach & Tidepools

Pine Trees
Detailed map on page 164

Honokohau Bay
'Alula Beach
Old Kona Airport Beach Park

Kaiminani Dr

Hina Lani

4WD

19

Costco

Kmart

180 **Holualoa**

Kailua-Kona

190

Walmart

11

Alii Drive

Detailed map on page 61

0   5 MILES

© 2014 Wizard Publications, Inc.

North Kohala

Often 4WD from here

Kamehameha Birth Site

'Upolu Airport
Mo'okini Heiau
Hawi Wind Farm

Akoni Pule Hwy

Hawi

Kapa'au

Kauhola Pt.
20°14.777'
155°46.284'

(270)

Kapa'a Beach Park

Kahikolo Church

Kapanai'a Bay
Keokea Beach Park

(250)

Navigational Heiau

Mahukona Beach Park

Kohala Ditch

Waikama Falls (2nd)

Pololu Beach

Lapakahi State Historical Park

Pololu Trail

Kaiholena Cove

Kohala is the oldest surviving Big Island volcano. The mountain last erupted 60,000 years ago and is considered "extinct," but will probably cough back to life in a million years or less for a last gasp at island-making before it is pronounced truly dead. Haleakala on Maui is now in that final phase. Diamond Head on O'ahu is the product of its volcano's last gasp phase.

Kohala Mountain Road

1 Kohala Village Inn
2 Hawai'i Island Retreat
3 Kohala Club Hotel

Pololu Valley

Honokane Nui Valley

Kohala Mountain

0   2 MILES

Road Crest at 3,564'

Crystal Cove

꙰ Indicates Foot Trails
10 Roadside mile markers
⋯ Unpaved Roads

It's not hard to guess which is the wet, windward side, and which is the dry, leeward side.

(270)

Kawaihae

Pu'ukohola Heiau
Spencer Beach Park
Mau'umae Beach

(250)

Waimea
(Kamuela)
Detailed map on page 135

(19)

Mauna Kea Beach (Kauna'oa)

Kawaihae Road
Queen Ka'ahumanu Hwy

(19)

56 Miles to Hilo

Hapuna Beach

32 miles to Kailua-Kona

Mamalahoa Hwy

36 miles to Kailua-Kona

(19)

(190)

Map continued on page 45

© 2014 Wizard Publications, Inc.

chapter. Waimea has an incredibly colorful history and is worth exploring. If you do it now, turn to page 133 before continuing on.

KOHALA MOUNTAIN ROAD

[C] See map on facing page or on page 135 to get to Highway 250 (left at the Shell station onto Lindsey Road first). You are traveling up the spine of the sleeping Kohala Volcano. (They say you shouldn't honk your horn, or you may wake it up.) You're still on the dry, leeward side and will crest at 3,564 feet before descending to the sea.

Around the 14 mile marker you'll start to see a huge mountain looming in front of you. That's not on this island; it's **Maui**, 30 miles across the sea. On clear days, the island of Maui seems to tower over the little town of Hawi even more than the Big Island's own volcanoes. Sometimes it looks gigantic, and sometimes it's less impressive. It's the same reason the moon always looks enormous when it's near a mountain horizon or through trees—it gives your brain some scale to compute its size. Maui looks biggest when you see it *with or through* something other than on the ocean's horizon.

NORTH SHORE OF KOHALA

[D] Be sure to take the road to Hawi, not Kapa'au, near the 20 mile marker. As you pull into Hawi, you're greeted by a couple of old banyan trees on your right. You'll want to head right (east), but if you're hungry for a treat, across the street from **Bamboo Restaurant** on your left is **Kohala Coffee Mill**, which has **Tropical Dreams**, an *outstanding* ice cream made here on the island. We unselfishly review it every time we are on the north shore, just to be thorough.

The sleepy little towns of **Hawi** and **Kapa'au** lie at this northernmost point of the island. Until the '70s, this was sugar country. When Kohala Sugar pulled out, this area was left high and dry. Rather than let their towns die, residents stuck it out, opening shops and other small businesses. Today, this area is enjoying a comeback of sorts. There are lots of artists who call this area home. A Japanese investment company bought most of Kohala Sugar's land assets (19,000 acres) in 1988 when land here was cheap and has *plans* for a resort and golf course at Mahukona, a restaurant at the end of the road overlooking Pololu Valley and more. But they've been *planning* for a long time. In the meantime, this is a quiet, peaceful community. It's said that the investor bought all this land after simply flying over it in a helicopter—without ever touching it!

Heading east, you come to the town of **Kapa'au**. Watch your speed in this area. Police commonly nab people caught by surprise in some of the slower posted areas. On the mauka side of the highway in Kapa'au is a statue of **King Kamehameha the Great**. If it looks just like the famous one standing in front of the Judiciary building in Honolulu, that's because it's the same...sort of. When the Hawaiian Legislature commissioned the statue in 1878, it was cast in Paris and put on a ship. Unfortunately, the ship and its cargo were lost at sea near the Falkland Islands in the South Atlantic. Since they had shipping insurance, they used the money to order a new one. Meanwhile, the captain of the wrecked ship later spotted the "lost" statue standing in Port Stanley (somebody had salvaged it). He bought it for $500 and shipped it (this time successfully—must have FedExed it) to Hawai'i where its broken arm was repaired, and it was erected where you see it now. On King Kamehameha Day (June 11) the statue is piled high with leis and other decorations and is quite a sight to see. There are public restrooms here behind the building.

Continuing east, just before the 24 mile marker, is the road to **Kalahikiola Church**, originally built in 1855. It was ravaged by a strong earthquake in 2006. The current building is new, but the stones from the original building, hand-carried from the ocean and rivers of the area in 1850, were used to build the wall around the new church.

If you want to see some raw coastline and have a 4WD vehicle, take a left ½ mile past the 24 mile marker onto Maulili (which is just after Old Halaula Mill Road). After ⅓ mile it becomes dirt. Turn right when it ends and the short paved section leads to an unpaved road that goes to Kauhola Point. In 1933, they built a lighthouse at this point that was 85 feet away from the edge of the cliff. In 2009, they had to destroy the lighthouse because it was only *20* feet from the shoreline and ready to topple into the sea. If you look at the sides of the cliffs, you can *see* how they're getting munched away by the waves. This area is wild and undeveloped and sports nice views of the sea cliffs that wrap around the north shore. The area a few hundred yards to the right (east) is full of abandoned sugar equipment and cars. Many are actually embedded in the *side* of the cliff, evidence of the rapid pace of cliff erosion. Just a few decades ago the cars

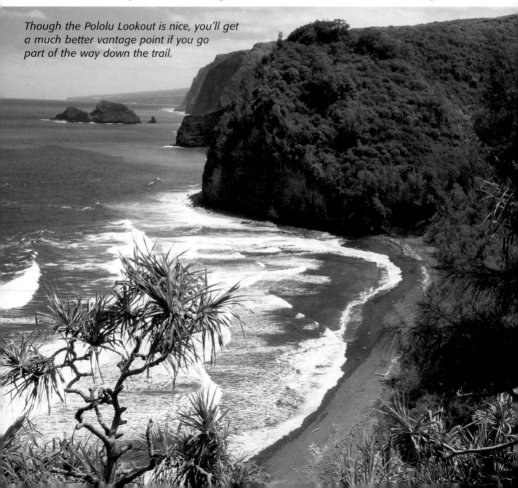

Though the Pololu Lookout is nice, you'll get a much better vantage point if you go part of the way down the trail.

were buried in "stable" ground and the cliffs were farther out.

Back on the highway, look to your left just before the 25 mile marker. There is a large banyan tree with an old **tree house**. Wouldn't you have *loved* a tree house like that when you were a kid?

There are ATV **Tours** of the coastal cliffs along here as well as other **Land Tours**, all described in ACTIVITIES.

POLOLU VALLEY

E The end of the highway (which lacks a turnaround for some reason, so expect vehicular confusion) is the **Pololu Valley Lookout**. This outstanding vista displays the raw, untamed side of the Big **A REAL GEM** Island. (Unfortunately, the state sometimes lets the vegetation block out some of the view. The view's *much* nicer halfway down the trail mentioned below.) Nearly vertical cliffs are battered unmercifully by the winter north shore surf. Four hundred feet below is **Pololu Beach**, accessed via a 15–20 minute trail down through lush vegetation. (If you make it back *up* in 15 minutes, we're proud of you. It means you didn't stop once.) If it's been raining much, the trail may be slippery. At the bottom, in several spots, you'll find black sand dunes over 100 feet high, now mostly covered with vegetation. This type of black sand beach is formed as water constantly chips away at the lava river bed. Though the beach is not very swimmable (the surf and current are usually too violent), it's very picturesque and a nice place to observe Mother Nature's force. During the week you may have it nearly to yourself down there. Halfway down the trail is a small natural platform that looks out over the beach—a good photo op.

The beach is prettier from below than above and there are some rope swings in nearby trees. On the opposite side of the valley, a trail leads up the wall over

to the next valley, called **Honokane Nui**. These seven valleys, from Pololu to Waipi'o, are the only part of this new island that show much sign of erosion.

In ancient times Pololu Valley was a bountiful source for waterworn stones. Thousands of tons of stones have been hauled from here to build temples, houses and other structures. The massive Pu'ukohola Heiau, 25 miles away at Kawaihae, was built from stones from this valley. A gigantic chain of people passed stones hand to hand all the way. If one was dropped, it was left where it lay (unless it was on his foot) to prevent the cadence from being interrupted. When you're ready, head back west past Hawi.

MO'OKINI HEIAU

F Near the 20 mile marker is a sign saying simply "Upolu Airport." This road (unpaved *past* the airport) leads to the northernmost tip of the island and past two important sites. The impressive 10½ megawatt **Hawi Wind Farm** is just before the airport. Though it looks peaceful, to any pilot who has ever landed at 'Upolu, the location is horrifying. That's because during normal winds, your approach to the airport places you in the gut-wrenching, scream-for-Mama prop wash from the turbines, turning a previously turbulent runway (before they built the turbines in 2006) into a delightfully terrifying experience.

You head left when you reach the quiet 'Upolu Airport. The county does a *terrible* job maintaining the unpaved portion. If it's dry and they've scraped it lately, you *may* make it in a regular car the 1½ miles to the heiau described below. Otherwise, it's 4WD on at least *part* of the unpaved section, and the last part might even scare 4-wheelers. Puddles last a *long time* here, and some of them are large enough to have nearly spawned their own unique ecosystem. Even during bad weather

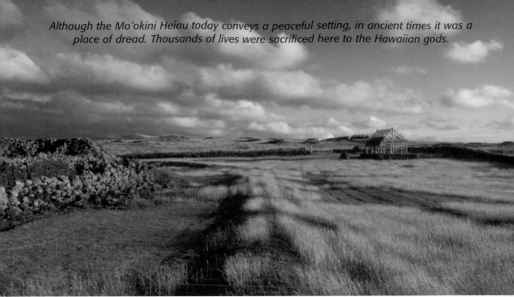

we've seen rental cars back here, giving legitimacy to the question: *What's the difference between a rental car and a 4WD? A rental car can go **anywhere**...*

This area is dominated by the legacy of two influential men—an ancient priest named **Paʻao** and **Kamehameha the Great**. Paʻao is said to have arrived in the 11th or 12th century and changed the islands. He was born in Tahiti or on one of its neighbor islands. It is said that the islands were in a state of anarchy when Paʻao arrived. He restructured society, introduced the concept of human sacrifice and brought other similar traditions. Here he built the Moʻokini Heiau, where countless people were put to death to please Paʻao's hungry gods. You'll have to park at the gate and walk five minutes to the heiau.

Even before we knew the gory details about Moʻokini Heiau's history, the place gave us the heebie-jeebies. We aren't the only ones who have noticed that the area around the temple is filled with an eerie, ghostly lifelessness, and it's the only place on the island that we like to avoid (not counting the Department of Motor Vehicles). Used for human sacrifices, the area feels devoid of a soul. The quiet is not comforting, but rather an empty void. The walls of Moʻokini are extreme-

ly tall and thick—oral tradition says that some of the rocks were passed by hand from Pololu Valley, 9 miles away. Just in front of the heiau is a large lava slab with a slight dip in it. In front of it is a raised stone. It takes little imagination to see that this slab was the *holehole* stone, where unfortunate victims were laid while the flesh was stripped from their bones. These bones were then used to make fishhooks and other objects. The number of Hawaiians sacrificed here ran into the tens of thousands.

There were no signs at this heiau at press time to orient you to the timeline here. Although people from the Marquesas Islands settled on the Big Island around 300 AD, they were eventually overwhelmed by the Tahitians who came with Paʻao around 1000 AD. It was the Tahitians who built this heiau and became the Hawaiians we know today.

Farther down the road is the **Kamehameha Akahi Aina Hanau Heiau**. This is where Kamehameha the Great, who conquered all the islands, was said to have been born. (Actually, many think he was born nearby, but not right here.) Kamehameha means "the lonely one," which seems ironically fitting given the almost palpable loneliness this area of the island exudes.

After Kamehameha's birthplace, you will come to an old Coast Guard LORAN station where you'll probably encounter boulders blocking the road. If so, retrace your route to the highway.

As you pass the tip of Kohala on 270, take note of how quickly you go from green to lots of dry scrub and an arid feel. That's the rain shadow effect, when the mountain causes it to rain more on one side than on the other.

There are a couple of places along this stretch to swim or snorkel—**Kapaʻa Beach Park** and **Mahukona**, both described in BEACHES.

Near the 15 mile marker, look toward the ocean in the distance, and you can see stones sticking up in the air from a fascinating *navigational* heiau where the stones are aligned to point to other Hawaiian islands, Tahiti and more. You can walk to a position below it from Mahukona Beach Park. We took a GPS here and were able to verify that the stones *really do* align with Polynesian destinations. Pretty impressive.

By the way, Mahukona is also the name given to the Big Island's first and now-forgotten volcano, located offshore. This volcano started it all but sank beneath the water less than half a million years ago.

On a clear day, you can't miss seeing Maui from here. But on *very* clear late afternoons, in addition to Maui's two mountains, you may see the islands of Lanaʻi, Kahoʻolawe (in front of Lanaʻi from this angle) and Molokaʻi between Lanaʻi and Maui. Look at the island chain map on the front inside cover to orient yourself. Sunsets from this area can be superb.

LAPAKAHI STATE HISTORICAL PARK

G At the 14 mile marker is **Lapakahi State Historical Park**, which consists of the remains of an old Hawaiian village. There is a trail running through the vil-

lage, complete with markers noting interesting spots. Open 8 a.m. to 4 p.m., admission is free. This self-guided tour takes around 45 minutes, and the brochure does a reasonable job of explaining what you are seeing. Lapakahi is interesting at times and worthwhile for anyone interested in a taste of how the ancient Hawaiians may have lived in such an inhospitable place. The park rangers here can be inhospitable as well. Sometimes surly to the point of being comical, they occasionally convey some of the worst and most inaccurate information we've run across in any park in the state. An example: "This area was once lush rain forest until western man came along and cut it down, causing the rainfall to go from 100 inches to 10 inches annually." (In reality, this was originally a thin, rocky and scrubby *dryland* forest until *the Hawaiians* burned it down to plant crops after they discovered Hawaiʻi. This area is dry because it is, and always has been, in the rain shadow of Kohala Mountain.)

One often overlooked aspect to Lapakahi is the fabulous water in **Koaiʻe Cove** (described in BEACHES). But don't expect to get the warmies from the staff, who seem to resent snorkelers here.

The highway between the 14 mile marker and Kawaihae (4 mile marker) is replete with dirt roads leading toward the ocean. You may be tempted to explore them, especially if you have 4WD. With that in mind, using a variety of vehicles and on foot, we traversed nearly every inch of all of them, including their branches (and we can cough up the dust-balls to prove it). The result? We can say with complete confidence that most of these roads are utterly wretched and lead to absolute squat. The entire coastline in this area is rocky and mostly unprotected. There are *no* beaches. It's pretty but not beautiful, and the land is harsh and unforgiving. (The real beauty of this area is underwater, with lots of extensive coral formations and ultra-clean water.) The only people who bother to make their way to the coast along this stretch are shoreline fishermen or hopeful whale watchers. So don't bother unless you have *way* too much time on your hands. The only exception is **Kaiholena Cove** between the 11 and 12 mile markers. The snorkeling is outstanding and fairly easy to access. (See BEACHES for more.)

Look to the shoreline from this area. Somewhere around here you'll usually find a place where to the left, the ocean looks calm and inviting, whereas to the right it looks choppy and frothing, and the line of demarcation is pretty defined. This is a terrifying place (if you're a pilot). It's the transition zone from waters that are wind-protected to waters that are whipped up from nukin' gales that slither around the tip of North Kohala. The turbulence in this area would make the toughest ULTIMATE FIGHTER scream like a little girl if he were flying here. (I've tried taking aerial photos of Kai-

holena Cove, but that pesky emotion called *fear of death* keeps turning me away.) So if you see any low flying aircraft around here—salute 'em.

Like an old commercial says, sometimes you feel like a nut. If so, just over ½ mile past the 5 mile marker is a road that leads to the **Hamakua Macadamia Nut Co.** (882–1690). They have all things mac nut. Super friendly folks, they'll give you a quickie tour of the processing facilities behind the glass.

KAWAIHAE

H The tiny port town of Kawaihae has a few places to eat and shop and is the launching area for some fishing and SCUBA operations. Otherwise, there's not much to see. There's an ice cream place on the back side of Kawaihae Center that has really good ice cream. **Café Pesto** is your best bet for food.

This is the driest part of the state, with annual rainfall averaging less than 10 inches. (Contrast that with 240 inches on the slopes northwest of Hilo.)

Kamehameha was instructed to build Pu'ukohola Heiau in order to conquer all the islands.

Kohala Resort Area
Waikoloa & Mauna Lani

Puako Road

Puako / Malama
Petroglyph Trail

Fairmont
Orchid

Parking

Pauoa
Bay

Fairways at
Mauna Lani

Mauna Lani North
Golf Course

Villages at
Mauna Lani

Shops at
Mauna Lani

Mauna Lani Bay Hotel
& Bungalows

Public
Parking

Pauoa Rd

Mauna Lani Dr

Islands
at
Mauna
Lani

Mauna Lani
Terrace

Makaiwa
Bay

Secret
Pond

Mauna Lani
Point

Kaniku Dr

0   1/2 MILE

Indicates Foot Trails

75   Roadside mile markers

Unpaved Roads

Ala Kahakai Trail

Mauna
Lani
South Golf
Course

Gate

Na Ala Hele

49 Black
Sand Beach

Honoku'ope
Beach

Honokaope

Lava Freshwater
Pool

Parking

Ala Loa / King's Trail

Hali'i Kai

Colony Villas

Hilton Waikoloa

Waikoloa Kings'
Golf Course

Waikoloa Beach
Golf Course

Shores at
Waikoloa

Vista
Waikoloa

Fairway
Villas at
Waikoloa

Waikoloa
Beach
Villas

Parking

Kings'
Shops

Waikoloa Beach Dr

Kolea

Waikoloa Beach
Marriott

Gas

Queens'
MarketPlace

'Anaeho'omalu Bay
(A Bay)

Parking

19

Note: From this area
(clouds permitting) you can
see four of the Big Island's
five volcano mountains.
Looking away from the ocean,
from left to right, they are
Kohala, Mauna Kea, Mauna Loa
and Hualalai. The most massive,
Mauna Loa, seems the least
impressive from this perspective.
Offshore, Haleakala on Maui is often
seen.

73

19

74

75   Waikoloa Road

Queen Ka'ahumanu Hwy

76

© 2014 Wizard Publications, Inc.

At the junction of Highways 19 and 270 is the impressive **Pu'ukohola Heiau** (882–7218). Entry is free and a very impressive visitor center is open 8:15 a.m. to 4:45 p.m. Check out their incredible weapons display. This massive structure was built by King Kamehameha in 1790–91. He had sent his wife's grandmother to visit a kahuna on Kaua'i to ask how he could conquer Hawai'i. The kahuna said that if he built a fabulous heiau (temple) at Kawaihae and dedicated it to his war god, he would prevail. Thousands of "volunteers" worked on the project, carrying boulders from miles away. Workers were routinely sacrificed at different portions of the structure during construction to ensure that the gods would be pleased. When the temple was completed, Kamehameha dedicated it by inviting and then sacrificing his enemy Keoua (see page 90). During construction Kamehameha himself participated to inspire his workers. When his brother picked up a boulder to help, Kamehameha slapped the rock out of his hand saying, "No, brother, one of us should keep the kapu" (meaning staying pure). Kamehameha then instructed that the rock his brother had touched be taken far out to sea and dumped into deep water. Pu'ukohola Heiau is best viewed from Kawaihae Harbor Road (the one that leads out to the breakwater) in the late afternoon with Mauna Kea in the background. Just offshore are said to be the remains of a shark heiau, called **Hale-o-Kapuni**, where human remains were offered to sharks. Its precise location is unknown, and it has been buried for decades.

KOHALA RESORT AREA

I Continuing *south* onto Highway 19 (called *Queen K* by most locals, short for Ka'ahumanu) toward Kailua-Kona, you will pass the **Kohala mega-resort area**.

Ensconced in this desolate sea of lava and scrub, multi-zillion dollar resorts dot the coastline offering the luxury and amenities that have made this region famous. Golfing is top notch (and *expensive*) here; see ACTIVITIES. Ocean activities, such as snorkeling and SCUBA, are very good. Though you wouldn't suspect it from the road, some of the best beaches in the state lie between here and Kailua-Kona. Some, such as Hapuna and Mauna Kea, are well known. Others, such as Manini'owali and Makalawena, are less known or deliciously secluded. The chapter on BEACHES describes them all in detail and tells you *exactly* how to get to each one of them.

See that barren lava field on the mauka (mountain) side of the highway? A Japanese company purchased the 3,000 acres in 1990 for a *mere* $45 million. They had big plans for it, including six golf courses and 2,600 homes. After paying taxes on it for nine years, the shrewd investors unloaded it in 1998 for $5 million.

Most of the lava you see here flowed thousands of years ago. In other parts of the island it'd be covered with forest. But the very thing that brings visitors here—the utter lack of rain—keeps the lava looking so uninviting.

Hold on to your hat along this stretch. The wind can be fierce in the afternoon. As the lava fields heat up during the day, it causes the air to heat and rise. Air from the ocean rushes in to fill the void, creating strong afternoon breezes.

Hapuna Beach is off the road near the 69 mile marker. This beach is often featured in travel shows and is a *superb* place to frolic. We like to snorkel from there to Beach 69 on calm days, or boogie board till we're raw. Otherwise, just gallivant on the fine sand.

The road to the Mauna Lani between the 73 and 74 mile markers is worth consideration. See map on page

Even where the land is bone dry and harsh, the exquisitely clear ocean makes up for it.

53. To the north is the **Puako/Malama Petroglyph Trail**. This simple 25-minute walk through kiawe forest leads to a very large field of petroglyphs—or carvings—in the lava. Though not as extensive as the Pu'u Loa field at Kilauea Volcano, it's one of the largest in the state and worth a stroll if you want to see how ancient Hawaiians expressed themselves through their tenacious carvings.

The **Mauna Lani Bay Hotel** sits adjacent to some of the most fascinating grounds of any Big Island resort. Huge fishponds surrounded by palm trees to the south make for wonder-filled strolling. We like to wander back to Secret Pond (see map on page 53) for a cool, refreshing dip in the crystal clear water. (I know: The other ponds aren't clear—*this* one is.) Park at the public parking area (6:30 a.m. to 6:30 p.m.) and wander along the trail toward the fishponds. Allow an hour for this pleasant diversion.

Continuing south, the road at the 76 mile marker leads to **'Anaeho'omalu Beach**. If you're low on gasoline, there is relief on this road. 'Anaeho'omalu has a gorgeous palm-fronted fishpond behind the beach. If you're looking for the perfect location to take a **sunset photo**, the backside of the fishpond is as good as it gets. When clouds cooperate, even the most photographically challenged (present reader excluded) can take postcard-quality shots.

KOHALA LAVA DESERT AREA

[J] Back on Highway 19 heading south, the large cluster of palms toward the ocean at the 79 mile marker surround a large freshwater pond and a pretty but secluded beach called **Ke-awa-iki**. The pond itself is not available to visitors (the barbed wire, half-starved Dobermans, and snipers with night vision glasses see to that), but the beach is accessible via a 15-minute walk, and there is a special freshwater golden pool available to hikers. (See Ke-awa-iki hike in ACTIVITIES.)

You may see "graffiti" strewn about the lava field. It's sort of an island tradition to compose messages from pieces of coral on the black lava canvas, and families often come out here to do it together. They're almost always friendly messages, like *Al ♥ Sandy, I Love You Mom,* or *In Memory of Dan,* and rarely contain the nasties often seen in real mainland graffiti. It used to stretch all the way to Kona, but some in the community consider it *kapulu* (messy) and have been removing the coral.

The scenic turnout at the 82 mile marker overlooks **Kiholo Bay**. Down there you will find a saltwater bay with freshwater calmly floating on top, lots of turtles and a lava tube with fresh spring water just 80 feet from the ocean. Intrigued? I hope so. You can drive part of the way during daylight hours and hike around. (See HIKING on page 199.)

Throughout this part of the island you'll occasionally see palm trees along the barren coastline. These are almost always an indication of freshwater spring-fed pools. Since there's no permanent stream on the entire west side of the island, water percolates into the lava and often bubbles to the surface near the shore, forming pools. We look for them when we're hiking along the coast. When you're hot and tired, you can't beat splashing like a fool in a cold, clean freshwater or brackish pool.

If you're looking for a stunning, secluded beach, and don't mind walking for 15–20 minutes, **Makalawena Beach** (described in BEACHES) is west of the 89 mile marker.

You may still see some DONKEY CROSSING signs along here. Until the turn of the century there was a small herd of wild donkeys that crossed the highway at night and early mornings on the older lava north of the 85 mile marker. They came down out of the mountains to lick the salt off rocks by the shore, drink from springs and occasionally putt on the Hualalai Golf Course. (Now *there's* a hazard.) Known locally as **Kona Nightin-**

gales, (because they would call, or "sing" to each other at night), they were the descendants of coffee-hauling pack animals that escaped a century ago. Every so often one got whacked by a passing car, leaving both pretty bent out of shape. They were finally rounded up and hauled away to a corral near Waikoloa Village, but many have escaped and now similarly terrorize the golf course off Waikoloa Road. Wild goats still work this area and are fairly easy to spot.

Just north of the 91 mile marker is a **large lava tube** from the Hualalai lava flow of 1801 that bisects the highway. On the ocean side of the road it has collapsed, leaving a large chasm in the lava. On the mauka side it forms a cave, which is collapsing in several spots. This cave looks rickety and unstable.

Located just south of the Kona airport is the **Natural Energy Laboratory**. This is a classic example of unintended consequences. Started by the government in the 1970s, they monkeyed with making electricity using temperature differences between 80° surface water and 37° deep sea water. Yeah, it worked. But the technology wasn't particularly scalable and has since been abandoned at this location. But their giant 55-inch pipe sucking water from 3,000 feet down has become a magnet for dozens of private companies taking advantage of easy access to cold seawater and year-round sunshine. Industries, such as those raising clams, coral, sea horses, blue green algae, oysters and mushrooms, are thriving out here.

An example is **Kona Cold Lobster**. When the lobsters arrive from the mainland, they have a nasty case of jet lag. (If you flew here from the East coast, you can probably relate.) The beasties are put in the cold water to rejuvenate so that they are bright and alert when you boil them for dinner.

A nice tour here is at **Ocean Rider** (329–6840). They have 1-hour tours of their seahorse farm *(Hey, shouldn't this be called a ranch?)* for $42. The price is pretty steep, but there's something undeniably endearing about these critters that have been nearly wiped out in the wild. At the end of the tour you'll get to have one of them wrapped around your finger. (More likely it'll be the other way around.) Good for kids and adults.

Surprisingly, once you pump seawater out of the ocean, federal environmental laws make it *illegal* to return it, even if it's perfectly clean. So they're forced to pump it into a deep hole (more like a *loop*hole) where it naturally seeps back into the ocean. The energy lab gives tours, but they are pretty dull. Reserve at 329–8073 if you like. A mile offshore here is **Blue Ocean Mariculture**. It's an open-sea fish farm that raises a delicious fish called *Hawaiian Kampachi*, which is available at Roy's and Merriman's restaurants. Normally tasty but inedibly wormy in the wild, these farm-raised kahala fish are worm-free.

An excellent tide-pool is nearby at **Wawaloli Beach**. (See page 163.)

Near the 97 mile marker is the parking lot for **Kaloko-Honokohau National Historical Park**. Despite its appearance, this area was once a thriving community, and Hawaiian artifacts are still scattered about the lava field. There's even a holua

The Green Flash

Ever heard of the green flash? No, it's not a super hero. We'd heard of the Green Flash for years and assumed that it was an urban myth, or perhaps something seen through the bottom of a beer bottle. But now we know it to be a real phenomenon, complete with a scientific explanation. You may hear other ways to experience the Green Flash—but this is the only true way.

On days when the horizon is crisp and clear with no clouds in the way of the sun as it sets, you stand a reasonable chance of seeing it. Avoid looking directly at the sun until the very last part of the disk is about to slip below the horizon. Looking at it beforehand will burn a greenish image into your retina, creating a "fool's flash" (and possibly wrecking your eyes). The instant before the last part of the sun's disk disappears, a vivid flash of chartreuse is often seen. This is because the sun's rays are passing through the thickest part of the atmosphere, and the light is bent and split into its different components the way it is in a rainbow. The light that is bent the most is the green and blue light, but the blue is less vivid and is overwhelmed by the flash of green, which lingers for the briefest of moments as the very last of the sun sets.

For a variety of reasons, including our latitude, Hawai'i is one of the best places in the world to observe the Green Flash. North Kohala is usually better than Kona due to the clarity of the horizon, but we've seen excellent Green Flash from all along the West coast.

If you aren't successful in seeing the real Green Flash, try the beer bottle method—at least it's better than nothing.

(stone slide) that was used by chiefs. (See page 67 for more on holua.)

If you are into deep sea fishing, you'll want to check out **Honokohau Harbor** listed in the BEACHES chapter. Fishing boats leave from here, and weigh-ins take place daily at 10 a.m. and 6 p.m. (You can tell what they caught by the fish flags they hoist.)

KOHALA SHOPPING

While in Hawi, pick up some **Tropical Dreams** ice cream at **Kohala Coffee Mill**. If you are looking for an 'ukulele, **Hawi Gallery** is the place. **L. Zeidman** has wood bowls and vases. **Mother's Antiques & Fine Cigars** is a good place to stop if you appreciate a smoke. Their Hawaiian brand cigars ironically are rolled in Nicaragua. We really love the jewelry designs at **Olivia Clare**. See **Elements Jewelry & Fine Crafts** for exciting artwork, jewelry and items made from recycled materials. On the other end of town, don't miss the excellent contemporary galleries **Kohala Mountain Gallery**, **Ipu Kane Gallery** and **Kohala Artworks**.

Heading north in Kapa'au, grab a coffee drink or sandwich at the **Nanbu Courtyard**. There are a few great galleries in town. Our favorites are **Ackerman Galleries** for paintings and further down the road, **Ackerman Gift Galleries** has a great assortment of original artwork, glass and woodwork.

All of the mega-resorts have shopping areas. In the **Shops at Mauna Lani**, stop in at **Tommy Bahama** for clothes, and **Lahaina Galleries** and **Third Dimension** for art. We also love **Oasis Lifestyle** for a bit of everything for everyone. For groceries, try **Foodland Farms** where you can also pick up a meal for the beach.

The main shopping area in South Kohala is the **Kings' Shops** located at the Waikoloa Beach Resort. Just about anything can be found here from **Tiffany & Co.** to **Sunglass Hut**. Don't miss **Noa Noa** for Polynesian print clothes for both men and women, and **Jourabchi** for contemporary women's clothing. **Making Waves** is a good place to get a new swim suit, while **Walking in Paradise** is a sandal collector's dream. An art gallery worth mentioning is **Genesis Gallery**. **Martin & MacArthur** has everything in woodworks. **Hawaiian 'Ukulele & Guitar** has a nice selection at reasonable prices. **Mary Jane's** is a fun girly-girl store; leave the guys outside. Directly across the street is **Queens' MarketPlace**. We love **Giggles!** for anything kid-related. **Hawaiian Quilt Collection** has some outstanding examples of quilts and home decor. **Kona Surf N' Sandals** has all the great new styles. There's also a food court and **Island Gourmet Markets** if you're hungry and check out their extensive wine bar, too. Expect higher prices here.

KOHALA'S BEST BETS

Best Sunsets—Behind the fishponds at 'Anaeho'omalu Beach

Best Place to Get the Willies—Mo'okini Heiau, Hawi

Best Treat—Tropical Dreams, Hawi

Best Pizza—Café Pesto, Kawaihae

Best Secluded Beach—Makalawena

Best Resort Grounds to Stroll Around—Mauna Lani Bay Hotel & Bungalows

Best Golf—Mauna Kea Golf Course

Best View of Maui—Coming down Highway 250 into Hawi

Best Overlook—Pololu Valley

Best Boogie-Boarding—Hapuna or Mauna Kea Beach

Best Remnant of Ancient Hawaiian Art—Puako Petroglyph Field

Kamehameha the Great, the first king to rule all the islands, could live anywhere he wanted. He chose Kailua-Kona. This is his 'Ahu'ena Heiau.

Kailua was a tiny fishing village in days gone by. Fishermen would haul in giants from the deep, bountiful waters, while farmers tended their fields up the slopes of Hualalai. Many of the great chiefs of old chose this part of the island as their home. Kona weather and Kona waters were known throughout the islands as the very best, and that hasn't changed. Though no longer the sleepy little village of yesteryear, this is a charming seaside town where the strolling is pleasant, the sunsets are mesmerizing, the food is diverse, and the activities are plentiful. Some people badmouth Kona because it's not the same as it was 20 years ago—what is? Kona is still great; there are simply more people who know it.

The town is alternately referred to as Kailua-Kona, Kona, Kailua, or sometimes Kailua Town. See page 29 for an explanation of this confusing situation.

Kailua-Kona is nestled in the lee of Hualalai Volcano, meaning that it is sheltered from the trade winds coming from the other side of the island. The winds it does get are usually from wraparound sea breezes. The rains from them have already been wrung out.

The heart of Kailua-Kona is the mile-long oceanfront stretch of Alii Drive starting at the Kailua Pier. As with any town, traffic can be heavy. Alii Drive is a particularly good area to take a walk after a meal. There have been times that unsavory-looking characters made night walks intimidating, but shop owners have banded together to hire private patrollers, and it has helped tremendously. Public parking is pretty limited and is shown on the Kailua-Kona Map. This part of town has lots of shops and restaurants overlooking the water. If you start strolling from the Kailua Pier, keep an eye out for some of these sights.

AROUND DOWNTOWN KAILUA-KONA

A To the right (north) of the pier is the ʻAhuʻena Heiau. Now wonderfully maintained and very picturesque, this was King Kamehameha the Great's personal heiau (temple) that he had restored in 1812, and it was here that he spent his later years until his death in 1819. Note the bird on top of the tallest kiʻi akua (statue of a god). It is a golden plover, the bird that may have guided the first Polynesians here. (See page 15.) Kamehameha dedicated this heiau to the god Lono and filled it with European and Chinese furniture. Nearby is Nane Mahina ʻAi, where the king went to get away from it all. There was a famous portrait painted here of Kamehameha wearing a red vest, white shirt and a yellow silk necktie. The artist

Letters (A) correspond to paragraphs in text.

pleaded with him not to wear the fancy sailor's outfit, but Kamehameha insisted.

The tiny beach in front of the heiau is Kamakahonu Beach, one of the calmest beaches on the island. There you can rent kayaks, paddle boats, stand-up paddle boards, snorkel gear, etc. (though at confiscatory prices).

To the left of the pier is the starting gate to end all starting gates. Every year in October an athletic event occurs on the Big Island that draws world-wide attention. The Ironman Triathlon is a profound testimony to the power to challenge, to the ability to reach down to the very core of our spirit and summon the impossible. Three events, any one of which would seem *insurmountable* to most of us mere mortals, are stitched together in a triathlon that seems almost ludicrous. Swim 2.4 miles in the open ocean, then get out and ride a bike 112 miles on a hot road cut through a lava field. Finally, dismount and run a 26.2 mile marathon. All this is done consecutively under the tropical sun. This is the best opportunity you'll ever have to look into the faces of mass excellence, and not just the young. We had a friend who, even in his mid-60s, would blow by most of the 25-year-olds and complete the race in under 12 hours.

The seawall near the pier is usually a great place to fish. During abnormally high seas, water crashes over the wall and is quite a sight to see. Even better fishing is at the wall in front of the Huliheʻe Palace (329–1877) farther down. This palace,

A REAL GEM built in 1838 by Governor Kuakini, quickly became the house of choice for vacationing Hawaiian royalty until 1914. Now a museum lovingly run by the Daughters of Hawaiʻi, inside you'll find a nice collection of koa furniture, including some stunning armoires, and a 6-foot diameter table cut from a single piece of koa. Most of the furniture was auc-

Kailua-Kona

Old Kona Airport Beach Park

Old Airport Runway

Kona Commons

Makala Blvd

Target

Kmart

Kona International Market

Na Kamalei Toddler Playground

Kaiwi St

Queen Ka'ahumanu Hwy

Kamakaeha Ave

Kailua Park

Old Industrial Area

Pawai Place

Alapa St

Luhia St

Eho

Gym

Kona Coast Shopping Center

19

Keiki Beach

King Kamehameha Mall

Ilima Court

Palani Rd

100

190

Mamalahoa Hwy

King Kamehameha's Kona Beach Hotel

Kona Square

Post Office

Kona Crossings Shopping Center

Safeway

'Ahu'ena Heiau

Seawall

Likana

Kuakini Hwy

Kopiko Plaza

Lanihau Center

Walmart

CrossRoads Shopping Center

Kailua Pier

Kona Banyan Court

Kailua Bay

Mokuaikaua Church

11

Henry St

Hulihe'e Palace

Hanama Sarona

Kona Inn Shopping Village

Kona Marketplace

Kalani

122

Hale Halawai Beach Park

Hualalai

Hualalai Rd

Waterfront Row (Parking Underground)

Farmer's Market

W   N

S   E

Alii Sunset Plaza

Oneo Bay

0   1/4 MILE

Royal Kona Resort

Coconut Grove Market Place

Kahakai Rd

Kuakini Hwy

Aloha Kona Dr

Walua Rd

Nani Kailua St

Alii Drive

The Pines Plaza

Swim portion of Ironman Triathlon

25 Mile Markers
⬤ Parking Lots

Lunapule St

Hualalai Rd

11

121 Map continued on page 63

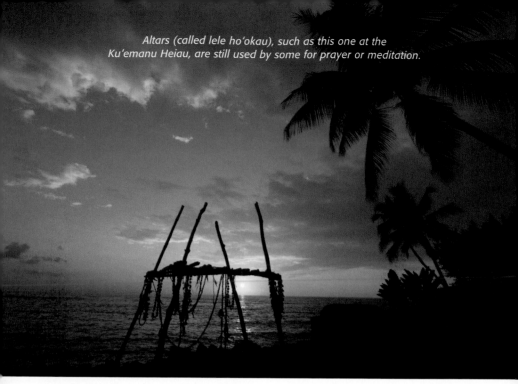

Altars (called lele hoʻokau), such as this one at the Kuʻemanu Heiau, are still used by some for prayer or meditation.

tioned off in the 1920s but fortunately was cataloged. Later, the buyers were contacted, and many have graciously lent the items to the museum for display. There are many photos of Hawaiian royalty, including Princess Ruth. (History books *never* mention her without mentioning her size, but we're above that... no, we're not. Estimates range from 6-foot-2 to 6-foot-10, 400–450 lbs. She slept in a hut outside.) Spears, fishhooks and other artifacts make this museum a worthwhile stop. Most who give the tours (under an hour) are very knowledgeable and friendly, but occasionally you'll get some bad historical information. Admission is $8–$10. Open Monday through Saturday. The Palace Gift Shop next door has interesting items and hard-to-find books and is worth a peek.

Outside, on the south side of the Palace *was* a rock with a hole in it. It was the top of a Pohaku Likanaka. This was used for executions out at Kahaluʻu Beach Park. People would be forced to stand in front of it while a rope was passed through the hole, around the neck, and back out. The executioner would then pull back for a few minutes...and that was that. Some palace personnel used to grumble that the darkly historic stone shouldn't be there. In 2006 an earthquake damaged the palace, forcing its closure and refurbishment. When they reopened, *whaddayaknow?* The stone had simply vanished. They don't know where it went, and they don't seem too unhappy about it.

Across the street from Huliheʻe Palace is the Mokuaikaua Church. This was the first Christian church built in the islands, in 1820. The initial building was a thatched hut, with the current structure erected in 1837. You're welcome inside; admission is free. Built of lava rock and crushed coral with koa hardwood gracing the tall interior, this is a magnificent remnant of the era. Look at the joints inside the building, which were painstakingly attached with pins made from gnarly ʻohiʻa trees. There are exhibits relating to early Hawaiʻi and the work of the missionaries, along with a model of the *Thaddeus*, which brought the first missionaries here. Sometimes referred to as the Mayflower of Hawai'i, the *Thaddeus* left Boston in October 1819 for a five-month trip to the islands. These men and women left comfortable lives in the United States to come to an alien and mysterious land. Unbeknownst to them, their chances for success were greatly enhanced en route when Kamehameha II and his step-mother Ka'ahumanu orchestrated the overthrow of the Hawaiian religion less than a month into their journey to the islands.

There's a large shopping area at Kona Inn, though it looks as though it could use a good sprucing up. If you're looking for a place to watch the sunset or have a picnic, the grass on the ocean side of this center is ideal.

If you want to watch the sunset from a restaurant along here, the best views (from south to north) are: Don the Beachcomber, Huggo's, Bubba Gump, Kona Inn and Kona Canoe Club. See individual reviews in ISLAND DINING. During months around the summer solstice (June 21), the sun may set behind the point from the northernmost restaurants.

ELSEWHERE ALONG ALII DRIVE

As you drive farther south along Alii Drive, keep an eye out for joggers. They trot up and down Alii Drive in large enough numbers to constitute a flock. (Or is it a gaggle?) There are mile markers every half mile here, which we put on the Alii Drive map. Between Kona By The Sea and Kona Isle is a 100-yard access trail that leads to something that even most longtime Alii Drive residents don't know about. It's a public saltwater swimming pool fed by the splashing of waves. It was privately built decades ago and reverted to the state when the owner died without heirs. The pool directly abuts the

Alii Drive

1 Courtyard King Kamehameha
2 Kona Seaside Hotel
3 Uncle Billy's Kona Bay Hotel
4 Kona Islander Inn
5 Kona Alii
6 Royal Kona Resort
7 Hale Kona Kai
8 Kona Reef
9 Kona Pacific
10 Kona Tiki
11 Sea Village
12 Alii Villas
13 Kona Makai
14 Royal Sea Cliff Resort
15 Casa de Emdeko
16 Kona Isle
17 Kona By The Sea
18 Kona Nalu
19 Kona Bali Kai
20 Banyan Tree
21 Kona Magic Sands
22 White Sands Village
23 Kona Seaspray
24 Kahalu'u Bay Villas
25 Makolea
26 Kahalu'u Beach Villas
27 Keauhou Kona Surf & Racq
28 Na Hale O'Keauhou
29 Kona Coast Resort
30 Kanaloa at Kona
31 Keauhou Palena
32 Keauhou Resort
33 Country Club Villas
34 Sheraton Keauhou Bay
35 Keauhou Akahi
36 Keauhou Punahele

25 Mile Markers
23 Resorts

Kailua Bay
Henry
122
11
Aloha Kona D
Nani
Kailua
121
Downtown
Kailua-Kona
shown in grey.
(Detail Map
Page 61)
Honl's
Hualalai Rd
Kuakini Hwy
Walua
Alii Dr
Lunapule Rd
120
Saltwater Pool
Alii Gardens Marketplace
2.5
Royal Poinciana Dr
Lako St
119
Pahoehoe Beach Park
La'aloa Bay Beach Park
3.5
118
4.5
Kahalu'u Beach
5
Ke'eku Heiau
Petroglyphs
5.5
Kamehameha III
11
117
Keauhou Shopping Center
Keauhou Bay
33
Kona Country Club Golf Course
Holua (Hawaiian Slide)
116
180
N
W   E
S
0   1/2 Mi.
11
End of the World
Burial Grounds, Kuamo'o Battle
Mamalahoa Bypass Road
Kealakekua Bay map on page 66
115

© 2014 Wizard Publications, Inc.

ocean and even has some fish in it most of the time. There's a smaller tide-pool to the left. If you want to swim in seawater but are hesitant to go into the ocean, here's your chance. Unmaintained, the pool occasionally isn't refreshed enough if the surf has been flat for too long, meaning it sometimes gets green and yucky.

Keep an eye out on the mauka side of Alii Drive for a farmers' market called Ali'i Gardens. Near the 3½ mile marker is Pahoehoe Beach Park. No sand here, but it's a nice place to have a picnic, or to just sit on a bench and watch the surf. White Sands Beach (as it's known by locals or La'aloa as the sign says) is a little farther down with good boogie boarding when the sand is in town. (See BEACHES.)

There are scads of oceanfront condos and apartments along this road. Traffic noise is going to be your penalty for staying on Alii Drive, but it's a penalty most are quite willing to endure.

Soon you'll come to the quaintest little church you've ever seen. St. Peter's Catholic Church is known locally as the "Little Blue Church." This tiny building, with its picturesque location and less than a dozen simple *small* pews, is the most photographed in the islands. Weddings of all denominations take place there almost every weekend. If the doors are unlocked, sunsets through the etched glass can offer dramatic photo opportunities.

To the right of the church is the Ku'emanu Heiau. This is the only heiau (temple) in the state known to be associated solely with surfing. This surf spot was available only to chiefs (commoners caught surfing here were put to death), and they came here to pray for gnarly conditions. (They usually got them, too. Even today this is one of the most dependable breaks in Kona.) To this day, Hawaiians still come here to pay homage to the spirits. The small notch in front was a luapa'u, where discarded bones were tossed—perhaps bones of commoners caught surfing. Incidentally, surfing in the old days was usually done naked (giving new meaning to the term *hang loose*).

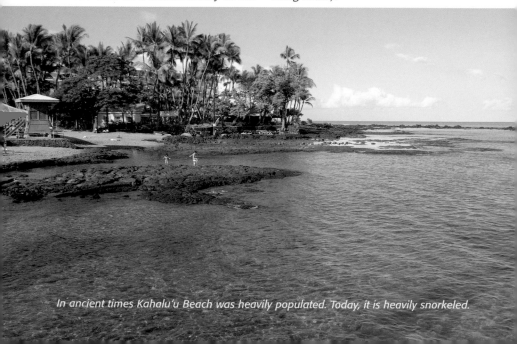

In ancient times Kahalu'u Beach was heavily populated. Today, it is heavily snorkeled.

A Fish Story

Keauhou was dominated by the legacy of a king in the 1600s named Lonoikamakahiki (called Lono by his friends). Lono (not to be confused with the Hawaiian god of the same name) made a series of bets with the king of O'ahu. Each time Lono won. On one occasion, Lono and the O'ahu king were out fishing. Lono's advisor told Lono not to go because he (Lono) didn't know how to fish. They went anyway, and while fishing, Lono got all worked up while the O'ahu king was hauling in a beauty and asked to borrow fishing gear. As Lono's advisor feared, the O'ahu king mocked Lono for not bringing his own gear. Lono's advisor, in order to save his master's honor, volunteered the solution to Lono. He whispered it into his ear and Lono agreed. Lono then shouted, "Hey, I don't need your gear. I'll bet you I can catch a fish on my own." The O'ahu king accepted, knowing that Lono had not brought any fishing gear with him. Then Lono, at his advisor's suggestion, clubbed his advisor to death, ripped open his belly and used his intestines for fishing line. Lono splintered the man's thigh bone for a fishhook. His flesh was used for bait and his head for a sinker. He lowered the gear into the water and immediately caught an ahi. Lono won the bet (a large piece of O'ahu) and later went on to win all of O'ahu in another bet.

The moral: If you think you sacrifice a lot for your boss, try working for Lono.

(Incidentally, Lono's bones were in the Bishop Museum in Honolulu until 1994 when they were stolen by Hawaiian activists and buried in Waipi'o Valley.)

Next to the church is Kahalu'u Beach Park where you'll find some of the easiest access to good snorkeling on the island. It gets crowded on weekends. See BEACHES for more on this gem. Kahalu'u had a large population in the old days, and there are very extensive lava tube caves tucked away in the jungle up mauka (toward the mountain).

After you pass the closed hotel next to Kahalu'u Beach Park, you'll see a parcel of land to its left. Fronting this parcel on some of the lava at low tide, you can see petroglyphs carved in the rock. They are at the northern end of the salt-and-pepper sand and gravel beach kitty-corner to the heiau described below. In the 16th century, Kamala-lawalu, the King of Maui, was impaled alive by Lonoikamakahiki at Ke'eku Heiau for 10 or 11 days. Kamalalawalu was then taken to a flat rock nearby and slain. His body was towed out to sea and fed to the sharks. The petroglyphs on the rock date back to that incident and detail the event. (Lonoikamakahiki had a good reason to be miffed at Kamalalawalu. His general had been captured by invading Maui forces, had his eyes gouged out and his eye sockets pierced with darts *before* being killed. That was considered uncool even by the standards of the time.)

The land contains several heiau, including one where thousands of Hawaiians were sacrificed to their gods. Local lore says that any business that operates there is cursed. If you don't believe it, ask the Japanese company that paid millions for the lease to a 454-room hotel here in 1988. They closed the hotel, called the Kona Lagoons, planning extensive renovations. Then they ran out of money. It

Kealakekua Bay to Honaunau

Greenwell Coffee
Farm 1 mile north
on Hwy 11.

Alii Drive map on page 63

Ka'awaloa Flats Trail to Captain Cook
This trail is hot and unrelenting

1300'

11

110

11

Mamalahoa Hwy

109

108

Napoopoo Rd

10

Captain Cook Monument

Exceptional snorkeling here

Kealakekua Bay State Historical Park
(Great place to spot dolphins)

Hikiau Heiau

Napoopoo Rd

Napo'opo'o Beach Park
(Sand mostly gone now)

Manini Beach

Grandma's Little Beach
Kayakers can launch here

Keawiki

Kahauloa Rd

Old Coffee Mill

160

8

11

107

Ke'ei Beach

Middle Keei Rd

Moku-a-Kae Bay

Moku'ohai Battlefield

160

Paleaku Peace Gardens

Painted Church Rd

106

1

N
W   E
S

19°26.016'
155°55.215'

† **Painted Church**

105

Arch City

0   1/2 MILE

Ke Ala o Keawe Rd

1

Honaunau

2

3

160

104

Honaunau Bay
Two-Step
Keoneele Cove

Pu'uhonua o Honaunau
National Historical Park
(AKA **Place of Refuge**)

11

〜 Indicates Foot Trails
3 Roadside mile markers
⋯ Unpaved Roads

Picnic Area

1871 Trail

sat vacant and dilapidated, until they finally gave it up in 1994 to the landowner, Bishop Estate, which bulldozed it a decade later. The re-created heiau you see here are a far cry from the rubble you would have seen at the turn of the century. They are part of a long rebuilding project begun in 2008 by the landowner.

As you ascend Alii Drive toward the Keauhou Shopping Center, keep an eye on your right, in the golf course, for the strangest corkscrew-shaped palm tree we've ever seen. No interesting story here—just weird. There's a flock of imported wild parrots that cruises around these parts. Keep an eye (and ear) out for them.

If you stay on Alii for a moment, pull over at the service entrance for the old Kona Country Club golf course and look up mauka. It looks like a wide path that was bulldozed through the lava. That was done *by hand* to create the Keauhou Holua. In ancient times Hawaiians would fill these holua (slides) with dirt and wet grass, then ali'i (Hawaiian royalty) would race down these slides at rippin' speeds on wooden sleds while commoners screamed and cheered them on. These holua remains are 2,500 feet long (not 1,200, which is listed in most references) and at one time extended to Keauhou Bay.

Soon after this, Alii ends near the shoreline. (The road extending south is a bypass used by folks living up in coffee country.) There is a lava road near the dead end. If you walk on the road for a minute (actually you can see it from your car), you'll be able to see, on your left, terraces in the side of the mountain. You are at an extraordinary place. It might not look like much, but this is where the battle between Hawaiians to kill their religion took place one day in 1820. (See page 17 for the amazing story.) The terraces are the graves from that battle.

With a name befitting the area, a cliff-jumping spot past the battlefield called *End of the World* is listed in ADVENTURES on page 235.

UP MAUKA OF KAILUA-KONA

B Hualalai Volcano erupts sporadically every few hundred years. The last time was in 1801 when it covered part of what is now Kona International Airport. The top of Hualalai is mostly covered with 'ohi'a and eucalyptus forest with occasional koa and pine. The clouds usually roll in around mid-morning, blanketing the 8,271-foot summit in a rich fog that can reduce visibility to zero. Wild goats and pigs scramble about the uninhabited top portion of the mountain. The views of Mauna Kea and Mauna Loa, as well as its own caldera, make Hualalai a hiker's haven. Unfortunately, it's all owned by Bishop Estate, which routinely denies access to the public. (Bishop Estate is a trust set up in the 1800s to help Hawai'i's kids. It has grown to now own 11% of the state and has astonishing power. Many of the houses you see on the island are actually on Bishop land leased for several decades by individuals.)

Hovering above the town of Kailua-Kona is the "artist community" of Holualoa on Highway 180. There are several galleries (and one excellent restaurant called Holuakoa) worth stopping for if you are in the neighborhood. Hours can be sporadic. Otherwise, there is not as much to offer the visitor in this quiet, peaceful bedroom community as visitor literature might imply.

Although Kona itself doesn't convey the lushness many associate with Hawai'i, it *does* exist on this side of the island. Kaloko Drive meanders up into a luxuriant cloud forest. See page 43 for more.

SOUTH OF KAILUA-KONA

C If you head south out of Kona, you'll come to a series of small towns, all above 1,000 feet. It's usually cool up here,

Kona Coffee

Of all the products produced on the Big Island, none is more well known or has received more accolades than Kona coffee. Though now out-produced in quantity by

Kaua'i, Kona coffee is unmatched in terms of quality. With the possible exception of Jamaican Blue Mountain coffee, Kona coffee is widely considered to be the best in the world. Good Kona coffee lacks the bitterness of coffees from other parts of the world. By the way, contrary to nearly everyone's belief, lighter roasts have more caffeine than darker roasts. (Caffeine cooks away during the roasting process.)

A quality cup of coffee has little resemblance to mass-produced coffee you see on most supermarket shelves. (Of course, you pay more for the good stuff.) Good Kona coffee will set you back $20 or more per pound. Surprisingly little profit is made by the farmer at that price. Most small farmers grow coffee as a labor of love. If you see 100% Kona coffee (not a blend) selling for $12 per pound, it might be poorly chosen, broken or contain poorly roasted beans. You usually get what you pay for. And if you're told in a restaurant that they serve Kona blend because pure Kona is too strong, it's like saying that champagne needs to be blended with gasoline because pure champagne is too strong. Kona blends (which are blended with cheap beans from elsewhere) are less mellow than pure Kona. Blends are usually served because they're cheaper, not better.

Being wretched coffee addicts, we've tried them all. For what it's worth, we like **Pau Hana Estate** (808–328–8099), **Fike Farms** (808–328–2265), **Holualoa** (800–334–0348), **Greenwell** (808–323–2275) and **Kona Blue Sky** (877–322–1700). Some aren't available in stores, only by phone or mail order. **Kona Joe** (808–322–2100) grows their trees on a trellis, like grapes, and the Trellis Reserve medium roast is very good. But at $75 per pound you'll be forgiven if you want to pursue less expensive vices, such as caviar or Cristal champagne.

Coffees that we've tried and didn't like are Bad Ass Coffee, Ferrari Mountain Gold, Royal Aloha, and Starbuck's Kona coffee. (The last one is surprising.) We are not saying that these companies are bad, just that we didn't like their coffee and didn't think it was worth the money.

Coffee tours are available from many growers, but coffee farms that claim to offer tours are often poorly marked, and owners and employees sometimes seem shocked when you show up to buy coffee. **Greenwell** and **Hula Daddy** (327–9744) have good tours. Greenwell is on the map on page 66.

sometimes even foggy. The theme of these towns is often coffee. Free samples are offered at many establishments. Some are mediocre. Others, such as Greenwell, sell very good quality coffee to take with you. There are places to eat along here, such as Ke'ei Café (for dinner) and The Coffee Shack, (for breakfast). Look for Discovery Antiques—Ice Cream on the ocean side of the highway in Kealakekua. They serve Tropical Dreams ice cream, as sinful here as in Hawi on the north shore. Just after the Aloha Theater in Kainaliu, stop at the Donkey Ball Store for some of their namesake treats. (Wonderful chocolate covered mac nuts with thick chocolate.) Available in any quantity. (Not just pairs.)

In Kealakekua (you'll be forgiven if you don't readily see the transition between towns up here) between the 112 and 111 mile markers on the ocean side of the road is the Kona Historical Society Museum (323–3222). Located in an old general store built during the 1800s, there are lots of old coffee-related photos and other items of historical interest. Worth a stop if you have an interest in the past. Open Mondays and Thursdays, $7 admission ($3 for kids).

There are good views down the coast from some spots along here. You've transitioned from Hualalai to Mauna Loa Volcano and up the mountain there are vast ranches that you'd never know were there. After you pass the 111 mile marker on Highway 11, you'll see Napoopoo Road on the ocean side of the road—take it. There are lots of coffee farms down here. (See gray box on facing page.) A coffee tour might be worth the effort. You may get to try delicious coffee or meet offbeat characters you'll remember for years to come.

Napoopoo comes to an intersection of itself and Middle Ke'ei Road. Turn right here and head toward the ocean. The old

Mauna Loa Coffee Mill near the 8 mile marker is now a farmer's co-op and they are generous with their free samples of various goodies. They also have a small but well-represented botanical garden.

KEALAKEKUA BAY & PLACE OF REFUGE

D When you get to the sea, hang a right to Napo'opo'o Beach Park. The

A REAL GEM

stone structure you see in front of you at this southern end of Kealakekua Bay (at the end of the road) is Hiki-au Heiau. This was a luakini (a temple where human sacrifices were made). Here Captain Cook was first worshipped as the returning god Lono. During the ceremony, an elder priest named Koa, in the honored tradition of the Hawaiians, chewed the food first before spitting it out and offering it to Cook. (He politely declined.) It was also here that the first Christian ceremony was held in Hawai'i. Ironically it may have contributed to the death of Captain Cook. When one of his men died, Cook ordered him buried near this heiau and personally read the service. This event was proof to some Hawaiians that the strangers were mere mortals, not the gods others felt them to be.

Napo'opo'o Beach used to be a fabulous beach fronting the heiau. It had been eroding for years, being gradually replaced by boulders. When Hurricane 'Iniki sideswiped the island way back in 1992, its surf removed most of what sand was left. Over the decades very little has returned.

One mile across the bay you can see a white obelisk, the Captain Cook Monument, which was erected in 1874 by British sailors. It was near this spot (a rarely visited plaque to the left of the monument marks the *actual* spot) in 1779 that Cook was killed by the Hawaiians. (See INTRODUCTION for more on this event.) You won't need your passport to go there, even though it is British soil that the monument rests on. The small plot was deeded to the United Kingdom by Princess Likelike.

Kealakekua Bay is also popular with dolphins. A large number of spinners reside in the bay, so keep an eye out for them. We see them almost every time we kayak to the monument. Toward the monument side on the bay, up the steep cliff, there is a grayish impression. Local lore says this was made by a cannonball fired from Cook's ship.

These cliffs hold even more secrets. In the past, important chiefs were buried in small caves in the cliff face. After the bones had been separated, volunteers were lowered down the face of the cliffs by rope to place the bones in crevices. No one had a long résumé in this line of work. That's because the person doing the burying, once finished with his task, would signal to those above that he was done. The officials on top would promptly cut the rope, sending the burial person, and all knowledge of the location of the bones, crashing to the rocks below. (It was actually considered an honor to be the volunteer at the end of the rope.) All this was to prevent the bones from being desecrated. Bones were often turned into fishhooks and other implements. Skulls were turned into refuse pots or toilets. (Really good joke edited out here upon further reflection.)

Today, if you hear something fall from the cliff, it won't be a person. Brainless cows from above occasionally wander off the ledge, pleasing the fish below with a refreshing change from their seafood diet.

The waters near the monument are crystal clear and teeming with coral and fish. This is some of the best snorkeling in the state. The local community wants to keep it somewhat difficult to access to prevent it from being overrun with "casual" visitors. If you are wondering how to get there, you have several choices:

You can swim it. This takes us about an hour each way with fins and is guaranteed to tucker you out.

You can walk along the edge of the bay for about 98% of the distance. You'll have to scramble on boulders the whole way and will have to swim for a couple of short patches. You expose yourself to the ocean's whims and

Is there anything more tranquil than coconut trees, like those here at Honaunau?

falling rocks with this method. Not a great way to get there.

You can kayak over. (See KAYAKING on page 208.) It's a relatively easy 30-minute paddle across the usually peaceful bay, and you stand a good chance of cruising among dolphins along the way.

Another way to get to the monument is to take the trail near the intersection of Highway 11 and Napoopoo Road. The trailhead is a little over ⅒ mile from the highway across from 3 large palm trees. See map. You may have to park a short distance up the road as this hike has gotten much more popular since they limited kayaking to the monument. It used to be a road but is now suitable only for hiking. It's 2 miles each way with a 1,300-foot constant descent to the water. It's a pretty good puffer coming back up with little shade and some obnoxious footing. It takes most people more than an hour each way. Drink *plenty* of water before and during the ascent, and be careful not to pull your calves during the steady, grueling climb. Along the way you'll pass (but won't see due to brush) the Puhina o Lono Heiau. It was here that Cook's bones were...well, cooked. (See below.)

Lastly, you can take one of the boat trips on page 210. They stop for snorkeling near the monument. They also offer SCUBA, SNUBA, and all-around fun.

What Finally Happened to Cook?

The Hawaiians traditionally scraped the flesh off the bones of great men. The bones were then bundled together and burned or buried in secret so they wouldn't be desecrated. If the dead person was really loved, the bones were kept in a private home for a while. Because Cook was so respected by the Hawaiians, his body parts were distributed among the chiefs. His head went to the king, his scalp went to a high-ranking chief, his hair went to Kamehameha, etc. Some of his organs, including his heart and liver, were stolen and eaten by some local children who mistook them for dog innards. *(Yuck!)* Eventually, when two Hawaiians brought a bundle to the ship, the British solemnly unwrapped the bundle and discovered a pile of bloody flesh that had been cut from Cook's body. Even though the Hawaiians were bestowing an honor upon Cook, the British sailors didn't see it that way and were naturally shocked and horrified. The anguished sailors begged Captain Clerke to allow them to go into the village and extract revenge, but he refused, fearing a bloodbath. Some went anyway, killing several villagers. Most of the bones were eventually returned to the British, and Cook was buried at sea in Kealakekua Bay. The ship's surgeon wrote, "In every situation he stood un-rivaled and alone. On him all eyes were turned. He was our leading star which, at its setting, left us in darkness and despair."

The steep cliffs around Kealakekua Bay seem strangely out of place on this otherwise gently sloping mountain. There's a good reason, and it happened in one day. See page 77 for the explanation.

As you leave Napo'opo'o Beach, stay on the oceanmost road heading south. There is a side road leading to Ke'ei Beach. Pretty but not real usable, its historical legacy is a Hawaiian legend, bolstered by Spanish records, which states that white men straggled ashore in the 1520s, 250 years before Cook arrived.

Lots of blood has been spilt on this part of the island. One particularly important battle took place just south of Ke'ei Beach at Moku-a-Kae Bay called the Moku-'ohai Battlefield. You only access it via a hike, but it was near here in 1782 that Kamehameha the Great finally became king of this half of the island after defeating Kiwala'o. During a bloody battle, one of Kamehameha's generals, named Ke'eaumoku (call him Ke for short), got

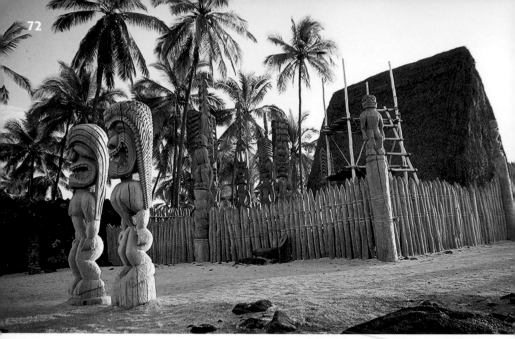

Lawbreakers had one chance to escape the inevitable death penalty: Reach the area's place of refuge before your enemies reached you, and all was forgiven.

tangled in his own spear and tripped, savagely impaling himself. Presuming Ke to be mortally wounded, Kiwala'o ran over to the enemy general to finish him off and seize his prized neck ornament. (Taking it off your enemy's body was symbolic of defeating him.) As he was leaning over Ke's body, Kiwala'o was beaned on the head by a sling stone hurled by one of Kamehameha's warriors, and fell backward. Ke, who wasn't dead from his spear wound, painfully crawled to the unconscious Kiwala'o and slit his throat with a leiomanu (a Hawaiian version of brass knuckles, but with razor-sharp shark's teeth embedded on the outside). Thus Kamehameha was able to defeat his nemesis and rule western Hawai'i.

Battles such as these are a constant throughout Hawaiian history after the 12th century. Rival chiefs or kings were quick to take each other on. Warriors would often congregate on opposite sides of the battlefield and shout insults at each other in an attempt to intimidate. (Insults about lineage were always a real hit.) During battles, spears, sling stones and clubs were used with remarkable efficiency. Shark tooth-studded leiomanus were often given to old men who would go out onto battlefields after the fighting was over to slit the throats of those still alive. Though it may sound harsh (OK, OK—it *is* harsh), this was their way and not considered abhorrent to them.

Soon you come to Pu'uhonua o Honaunau (pronounced HOE-NOW-NOW). Also called Place of Refuge, this is an *awesome* spot to visit. It is a site of great importance and a fun place to explore. In ancient times, commoners' lives were governed by the kapu system. There was a dizzying number of laws to observe. Those of lower classes weren't allowed to look at or even walk on the same trails as the upper classes. Men and women were forbidden to eat together, citizens were not allowed to get close to a chief or allow their shadows to fall across them, etc. All manner of laws kept the order. The penalty for breaking any of the

NOT TO BE MISSED!

laws was usually the same—death by club, strangulation, fire or spear. (Well, it's nice to have choices, at least.) If the offense was severe enough, the offender's *entire family* might be executed. It was believed that the gods retaliated against lawbreakers by sending tidal waves, lava flows, droughts and earthquakes, so communities had a great incentive to dispatch lawbreakers with haste. If a lawbreaker could elude his club or spear-wielding pursuers, however, he had one way out of his mess—the area's Pu'uhonua (Place of Refuge). This predesignated area offered asylum. If a lawbreaker could make it here, he could perform certain rituals mandated by the kahuna pule (priest). After that, all was forgiven and he could return home as if nothing had happened, regardless of the violation. Defeated warriors could also come here to await the victor of a battle. They could then pledge their allegiance to whoever won and live out their lives in peace.

Pu'uhonua o Honaunau is such a place. Designated as a national park by Congress in 1961, it is the finest example of a Place of Refuge in all the islands. Here you will find neatly kept grounds featuring a remarkable stone wall, called the Great Wall. Built in the 1500s, this massive wall is 1,000 feet long, 10 feet high and 17 feet thick in most places. It separated the Pu'uhonua from the Ali'i's palace grounds. Though the wall has a chiseled appearance, it was made without dressed (cut) stones and without mortar. Also on the grounds you will find reconstructed Hawaiian houses, temples, and a few petroglyphs (rock drawings). There are wood carvings of gods (including one that is anatomically correct, assuming that's how the gods were endowed). The reconstructed thatched structure called Hale-o-Keawe was originally a mausoleum, containing the bones of 23 chiefs. Bones were thought to contain supernatural power, or *mana*, and there-

fore ensured that the Place of Refuge would remain sacred.

There are many other sights here, as well. Overall, this place is easy to recommend. The walk around the grounds is gentle, and there are facilities such as drinking water and restrooms. Coconut trees (which have an almost magical, calming effect) are scattered all over. There is a $5 per car entrance fee, but sometimes no one is there to collect it because they "can't afford the manpower to collect the money." (Only the government could come up with that kind of logic.)

Honaunau is particularly enchanting an hour before sunset, the best time to visit. Swaying coconut trees have a golden glow as large turtles munch limu in the water near the canoe landing. You won't find a more relaxing or soothing place to finish off the day. Then head over to the middle/southern end of the park where picnic tables and BBQS await. Local families often bring their keiki (kids) to play in the nearby tide-pools, some of which have coral. Drive to that area using the dirt road to the left of the visitor center after you enter the park.

For the less cerebral, you'll find unbeatable snorkeling and SCUBA diving in Honaunau Bay to the right of the boat launch. There are also hiking trails, including the 1871 Trail, so named because area residents paid their taxes in 1871 by fixing up this formerly dilapidated trail. (We have a call in to the IRS to see if the offer's still good.) The trail goes all the way to Ho'okena Beach, but the portion *outside* of the park is pretty bleak and not worth your time.

Leaving Honaunau, you'll continue up Ke Ala o Keawe Road to Painted Church Road. Hang a left onto it to get to St. Benedict's Catholic Church, known simply as the Painted Church. It's a charming little building dating back to the

A REAL GEM

Wake me when the mai tais are ready.

1800s. Between 1899 and 1904, Father John Velge dedicated himself to creating frescos on the inside walls and ceiling. Everything from hell to the Temptation of Christ is represented in loving detail. There is a sign on the door explaining in detail Father Velge's efforts. Termites and age are starting to take their toll, but this is always worth a stop.

Still on Painted Church Rd. you'll come to the Paleaku Peace Gardens (328–8084). We've never seen someone do so much with only 7 acres. Formerly a Buddhist retreat center, the way the sculpted grounds blend with their indoor settings creates an amazingly tranquil and serene setting. Worth the $10 entrance fee for those looking for a calm, cerebral experience. Closed Sun. and Mon.

Either continue on Painted Church Road to Middle Keei Road, or backtrack to get back up to the highway. (See map.)

When deciding where to eat in Kailua-Kona, see ISLAND DINING on page 248.

KAILUA-KONA SHOPPING

There are many small shopping areas in, around and south of Kona to keep your stomach filled and wallet emptied.

Kona Commons is a shopping center north of Kona on Makala Blvd. off Hwy 19. The main store is Target and there is a Sports Authority for all things related that you may need for your trip.

The Kona International Market in the old Industrial Area north of Kona on Kaiwi and Luhia Streets has small vendor stalls. Some are so-so, others are pretty nice. Trini's Market for Asian foodstuffs and good prices on fresh produce.

Continuing south on Kuakini is the King Kamehameha Mall where you will find Quilt Passions for original quilts and quilting supplies and don't miss Music Exchange for great prices on 'ukuleles. Across the street from the Courtyard King Kamehameha Kona Beach Hotel at the Kona Seaside Shops is the Cindy Coats Gallery, whose whimsical artwork reflects the colors of the island. By the Sea is a good place to pick up sandals and clothing for men and women.

Along Alii Drive there are many shops. A few of our favorites: At the Kona Square is Country Samurai Coffee Company, where you can get the shakes off their Buzz Beans, a coffee and chocolate jolt that will wake the dead. At the Kona Banyan Court, Big Island Jewelery, Ltd. makes all their pieces right there and is very helpful. Other shops to visit along the north end of Alii Drive are Lava Light Galleries for photos of the island that you can't capture with your pocket camera. Sugar Momo (just off Alii Drive) for unique jewelry by local artists and other fair-trade items. At Kona Marketplace, a good artists' co-op is Kailua Village Artists Gallery. Across the street at the Kona Inn Shopping Village you'll find Honolua Surf Co. for casual island-style clothing. Try Kona Inn Children's Wear for kids' clothes and books, Tropical Heat Wave for island-style housewares and Mermaids Swimwear, which is great for women's swimsuits. Surf N' Sandals has tons of sandals in case you need a new pair. Don't miss Makau Nui for fabulous Polynesian bone carvings and helpful staff. Just Ukes has 'ukuleles, of course. Pacific Fine Art and Krazy About Kona are two good art galleries.

Other stops in Kona include Walmart in the Crossroads Shopping Center offers good prices on souvenirs. Costco (near the airport) has the best gasoline prices.

South along Alii Drive, on the mauka side of the road, is Ali'I Gardens Marketplace, where there's a place to create that coconut postcard you've wanted to send. (Other stalls there are hit or miss depending on the day you visit.) In Keauhou Shopping Center, visit Kona Stories, a well-stocked bookstore with many gift items and cats (not for sale).

Above Kona in Holualoa there are some of the most original galleries on the island. Ipu Arts Plus, on the north end of town, for bowls and vases made from gourds dyed in a traditional Hawaiian way. Some of our other favorites are: Dovetail for contemporary art and Holualoa Gallery. At Holualoa 'Ukulele Gallery you can make your own 'uke, if you have a spare 8 to 10 days in your schedule, or just buy one created by their many artists.

In Kainaliu, there's Showcase Gallery for paintings and sculptures by artists from all over Hawai'i. Lavender Moon has works by Big Island artists, Kathleen Dunphy Studio has works made from a collage of objects. Also check out Blue Ginger Gallery. To pick up an 'ukulele, try Kiernan Music. At Paradise Found, Yoganics Hawaii and Lucky Cat Boutique you'll find island-style clothing for women—sorry, guys. Kimura's Fabrics has an outstanding selection of Hawaiian print fabrics and quilting supplies. Further south in Mango Court is Cliff Johns Gallery, which has nice woodworks.

Past the 111 mile marker on your left is a beautiful antiques shop called Antiques & Orchids. Other great antiques stores in the area are: Vintage Adventure, Discovery Antiques and Mayme's Antiques Boutique. Before the 109 mile marker on the makai side of the road is Sacred Grounds Coffee Farm & Paradise Pottery Studio. They grow mac nuts here, too. Their reasonably priced ceramics are covered with ginko leaf patterns.

KAILUA-KONA'S BEST BETS

Best Place to Meet Fish for the First Time—Kahalu'u Beach Park
Best Pizza—Kona Brewing Company
Best Fish Sandwich—Quinn's (cajun)
Best Treat (Despite the Name)— Donkey Balls
Best Place for a Coffee and Cinnamon Roll in the Morning—Island Lava Java
Best Snorkeling—Captain Cook Monument or Honaunau
Best Place to Spot Dolphins— Kealakekua Bay
Best Sunset Picnic—The BBQS at Honaunau or the tide-pools of Wawaloli Beach, if the surf's crashing
Best SCUBA Adventure—Manta Ray Night Dive
Best Way to make your Lips Numb— Kanaka Kava

Bring your extra-strength hairspray when you visit South Point.

The southern end of the island from Honaunau (near the 104 mile marker on Highway 11) to Hawai'i Volcanoes National Park is the least developed part of the Big Island. Long stretches of lava fields on the western side of Mauna Loa's flank give way to green as you round the southern part of the island, where rain is allowed to fall with less interference from Mauna Loa volcano. Along the way you'll pass roads leading to, among other things, a (usually) deserted black sand beach, a lightly inhabited 11,000+ acre housing subdivision and the southernmost place in the United States. Since most people drive this stretch on their way to the volcano from Kailua-Kona or Kohala, we'll describe it from that direction.

These districts, called **South Kona** and **Ka'u**, are littered with the financial corpses of big businessmen with big plans and big wallets who took a big bath. Most didn't have a clue how business in Hawai'i works and lost their 'okoles as a result. Three examples, all mentioned in detail later, are:

HOVE—*If you build it, they won't come...not for a generation.*

Hawaiian Riviera—*He who underestimates his opponents will ultimately be crushed by them.*

SeaMountain—*How to turn $30 million in cash into $3 million in real estate.*

[A] From Highway 11 heading south from Honaunau, you'll have several opportunities to visit beaches below the road. **Ho'okena** (a decent gray sand beach) and **Pebble Beach** (a violent 'okole kicker) are described in BEACHES. Distances between gas stations are large, so gas up when you can. Just after Honaunau between the 104 and 103 mile marker is the best fruit stand we know of on the west side. **South**

Kona Fruit Stand usually has excellent quality fruits all organically grown on the adjacent farm.

While driving along the flanks of Mauna Loa along here, consider this: Mauna Loa was built from countless thin layers of lava flows, usually less than 15 feet thick. (Flows since 1800 are shown on the map.) About 120,000 years ago, there was a plain below you where there are now steep hills. At that time, a humongous piece (that's a technical term) of the island, from roughly around the 109 mile marker to an area north of Miloli'i (20 miles to the south), broke off and slid into the ocean, creating what is now Kealakekua Bay and the steep hills south of Honaunau. The resulting tsunami (tidal wave) was so huge that it washed completely over the 1,427-foot-high island of Kaho'olawe, continued on and washed almost completely over the 3,370-foot-high island of Lana'i, where it deposited chunks of coral over a thousand feet up

the mountain. This area is, geologically speaking, still unstable. Just didn't want you to run out of things to worry about.

Be extra careful driving from the 100 mile marker to the 90 mile marker. Though most of it is wide open, it's also 35 MPH and full of speed traps.

Usually referred to as the last remaining fishing village on the island, **Miloli'i** is just past the 89 mile marker. As a beach destination, it won't offer you much (especially on the weekends—see BEACHES for more information). From the highway, 2²/₁₀ miles into the beach access road, look off to your left, and you will see a narrow a'a lava flow. The nearby village of **Ho'opuloa** was wiped out entirely when the lava marched down the slopes of Mauna Loa in 1926. Miloli'i's residents gained notoriety when they and their lawyer managed to kill the Hawaiian Riviera Resort, 17 miles to the south. (See below.) A 20 minute walk from Miloli'i leads to what *was* an exceptionally picturesque coconut-lined bay called **Honom-alino** until it got whacked by a tsunami in 2011. See page 170 for more.

The main highway, called the Hawai'i Belt Road, follows an old Hawaiian road called the Mamalahoa Highway. If you want to see what driving this area *used* to be like (and why it took so bloody long to circle the island), take the 2-mile stretch of the old road. The intersections are at the 88 and 86 mile markers on the mauka (mountain) side of the road.

You'll see lots of macadamia nut trees along this stretch of the island. (By the way, keep the mac nuts away from dogs; they cause paralysis in certain breeds.) The Big Island is a major player in the macadamia nut world though trees in this area show signs of distress from the vog. The inner shell of the macadamia nut is impossibly hard. We've been told by nearly every macadamia farmer we know that if you roll over them with your car, they won't break. So we did it. The result? They all broke. Another urban legend shot to…

Back on the highway, **Manuka State Park** is near the 81 mile marker. There's a 2-mile loop trail that wanders through lava flows of several ages, giving you perspective on how things grow over different times. There are restrooms and phones.

The arrow-straight dirt road ⅔ mile past (south of) the 80 mile marker off Highway 11 is a perfect example of why 4WD vehicles are so useful here. It's called **Road to the Sea**. (Gee, I wonder where it goes…) Two stark, deserted black sand beaches, unknown even to the vast majority of island residents, are at the end. (See BEACHES on page 171 for an explanation.) It's hard to conceive of a lifeless, arid area being inviting, yet these beaches somehow are. We've even seen plankton-eating whale sharks more than once near the beach. The road is a *public access*, misleading sign notwithstanding.

Another beautiful bay south of here is called **Pohue**, but access to it from the lava road has been scuttled for decades by lawsuits and general bickering. Separately, there was a several *thousand* acre resort called **Hawaiian Riviera** slated to be built from Road to the Sea to Pohue Bay. Even though the developer had big bucks, he was thwarted by a handful of residents from Miloli'i, 17 miles to the north, who protested that a planned marina here (and the resort in general) would interfere with their rich fishing grounds and their way of life. They got a lawyer to take up their cause, and together they successfully killed the project. The land has changed hands several times since then, the last time for $13 million, and the current owners resurrected giant development ideas (including an airport) for the area in 2009, but so far it's going nowhere.

Continuing along, Hawaiian Ocean View Estate (known locally as HOVE) lies up mauka of the highway along here. They have gas, nice grocery stores (we prefer Malama Market) and a few restaurants. HOVE is sort of a new community and an old one at the same time. Look at the map on the previous page. Notice all those roads? About 11,000 one-acre parcels on harsh lava are spread among those roads. An oil company built it in the '60s, with the dream of creating a new community. Acre lots originally sold for $995 each, and until the early 2000s you could still pick up lots for $1,500. Prospective buyers were lured by photos of palm tree-backed Pohue Bay (which is distant, private and not reachable) and talk of the HOVE Yacht Club (which never existed). For over 30 years the vast majority of the lots remained unbuilt. They used party line phones until 1998 and around that time they got electricity. Rain catchment has been their lifeline. There's not even a school. Streets have lovely sounding names like *Paradise Parkway* and *Tree Fern Avenue*. But after driving around, you'd expect names like *Lava Lane* and *Rocky Road*.

Most of the lots were sold or given away free with a full tank of gas (just teasing). Not to be outdone, another company built a subdivision below the highway (also shown on the map) with 1,200 three-acre lots. It took the short-lived land boom of around 2005 to finally shake up HOVE real estate values and draw residents.

To be fair, everyone we've met who lives in HOVE loves it there. They have formed a tight-knit community and seem happy as can be with their location. Whenever we drive around here, however, we're reminded that the Big Island is often rumored to be one of the largest repositories of people from the FEDERAL WITNESS PROTECTION PROGRAM. What a perfect place to lose oneself.

SOUTH POINT

B Between the 69 and 70 mile markers is the road to South Point (called Ka Lae meaning "the point"). This is the southernmost part of the island, making it the southernmost spot in the entire nation. (Not the Florida Keys, as most trivia books claim.) At one time the road was nasty and very hard on rental cars. It has since been repaved and is in fine condition the whole way. The only hazard is that the road is one lane for much of its length. It is mostly straight, and there is space to pull over for on-coming cars. Try to resist the temptation to speed on the seemingly wide open parts of this road; there are some surprise blind hills and turns.

NOT TO BE MISSED!

The wind is always blowing out on this grassy plain, hence this location for the Pakini Nui Wind Farm in the distance. The trees here are all wind-blown in the same direction (west), vividly showing what happens to deflected trade winds coming from the northeast. (The foldout back cover map puts it in perspective.)

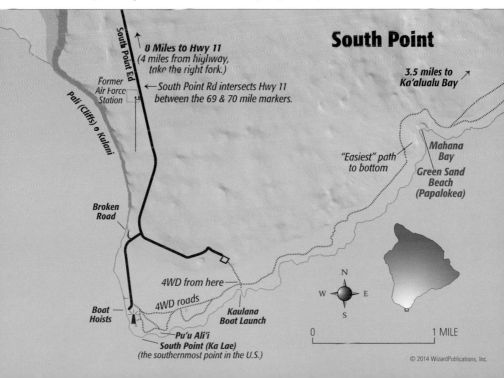

South Point

0 Miles to Hwy 11
(4 miles from highway, take the right fork.)

South Point Rd
Former Air Force Station
Pali (Cliffs) o Kulani

←—South Point Rd intersects Hwy 11 between the 69 & 70 mile markers.

3.5 miles to Ka'alualu Bay

"Easiest" path to bottom

Mahana Bay
Green Sand Beach (Papalokea)

Broken Road

4WD from here
4WD roads

Boat Hoists
Kaulana Boat Launch

Pu'u Ali'i
South Point (Ka Lae)
(the southernmost point in the U.S.)

N W E S

0 _____ 1 MILE

© 2014 WizardPublications, Inc.

Massive turbines are one indication of the ever-present winds in this area.

As you get near South Point, turn right at the fork after the KALAE entrance sign. (The sign looked rickety at press time—the fork is a mile south of some abandoned buildings on the right.) South Point is the site of some of the oldest artifacts yet discovered in Hawai'i (as early as 300 AD) and was probably the first place the Polynesians came ashore and settled when they discovered these islands. Dry and desolate with no permanent streams, this might seem a surprising place for people to settle. The reason for its settlements, however, lies offshore. The waters off South Point are incredibly rich fishing grounds. Large pelagic game fish, such as tuna, mahimahi and marlin are plentiful. The ancient Hawaiians quickly discovered this but had a problem harvesting the fish. The wind and current together form such a strong offshore force that it would require all the fisherman's attention just to stay put in a canoe. Those who went out too far were considered lost due to these forces since fishing canoes were not as maneuverable as voyaging canoes, and since the currents are uninterrupted all the way to Antarctica. The bottom drops to great depths quickly, so anchors aren't the answer. Their clever solution was to carve holes into the rock ledge and feed ropes through them so their canoes could be tied to shore while fishing. Some of those holes are still visible near the boat hoists at the cliffs.

Freshwater is very scarce here, even from wells, and what is available is barely potable. In the 1700s a chief named Kalani'opu'u, tired of having to bathe several miles away, asked his kahunas if there was water under the ground. One know-it-all assured him there was water at a certain spot if he dug *really* deep. After much digging, they found nothing. The big-mouth kahuna was promptly executed for his bad advice.

Today, you're likely to see long lines strung from the sea cliffs just to the northwest of the actual South Point. These lines are usually held afloat by empty bleach bottles and are sometimes pulled so taut by the wind and current that you'd swear you could walk on them. Fishermen use toy sailboats or balloons to drag the rope out to sea and dangle 10 foot leaders from the main line at every bleach bottle. When they get a strike, they haul the whole line in.

At the cliffs near South Point are old hoists, used to lower small boats from the low cliffs. A metal cliffside ladder is present, as well. Larger boats use the Kaulana boat launch less than a mile to the east.

People lived at Kaulana until the beginning of the 20th century. Most visitors make the mistake of assuming that the cliffs with the boat hoists *are* South Point. The real South Point is past the light beacon to the left of a place where a rock wall trails down into the sea. There is no cliff there. The beacon will be behind you. Next to the beacon is the small Kalaea Heiau.

Since ancient times this entire area has had a reputation for having exceptionally strong currents, and during all but calm seas this is no doubt true. Even so, we know people who love nothing better than to leap into the water from the boat hoist area and come back up via the metal ladder adjacent to a boat hoist. They also jump into the sketchy hole near the cliffs, though I have to confess to not having the stones to do the latter myself. There are also a few spots along the cliffs where you can scramble down

to the water. Some people even like to snorkel here at night when fish and clouds of small, beautiful shrimp greet the eye. The water is unbelievably clear and seems quite inviting when calm, especially when you can see lots of fish swimming below.

With this in mind, I've repeatedly snorkeled here below the boat hoists to assess the currents. I was so wary the first time out that I tied myself to the cliff ladder with a long rope—just to be safe. It turned out to be unnecessary. *When calm, I have yet to detect much current below the boat hoist area,* probably because it's protected by the point. The water is teeming with life and visibility is usually over 100 feet. But (and I can't stress this enough) I've *never* gone into the water when it's not calm, I don't swim too far, and I don't endorse swimming there. The surge here demonstrates the extreme

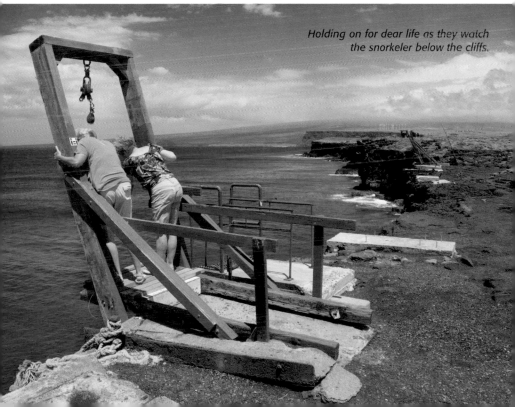

Holding on for dear life as they watch the snorkeler below the cliffs.

power of the ocean, and I'm excited and nervous every time I swim at that spot. South of the cliffs at the actual South Point, the water is always violent and unswimmable. I mention all this so you will know what I've experienced here in case you are crazy enough to do it on your own. Check to see that your life insurance policy is in order before you go, and buy a good guidebook to Antarctica—just in case.

South Point was used during WWII for army barracks. Later, the Navy installed a missile tracking station on 33 acres. Not to be left out, the Air Force later took over the facilities and renamed it South Point Air Force Station. The station was closed in 1979, and little remains except the shabby buildings on your right as you approach South Point. Look for horses in the buildings' remains.

Just north of the boat hoists (see map) is a road that leads off a cliff. The road was built in 1955 along with a concrete landing below to service fishing boats. Representing the finest county quality, it lasted less than a year. The surf erased the landing and part of the road. What remains is called (you see this one coming, don't you?) **Broken Road**. The view from the end of Broken Road is spectacular, but the snorkeling isn't as good here as it is below the boat hoists. Off in the distance you see Pali o Kulani, which rises 350 feet from the ocean. At the place where the cliff appears to end, it actually turns inland and runs north to an area just south of Highway 11. The inland cliff was caused by another catastrophic landslide, similar to (but pre-dating) the one described earlier. It slid to the west and caused a similar splash.

If you had gone left at the aforementioned fork, you'd come to all that remains of former military housing. We were thrilled when state authorities leveled them a while back. Until then, militant squatters had occupied the crumbling buildings for many years, extract-

ing "Green Sand Parking Fees" from visitors and often threatening car break-ins if they didn't comply. It was a well-known problem and generated over 150 police reports in one year alone. Authorities seemed paralyzed until finally, in 2007, 21 officers converged here, brought a BBQ, grilled up burgers for themselves and the squatters, then proceeded to bulldoze all the structures.

When the pavement ends, a dirt road leads to a boat launch ¼-mile away.

Off to the east of South Point is a strange phenomenon called **Green Sand Beach**. (See BEACHES.) It fea-

A REAL GEM

tures a beautiful mixture of green and black sand and is a fascinating place to visit. If you have 4WD (and insurance) you *might* be able to drive it. It's 2¼ miles each way on the flat but sometimes *deeply* rutted, grassy plain. Sometimes even timid 4WD-ers can make it. Other times, you'll want to bring along four sumo wrestlers to help you carry your car out of the ruts. During extended dry times the government often prohibits 4WD vehicles in the name of fire safety, though local residents seem to ignore the prohibition and will often charge a fee to drive you out. Many readers have written us to say we're *way* off on that distance, by the way. We promise, we're not. We've checked it by car odometer and on foot with GPS. It just *seems* longer since the wind is in your face going out.

Back on Highway 11, as you continue, you'll wrap around the island and enter the wetter, windward side. Almost instantly, our old friend green has returned to the scene. This was the edge of sugar country. Big Island sugar died here in 1996 (as a business—some of the cane still lives on), and many of the fields here have been replaced with the more profitable macadamia nut trees. Coffee has also been planted upslope of the highway. It's not in the same league as Kona coffee. We've

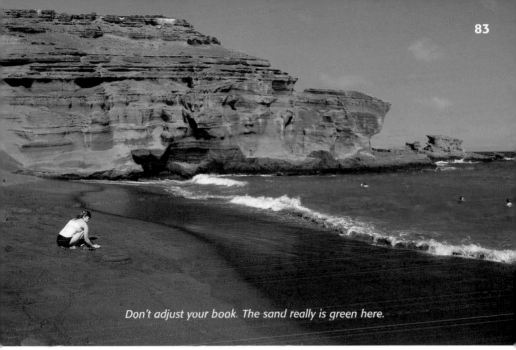

Don't adjust your book. The sand really is green here.

had some good Ka'u coffee, but a lot of bad cups. (Ka'u growers write to us telling us we're dead wrong and have no taste. *Sorry*, it's just our opinion.) Both coffee and mac nuts can be found at roadside stands and local markets.

Waiohinu and Na'alehu are the first towns you come to. Waiohinu's claim to fame was the **Mark Twain Monkeypod Tree**, planted by the author himself. It blew down in the '50s, but its shoots have grown into a respectable new tree. You'll find restrooms down the road at Waiohinu Park.

While in Na'alehu, stop by the best restaurant along this part of the island, **Hana Hou Restaurant and Bakery**.

As you come down the hill near the 62 mile marker, you'll see **Whittington Park** and the remains of its wharf in the distance. From the vantage point up the hill you truly appreciate the vastness of this Big Island. Whittington is picturesque from a distance and makes a decent rest room pit stop if you're in need.

Just after the 56 mile marker is the road to **Punalu'u Black Sand Beach**. This is the easiest volcanic black sand beach to access on the island now that the

more famous one in Puna is gone. (That one was buried by lava in 1990—see page 119.) The water here is cold due to the large amounts of freshwater percolating from the floor just offshore. At one time the ancient Hawaiians at Punalu'u (which means *spring dived for*) obtained their freshwater here by diving down with an upside-down, dried, hollow gourd to where the freshwater was streaming out. There they would flip the gourd, fill it with fresh water, put their thumbs over it, and come to the surface.

NOT TO BE MISSED!

There are scads of turtles in the bay, and it's one of the few areas where we've seen them beach themselves. There is also a picturesque fishpond backed by lots of coconut trees. (Incidentally, there were no coconuts in Hawai'i before the Polynesians came. Though ubiquitous in the South Pacific, Hawai'i is fed by the North Pacific Current, precluding the possibility that a live coconut could have floated here from any place warm. Just thought you needed to know that for your next appearance on *Jeopardy*.) The only eyesore at this exotic black sand beach is the closed and ramshackle restaurant behind the fishpond, whacked by a tsunami in 1975. Fortunately, it's mostly covered over from the beach side, which tells you how long it's been closed—long enough to choke off their lovely view with vegetation. It's been condemned and might be bulldozed by the time you arrive.

When the Japanese attacked Pearl Harbor in 1941, Army troops dynamited the concrete wall over near the boat launch to keep it from being used by the enemy in case of an invasion.

Tour buses sometimes bring groups to Punalu'u, but it *usually* isn't crowded since it is 60 miles from both Hilo and Kona. Forgive us for nagging, but please resist the temptation to take black sand home as a souvenir. Since it is finite, it would eventually deplete the beach for everyone. (Or you can see CURSES in BASICS.) The sharp edges of the sand grains ensure that swimmers will inadvertently take some home anyway. You will find plenty of stowaways in the lining of your bathing suit, which will stay there for years. The concessionaire at Punalu'u sells black sand and, though they *claim* it's from another beach consumed by the volcano, that certainly can't be said of their green sand, so we hope you won't buy any. OK, end of nag.

This area is sometimes called **Sea-Mountain**, named by a developer for the **Lo'ihi Seamount**. That undersea volcano, 20 miles offshore from here, will be the Big Island's next volcano attraction. It's still 3,200 feet underwater and won't surface for another 100,000 years, but be sure to look for it when we release our 99,000th edition of this book. (Call now to reserve your copy early.) The whole property was purchased by a Japanese investment company for more than $30 million at the height of a real estate boom in 1989. After five years and countless challenges to their plans by local residents, they sold it for less than $3 million,

not even a *tenth* of what they paid for it. *(Ouch!)* There are older condos here and a golf course. See BEACHES for more on Punalu'u.

From Punalu'u you'll start your gradual 4,000-foot ascent to Kilauea Volcano. Along the way you pass **Pahala**, a former sugar town. Though friendly, the town is quiet and a little depressing, and the economic harm is, to a certain degree, self-inflicted. Pahala residents were crucial in killing the expansion plan at Punalu'u in the mid-'90s, confident that their sugar plantation jobs were sufficient and fearful of altering their way of life. After that, the coastal land below Pahala was slated to be a spaceport where private satellites would be launched. Again Pahala residents were able to successfully fight the plan, even though it was backed by the state, the governor and the mayor.

Then in the late '90s the last Big Island sugar plantation opened the books and told the workers they either needed to accept a 15% pay cut or the company would have to close down due to ongoing losses. (Every other sugar plantation on the island had failed in the previous years due to a changing marketplace.) The sugar workers voted to reject the pay cut, and the sugar company promptly shut down, putting nearly every resident of this one-industry town out of work. Their way of life changed anyway, but they had nothing to fall back on. For a decade they paid the price in the form of a downward economic spiral. Only after the short-lived 2005 land boom did some prosperity finally start to trickle down to this part of the island.

C A couple miles past the edge of **Hawai'i Volcanoes National Park**, take note of the rugged looking a'a lava. It's hard to believe that barefoot armies marched through this stuff, but they did—sometimes under extraordinary circumstances like those described on page 90.

Lava sometimes forms surreal images as it's flowing.

If you had to name the one thing the Big Island is most famous for, it would undoubtedly be **Kilauea Volcano**. In all the world there isn't a more active volcano, and none is as user-friendly as Kilauea. People often refer to it as the drive-in volcano.

Kilauea is an enigma—you can't really see the mountain from anywhere on the island, or even recognize it when you are standing on it. It seems more like a wound on Mauna Loa, whose flanks it resides upon. In the past, everyone thought that it was *part* of Mauna Loa, but today we know that it is separate and distinct, with its own separate (though possibly interrelated) magma chamber. One part of Kilauea, the actual Pu'u 'O'o vent itself, is teasingly inaccessible. You can't get very close to it without a long hike.

The "quickest" way is described in ADVENTURES on page 232.

We feel strongly that most people allow far too little time for visiting **Hawai'i Volcanoes National Park**. Many simply blow through on an around-the-island driving frenzy, stopping long enough to snap a shot of Kilauea Caldera. There is much more here than meets the eye, and this might be the highlight of your Hawaiian trip. Whether Kilauea is erupting or not, this park is the most fascinating place you may ever visit, and you *surely* don't have anything like this back home. The finest hiking on the island is here. The lushest rain forest you've ever seen is here to stroll through. Vents spewing steam, brand new land, birds-a-plenty, giant chasms, ancient Hawaiian petroglyphs, lava craters, walk-through lava tubes, un-rivaled vistas—it's all here. Once you know what to look for, you will want to spend *at least* a whole day, preferably two. Since driving to the volcano can take four hours round trip from Kona and five hours from Kohala, consider reserving a place to stay in the town of Volcano (see WHERE TO STAY). This allows you to ex-perience it at a more leisurely pace and is a nice way to go, if you can swing it. You'll probably want to stay until after dark if there are accessible surface lava flows, and the drive back to Kona or Ko-hala is a drag. If you are staying in Hilo, it's an easy drive back.

WILL I GET TO SEE LAVA FLOWING?

Historically (meaning since 1778), most eruptions have lasted days or weeks, rarely months. Until this erup-tion, only once, from 1969–1974 at Mauna Ulu, has an eruption outside the crater lasted more than a year. The cur-rent eruption, originating from a newly created vent called Pu'u 'O'o, is redefin-ing our understanding of an eruption. It started on January 3, 1983, shifted to a vent called Kupaianaha from 1986 to 1992, then shifted back toward Pu'u 'O'o and was flowing outside the park into lower Puna at press time with an oc-casional hiccup in its flowing activity.

When you visit Kilauea, you either *will* or *won't* get to see a surface lava flow. (Now *there's* a gutsy prediction!) Hawai'i Volcanoes National Park has a recording at 985–6000. They also have weather info. You can also get updates from the USGS at 967–8862. As we went to press, there were no signs of an impending work stoppage by Madame Pele, the fire goddess of Hawai'i, but that doesn't mean you can come here and be assured of being able to stick your toe into liquid lava. Madame Pele can be kind of a tease. The lava has stopped and started many times, shifted from vent to vent, gone straight into the ocean from underground lava tubes, and flowed in inaccessible places. It has also flowed just feet from the end of Chain of Craters Road, in Kilauea Caldera and other very accessible places. It's a gamble as to whether you will get to see it. Kilauea might go months without *accessible* lava flows, then put on a flawless show for months after that. If you have Internet access, we have an eruption update on our web-site at **www.hawaiirevealed.com**. We also have links to other eruption websites.

When you hear that the volcano is erupting, you might think of a cone-shaped mountain, of going up to the top and peering into a boiling lake of molten

Light brown indicates major trails

Beaches of jet black sand can form almost overnight when lava shatters as it's quenched by the sea. A month later, this beach was gone.

rock. Maybe some will be pouring rapidly down the mountain, consuming everything in its path as people flee in panic. In Hawai'i, things are *far* different. Here, even the volcano is laid-back. Though it has erupted from the main crater in the past, most of the time (including the current eruption) the lava breaks out from a vent along what's called the rift zone, a linear belt of fractured rock on the flank of the volcano. From this vent the lava travels downhill, usually to the sea. After it starts flowing, pahoehoe lava rivers crust over, forming tubes. These tubes act as excellent insulators (the lava usually loses a mere 20°F over miles of travel in these tubes) and carry the lava to the ocean. Sometimes these tubes break the surface downhill of the source, forming surface flows. When this happens, you can often walk right up to it. Otherwise, there might be an enormous steam plume at the sea (which glows at night).

Many activity companies and nearly every guidebook show photos of a helicopter or viewer directly in front of gigantic fountains of lava. You won't see any pictures like that in our book for two reasons. One, you're more likely to see a *balanced federal budget* than to see that. It might happen a few times each decade for a few hours. What are *your* chances? The other reason is that a few of those photos are fake. (A stock government photo of a Kilauea lava fountain taken by scientists, a shot of a helicopter or person, a computer, and *voilà*—the unreal looks real.) The close-up photographs of surface lava flows you see in this book were all taken by us at accessible sites. We didn't get special permission to go to special spots or go through unusual procedures. We didn't use a camera lens longer than a rental car to make it *seem* like it was close (and I've had the singed leg hairs to prove it). We also didn't charter helicopters and use zillion dollar cameras on loan from NASA. Granted, we didn't get to see this kind of lava our first time out there, but these are the kinds of things that mere mortals like us might get to see *if* Madame Pele is cooperating.

THE SCENE

We've been to the volcano countless times, with and without surface lava. It's always a fantastic experience, though not what people expect.

During a relatively calm flow, pahoehoe lava is silvery coated, red or yellow as it oozes its way toward the sea. It is a humbling experience to stand there and observe Earthly creation, like seeing the planet during its fiery adolescence. In most parts of the world, people dread active volcanoes, fearing death and destruction. A huge explosion will send clouds of ash and pumice into air, killing everything in its path. (Or screwing up travel to Europe.) In Hawai'i, people drop whatever they are doing and drive out to see it. Rather than apocalyptic explosions, Kilauea mostly drools and dribbles. (In historic times, it has exploded only a few times, and one had astonishing consequences—see page 90.) Though the total volume of lava erupting ranges from 300,000 to more than a million cubic yards *per day,* it is so spread out that it rarely rushes down the mountain in a hellish river of liquid stone. Usually, it's small rivulets of molten lava separated by large distances from other rivulets. When it hardens (which occurs very quickly), it crunches beneath your feet like shards of glass.

There are not many places on this planet where you can walk on ground younger than you are, where you can be assured that there is absolutely nothing alive beneath your feet except for the earth itself. We've been there when people from all over the world stand in awe, tears streaming down their cheeks as they tell their children, "You may never see anything like this again in your lifetime."

As freshly hardened pahoehoe lava cools, it stresses the silica coating on the outside. This natural glass then crackles and pops off the rock, creating subtle sounds that bewitch viewers. Heat from the flows can be intense. Many times we've been less than a yard from the molten lava and felt like we would suddenly burst into flames. Other times, the wind has blown from the other direction so we could enjoy the liquid earth in comfort. Sometimes there is unpleasant black smoke and fumes (especially when the volcano is gobbling up more road or forest). Other times it seems to have absolutely no fumes or smoke and no offensive smell. (What smell it does have is hard to describe but never forgotten.)

At night, the lava may glow in numerous spots like a prehistoric scene from yesteryear. Sometimes, as the lava flows into the ocean, brilliant red and orange steam clouds light up the immediate area, creating dazzling light shows as the flow drips or gushes into the ocean. Sometimes, when it burns scrub vegetation at night, the methane emits a blue flame. A night scene might go like this: A crowd of about 50 people on a bluff overlooking a field of fresh pahoehoe. It pops, crackles and glows as the night consumes all. What amazes us is how reverent everybody is. Couples hold each other tight. People speak in soft whispers. They try not to move much for fear of disturbing others as they watch Earth's most primordial show. Nobody wants to leave. Watching the lava enter the sea at night never fails to impress, and we've been told more times than we can count by visitors that it is an unsurpassed highlight.

A FEW BASICS

Despite the fact that it is operated by the federal government, the park seems very well run. Much of the staff are friendly and professional. (We've seen other parks where the staff can be real curmudgeons.) The rangers are pretty good at letting you see the action close up. We've been there when they lead people across smoldering lava, the heat

Lava comes in many flavors and textures.

coming up through their shoes. They will only keep you away if they *truly* perceive danger, unlike some other parks where they sometimes keep you away from imaginary dangers on orders from the lawyers. Because of this, you should heed their cautions seriously. If they say you can't go to a certain area because they expect a lava bench might collapse, don't go there. At least one person has died because he didn't heed this warning. (The ocean drops quickly off the coast of the park, and new lava land is usually destined to break off when it reaches a critical mass.) If rangers say an area is off limits because of the dangers

The Explosion That Changed History

Mild-mannered Kilauea has exploded on a large scale only twice in recorded history, once in 1790 and once in 1924. (There is evidence that it may have exploded more often in the distant past.) These eruptions are phreatomagmatic, meaning steam-induced (but you knew that).

In 1790, Kamehameha ruled much of the island. While he was distracted with plans to invade Maui, a rival chief named Keoua seized control of this part of the island. Kamehameha sent troops to do battle. Eventually both armies pulled back to their strongholds. As Keoua's troops and their families camped at Kilauea that night, fire and rock spewed from Kilauea Caldera. Keoua thought he had offended Pele, the volcano goddess, by rolling stones into the crater the day before and spent two days trying to appease her. It didn't work. On the third day they tried to leave, organized in three divisions. Right after the first division left, the mountain exploded. Darkness enveloped the area, punctured by volcano-induced thunder and lightning, and streams of red and blue light from the crater. Huge amounts of hot ash rained down, then a suffocating gas belched up from the volcano.

The first division to depart escaped mostly intact. The second division disappeared. When the third division came to the scene, they found their comrades of the second division huddled in circles, some hugging each other with their noses pressed together. Relieved, the third division rushed forward to greet them, only to discover that every last member of the second division—around 400 men and their wives and children—were dead. (Not 85 as the park sign says.) Most had been asphyxiated by the noxious gas. The only survivor was a solitary hog. If you take the Ka'u Desert Trail (page 102), you can see the faint outline of steps preserved in the ash—steps created by other soldiers at the time of the disaster.

As for Keoua, everyone now knew that Pele was against him and his army. He kept fighting more battles but never turned the tide. Not yet defeated, he was invited by Kamehameha to peacefully dedicate the new Pu'ukohola Heiau in Kawaihae. When Keoua's boat approached the shore of Kawaihae, he was immediately murdered by one of Kamehameha's officers and had the dubious honor of being the temple's first official human sacrifice. Thus was Kamehameha's rule over the island forever solidified.

of methane explosions, believe it. Methane from plant matter in older flows can heat up when a new flow covers it. This usually escapes by hissing or by small pops, but sometimes it can be more dramatic. We were there once with many other visitors when a large methane explosion occurred 25 feet from us. It was powerful enough to rip through 12-inch thick lava, pieces of which jumped into the air. Under certain circumstances, these explosions occur 100 yards in advance of a lava flow.

In the park we like to arrive at surface flows about an hour or two before sunset. That way we get to see it during the day and at night. As the sun sets, the light-emitting lava doesn't have to compete with the sun, resulting in brighter and seemingly more abundant lava. Bring a polarizing filter if you have a camera that will accept it. (Wipe your camera off when you are finished; the air can be acidic and is hard on electronics.) The best shots will be late in the afternoon. If you get close to the lava, the heat might consume your camera battery faster than you think. (Trust me on that one.) Bring water—you'll get hot and thirsty. If it rains, you'll be grateful for something waterproof, and so will your camera. Depending on the flow, a flashlight might be invaluable. At times, they let you walk to places at night that can be spectacular. Contact lens wearers will want to bring drops—maybe even your glasses if it gets uncomfortable. Bring sunscreen if you are there for the day. Add more water.

What you don't want to bring are your preconceptions. No matter what you expect, the flow will be different. Come with a blank slate, and you will leave full of wonder.

And remember, if there are no accessible surface flows (which is quite possible), don't despair. The volcano area is eminently fascinating and exciting, with or without surface flows, and is always worth at least a day of exploration. Below are some of the other delights waiting for you at Hawai'i Volcanoes National Park.

HIKING IN THE PARK

Much of the best hiking on the island is in Hawai'i Volcanoes National Park. The ACTIVITIES chapter has a HIKING section on page 193, which lists scads of great hikes in the park. There are also a couple spookier park hikes listed in ADVENTURES. Note that strolls of less than 30 minutes were described below in the tour of the volcano.

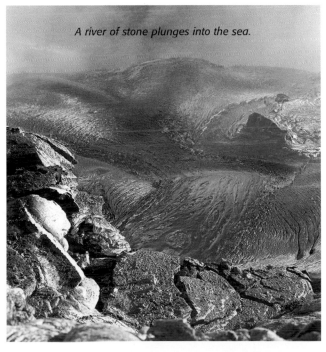

A river of stone plunges into the sea.

Kilauea Crater

This map is rendered at an angle in order to convey the lay of the land at Kilauea. Visualize it as a solid cast of the land sitting on a table. Each "terraced" contour line represents an elevation change of 20 feet.

Volcano Village

Gas

26 miles to Hilo

11

27

Old Volcano Rd

Park Boundary

Escape Rd

Thurston Lava Tube

Kilauea Iki Overlook

Crater Rim Dr

Kilauea Iki Trail

Kilauea Iki Crater

Kilauea Iki Trail

Devastation Trail

Crater Rim Trail

Pu'u 'O'o Vent is 8 miles this way. It's not easily accessible. The hike to Pu'u 'O'o, from outside the Park is described on page 233:

Puhimau Crater

Park Visitor Center

Park Entrance

28

Crater Rim Trail

Chain of Craters Rd

1

Sulphur Banks

29

Crater Rim Trail

Volcano House

Byron Ledge Trail

Pu'u Pua'i

No Cars from here

Road Closed

Keanakako'i Crater (Walkable)

Lua Manu Crater

1 MILE

Kilauea Military Camp

'Iliahi (Sandlewood) Trail

Old Crater Rim Rd now collapsed & part of Crater Rim Trail

Dashed Lines Indicate Trail Closed

0

Gas

30

Steam Vents

Kilauea Caldera

Halema'uma'u Trail

Tree Molds

Kilauea Overlook

Hawaiian Volcano Observatory

Jaggar Museum

Crater Rim Trail

31

Crater Rim Dr

Kipuka Pua'ulu — Volcano Golf & Country Club

Mauna Loa Scenic Rd

Halema'uma'u Crater

Crater Rim Dr

Crater Rim Trail

Namakani Paio Campgrounds Cabins

Road Closed

11

88 miles to Kailua-Kona

32

Ka'u Desert Trail

Crater Rim Trail

N E S W

Indicates Foot Trails

25 Roadside mile markers

Closed due to fumes

© 2014 Wizard Publications, Inc.

AROUND KILAUEA CRATER

A quick note: We decided not to use our **Real Gem** and **Not To Be Missed** icons in this section because they would fill the pages. The entire park is *a real gem* and is *not to be missed*.

A REAL GEM

Remember that Kilauea Caldera is located at an altitude of 4,000 feet, so make sure you bring your warmies for those days when it's misty and chilly at the summit.

After paying your $15 car entrance fee (what a deal, and it's good for a week!) at the gate, stop by the Visitor Center on your right. They have up-to-date information, a nice display of books, videos, artifacts, a movie showing and—most important if you've driven a long way—restrooms. Check out the 3-D miniature of the island near the restrooms to get a perspective of the island. Some guided hike notices are sometimes posted at the Visitor Center if you're interested. From there, you might want to walk across the street to **Volcano House** for your first peek of Kilauea Caldera from their enviable view.

We should probably take the opportunity to confess here that the park used to sell this book at the Visitor Center. After undergoing a lengthy reviewing process, they called it the most accurate book they'd ever seen on the Big Island, and it became the only guidebook sold there. Quite a coup. The book's not there anymore. Why? Because some park bureaucrats became upset when they realized that we revealed things, such as a trail to Pu'u 'O'o that doesn't go through their park, the hike to Mauna Ulu, and several other things. Well, we're not going to stop telling you about these attractions even if it means they won't carry our book at the Visitor Center. The trail to

Pu'u 'O'o is described in ADVENTURES on page 232; Mauna Ulu is on page 231. (A few other things we revealed also got under their skin.)

Crater Rim Drive is closed at the Jagger Museum, so you'll want to do a counter-clockwise tour of the caldera to start. Take a right from the Visitor Center, and the first thing you come to are the **Steam Vents** on your left. Here, rain that has seeped into the ground is heated by Kilauea and issues forth as steam. The amount varies daily depending on the level of rain in the past few days, and it is rarely smelly like Sulphur Banks listed below. In fact, there is usually no smell at all. Make sure you take the trail for 2–3 minutes toward the crater rim for a smashing view of the crater, and where additional, more powerful and unobstructed steam vents are present.

From the steam vent parking lot you can walk across the road along a paved path called the Sulphur Banks Trail. It leads 5 to 10 minutes through a pretty forest to a boardwalk at the **Sulphur Banks**. This colorful but stinky phenomenon is where hydrogen sulphide gas and steam form deposits of sulphur, gypsum and hematite on the ground. This should be avoided by those with a heart condition, respiratory problems, children or anyone eating lunch.

Continuing on Crater Rim Dr. you'll see **Kilauea Military Camp**. Though you gotta be active or retired military to stay here, multiple visits by us as well as phone calls confirm that visitors are welcome to buy from their relatively cheap credit card-only gas station as well as their general store, restaurant, lounge and bowling alley (though they reserve the right to bump you from the latter if a guest wants to bowl). Small handmade signs asking for military ID seem at odds with their warm welcome.

A young couple standing around watching the world get made. Not a bad way to spend the afternoon.

Rounding the crater, you come to **Kilauea Overlook**. This is a different perspective on Kilauea Crater and its progeny, **Halemaʻumaʻu Crater**, and is definitely worth a stop. Look for white-tailed tropic birds soaring on the thermals down in the crater.

Just past the overlook is **Jagger Museum** and the **Hawaiian Volcano Observatory**. The museum has some very interesting exhibits and is worth a stop. (The view is *da kine*, as well.)

When Halemaʻumaʻu started spewing nasty gases in 2008, park officials closed the road from here, and it will likely be closed during your visit. This is as close as you'll be able to get to **Halemaʻumaʻu Crater**. This crater-within-a-crater is said to be the home to Madame Pele, the Hawaiian volcano goddess. Though crusted over now, for most of the 19th century this was a boiling lava lake. Mark Twain and other celebrities of his time vis-

ited here and described it as viewing the fiery pits of hell. When Isabella Bird saw it in 1873, she wrote:

Suddenly, just above, and in front of us, gory drops were tossed in air, and springing forwards we stood on the brink of Hale-mau-mau, which was about 35 feet below us. I think we all screamed, I know we all wept, but we were speechless, for a new glory and terror had been added to the Earth. It is the most unutterable of wonderful things. The words of common speech are quite useless. It is unimaginable, indescribable, a sight to remember forever, a sight which at once took possession of every faculty of sense and soul, removing one altogether out of the range of ordinary life. Here was the real "bottomless pit"–the "fire which is not quenched"–"the place of hell"–"the lake which burneth with fire and brimstone"–the "everlasting burnings"–the fiery sea whose waves are never weary. There were groanings, rumblings, and detonations, rushings, hissings, and splashings, and the crashing sound of breakers on the coast, but it was the surging of fiery waves upon a fiery shore.

Halemaʻumaʻu is quieter now, though still steaming and occasionally with a lava lake rising high enough to glimpse. The crater has risen and fallen over time—going from 1,335 feet deep to overflowing its top. It's 3,000 feet across, but we can't predict how deep it will be during your visit.

Until the road closure Hawaiians still made offerings here to Pele. It is said that Pele will appear as a beautiful young woman in the mountains and as a very old and ugly woman at the shoreline. (Hence the Hawaiian saying, "Always be nice to an old woman; it might be Pele.") Though Halema'uma'u is said to be her home, she seems to be spending more time these days at her summer house at Pu'u 'O'o.

You're gonna have to backtrack toward, then past, the visitor center, then hang a right before the park entrance to stay on Crater Rim Dr. If you need a break, you could stop by the **Volcano Art Center Gallery** near the visitor center. Built in 1877, this was the original Volcano House before it was moved here to make way for another building. Now an art gallery, they have an exquisite selection from some of the island's top artists, including higher-end wood carvings, glassworks, paintings and more. This is also a good place to check out what's going on in the area in terms of events and demonstrations. Open 9–5.

Now you're going clockwise around the crater. There is a nice hike called the **Earthquake Trail** that starts near Volcano House. (See HIKING on page 196.) Part of it is on the *old* Crater Rim Drive—before it fell into the crater in 1983—and the results are dramatic.

Watch for the **Kilauea Iki Overlook** on your right. This is definitely worth stopping for. This crater (meaning "little Kilauea") had been asleep for almost a century when it became active in 1959. Then it erupted into gargantuan fountains of

'A'a lava on the left (named by the first Hawaiian to walk on it barefooted?) is rough and clinkery. Pahoehoe on the right is smooth and ropy, like thick cake batter.

lava, some reaching a staggering 1,900 feet—that's more than four times the height of the crater walls and is the highest on record. Scientists had warnings that an eruption was going to occur. Earthquake swarms and a swelling of Kilauea told them it was coming. So they set up their instruments and waited for the inevitable—*at Halema'uma'u*. They were stunned when the lava instead shot from the southwest wall of Kilauea Iki (across from you) 2 miles away from Halema'uma'u. Ground zero was near the Pu'u Pua'i (meaning gushing hill) cinder cone on the other side. It was created as fountains of lava, blown southwest by the trade winds piled high into a cone. The vent spewed enough lava at one point to bury a football field 15 feet deep in lava—*every minute!* Each time the showers ended, the lava would drain back into the vent opening, only to be shot out again. When it ended, 36 days after it began, the crater floor was a dead zone with a lava bathtub ring above the floor to show how high the lava lake had reached. The lava lake cooled and cracked as sheets of lava buckled and warped, giving the crater the look of dried, crusted-over gravy. Today, steam usually issues from cracks in the crater floor, and the rock is still molten a couple of hundred feet down. There are still vents on the crater, though the main vent was covered by falling cinders. Kilauea Iki offers one of the best hikes on the island. See HIKING on page 194.

Kilauea Iki is separated from Kilauea by a narrow shelf of land called **Byron Ledge**. It was on this ledge in 1824 that Princess Kapiolani publicly stood and, to the horror and fear of many, denied the volcano goddess Pele and embraced Christianity. She initiated this by eating 'ohelo berries without offering any to Pele first. (It was thought that Pele would strike you dead if you didn't offer her some first by tossing a fruiting branch into the crater.) When the Princess didn't die after snubbing and denying Pele, Christianity was more widely embraced by her people.

Back on Crater Rim Road, you come to a parking lot (probably full of buses). This is **Thurston Lava Tube**. If you are looking for an easy way to see what the inside of natural lava plumbing looks like, Thurston Lava Tube is worth a stop. It is considered one of the "must sees" at the volcano. If you get there between tour buses, it can be an interesting experience. The entrance is a few minutes walk from Crater Rim Drive (see map). This part of the tube is lit and is the most widely visited. Most of the lava stalactites have been removed over the decades, but you can still see enough tube detail to get the idea of how the lava travels. Undisturbed tubes often have floors littered with rocks that fall from the ceiling (either from when the tube cooled or from rainwater seeping through the cracks over the years). Thurston has been cleaned up and lighted to make it easy to visit. You exit about halfway through the tube. It's a shame they put up a fence to Thurston's *darker* half. At the stairs at the end of the tube tour and past the gate, Thurston continues for another 1,000 feet (it seems like more) before it ends abruptly. If the park reopens the gate, make sure you bring a good flashlight (or two) for the journey, as you will be in total darkness most of the way. At the end, turn off the light. You've never seen *real* blackness until you've seen *this* blackness.

That dirt road that leads south of Thurston Lava Tube is an **escape road**. It is well-maintained in case Chain of Craters Road is ever obliterated by a lava flow (again). That dirt road is the only

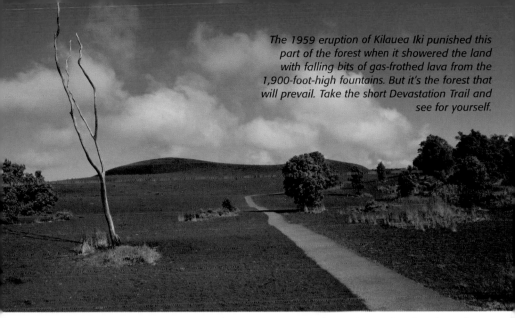

The 1959 eruption of Kilauea Iki punished this part of the forest when it showered the land with falling bits of gas-frothed lava from the 1,900-foot-high fountains. But it's the forest that will prevail. Take the short Devastation Trail and see for yourself.

place in the park where **mountain bikes** are allowed. It goes through very lush forest and is a delight. Just make sure you close all gates behind you. Some areas are fenced off to prevent pig damage. Wild pigs are amazingly destructive, and rangers fight an unending war to minimize their impact.

Driving past Thurston Lava Tube, on your right will be a road to the **Pu'u Pua'i Overlook**. The overlook just past the parking lot is great. You're right next to the cinder cone where all the debris from the eruption piled up. From here you can stroll for 10–15 minutes along the **Devastation Trail**. This is where the fallout from the 1959 Kilauea Iki eruption killed the fern and 'ohi'a forest. The line of demarcation is abrupt, going from healthy forest to a field of **tephra** littered with bleached tree trunks. Tephra is airborne gas-frothed lava from fountains, which cools as pumice cinders. The forest is working to come back, and you will see the results along the way. You can either walk back the way you came, loop around on Crater Rim Road, or have someone pick you up at the other end.

Soon you're confronted with the other Crater Rim Dr. road closure. If you want-

ed to walk ⁸⁄₁₀ mile on the closed road you'd come to another crater called **Keanakako'i**. The Hawaiians used to fetch abnormally hard rock from here until it was covered by subsequent lava flows. Across the road from Keanakako'i is a lava fissure. These fissures are usually long cracks where lava erupts in a curtain of fire, as this one did in 1974.

DOWN CHAIN OF CRATERS ROAD

At the road closure you're at **Chain of Craters Road**, which leads 19 miles down to the shore and ends abruptly where the current lava flow has cut it off. (At least it was 19 miles when we went to press, and getting shorter from time to time.) The road was so named because it passed numerous craters along the rift zone before veering off to the shore. It was rerouted after Madame Pele repaved 12 miles of the road with lava during the 1969–74 Mauna Ulu flow and now visits fewer craters than it used to. Mile markers are on alternating sides of the road, and we will refer to some of them. There are still some craters along the way you might want to check out (but don't bother with Ko'oko'olau). Remember to check your gas gauge; we've seen people run out of gas coming back up.

A little more than 2 miles into Chain of Craters Road is **Hilina Pali Road**, 8³/₁₀ miles long. It may be closed during nene nesting or if there is a perceived fire danger. The drive isn't impressive, but at the end is **Hilina Pali Lookout**. Walk down the path for 100 feet or so, and you are treated to an amazingly expansive view. You're perched above the vast shoreline below, and on a clear day you can see the entire shoreline for over 30 miles south. It's very quiet, desolate and peaceful, with the sound of the distant ocean sometimes present. If you take it, please drive very slowly as the endangered nene are usually in the road and aren't very impressed by cars. The Kulanaokuaiki campgrounds are also on Hilina Pali Road.

Less than ¹/₁₀ mile past Hilina Pali Road, on the left (east) side is a 60-second walk to **Devil's Throat**. (It's unmarked.) This small collapsed crater is impressively sheer and a genuine heart-stopper. It's *straight* down. Be careful at the edge; it looks pretty fragile.

Lava sometimes bursts from fissures such as this one from the 1970s Mauna Ulu eruption. But life always reclaims the land.

Along this stretch of Chain of Craters Road, keep an eye to your left. You *might* see steam coming from a hill. This is **Mauna Ulu**, the source of the second longest flank eruption of Kilauea. From 1969–1974 it poured lava and harassed park road builders, forcing Chain of Craters Road to be rerouted. There is a trail off the spur road past Pauahi Crater that goes near Mauna Ulu. (See ADVENTURES on page 231.) In 1997 a couple camping way out at Napau Crater (3½ miles east of Mauna Ulu) was awakened when lava suddenly began gushing from the ground half a mile away.

Just east (to the left) of the 4 mile marker is a field of gravel-like tephra. We've walked along here (staying mostly to the left side of the flow) and discovered incredible lava fissures and colorful blobs from four decades ago (such as the one shown in the photo), with ferns and trees already growing in them. But there is no trail, so you are on virgin, and untested, ground. This is an area where lava fountains shot into the air, and the violence from the event is evident.

Proceeding down the road, you will get an appreciation in several spots of how lava actually flowed down the mountain during the 1969–74 Mauna Ulu eruption. At the **Alanui Kahakai turnout** (near the 14 mile marker) you will see a segment of the old, partially covered Chain of Craters Road. At the **Holei Pali Lookout**, just before the 15 mile marker, there is a great view of the mountain lava flows, where you get a feel for the volume of 'a'a and pahoehoe that drooled down the mountain. The newer highway cutting through the lava flow is dramatic.

About ⅓ mile past the 15 mile marker, you will pass a lava tube on your left. Road crews bisect them every time they cut a new road in this area.

Past the 16 mile marker you will see the **Pu'u Loa Petroglyph Trail**. This 15–20 minute walk is over an old pahoehoe lava flow with cairns (mounds of rock) marking the way. (The undulating lava is a bit more tiring than flat ground.) It leads to an area studded with thousands of petroglyphs (rock carvings) representing everything from birth to death. This is the largest petroglyph field in the state. A circular boardwalk has been built near some of them to allow you to view them without walking on them. If you circle the boardwalk from both directions, you notice some you didn't see on the first pass. *Many* more carvings are located past the boardwalk, but they request that you avoid walking around to pro-

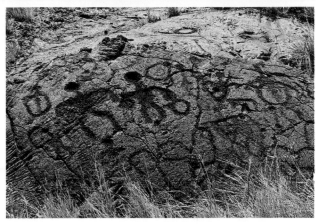

The Hawaiians, like people since the dawn of time, were compelled to leave a lasting legacy of themselves to the ages. These ancient petroglyphs are on the short Pu'u Loa trail.

tect the perishable petroglyphs from wear. The small holes bored in the rock were usually cut by parents who placed the umbilical cords from their newborns there for good luck. The area is very peaceful and worth your time if you wish to see a direct expression of ancient Hawaiian life. It's 1½ miles round trip.

At the 18 mile marker you'll probably have to park and can walk to your right to see the **Holei Sea Arch**, where the ocean has undercut the rock, leaving an arch.

Past here should be the **end of Chain of Craters Road** (unless the lava advances to the sea arch). This is where the lava flows, at times on the surface nearby, often into the sea, sometimes too far inland to walk to, at other times outside the park boundary, many miles away. Old maps showing Kamoamoa Campgrounds, a visitor center, Waha'ula Heiau, Lae 'Apuki, Waiaka Pond, Queen's Bath, Royal Gardens, Kalapana Gardens and more are all tragically out of date.

1983–1986 Flow

2014 to Present Flow

2007–2011 Flow

Kupaianaha

10 miles to Kilauea Caldera

Pu'u 'Ō'o Crater
(Heart of current eruption)

2500'

2000'

2007–2011 Flow

Park Boundary

2011–2014 Flow

1992–2007 Flow

2000'

1500'

1000'

500'

Only road segments
of subdivision not
covered with lava

Royal Gardens
Subdivision

Visitor Center
(Closest Parking)

End of Chain of
Craters Road

19

New Road Scraped in 2014

Former
Campground

Kohola

Wilipe'e

W. Highcastle

Laeapuki

Kamoamoa
Pre-eruption coastline

Brand new land

Kamokuna

Waha'ula Heia
(now destroyed)

0   1 MILE

© 2014 Wizard Publications, Inc.

The Current Eruption

Since the eruption began at Pu'u 'O'o (which conveniently materialized just within the park boundary) on January 3, 1983 the lava flows have been quite prolific. Each day 300,000 to 1,000,000 cubic yards of lava erupts, which has dramatically changed the landscape. Note how the lava concentrates in one area until another area opens up. The town of Kalapana was erased from the map in 1990. The famous Black Sand Beach at Kaimu is gone, now under 50–75 feet of lava. But a new, unnamed black sand beach now exists a third of a mile in front of where the old one was.

One of the most important heiau on the island was Waha'ula Heiau. Oral tradition states that it was constructed by Pa'ao, a priest from Tahiti who arrived during the second wave of colonization in the 12th century. It was he who was said to have introduced the concept of human sacrifice. Mu, whose role was to gather people to be sacrificed, would go out at night in parties of three and eavesdrop on houses, listening for any breach of kapu (rules of conduct). When one occurred, they would rush in and seize the victims and lead them off to this heiau. Sacrifices here were deemed so important that priests were sometimes sacrificed if others could not be found by the required time. Even smoke from its altars was sacred, and it was death to anyone who passed under the shadow of the smoke. Abraham Fornander states in his epic work of the late 19th century that this was the last heiau to be destroyed after the kapu system was abolished by King Kamehameha II in 1819. The heiau's foundations were finally buried by lava in 1997.

The doomed village of Kalapana is said to be named after an old man from Kaua'i trying to make a pilgrimage to Pele. He landed at what was Kaimu Beach and tried to make it to Kilauea but was unsuccessful due to severe storms. That night Pele came to his hut and appeared to him. The next morning nearly all of the old man's long hair was burned off. When he died some time later, the people named their village after him. It is said that because Kalapana could not make it to Pele's house, she sometimes visits his.

Interesting facts at a glance...

Total lava erupted since 1983–4,600,000,000 cubic yards
Number of dump trucks that would fill–Over 300 million
Temperature lost while traveling in lava tubes–20 °
Average temperature of flowing lava–2,000 °
Length of public highway covered–8.5 miles
Amount of new land created–500 acres
Owner of all new land–State of Hawai'i
Total area covered–48 square miles
Number of structures destroyed–214

1500'

1986–1992 Flow

1000'

500'

Kalapana Gardens and most of Royal Gardens were destroyed by lava flows in 1990. The last resident was driven out of Royal Gardens in 2012.

Kalapana

Kalapana Gardens Subdivision

Former Kaimu Black Sand Beach

18

130

19

20

21

21

22

137

Pre-eruption coastline

New Kaimu Black Sand Beach

Brand new land

Cave of Refuge

Brand new land

Kupapau Point

These were victims of the current eruption. Before you is a newly paved lava wasteland, where liquid rock has poured above and below ground, reaching the ocean and building more land. The park "Visitor Center" at the bottom is now a movable temporary building, which has had to be moved many times to avoid the fate of the last visitor center down here. Check with the rangers to see what's shakin'. Ask if nighttime offers good viewing conditions. Often at night the skylights, holes in the ceiling of a lava tube, are visible in the distance. Usually the only way to see a skylight during the day is on a helicopter flight. When the lava is flowing inland, you are usually allowed to hike to it. (They may *imply* that you can't but will usually admit that it is permitted if pressed.) See ADVENTURES on page 242. They may have beverages and souvenirs available.

OUTSIDE THE PARK ENTRANCE

Just outside the park entrance there are a few sights that are worth checking out, either before or after your park visit.

If you were heading back toward Kona, **Mauna Loa Scenic Road** leads past the **Tree Molds**. These holes are created when a lava flow encounters a sopping wet tree trunk, which resists bursting into flames just long enough to harden the lava around it. They look a little like water wells with the texture of the tree bark and some of the trees must have been pretty large. No walking required, the tree molds are right at the parking area. Farther up the road is **Kipuka Puaʻulu (Bird Park)**. A trail goes through a kipuka, an old growth of forest surrounded by newer lava flows. This kipuka features many native trees and plants, but is less visually dazzling than other hikes nearer the crater. Birds abound in this park—hence its nickname, Bird Park. The entire 1-mile

stroll takes only 30 minutes plus stopping time. There are several benches scattered along the trail, which ascends gently for the first half.

Mauna Loa Scenic Road becomes very winding past here and switches to one lane (with several blind turns), as it passes through a pretty forest that is different from other forests in the area. No big payoff here, just a lonely road that often ascends into the clouds, usually with lots of pheasants around. At the end of the 13-mile road (at 6,650 feet) is the trailhead to **Mauna Loa Trail**. This is where you start your multi-day trek through the cold and altitude to ascend the summit of Mauna Loa. (Maybe another day.) There are picnic tables and a nice view of the park at the road's end. Though pleasant, this road is dispensable if you are budgeting your time.

Off the main highway south of the park entrance near the 38 mile marker is the **Kaʻu Desert Trail**, which leads less than a mile to **Footprints**. Most of these were created during the explosion of 1790 (plus a few from an earlier explosion in the 1500s). You may read or be told that the footprints are worn away because they were vandalized. The truth is apparently a little more embarrassing. Park sources have told us that park personnel tried to protect the footprints many years ago by placing a glass case over them. Their intentions were good, but when it rained, water condensed on the underside of the cracked glass and dripped onto the prints, wearing them away. That's why the display case is gone, but the vandalism rumor persists. Most personnel believe the vandalism explanation to be true to this day. Regardless, if you look around, you can still find better footprints elsewhere when shifting ash dunes permit.

Creation meets destruction. The ocean begins dismantling the land even before it cools.

Why you Shouldn't Pick a Lehua Blossom off an 'Ohi'a Tree

According to legend, 'Ohi'a was a young, handsome Big Island chief. The volcano goddess Pele knew that 'Ohi'a was courting a beautiful young girl *named Lehua. Pele became enamored with 'Ohi'a and desired him for a husband. One day as 'Ohi'a went up into the mountains to cut kukui bark to stain his surfboard, Pele appeared to him. She was dressed in her finest clothes and was quite striking. After a time, she announced to 'Ohi'a who she was and asked him to be her husband. Nervously but very diplomatically, he turned her down, professing his eternal love for Lehua. In her anger, Pele told him he was as gutless as a piece of wood, and changed him into a gnarled tree with grey-green leaves. When the other gods saw what Pele had done, they felt bad and tried to reverse it, but failed. The best they could do to reunite the broken-hearted Lehua with her beloved 'Ohi'a was to turn Lehua into a beautiful blossom on the same tree. To this day, it is said that picking a lehua blossom off an 'ohi'a tree will produce rain. These are the tears from heaven for separated lovers everywhere.*

Just outside the park is **Volcano Golf and Country Club** (see GOLFING in ACTIVITIES). Their golf course has seen better days. A mile down Piimauna Road, you'll find **Volcano Winery** (967–7772). This is a good place to stop for a sip of some locally made wines. They have several unusual wines, including a local favorite, Mac Nut Honey Wine. They also have wines made from fruits—*even grapes.* Hard-core oenophiles might turn up their noses, but less finicky palates might enjoy a snort or two of the exotic. A sign there says NO LARGE TOUR BUSES. Wow, *that's* a switch. We also like their sign that says RESERVED FOR WINOS.

THE TOWN OF VOLCANO

When you first see the town of **Volcano** on a map, you figure they must spend all their time biting their nails over the active volcano crater less than 2 miles away. In fact, since they're upslope of the crater, they're safer from lava flows than Hilo or even the Kohala Resort area 50 miles away, as far as the geologists are concerned. Though extensive lava flows did cover this area about 500 years ago, the summit has since been reshaped so that today nearly all the lava flows happen on Kilauea's southern flank (away from the village). Their main threat is from falling tephra or ash from the occasional crater explosion like the one in 1790—annoying, but not as bad as a lava flow. And as for volcano smoke, normal trade winds send the smoke around the bottom of the island and up the coast where it harasses Kailua-Kona. It's ironic that this dreamy little community, set in a misty, lush fern-filled forest, can be so snug living on an active volcano.

Volcano is also a convenient place to pick up some supplies and gas (which is *breathtakingly* expensive here). If you enter the loop road from near the 27 mile marker, you pass by the **Volcano Store** and **Kilauea General Store and Gas Station** farther down. If you're driving back to the west side of the island, you can grab some gas or a snack before the long drive back. We often pick up some tasty pumpkin bread, mac nut bars, ginger cookies, or sandwiches on Hawaiian sweetbread at Kilauea General before heading back. Baked Mon., Wed. and Fri.

In addition to the hotels and inns, there are cabins and $15 tent camping at **Namakani Paio Campgrounds** (866–536–7972) and **Kulanaokuaiki**, both in CAMPING on page 179. Current and retired military can rent clean cabins at **Kilauea Military Camp** (967–8333) right in the park. Higher rank, higher rent.

Looking more like the gates of hell, a rare vertical skylight allowed us to peek into a lava falls. You never know what you'll discover on an ever-changing lava field.

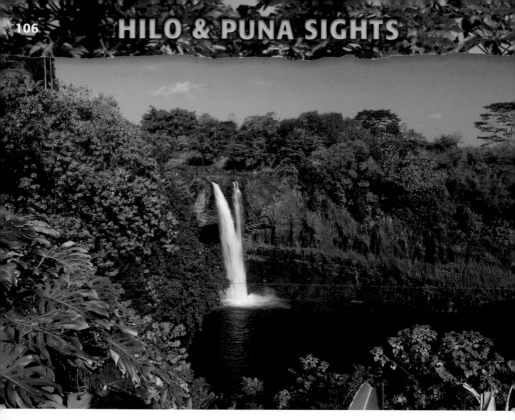

If you like waterfalls, Rainbow Falls is a perfect example of why you'll want to drive to the Hilo side.

Hilo is a charming mix of old and new Hawai'i. Once a thriving town bolstered by limitless sugar revenues, the demise of the sugar industry has kept Hilo in a time warp. And that's the charm. Though a full-fledged city, things move slower here, and the community is tight. They've been through a lot. Lashed by tsunamis, threatened by lava flows, racked by a changing economy, Hilo has withstood it all. Hilo is also a strikingly beautiful town. Abundant rains give the flora a healthy sheen that soothes the soul. Though the exodus of business has left many of its buildings looking worn and neglected, Hilo's charms lie deeper.

Hilo's Achilles' heel is weather. Only in Hilo would water officials quake in fear and declare a drought, even encouraging water conservation, when they receive *only* 70 inches of rain in a year. (All you Arizona residents can stop laughing now!) This rain translates to an unacceptable gamble to many visitors. People are hesitant to spend precious Big Island days in a soggy place. But they forget that even if it's rain-city here, elsewhere along the eastern side things might be sunnier. Hilo is the logical gateway for exploring Puna, the easternmost part of the island, where you'll find lush rain forests, a black sand beach, thermally heated pools and volcano-ravaged towns. Puna is also famous for its outlaws from the 20th century, guerrilla gardeners and bizarre characters.

Hilo has a reputation for being less friendly to visitors than other parts of the island. Sort of a *let da buggahs go to Kona* mentality. Though this reputation is not entirely unearned, it is also not entirely accurate. Some of the friendliest, nicest and most helpful people we've run into have been in Hilo. But we've also gotten more blank expressions and outright nastiness here.

Hilo is a ghost town on Sundays. Don't expect much of anything to be open. We'll describe sights around Hilo in a scattershot manner before heading toward Puna.

AROUND HILO TOWN

[A] Starting at the corner of Kamehameha (which fronts the bay) and Waianuenue (in northern Hilo), head southwest on Waianuenue. (See map on next page.) When you pass the Hilo Public Library on your right, take a look at that oblong stone out front, six full strides long.

Think you can move it? At age 14, Kamehameha risked death (if he failed) and agreed to try to move that Naha Stone (estimated at 7,000 pounds). He did it because legend said that whoever could overturn the stone would be the first king of all the islands. At that time the stone was slightly imbedded in the ground. The ox-like youth, whose strength was unprecedented, squatted and gave a huge push—nothing. He tried and tried but could barely nudge it. As people gathered round and the priest started to come over (to condemn him to death), he summoned a final burst of strength and overturned the boulder, shocking everyone and beginning the fulfillment of his destiny.

Just off Waianuenue Street, on the corner of Haili and Kapiolani, the Lyman Museum (935–5021) is worth a stop. The Earth Heritage exhibit alone justifies the $10 admission. It has incredible displays of Hawaiian geology, plant,

Letters ([A]) correspond to paragraphs in text.

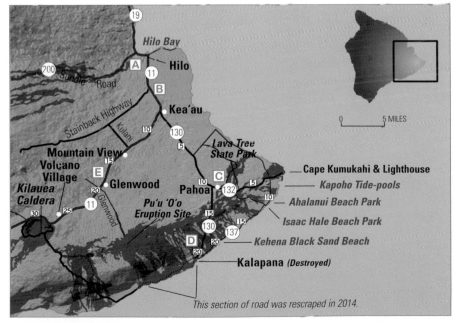

This section of road was rescraped in 2014.

Hilo

Hilo Bay

Reeds Bay

Kalanianaole Ave

Ice Pond

Hilo International Airport/(General Lyman Field)

Banyan Dr

Coconut Is.

Lili'uokalani Gardens

Hilo Bayfront Beach Park

Naniloa Golf Course

Clock

Lihiwai

Kanoelehua

Kalanikoa

Ho'olulu Park

Manono St

Kekuanaoa St

Hinano

Kawili

Waiakea Center
Walmart

Maka'ala

Prince Kuhio Plaza

Puainako Town Center

Kanoelehua

To Puna & Kilauea Volcano

Lower Puna map on page 113

Maka'ala

Kilauea Ave

Kinoole

Kawaiiani

Bayfront Hwy

Kamehameha

Pauahi

Kilauea

Hualalai

Kinoole

Wailoa River State Park

Kunpum

Hilo Shopping Center

University of Hawai'i at Hilo

Lanikula

Kawili

Puainako St

Keawe

Kapiolani

Mohouli

'Imiloa Astronomy Center

Kumukoa

Nowelo

Komohana

Wainaku

Naha Stone

Lyman Museum

Haili

Ponahawai

Punaheke

Lava Flow of 1881

Hamakua Coast map on page 125

Wailuku River

Rainbow Falls

Kaumana Dr

Waianuenue Ave

Boiling Pots

Pe'epe'e Falls

Waiole Falls

Pe'epe'e Falls Street

Akolea Rd

Kaumana Cave

Bayfront Hwy

Kamehameha

Wailuku

Shipman

Kalakaue

Keawe

Kilauea

Kinoole

Haili

Mamo

Ponahawai

Waianuenue

1 Inn at Kulanaiapia Falls
2 Shipman House
3 Dolphin Bay Hotel
4 Wild Ginger Inn
5 Hilo Bay Hostel
6 Hilo Hawaiian Hotel
7 Uncle Billy's Hilo Bay Hotel
8 Hilo Naniloa Hotel
9 Country Club Hawaii Condo Hotel
10 Hilo Seaside Hotel

1/2 MILE

Indicates Foot Trails

Roadside mile markers

Bypass Starts Here
(You'll have to watch for your chance to stay on Kaumana Drive/Hwy 2000.)

© 2014 Wizard Publications, Inc.

animal and fish life (nicely done), plus an exceptionally beautiful rock and mineral collection from around the world. Elsewhere they have Hawaiian history displays and a few other interesting items. **A REAL GEM** Tours of the Lyman missionary house next door are given at various times throughout the day.

Take the right fork after the 1 mile marker and follow the signs to Rainbow Falls. These falls change dramatically depending on water flow. Moderate flow is best. (Too little and the wishbone shape is gone; too much and it's an undefined, roiling mess.) The falls are best seen in the morning when the sun is behind you. (Rainbows can only be seen when the sun is behind you, so if you ever see a photo with the sun and a rainbow in the same frame, it's fake.) The cave below the falls is where Kamehameha is said to have buried the bones of his father. Take the trail to the left for different views and the shady comfort of a large banyan tree. From the left, a trail leads to the top of the falls, but you are on your own in assessing whether to go down there.

A mile farther up the road is Wailuku River Boiling Pots State Park. This series of bowl-shaped depressions roil and boil when the water flow is heavy, creating dramatic photo opportunities. From the lookout, odds are you *won't* be able to see the boiling pots because of the state's perpetual lack of vegetation grooming, which virtually ensures that you'll have to take the trail to the right of the railing. To the left of the railings, you *will* see Pe'epe'e Falls. (No, it's *not* pronounced pee-pee, but rather PEH-EH PEH-EH, so wipe that smirk off your face.) If you go down the trail, one look and it's obvious you can't swim in Boiling Pots when it's boiling. (During calmer times we see daring dudes jumping from pot to pot to pot, but even

in calm times Boiling Pots tends to claim the lives of swimmers.) From the trail you could scramble over the boulders to the other side (without getting your feet wet if the flow is low enough, as in our photo on the next page) and continue to Pe'epe'e Falls. This waterfall and deep pool are an idyllic place to sit in solitude and ponder. You'll usually have it to yourself. Be careful on the rocks; don't go if the river is raging, and don't fall in. Also, don't go down to the falls without mosquito repellent unless you've checked with your life insurance company to see if excessive bloodletting is considered an accident rather than suicide. While we're nagging, this is probably a good time to tell you that Boiling Pots and Rainbow Falls are common places for car break-ins. We often see thieving scum casing the lots looking for unsuspecting tourist cars to rob while they are away lost in the beauty.

Less than a mile up Waianuenue the road veers right. From a bridge you can see Wai'ale Falls. The amount of water is considerably more than what you saw downstream at Rainbow Falls, an impressive demonstration of how much actually seeps into the porous lava bed along the way. (It's *not* tapped at the nearby dam.) You can hike there and enjoy some wonderful pools. See HIKING on page 204.

Over on Kaumana Drive (see map) is Kaumana Cave. This lava tube can make for fun exploring and is described in detail in SADDLE ROAD SIGHTS on page 146 since it's usually visited by those coming into Hilo from the Saddle.

Off Komohana St. is the 'Imiloa Astronomy Center (969–9700), a good hands-on exhibit for kids and a pretty cool planetarium that will make you dizzy. $17.50 for adults, $9.50 for kids.

Along the bay, the grassy park fronting the town is the Hilo Bayfront. It used to be the main Japanese district, Hilo's Japantown. On April Fool's Day 1946 a

Offerings are common at Pe'epe'e Falls.

hands frozen in time—1:04 a.m.—from the 1960 tsunami. Townsfolk refurbished the clock but refused to rebuild it to working order in honor of those who died.) Tsunamis have unimaginable power. The water first recedes, exposing the ocean's floor, and then bulldozers of water come crashing in. The event can last for hours.

The **Pacific Tsunami Museum** (935–0926) is on Kamehameha and Kalakaua. (Open 10 a.m. to 4 p.m.) It's in the old First Hawaiian Bank Building. (You sit in the old bank vault while they show a movie of the tsunami.) They haven't had docents on recent visits, so you're probably on your own. Lots of photos, and you'll leave with a good understanding of what a tsunami is— and why it's not really a wave. Admission is $8, closed Sundays and Mondays.

Banyan Drive, where most of Hilo's hotels are located, is named after the graceful and stately banyan trees that line the road. If a tree can look wise, then banyan trees definitely qualify. Each tree was named after the person who planted it. Familiar names such as Amelia Earhart, King George V, Babe Ruth, FDR and Richard Nixon. (In one **A REAL GEM** of those ironies of life, the first tree Nixon planted was washed away on election day when he became VP.) Also on Banyan Drive is Lili'uokalani Gardens. This is one of several graceful and serene parks in the area and is our favorite place in Hilo for a great early morning or late afternoon stroll. If you're a bit warm, look for the nearby ice pond. (See map.) Cold water intruding into this part of the

tsunami (tidal wave) of unprecedented size was generated from a horrific earthquake off Alaska. The tsunami lashed the entire state, but punished this part of the Big Island the most. In all, 159 people, including 21 school children in Laupahoehoe, were killed in one of the worst natural disasters in Hawai'i's history. After another tsunami killed another 61 people in 1960, town fathers decided to make this area a park rather than risk more lives during the next tsunami. (The clock on the side of the road on Kamehameha Street in front of Naniloa Golf Course stands with its bay (you can sometimes see it percolating to the surface) creates water so cold it'll give you *chicken skin kine.*

If you were to continue east along the shoreline on Kalanianaole, you would pass most of Hilo's beach parks. See BEACHES for more on these. On your way out to the parks check out a beach access across from Lokoaka Street. It is very jungly and draped with vines. The beach is worthless, but the short walking road is kind of cool as is the trail on the left, which ends at the more desirable Carlsmith Beach Park. You'll also pass Hilo Homemade Ice Cream (935–3895) on the ocean side. Although owned by our favorite, Tropical Dreams, this ice cream is not as sweet or rich as other gourmet ice creams, has more air and less butter fat. Lots of exotic flavors like ginger and 'ohelo.

HEADING SOUTH ON HIGHWAY 11

B As you head out of town, you will pass by Hilo's biggest shopping area. Prince Kuhio Plaza, Waiakea Center, and Puainako Town Center are where you will find Safeway grocery store, Longs Drugs, Walmart and a zillion fast food restaurants. On Hinano Street off Kekuanaoa is Big Island Candies (935–8890). Their locally made chocolates and cakes are *excellent*, though their prices are confiscatory. (This is a favorite stopping place for tour buses.) Good place for chocolate if you don't mind paying double-extra-super-retail. You can see their impressive operations behind giant glass windows, but refrain from calling their chocolate makers *oompa-loompas.* On the highway before the 4 mile marker, Makalika Street heading east leads to Nani Mau Gardens (959–3500). This used to be 20 acres of flawlessly groomed tropical and sub-tropical plants, but our most recent visit found them unkempt and avoidable. Whereas the mother of all gardens, Hawai'i Trop-

ical Botanical Garden (on your way out of town heading north, described on page 124), is much more exotic.

The road past the 4 mile marker heading west leads to Stainback Highway and the Pana'ewa Rain Forest Zoo & Gardens (959–7224). We've never been very impressed with this zoo, but they've really put in the effort at places, and it shows. The grounds are lush and beautiful, to the point that they have added the word "gardens" to their name. It's a small zoo with few animals (they do birds the best), but kids should enjoy it as a brief diversion and parents will enjoy the price—it's free.

Between the 5 and 6 mile marker is Macadamia Road and the Mauna Loa Visitor Center (966–8618). This is the mac nut giant's main processing plant, popular with tour buses and cruise ships. You can see the process through the glass or pick up some of their products; otherwise, it's an expendable nut house.

If you're going to explore Puna, your best route is to take Highway 11 to 130, then take 132 to 137, and 137 to Kalapana where you link back up to 130. See maps on pages 107 or 113 if you aren't too dizzy to flip the page. If you want a meaningless diversion, you could continue along Stainback Highway past the zoo until it ends at the Big Island's least popular visitor attraction—our prison. This one-lane road goes for miles through an otherwise impenetrable forest, ending at over 5,000 feet elevation. There are signs saying that it is illegal to drive the road, but they were put up by the prison to cover their 'okole—they told us that it's perfectly OK to drive it as long as you're not planning to spring anyone. Some 13¾ miles into the one-lane (and dead-on straight) road is the Pu'u Maka'ala Forest Reserve. The roads in there are 4WD only, and the trails (if you can find them) are lush and wet.

EXPLORING PUNA

[C] Note that at press time lava was flowing in this part of lower Puna. Beyond the heartache it causes local residents who are affected, it's also causing traffic diversions. Look at our website (www.hawaiirevealed.com) for up-to-the-minute changes to this area.

Head south on Highway 130 and you come to the town of Pahoa. Known as the Big Island's outlaw town, this is where guerrilla gardeners (pakalolo farmers), dreadlock enthusiasts, FBI fugitives and the never-bathe crowd coexist without stepping on each other's toes—usually. You'd be surprised to learn how many homes you see are built on vacant land—at least according to the County Tax Assessor's Office. Permit? What's that? To be honest, Pahoa's reputation is a little exaggerated—probably. People-watching here can be a hoot sometimes. There are a couple places to eat here that you may like, reviewed in ISLAND DINING.

After Pahoa, turn onto Hwy 132 and you'll soon come to Lava Tree State Park. Lava trees form when fast flowing pahoehoe encounters wet 'ohi'a trees. As the flow drains away, it leaves a thick coating around the dying tree. Most of these free-standing tubes are moss-covered. You can saunter around the park in 30–60 minutes. Look for the huge chasms created during the explosive eruption of 1790. If you plan to go to Hawai'i Volcanoes National Park, there are better lava trees on the Napau Crater Trail, and here the state will probably greet you with a locked gate so you'll have to park outside and walk in.

If it's after sunset, pull over and listen. Millions of tiny coqui frogs fill the air with their whistle. Islanders consider these new arrivals a pest and have tried to eradicate them by spraying various chemicals, including caffeine. Though it gives you and me a morning lift, it'll make these little guys... croak. (Sorry, I just *had* to get that one in.)

Shortly after Lava Trees take the left fork (near a papaya grove) where Hwy 132 continues toward Kapoho. Ever wonder where people on an island get their electricity? Well, here on the Big Island, 20% of our juice is volcano-powered. They drilled a basketball-sized hole a *mile* deep, and when they did, steam shot up at pressures similar to what you'd find inside a SCUBA tank. They use the steam to turn

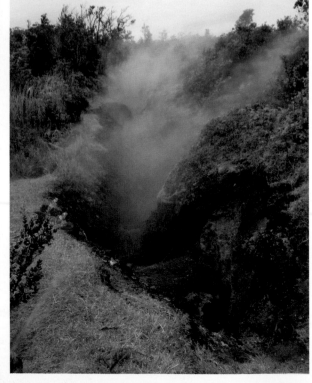

Free energy. In Puna they don't drill for oil; they drill for steam.

Lower Puna

5 miles
to Hilo

6 (11)

**Kea'au
Town**

7

(11)

1

2

Kea'au/
Pahoa Rd

(130)

3

Kaloli

4

Paradise

5

Makuu

6

**Huwaiian Paradise
Park Subdivision**

Government/Beach Rd

**Railroad Ave
Pahoa Bypass**

**Hawaiian Beaches
Subdivision**

7

8

Kahakai

9

19°32.747'
154°51.224'
**Natural Lava
Swimming Pool**

19°32.770'
154°51.030'
**Goddess
Pond**

1840
Flow

1790

1960

**Cape Kumukahi
Lighthouse**

**2015
Lava Flow**

10

11

**Pahoa
Town**

12

1840

1790

(132)

2

3

Frogs

**Lava Tree
State Park**

4   5

6

7   8

*Grey Lava
4WD Road*

**Champagne
Pond**

1955

9

(137)

10

**Kapoho
Tide-pools/
Wai'opae Ponds**

Kapoho
Kai Rd

1790

Pahoa-Pohoiki Rd
(very pretty)

**Ahalanui
Warm Spring**

**Isaac Hale
Beach Park**

14

1790

12

13

Opihikao-Kamaili Rd

1790

15

**Black Sand
Beach
Community**

15

1955

1790

16

**Pohoiki Warm
Pool (small)**

16

17

(130)

17

1790

18

**MacKenzie
State Recreation
Area**

1955

18

19

**Star of the Sea
Church**

21

(137)

**Kehena Black
Sand Beach**

20 22

21

1990

N

W   E

S

**New Kaimu
Black Sand Beach**

Pre-1990 Shoreline

Chain of Craters Rd

Cave of Refuge

Pre-1990 Shoreline

Map continued on page 101

0   5 MILES

Kazumura Lava Tube Cave

© 2014 Wizard Publications, Inc.

turbines. The underground water source is naturally replaced by the ocean's pressure, so it'll last indefinitely—at least until the surrounding rock cools. Interestingly, though the land is private, *all* mineral rights in Hawai'i belong to the state government (as all first-time landowners here discover to their shock). This includes "any steam over 150°." So, even though the private company returns the water vapor back to the ground, they have to pay the state almost $2 million a year for the steam they temporarily borrow because it's considered *state steam*. (Just thought we'd pass that along, in case you were thinking of opening a gold mine here.) By the way, the cost of steam has risen proportionally with the price of oil.

Across from the 5 mile marker on the left (north) side is the lava vent from the 1955 eruption. The vent is interesting to walk on. It's made up of loose and cemented blobs of airborne lava (called tephra) that fountained out of the vent. It's worth a few minutes if you want to poke around. There are opportunities for a good fall, so be careful.

The end of Hwy 132 is on lava flows from 1960. A dirt road leads out to the point. Fountains of lava ³⁄₁₀ mile high produced enormous amounts of lava that wiped out the town of Kapoho, leaving only two subdivisions. Having hiked through countless lava fields on the island, this wins the prize as the harshest and most difficult to walk through we've ever encountered. (You'd have an easier time walking through the minefields of the demilitarized zone between North and South Korea than hiking through this stuff.) At the end of the unpaved road leading to the sea is a light tower.

Take a deep breath. This is the easternmost part of the island, and since our winds come from that direction, scientists use it to test "virgin air" that has drifted over the landless Pacific for many weeks. Air from here is considered as pristine as any in the world, and it is analyzed by governments around the globe and used as a benchmark to compare to their air.

While you're out on this point, you'll see a 4WD gray lava road on the right. If you take it and a right, then left onto the lightest gray oil pan-eating road at the first confusing intersection, it heads for 1²⁄₁₀ miles to Kapoho Bay. Why would you want to do that? Simple. A truly awesome experience called **Champagne Pond** awaits.

Imagine a calm, protected ocean inlet filled with *crystal* clear water. A scattering of fish and sometimes a turtle or two (or *nine,* our personal record here) await. Fine, you **A REAL GEM** say. There are lots of places with that. Maybe. But how many of them are *heated*? Sparkling clean freshwater heated by the volcano percolates from the ground. It's not Jacuzzi-hot, but rather relaxing-warm (around 90° on top) and changes with the tide. The more it's been raining lately, the deeper the floating warm water goes. Bring a mask and you can *see* the layers of temperature differences (warm is on top). This isn't Ahalanui Park (listed later). This is in a gated residential community, and the cove is next to

Champagne Pond

To Hwy 137 & Hwy 132

Light Beacon

Main Lava Road (Walk or 4WD)

N

Private Gated Roads

0   1/4 MILE

Champagne Pond   19°30.114'
154°49.000'

© 2014 Wizard Publications, Inc.

An oceanside natural lava swimming pool—the original black bottom pool.

an A-frame house. But from the 4WD public *lava* road, *anyone* can access it. Weekends and holidays are crowded with locals, and it's best to leave it to them during those days. But during the week it's *usually* lightly used. Make sure you take out anything you brought in, and wear water shoes in the water or you are *guaranteed* to stub your toes. Don't worry if the water's cool when you first get in, just head to the back of the cove where it's warmer. And remember: The best way to avoid scaring a turtle away is to act disinterested and keep your distance.

Back at the corner of Hwys 132 and 137, you'll want to head south on 137. But if you feel like a different kind of forest drive, head north first for 5 miles or so. It goes from stark lava to a luxuriant jungle filled with birds almost instantly. Along the way there's a delightful natural lava swimming pool if you don't mind walking ³⁄₁₀ mile (each way.)

The enormous pool (250 feet long) is naturally ensconced in a rugged lava shoreline. It's 5 feet deep in spots and backed by a thick grove of lovely hala trees. (Sometimes unusually ultra-low tides virtually erase it.) Meandering around the pool is fun while you scramble over the occasional lava obstacle. (If you don't have some cheap water shoes, navigating the rounded-

boulder floor will be unpleasant.) There is shade near the pool until noon. Water splashes into the pool from the ocean. Only during big surf or very high tide is it anything but gentle in the pool. Bring a mask (though the water is so incredibly clear, you almost won't need one). Fishermen sometimes use it on weekends, but it's usually vacant during the week.

To get there, drive about 1½ miles from the end of the pavement (or 2⁷⁄₁₀ miles from the corner of Hwys 132 and 137—see map on page 113). The beautiful jungle-side road (which looks more like a tunnel drilled through hau bush) is easy to find: It's the first road on the right at the bottom of a short paved segment on the otherwise unpaved main road. It's 1,500 feet to the shoreline, and the pool is another 100 yards to the left.

Return to Hwys 132 and 137 when you're done.

Heading south on Hwy 137 leads past Kapoho-Kai Road. This road goes to one of the more unusual locations on the Big Island. Dozens and dozens of spring-fed, brackish pools and tide-pools, some volcanically heated, are strewn throughout the area known as the Kapoho Tide-pools. Many of the land-locked pools have been incorporated into people's front and back yards as swimming pools.

The large pools adjacent to the ocean (called Wai'opae Ponds) are on public property and contain some of the most fascinating snorkeling around. If you wish to snorkel here, take Kapoho–Kai Road (just before the 9 mile marker). When it seems to dead end (on Waiopae), turn left to the parking lot. (If it's full, there's an access at the end of Kapoho-Kai Road.) Snorkel exploration is possible even for novice snorkelers. The largest pool snakes its way to the ocean and rises and falls each day with the tide. This creates slight currents that are fun to ride if the surf's not high. These pools are usually (but not always) very calm and protected. Closer to the reef edge brings more fish, but sometimes there's a current. We've spent many hours here and counted eight kinds of coral. Toward the back (west) a couple of pools are slightly heated by the volcano. The weather is sometimes snotty in the morning but usually clears up in the afternoon. Small, *voluntary* parking fees are requested.

Note that the tide-pools are best visited during the week. Weekends are crowded since Puna residents have comparatively few beaches to choose from. A couple hours *before high tide* is our favorite time. The water is deeper and usually very clear. It also coincides with local residents' belief that at *low* tide, septic systems from nearby houses could leach into the tide-pools, causing higher bacterial counts at *low* tide.

There are lots of vacation rentals available here (called Vacationland) and next door in the gated community of Kapoho Beach Community. Make *sure* you see what you're getting beforehand because there are a number of charming-sounding dumps there alongside wonderful vacation rentals.

Farther down Hwy 137 past the 10 mile marker is Ahalanui. (Formerly called Pu'ala'a, the state discovered that they had accidentally misnamed it for decades—*oops*.) **A REAL GEM** This delightful gem is definitely worth stopping for. It's a spring- and ocean-fed pool with a manmade wall and an inlet separating it from the ocean. Although the original builders created this

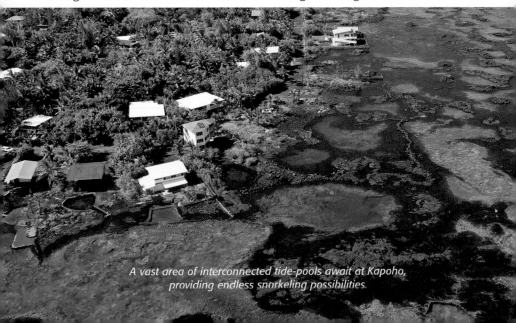

A vast area of interconnected tide-pools await at Kapoho, providing endless snorkeling possibilities.

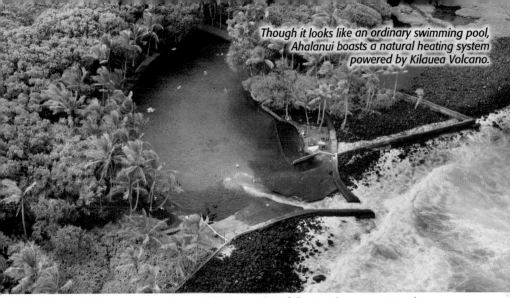

spot when the water was *ice cold*, the Kapoho eruptions of 1955 and 1960 reworked the lava plumbing here so that now, instead of coming out cold, this pool is *volcanically heated* to a toasty 91–95 degrees. The temperature is influenced by several factors, including tide. At high tide the ocean floods the pond with cooler seawater, making the pond more brisk. At these times, if you were to grope your way through the jungle to the left for 50 yards, you'd find the heater for Ahalanui in the form of a small, shallow warm pond in the lava where freshwater heated by underground rocks seeps to the surface.

With palm trees all around and the sound of the surf over the seawall, you may have trouble hauling yourself out once you've experienced this genuine Pele bath, and it's easier to access than Champagne Pond, though it's more crowded, as well. *On occasion* we've noticed a slight sulphur smell on the skin when we've gotten out, but even then it's worth it. Plus there's a shower there. Closed second Wednesday of the month.

As mapmakers we couldn't help but notice that this area called Puna, which receives *lots* of rain and is the size of Moloka'i, doesn't have a *single* river or stream—not even an intermittent one. The reason? The land's too new. Rain

that falls simply seeps into the porous lava. If you get a chance to hike in a lava tube, you'll see it dripping from the ceiling on its way to recharging the vast water table below.

Isaac Hale Beach Park farther down the road is where local fishermen launch their boats, and they are not known for extending gobs of aloha to visitors. (There's often a lunch wagon here that serves the worst shave ice we've had on the island.) The swimming is poor and the surfing is for experts. So why bother? Because if you take the shoreline trail to the right of the boat launch for two minutes, where it veers inland, you'll come to a surprise. There, set in the vine-covered jungle but only 40–50 feet from the shore, is a small (8-feet by 14-feet) warm water pool (called Pohoiki) similar to Ahalanui but completely natural. The setting is heaven sent. The only caveat is that some residents don't always appreciate the paradise that they live in and occasionally spoil the area with litter. But if you come during the week, there's a chance you may have it all to yourself. It's cut off from the ocean, but the level follows the tide, so it's deeper and more desirable (unlike Ahalanui) at high tide. You may encounter wild pigs in the jungle here. And being a surprise participant in a notorious pig-licking incident

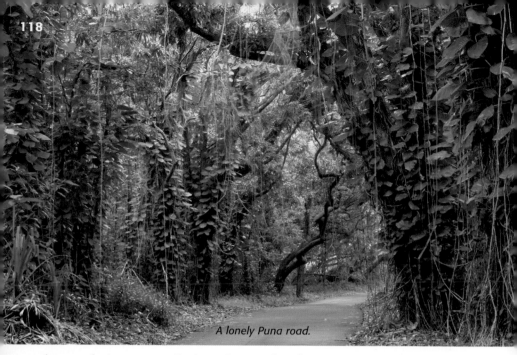

A lonely Puna road.

(no, we don't want to *talk* about it) is a memory that will never leave you.

As you drive along this stretch, realize that this is one of the least known parts of the Big Island. The vast majority of island residents and visitors never see this area, and that's a shame. It is mostly untouched and exceptionally beautiful. Take your time here.

Less than ²/₁₀ mile past the 13 mile marker is a turnoff to the ocean. Check out the massive squared-off rock at the lava bluff's edge. Then try to imagine the kind of wave it takes to *toss* it up from the ocean, because that's how it (and others you see around you) got here. This area is a nice place to watch the humbling power of the ocean when the surf's up. Just be careful not to let a monster wave surprise you. Another good wave-watching place is ²/₁₀ mile past the 14 mile marker. It's a 700-foot walk if you don't have 4WD and leads to a series of tide-pools that are created on this short bluff when waves explode against the lava, showering the pools.

If you look at the map, you'll see that this part of the shoreline was covered by a lava flow in 1790. The flow killed everything in its path, leaving nothing but barren, unforgiving rock for new life to work with. Yet look at what life has managed to accomplish in these two centuries. Remember this natural rejuvenating power when you come to the modern devastation that lies ahead on this road.

Near where the 19 mile marker *should* be (but was missing on our last visit) is **Kehena Beach**. This is a powerful testament to the changing nature of the Big Island. This beach wasn't even here until it was created by the 1955 lava flow you just drove through. Officials created stone steps leading down to the western part of the beach. Then an earthquake in 1975 sank the beach 3 feet all at once. The lower portion of the stone steps collapsed. The steps are still there (now blocked by vegetation), ending abruptly 10 feet above the shoreline. The trailhead to the beach itself is to the left of the parking area and has its own shorter dropoff at the end. Swimming is dangerous during high surf, and the beach is often used by nudists (who don't take kindly to cameras on the beach). Be careful not to leave anything in your car here, as we've noticed lots of thieving scum casing cars.

D Shortly after the 22 mile marker, you're confronted with the consequences of the current Kilauea eruption. A rolling sea of hardened lava stretches in front of you. This particular flow occurred in 1990, annihilating the towns of Kalapana, Kaimu and the Royal Gardens subdivision beyond. (See map on page 100 to get an idea of the scale of the devastation.) Kalapana was a treasured Hawaiian fishing village, richly steeped in the traditions of the past. Its loss was a stunning blow to those wishing to keep the old ways alive.

Until the 1990 lava flow, this was also the site of the most famous black sand beach in the world. A long curving bay of jet black sand with numerous stately palm trees sprinkled about, the black sand beach at Kaimu was universally regarded as the finest. Today, it is gone, forever entombed under 50–75 feet of lava.

When the road stops, get out and walk to the top of the lava and look toward the shore. You'll notice young, sprouting coconut trees in the distance. The campaign to bring the plantings was begun by a local resident. She encouraged others in the community to take trees out to the new black sand beach ⅓ mile in front of you to begin the process of rebuilding their precious beach. Even as she was dying of cancer, residents and school children continued the tradition in her honor. Today, there are vast numbers of sprouting coconuts along the new black sand beach, a testament to the vision of one resident who refused to let her community die, even in the face of her own death.

Like people, black sand beaches have limited life spans. Once the lava flow stops, the source of the sand disappears as well, and the ocean begins robbing the sand. The new Kaimu Beach was born in 1990, but after two decades, it is mostly gone. There is still some black sand that was tossed up beyond the low sea cliffs and a thin padding of sand that's best appreciated at low tide. But the new Kaimu Beach is now mostly a memory. A hundred years from now, when every grain of black sand is gone, visitors may wonder why there are so many coconut trees along a sandless lava shoreline.

Imagine what it must be like to have grown up in Kalapana. Sights that seemed so permanent to you like the freshwater queen's bath you played in as a child, the fishing shrine that your grandfather used every day before he went fishing, that beautiful coconut grove where you had your first kiss. All these things that seemed so timeless, that came before you, and you *knew* would always be there, are now gone, erased without a trace, as if your whole world had been nuked. Kalapana residents didn't just lose their home; they lost all traces to their past and share the unique experience of having outlived their world.

A 5–10 minute walk straight out across the lava field on crushed red rocks leads to what's left of the new black sand beach. Don't even consider swimming there for the surf is treacherous. To the right of the trailhead are some perfect impressions of palm trees. Their dying act was to cool and harden the lava around their trunks, forever capturing the bark texture of a vanished Kalapana coconut tree. There are even some hala tree fruit moldings in the lava.

If you look at the map on page 100 you'll see another road, Hwy 130, leading toward a demolished neighborhood. For two decades, the Royal Gardens Subdivision was an odd ghost town. Cut off from the rest of the island, most but not all of its homes burned and buried by lava, just a couple of hardy souls stuck around, living a surreal existence in an abandoned neighborhood. But today, all

The Star of the Sea Church had to be pulled from its foundations in Kalapana and moved to avoid being destroyed by an advancing lava flow.

of it is now buried under lava. (Just two tiny road segments were still left from the lava flow at press time.) The last resident of Royal Gardens was finally run off by Madame Pele in 2012. During the devastating lava flows, the media and the public focused their sympathy on the people who lost their homes. The *real* people to have felt sorry for were the people who *didn't* lose their homes. You see, insurance covers loss of property, not loss of *access* to property. Imagine an insurance adjuster walking up to your now-worthless house, surrounded but untouched by a sea of hardened lava and saying, "Nothing wrong with this house; claim denied."

The narrow paved access road at the end of Hwy 130 is a *public* road and you *are* allowed to drive on it, despite any misleading NO TRESSPASSING or RESTRICTED AREA signs you may see. (The land on *either side* is private, but not the road.) Depending on *where* the ever-changing lava is flowing during your stay, you might have to drive the state road to see lava flows. When lava viewing requires this road, the county *sometimes* charges $5 per car, which is very reasonable when you consider how much work it is to keep the road open. Less than two weeks after the state's grand opening of this road, lava crossed it again, requiring yet another trip for the bulldozers. See page 242 for more on lava viewing.

You may be wondering what happens if you own oceanfront property, and the volcano creates new land in front of you (called *accreted land* for the trivia-deprived). Do you now own a larger parcel? No. You don't even own oceanfront anymore! Apparently Madame Pele signed a quitclaim deed over to the state, because all newly created land goes to our hungry state government.

At that trailhead to the new Kaimu Beach you'll find some concessions, restrooms, a restaurant and a kava bar.

As you head north on Hwy 130 on your way back toward Hwy 11, look for the church on the right (east) side of the road near the 20 mile marker. Called the Star of the Sea Church, it was built in 1928 by the same priest who created the Painted Church near Honaunau. The building was in the path of an advancing lava flow in 1990. Community members had to wrench it from its foundations to save it just in the nick of time. After sitting on the side of the road for years without a home, it was finally placed on a foundation and can now be visited. Watch for aggressive wasps flying around inside.

Subdivisions in East Hawai'i often have names at odds with reality. Places like HAWAIIAN BEACHES SUBDIVISION (there are *no* beaches there), PARADISE PARK (it's not a park, and it sure ain't paradise) and our personal favorite up mauka of the 17 mile marker on Hwy 130. It's surrounded by jungle, miles from the ocean, and is called BLACK SAND BEACH COMMUNITY. (The lots were probably easier to sell than if they had named it SURROUNDED BY JUNGLE COMMUNITY.)

E When you take Hwy 130 back to Hwy 11, you can either head to Hilo or toward the volcano. If you head to the volcano, look for the easy-to-miss Hirano Store before the 20 mile marker. You used to be able to see Pu'u 'O'o belching 7½ miles away from their parking lot, and tour buses still stop here, but someone let vegetation block it across the street. Drive past the store to Glenwood Road on your left. About 100 feet down this road you should be able to see it, clouds permitting. This is the headline-grabbing vent that has been the lava source for most of the current eruption. Unless you hike to it or fly over it, this is as close as you'll come. If you *are* up to a long hike (and you're willing to jump through more hoops than most hikes), the trek through the virgin rain forest to Pu'u

This tiny segment of Prince Road is just about all that is left of the once large, thriving community of Royal Gardens at Kalapana. Kilauea Volcano has tragically erased it from the map.

'O'o is the trek of a lifetime. See ADVENTURES on page 232 for more on this beautiful hike.

Kilauea Volcano is just ahead.

HILO SHOPPING

Hilo has lots of shopping opportunities. The downtown has been going through some revitalization in recent years, and there is a wide variety of shopping.

Just south of the Farmers' Market on Kamehameha Ave. and Mamo St. on Ponahawai St. is Hilo Guitars & Ukuleles with a fabulous selection of just those. Then head north of the market on Kamehameha Ave. for the best shops. In the S. Hata Building is Burgado's Fine Woods for everything made of wood from doorstops to rocking chairs. Dreams of Paradise is an excellent gallery featuring local artists and has a very knowledgeable and helpful staff. Some other galleries to look at are High Fire Hawaii Gallery & Studio near the Tsunami Museum, Extreme Exposure for photography and One Gallery on Kilauea Ave. and Mamo St., a local artists' co-op with artwork, jewelry and pottery. In the same building is Still Life Books for used books. Fabric Impressions has an extensive selection of quilting fabrics, and Dragon Mama has great natural fabrics and bedding from Japan. Hawaiian Arts makes unique T-shirt designs. Hana Hou has boutique Hawaiiana clothing for women, men and accessories, and Sig Zane Designs, next to the Tsunami Museum, offers truly original clothing in native Hawaiian plant prints for men and women. Basically Books is a great bookshop for anything Hawai'i-related. Just off Kamehameha visit the helpful staff at Big Island BookBuyers for used and new books in all genres and Kathmandu Trading Co. for antiques from Tibet both on Waianuenue Street. Try some saltwater taffy from Sugar Coast Candy—only the Kona coffee and coconut flavors are made locally. (Whatever you do, don't leave it in your hot car!) Also on Kamehameha is Abundant Life Natural Foods if you're craving a healthy snack.

On Hwy 11 heading south you'll see Waiakea Center, which has a Walmart Superstore and a Walgreens. Across Maka'ala Street is Prince Kuhio Plaza, which has Sears, Macy's, Longs Drugs and other popular mainland chain stores.

If you're interested in the beautiful bonsai plants you've seen on many countertops around the island, Fuku-Bonsai (982–9880) is 10 miles south of Hilo in Kurtistown. Call first to be sure they'll be open.

HILO & PUNA'S BEST BETS

Best Cerebral Stimulation—Lyman
  Museum
Best Snorkeling—Tide-pools
  at Kapoho
Best Place to Soak Your Bones—
  Champagne Pond or Ahalanui Park
Best Way to Wrench Your Back—
  Duplicating Kamehameha's Feat of
  Lifting the Naha Stone
Best Waterfall—Rainbow Falls
Best *Secluded* Waterfall—Pe'epe'e Falls
Best Shakedown—State Charging for
  Use of Steam at Puna Geothermal
Best Healthy Food—Island Naturals
  Deli in the Hilo Shopping Center
Best Margarita—Luquin's in Pahoa
Best Chance of Finding Turtles—
  Champagne Pond
Best Place to Nuke Your Cholesterol
  Count—Café 100
Best Burger—Hilo Burger Joint
Best Place to Catch an Easy Glimpse
  of Erupting Pu'u 'O'o—Glenwood
  Road near the Hirano Store

The lush waterfalls of the Hamakua Coast contrast with this rolling countryside of Waimea, creating one of the best drives on the Big Island.

When local residents speak of driving between Hilo and Kona, they either "drive the saddle" or they "take the upper road." The upper road is the stretch of Highway 19 between Hilo and Waimea. It passes through magnificent country reminiscent of old Hawai'i. Along the way you can check out numerous waterfalls, drive along stunning gorges, gaze over (or go into) an Eden-like valley, or check out Hawai'i's premiere ranch town, home to one of the country's largest private ranch, Parker Ranch. Part of this drive is actually in the districts of North and South Hilo, but that distinction is lost on the driver.

We'll start our description from the Hilo side. (If you're coming the other way, just turn the book upside down.) It's best to start this drive in the morning since the waterfalls and much of the best scenery face east.

Highway 19 was constructed to make it easier and faster to travel this part of the island. Consequently, most people are totally unaware of the almost forgotten stretches of road that make up the old highway. We have a particular fondness for these diversions off the highway and point them out as DIVERSION ALERTS.

LEAVING HILO BEHIND

Ⓐ Heading north (see map on page 125) you will see a cemetery on the mauka side past the 4 mile marker. Take Nahala Street on the ocean side, then turn left at the T. You pass by **Honoli'i Beach Park**. This is the primo surfing and boogie boarding spot on this side of the island. There are stairs leading down to the black sand beach. The road continues around the back of the stream.

DIVERSION ALERT!

When it ends, hang a right to go back to the highway, then left. This is probably a good time to mention that, while stopping at scenic spots along here, during certain times of the year, it's a good idea to have mosquito repellent. Sometimes they are absent; other times they are ferocious. Feeling lucky?

Past the 7 mile marker is the only part of the old highway that is marked. This 4-mile **scenic route** is breathtaking—do *not* miss it—and leads past the **Hawai'i Tropical Botanical Garden** (964–5233). (Consider the 4-mile drive a NOT TO BE MISSED.) You don't have to be a "garden person" to appreciate this *stunningly* beautiful area that fronts Onomea Bay. For $15 ($5 for kids 6–16 years old), you wander on a self-guided tour for about an hour through over 2,500 exotic types of marked flora. (Umbrellas are thoughtfully provided, but mosquito repellent is extra.) Birds abound in this

A REAL GEM

Eden-like setting. The smell of flowers and fruit (especially mangos) fills the air. Onomea Falls is located on the grounds, which makes a nice place to stop and take in the surroundings. Views of the bay are unbeatable. $15 is pretty steep for a garden, but this is the Big Island's best. If you want a free taste of the environment there, a trail on the ocean side just before the HTBG visitor center leads to the shoreline. A guard will politely keep you from accidentally wandering onto garden grounds. A mile past the garden is a food stand called **What's Shakin'** (964–3080) that serves exceptionally good smoothies. (They make 'em the way you're *supposed* to make 'em—starting with frozen bananas, not ice—*oh, yeah...*) They also have a small lunch menu with dependably great food.

Back on the highway between the 13 and 14 mile markers is a 3¾-mile road through former sugar land to **'Akaka Falls**. This free-fall plunge of 420 feet is

Letters (**A**) correspond to paragraphs in text.

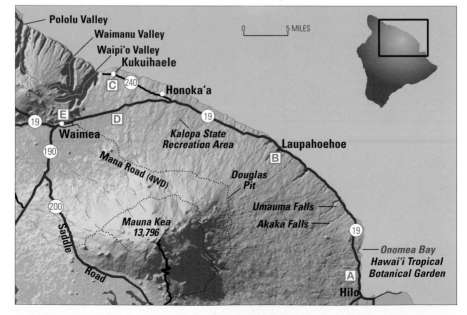

best seen in the late morning. It's $5 per car to park in the lot—free outside the parking lot—*and* $1 per person to walk in. Please don't rag on the attendant taking the money. It's not their fault the state charges for this. If you're in a hurry, walk left 3–5 *beautiful* minutes through lush vegetation and over streams to the falls. There you'll find silver/white strands forming as the water hits the rocks on the way down. Otherwise, there is a ½-mile, 15-20-minute amble (with *lots* of steps) through the lush bamboo-filled woods along with another waterfall. (Though the latter, **Kahuna Falls**, is largely blocked by vegetation.) The full loop is recommended if you have the time. Everything's paved. After visiting 'Akaka Falls, you'll want to stop at the **Woodshop Gallery and Cafe** for some homemade ice cream and the best collection of Hawaiian wood products we've seen on the island. Woodworkers can even purchase a plank of Hawaiian hardwood to take home. For food here, see ISLAND DINING.

NOT TO BE MISSED!

As you continue on Hwy 19, there is another piece of old road to take. It's shortly after the 14 mile marker on the mauka (mountain) side. It leads past **Kolekole Park**. The massive highway bridge in front of you was part of an old railway. The great tsunami of 1946 carried away many of the girders, rendering the bridge useless. This was the deathblow for the railway, sparking the construction for the entire highway. During the week this is a great place to bring your briquettes and cookables to make good use of the stone BBQs, full facilities and tranquil setting. (Though quiet during the week, it gets too rowdy on weekends to recommend.) The small waterfall and swimming hole is where most swim when the river isn't raging, since the black sand beach itself is too hazardous to swim. This is where the water from 'Akaka Falls ends up, so if you lost something up there, maybe you'll see it again here.

DIVERSION ALERT!

If you stay on this road, it crosses the highway, curves left and empties into **Hakalau Bay**. A rich, vine-filled forest dripping with life ushers you into the bay. The ruins at the mouth on the east bank are from a mill destroyed during the tsunami. The swimming here is poor, but you can't say that about the view. Backtrack to the highway.

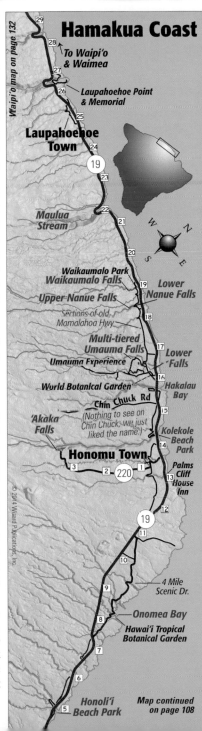

Hamakua Coast

To Waipi'o map on page 132

29

28

To Waipi'o & Waimea

27

26   Laupahoehoe Point & Memorial

25

Laupahoehoe Town   24

19

23

Maulua Stream   22

21

20

Waikaumalo Park
Waikaumalo Falls   19   *Lower Nanue Falls*

Upper Nanue Falls

18

Sections of old Mamalahoa Hwy

Multi-tiered Umauma Falls   17   Lower Falls

Umauma Experience

16

World Botanical Garden   Hakalau Bay

Chin Chuck Rd   15

'Akaka Falls   (Nothing to see on Chin Chuck, we just liked the name.)   Kolekole Beach Park

14

Honomu Town

3   2   1   220   Palms Cliff House Inn   13

19   12

11

10

9   4 Mile Scenic Dr.

8   Onomea Bay

Hawai'i Tropical Botanical Garden

7

6

© 2014 Wizard Publications, Inc.

Honoli'i Beach Park   5   Map continued on page 108

The bridge past the 16 mile marker boasts nice views of two waterfalls. As impressive as they are, they don't even come close to the multi-tiered beauty of **Umauma Falls** upstream. This may be the most stunning waterfall setting in the state. You can only see it by visiting the Umauma Experience (page 226) and paying $10 or going on one of their zipline tours. (See the photo on page 128 to see if it's worth it to you.)

Whether you want to pay for the falls or not, while you're on the highway, *be sure* to backtrack 2/10 mile from the highway bridge turnout, then take the road on the mauka side across from the 16 mile marker and turn right at the T. This 4-mile-long, one-lane country road passes through sugar land before it takes you to a small tree tunnel and several striking gulches. This is the Hawai'i of yesteryear, when life moved a bit slower. You might want to do the same. Stop at one of the old bridges and enjoy the peace. Vine-covered trees and ever-chirping birds give this area an unforgettable feel.

Early into this road is the **Botanical World Adventures** (963–5427). Started in 1995, it's still a bit stark for a garden, though it's starting to fill out. They used to control access to the Umauma Falls lookout, which was their most compelling asset. Now that they don't have the waterfall, it's hard to get excited about this garden.

Just past the botanical gardens, across from a sign that says THE UMAUMA EXPERIENCE, is a bridge. If you park across from that sign, there is a super-short, steep, treacherous (especially when muddy) trail that leads down to a pretty waterfall and perch from which to observe it. From looking at county TMK maps, it *appears* that the land here is part of a roadway easement, meaning you're allowed to be there, but it's hard to say for certain.

Still on this 4-mile back road, one of the small Depression-era bridges crosses **Nanue Stream** (it's stamped into the bridge). The nearside of the bridge has a crude and *steep* trail that leads down to the stream. From there a person could walk over to the top of the falls (don't fall off), or go

What a drop! 'Akaka Falls tumbles 420 feet.

DIVERSION ALERT!

From a picnic table at Kolekole Beach Park you can either watch the ocean or watch kids swinging off a rope swing next to a waterfall. Talk about an embarrassment of riches!

upstream where another waterfall awaits. (The upstream falls, though only 900 feet away, require *very* awkward stream hiking. See ADVENTURES on page 237.) If you don't have mosquito repellent, be prepared for the bloodletting of a lifetime.

Bypass any opportunities to reconnect with the highway until you pass rarely used **Waikaumalo Park** near a pretty stream.

When you reacquire the highway just north of the 19 mile marker, you may want to backtrack less than a mile to see the densely jungled gulch and waterfall visible from the highway that you missed before continuing north.

As you effortlessly cruise these gulches on our modern bridges of today, try to visualize what a nightmare it must have been to cross them in days gone by. It took many days to get from Hilo to Waipi'o Valley. When author Isabella Bird toured this area on horseback in 1873, she wrote of the utter dread she felt as she plunged down and then trudged up gulch after harrowing gulch on her way to Waipi'o, fording raging streams on a snorting, terrified horse. Today, the hardest thing about traversing these gulches is resetting the cruise control after a sharp bend.

B Just past the 25 mile marker is the road leading mauka to the town of **Laupahoehoe**. (The short road on the ocean side sports a nice view of the point mentioned below.) The town itself doesn't offer much other than a '50s-style restaurant (see ISLAND DINING), plus a store down a road on the *ocean* side of the Hwy ³⁄₁₀ past the 24 mile marker. It's just a store, and they usually only have one hot meal to eat, so just ask what's for lunch today. (Their curry stew's not bad.)

Also on the highway is the **Laupahoehoe Train Museum** (962–6300). This assortment of artifacts and photos of Hamakua's history with trains is somewhat interesting. They have over a dozen volunteers. Some are extremely knowledgeable...and some aren't. It's $6.

Just past the 27 mile marker is a road on the ocean side that leads 1 mile down the cliffs to **Laupahoehoe Point**. To many on the Big Island, Laupahoehoe is associated with tragedy. During the April Fool's Day tsunami of 1946, twenty-one schoolchildren and three

DIVERSION ALERT!

Umauma Falls is one waterfall on the island you have to pay to see. Is it worth it? You decide...

adults were swept to their deaths. Following this, the village was moved topside. The views from the road down to the rugged point sport dramatic views of the sea cliffs beyond and is well worth the stop. There is a memorial at the bottom to those who lost their lives. From out on the jetty, the ocean's energy feels raw and menacing. Waves come in with powerful anger. You feel (and are) exposed to the ocean's fury on the jetty. Here it's not the calm, soothing ocean of Kona, but rather the unpredictable, hot-tempered ocean of Laupahoehoe. Away from the jetty the surf pounds against the twisted and jagged lava and is spectacular to watch, especially when surf's up, but don't even *think* of swimming here at any time. In 1985 a barge full of brand new Toyotas broke loose from its tug and washed ashore near here, spilling the entire cargo. When an insurance adjuster from Lloyd's of London came to check it out, he insisted on landing on the deck of the wrecked ship in a helicopter. Then a wave knocked the chopper over, drowning the adjuster. Surf is almost always violent here.

This whole area was once dominated by sugar. Over 70,000 acres of the Big Island were under cultivation. Even with generous government subsidies, the last mill shut down in 1996, ending 150 years of sugar production. Today this area has a different look and a different crop. More than 24,000 acres of fast-growing eucalyptus trees were planted. Harvesting is ongoing, so you may see logging trucks carrying their loads to Kawaihae.

Between the 39 and 40 mile markers is the road to **Kalopa State Recreation Area**, which offers nice hiking and camping.

HONOKA'A

Near the 42 mile marker is a road through the town of **Honoka'a**. Most merely use it to get to **Waipi'o Valley**, described below. There are a few places to eat that are mentioned in ISLAND DINING.

WAIPI'O VALLEY

Ⓒ Waipi'o Valley is as beautiful a place as you will ever visit. With unimaginably steep walls on all sides, waterfalls etching the perimeter, fields of taro and a luscious **A REAL GEM** mile-long black sand beach, Waipi'o never fails to impress. The instant you arrive at the lookout above this awesome spectacle, you realize why this place was so special to the ancient Hawaiians. Because of its inspiring and tranquilizing effects, Waipi'o was often chosen as the meeting place for chiefs when important decisions, such as the succession of the king, were made. Even the kings who resided in sunny Kona had residences in Waipi'o Valley. According to Hawaiian legend, Waipi'o Valley was gouged out by a powerful warrior with his club to demonstrate his power. (Unfortunately, the warrior was himself clubbed to death by the one he was trying to impress.)

At one time thousands of people lived here, meticulously cultivating the lush valley floor with everything from bananas to taro to coconuts. Even Waipi'o pigs were considered tastier here in the Big Island's breadbasket. During times of famine, you could always count on Waipi'o Valley for much-needed sustenance. Fifty generations of Hawaiians have lived and died here, and they believe that the spiritual *mana*, or supernatural power left by those departed, is preserved and felt to this day.

The peace of Waipi'o Valley was shattered by the great tsunami of 1946 that washed away nearly everything. Most people moved away, and the valley was left mostly wild for two decades. Then in the '60s and early '70s people started trickling back in. Most were hippies and recently discharged veterans who wanted to "get away from it all." Others soon joined. These days Waipi'o is populated by a colorful assortment of 50 or so characters (including an inordinate number of guys named Dave). Many have turned their backs on traditional society; others simply live there to experience the grace of nature at its grandest. Lots of feuds take place down here, and it's not uncommon for one to result in a building getting torched. Police hesitate to get involved in Waipi'o disputes, so residents usually settle things on their own.

Those who live in the valley have no power, water, sewage, phones, cell or TV coverage. Solar power and generators provide the electricity they need. (A few nearside residents have phones and power courtesy of small lines stretching down into the valley.) They share their valley with two herds of wild horses (the swamp horses and the bush horses) that were left by the departing residents after the tsunami of '46. The horses can get pesky if they want something (such as apples, which they *love*), so don't turn your back on 'em. There are people who live "topside" and come down daily or on weekends to tend their taro patches.

Land ownership is a big issue. Even the biggest, most powerful landowner in Hawai'i, Bishop Estate, has trouble proving how much of the valley they own. Dueling surveyors keep boundaries in flux. When Bishop tried to block access to a beach parcel in 1997, all of their signs were torn down and Bishop gave up.

Today the allure of Waipi'o Valley is beckoning outsiders. Visitors and residents alike enjoy the splendor of Waipi'o. Experienced surfers and boogie boarders ride the waves off the black sand beach. Horseback rides are popular. And Waipi'o Valley Shuttle takes groups down the steep road. Does all this mean that Waipi'o is ablaze with activity? Not really. To you and me, Waipi'o is a quiet, peaceful place. But if

you've had the place all to yourself for years, even a few people a week would seem like a crowd. The residents here range from the friendly to the grouchy to the *very* weird. We've found that we are less likely to get a smile or a wave in this valley than anywhere else on the island, in sharp contrast to the friendly folks in Kukuihaele and Honoka'a above. Stink eye (dirty looks) and overall unfriendliness from some residents is common. Perhaps it's because they see visitors as antithetical to the reason they chose to live in Waipi'o in the first place.

Getting Into the Valley

Don't even *think* about driving a regular car down Waipi'o Valley Road. The paved one-lane road down into the valley has a ridiculously steep *25%* grade. Vehicles with 4WD and low gears (so you don't burn up your brakes) can make it down the 900-foot descent (in less than a mile). Regular cars simply can't. (There is a wad of metal that was once a two-wheel drive truck below one of the turns left by someone who thought otherwise. He miraculously survived by jumping from the vehicle just as it started tumbling down the almost vertical plunge.) You would probably be violating your rental car agreement if you brought your SUV down here, meaning that they won't come save your bacon if it breaks down. Downhill traffic yields to uphill traffic, so use the turnouts. While driving back up the road, the extreme angle makes it feel like the vehicle is about to flip over backward. (Lance Armstrong once biked up the road on a bet in just over 9 minutes.)

While the overlook sports an unforgettable view of the valley and along the coast, it gives you only a taste of what the valley has to offer. The view from the valley floor with its numerous waterfalls is even better. If you don't have an

SUV (or nerve), you can take **Waipi'o Valley Shuttle** (775–7121). For $55 they'll take you into the valley on a 1½-hour *limited* tour. You can get off and arrange for a pick up for $10. They are nearby in the town of Kukuihaele (shown on map on next page). A better way is **Waipi'o Valley Wagon Tours** (775–9518). For $60 they take you on the same 1½-hour tour in a mule-driven wagon. (A half hour of it gets you into and out of the valley by 4WD.) Wagons hold 8 passengers and the driver narrates the sights in a similar way, but with the added charm of being in an open-air wagon. Neither operate on Sunday.

If you want a better tour, **Na'alapa Stables–Waipi'o** (775–0419) has outstanding horseback rides in the valley. They'll shuttle you down into the valley and take you back a ways. See HORSEBACK RIDING.

If you want to hike down into Waipi'o Valley, just walk the road to the bottom. (Oh, is *that* all?) Though less than a mile going down, you'd swear it was 5 miles coming up. Just take your time. Waipi'o is a great place to spend the afternoon. At the bottom, the beach is to your right. **Waipi'o Beach** is often treacherous to swim unless the surf is real calm. Rip currents are a problem, and the power of the waves is impressive. Legend states that the door to the underworld is near Waipi'o Beach, so Hawaiians were always careful where they camped, lest they should take the one-way trip there themselves.

The back part of Waipi'o Valley is awesome. In the first nook you'll see twin falls of staggering heights. One of the falls are periodically shut off by Bishop Estate. *(Grumble, grumble.)* The falls on the right, **Hi'ilawe Falls**, is 1,450 feet high with a free fall of 1,200 feet, the highest on the island. You'll see it when you head inland after you've reach the bottom of the road.

Mosquito repellent should be required by law for visitors here. The bugs are not always around, but when they are in a foul mood—watch out!

Getting Around the Valley

Waipi'o seems so idyllic and peaceful you'll be forgiven if you feel compelled to dig in and explore. But the fact is that, other than the roads we show in yellow on the map, the rest of the valley is privately

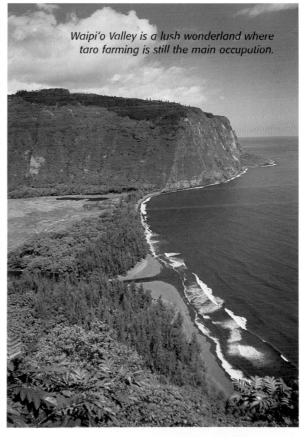

Waipi'o Valley is a lush wonderland where taro farming is still the main occupation.

Waipi'o Valley & Old Mamalahoa Hwy

Next map on page 125

40 Miles to Hilo

Old Mamalahoa Hwy

Hotel Honoka'a Club

1

Golf

19

42

43

Lehua

240

Honoka'a

2

Hamakua Ditch

44

Kalehua

Old Mamalahoa Hwy

Ahualoa

3

45

Kahana Rd

Hamakua Ditch

4

46

5

Mamane St

47

6

(New) Mamalahoa Hwy
(Hawaii Belt Rd)

Hamakua Coast Hwy / Mamane St

7

48

Indicates Foot Trails

25 Roadside mile markers

Unpaved Roads

S Public Access in Waipi'o

Cave

49

Cave #3
20°02.834'
155°32.563'

8

Kukuihaele

Hamakua Ditch

50

2WD Only

Dahana Ranch

240

9

Waiulili Falls

Kaluahine Falls

Unpaved 2WD usually OK

51

Exceptional view from this switchback

Waipi'o Bay

Nearly all of the coast in this area is composed of sea cliffs:

Mud Lane

Old Mamalahoa Hwy

52

To Waimanu Valley

Muliwai Trail

Waipi'o Valley

Hi'ilawe Falls

Falls

Gate

Note: Dirt roads shown as dashed yellow lines in Waipi'o Valley are county roads. The road to the beach from Waipi'o Valley Road is owned by Kamehameha Schools, which has traditionally allowed access to everyone.

53

19

1 Mile To Waimea

Map continued on page 135

N
E
W
S

2 MILES

0

owned and jealously guarded. Many Waipi'o residents get downright grumpy toward visitors wandering around. This has always been the case with Waipi'o, but we feel some responsibility for steering visitors into the back of the valley.

When we did our very first edition, we went down to the county building to diligently research road access in the valley. County personnel took out great big TMK maps and showed us that the roads leading to the back of the valley were "government roads," and we eagerly labeled them as such on our maps. For our last edition, we went back to the county and were shown the same TMK maps. But that time we dug deeper. We looked up ownership of every single parcel that *make up* the road. Lo and behold, most of the "government road" is actually private. So feel free to go to the bottom of Waipio Valley Road. Go as far back as the second stream crossing where you'll see an END OF COUNTY ROAD sign. If you want to head to the beach, visitors are traditionally allowed to go to and use the beach, despite a variety of odd signs over the years. (We like the far side of the beach best, if the stream is low enough to cross.) And if you're hiking to Waimanu Valley (see below), go right ahead. But that's it, unless you have the blessing of one of the residents or if you're on a commercial tour.

The trail you see zigzagging up the wall on the far side of Waipi'o Valley goes up, then down into the next valley, Waimanu. The third switchback (400 feet up the trail cut pretty deeply into the mountain) offers a far grander view of the valley than from the automobile lookout. You can see the back of the valley, the twin falls and lots more. Waimanu is much farther along the trail. It is utterly gorgeous, devoid of residents, and camping is allowed for those who are willing to make the trek. See ADVENTURES for more on accessing Waimanu Valley. Don't try to go and come back as a day hike. It's too long, and you can't see Waimanu Valley from the trail until you have mostly descended.

OLD MAMALAHOA HIGHWAY

D Leaving Waipi'o and Honoka'a behind, get back on Hwy 19. Along this stretch of the highway, between the 43 and 52 mile markers, there is another forgotten piece of the **Old Mamalahoa Highway**. Again the scenery on Old Mamalahoa is much nicer than Hwy 19 and worth the diversion. Lush, green hillsides bracket this old country road. Mist and rain mean that lovers of green will be very happy. If you like caves, there are several along Old Mamalahoa Highway. The best, by far, is labeled on the map as cave #3. You should bring two flashlights. (There are lots of long chambers snaking pitch black into the mountain and, though tall enough to walk upright in, you'd be groping till the cows come home if you lost your only flashlight toward the back of some of these chambers.) The entrances are often dripping with ferns Cave #3 has lots of structures inside (such as walls and platforms), presumably built by early Hawaiians, and a few empty drinking bottles, presumably left a bit later. It's 1½ miles from Dahana Ranch Road or 2¼ miles from where Kahana meets Old Mamalahoa Highway. The other caves labeled are much less impressive. These caves are in old Mauna Kea flows, and it's unusual for lava tube caves to last so long.

DIVERSION ALERT!

WAIMEA

E This town is often labeled Kamuela on maps. That's because there are two other Waimeas in the state, so the Post Office named the local branch Kamuela—Hawaiian for Samuel (as in Samuel Parker; see below). Many locals object to the use of Kamuela, so we will use the original name in deference.

On the surface, Waimea seems like the least Hawaiian town in Hawai'i. In fact, if Scotty had beamed you here and asked you where you were, Hawai'i would probably be the last state you'd guess. At 2,600 feet, the air has a cool crispness to it. Clouds slither over the saddle between Kohala and Mauna Loa volcanoes, often bathing Waimea in a cool fog. Evergreen trees and cactus sit side by side, and the trees all seem blown in one direction. (Kind of like your hair if you've rented a convertible.) Rather than seeing surfers in shorts and aloha shirts, you're more apt to see Hawaiian cowboys (called paniolo) wearing blue jeans and driving pick-up trucks. (A brief visit to a magazine rack, and you'll think, "Wow, I never knew there were so many *truck* magazines.")

Life runs a little slower here, and families are a bit closer knit. Many people compare its appearance to a Northern California rural town, but prettier. As you drive through town from the east side of the island, note how quickly the terrain changes from lush upland forests and green pastures to dry lava scrubland. If it's raining in Waimea (a common occurrence) and you're heading to Kohala via Hwy 19, it'll stop raining less than 5 minutes after you leave Waimea—*guaranz, brah*.

Don't be lulled into thinking that Waimea is a hick town. It is remarkably over-represented when it comes to fine shopping and has several restaurants that are utterly superb. Some of the homes up in the Waimea Homesteads where the descendants of cattle magnates live are absolutely beautiful.

Be careful if you take the Waimea Bypass. It *looks* wide open, but is a notorious 25 MPH speed trap.

PARKER RANCH

The town is dominated by the legacy of John Palmer Parker. When Captain George Vancouver brought long-horned cattle to Kamehameha as a gift in 1793, the king made them kapu (off limits) for 10 years to build up the numbers. By 1815 the wild herds that roamed Kohala were so ferocious that locals steered clear of them. Marauding cattle were known to drive Hawaiians from their homes by munching and goring everything in sight—even the homes themselves. Kamehameha the Great hired Massachusetts-born John Palmer Parker to shoot them, salt the meat and bring it to the harbor to sell to passing ships. This was no easy task. Long-horned cattle of that time were not like the tame, mindless morons we know today. They were wily, lean and stealthy. They would charge men on horseback, goring them. They lived in the valleys and canyons as well, making them very difficult to detect. Good horses became the equivalent of hunting dogs—they would smell the wild cattle before they saw them, and their ears would perk up, warning their rider to the danger. Because Parker possessed a musket and good shooting skills, Kamehameha made him the first person ever allowed to kill the cattle. Parker took great pains to select cattle with favorable traits and kept them for himself as payment. These he domesticated, starting the Parker herd.

As a totally irrelevant aside, one of the casualties of these cattle was the Scottish botanist David Douglas. He's the guy for whom Douglas fir trees were named. He was walking near Mana Road on the slopes of Mauna Kea one day when he fell into one of the covered pits used as a cattle trap. (Some said he was thrown in.) Although he was lucky enough to survive the fall, so was the bull already occupying the pit. The unhappy bovine made his displeasure known by goring Douglas to death. Douglas Pit is 28 miles into Mana Road from Waimea.

John Parker himself was a colorful character. A lover of adventure, he was a

Back of Waipi'o Valley

Map continued on page 132

∿ Indicates Foot Trails
25 Roadside mile markers
⋯ Unpaved Roads

N
W ⊕ E
S

0 _____ 1 MILE

Upper Hamakua Ditch

White Road

53

54

19

53 Miles → to Hilo

20 Miles to Hawi

3

250

60

19

59

Kawaihae Rd

9 Miles to Kawaihae

Waimea Park

Waimea Center

56

55

Mamalahoa Hwy

Kahilu Rd

Mana Road

Mana Road

Lindsay

Opelo

Kapiolani

58

57

Kamuela Inn

Restaurant Row

Parker Ranch Historic Homes

Mamalahoa Hwy

Kamamalu

Pukalani Stables

Parker Ranch Center & Visitor Center

To Parker Ranch Land
Dirt road leads 44 miles
around base of Mauna Kea
to Mauna Kea Road near Saddle Road.
After 18 miles, there is a
5-mile stretch that is 4WD
or mountain bike only.

1 Jacaranda Inn
2 Kamuela Inn
3 Waimea Country Lodge

36 Miles to Kailua-Kona

Paniolo Park

Waimea-Kohala Airport

190

Map continued on page 46

Kailua-Kona map on page 61

© 2014 Wizard Publications, Inc.

natural born risk-taker who, though a long-range planner, felt strongly that part of wisdom is to know the value of today. He was well loved and respected by his contemporaries. (But he sure wasn't very photogenic—in his sour photo he makes Ebenezer Scrooge look like Barney the dinosaur.)

In 1816 John Parker married Kamehameha the Great's granddaughter, forever cementing the bond between him and the royal family. He was eventually allowed to purchase two acres of land. His wife, because of her royal blood, was later granted 640 acres, and he bought another 1,000 acres. Thus was born what would become, until the 1990s, the largest privately owned cattle ranch in the entire United States, peaking at over 225,000 acres, 9% of the Big Island.

Parker and his descendants would go on to become very powerful on the island.

Later, when Kamehameha III realized that Hawai'i was lacking in people knowledgeable in the ways of cattle ranching, he arranged for three Mexican cowboys to come to the Big Island and teach the locals about ranching. Nearly all Big Island paniolo traditions descend from these three cowboys.

Parker Ranch was severely neglected by subsequent Parkers. John Parker's grandson, Samuel Parker, was a flamboyant playboy who spent money like water and had a genius for making profoundly stupid investments. Unlike King Midas, everything *he* touched turned to manure. As the aging Parker II saw money pouring down Samuel's many ratholes, he began to squirrel away funds as fast as he could. But when the time came to retrieve the money, the old man could not remember where he had hidden most of it. To this day, much of the fortune Parker II hid away has never been found. In 1900 the family hired a Honolulu attorney to manage and rejuvenate the ranch. This he did with a vengeance, turning a dying relic into a powerful and very lucrative operation.

The serenity of Waimea was broken in the 1990s when Richard Smart, the descendent of John Palmer Parker, died, leaving some of his $450 *million* estate to his family, but the bulk of the land (139,000 acres) to a non-profit trust. Lawsuits started flying from disgruntled family members angry about their share, and it was beginning to look as if the ranch might be broken up and fed to the lawyers and tax collectors. Fortunately, the dispute was finally settled, and peace once again returned to sleepy little Waimea.

Most of Parker Ranch is mile after mile of rolling, grassy hills and wide open plains interrupted by rows of trees for windbreaks. Owls, pheasant and wild turkeys crisscross the ranch, while ever-chewing cows wander about. The ranch consists of several non-contiguous segments of land, and its 35,000

cattle are controlled by a mere 12 paniolo (Hawaiian cowboys). The road across from the 55 mile mark (see Waimea map, on previous page, or graphic below) slices through Parker Ranch. Called **Mana Road**, it goes 44 miles around Mauna Kea mountain to Mauna Kea Road (off Saddle Road). 2WD vehicles can drive it for the first part to see what the ranch looks like. After 18 miles there's a bad 5-mile segment that requires 4WD (it'll seem like more than 5), plus there's an area with confusing but *presumably* parallel roads. Otherwise, you can go as far as your desire takes you. Close any gates that you open (all 4 of them). According to the county, it is a *public* right of way, despite any signs you may see that *imply* the contrary. Avoid it if it's been too rainy; some of the puddles can be big enough to waterski in.

A successful cattle ranch is first and foremost a grass farm. After being raised on sweet Hawaiian range grass for 5–6 months, most of the cattle are shipped by 747 to the mainland or by boat to Canada, then fattened in various areas before slaughter. (Ironically, cattle class on a 747 has more leg room than what you had in coach.) In the old days, just getting the cows to the ship was a traumatic process. They were driven to Kawaihae, forced into the ocean, then lashed to the outside of small boats, which ferried them to the main ship where they were belly-hoisted aboard. Now they simply walk onto an old cruise ship, into stalls, and off they go to Canada, where they are then trucked to Texas. Why Canada, which ain't exactly *on the way* to Texas? Because no shipbuilder in the U.S. makes cattle haulers. Yet a government law from 1920 makes it illegal for a foreign-built ship to sail from one

> ⚠️ **DIVERSION ALERT!**

Parker Ranch Shown in Dark Areas

Mana Rd—

U.S. harbor to another. Hence, they gotta go to Canada.

If you want to get an idea of what Big Island beef tastes like, the best (and most consistent) source is **Waikoloa Village Market** (883–1088) located in Waikoloa Village at the Waikoloa Highlands Center. The range-fed beef is darker and stronger than grain-fed beef and is particularly good marinated. Deliveries are usually Tuesdays and Fridays. Expect to pay *double* what you would pay for beef that is flown in by jet from the mainland.

Past Waimea heading into Kohala, sights are described in the Kohala section.

HAMAKUA & WAIMEA SHOPPING

The **Parker Ranch Center** in Waimea has lots of shops, including **Reyn's**, which offers men's, women's and keiki aloha wear. **Parker Ranch Store** has paniolo and Parker Ranch logo items. **Wishard Gallery** has works by local artists. There is also **Foodland** grocery store, **Natural Foods & Deli** and **Starbucks** here.

Across the street at **Waimea Center**, you should check out **Oshima Surf & Skate** for surf gear, **Top Stitch** for quilting fabrics and **Without Boundaries** is a fun place for knick-knacks of all kinds. There is also a **KTA Super Store**.

On Kawaihae Road is **Parker Square** with many outstanding shops. **Hula Moon** is a very nice boutique. **Bentley's** has women's clothing and home items as does **Gallery of Great Things**, which also has jewelry and artwork from around the world. And browse the **Waimea General Store**; it has a little bit of everything. **Sweet Wind Books 'n Beads** has self-help and cookbooks... and beads, of course. There is a huge **Longs Drugs** next door to the center. Across the street art lovers and collectors should visit **Isaac's Art Center Museum & Gallery**, it houses works by deceased Hawaiian artists; some are museum pieces, others are for sale.

After leaving Waipi'o Valley lookout, drive by Kukuihaele for **Waipi'o Valley Artworks**, which features an outstanding selection of Hawaiian woodwork and other gifts. Before your stroll up the road in Honoka'a on Mamane Street, pick up some fudge or baked goods at **Sweet and Savory Treats**. Try browsing **Honoka'a Trading & Antiques** or **Hula Moon**. Honoka'a Marketplace—**Mary Guava Designs** has a beautiful selection of Hawaiian quilts and just about every other item you can think of (from T-shirts to dinnerware), many designed for their store. Look at **Big Island Glass Gallery** for lava- or ocean-inspired glass pieces. Next door is **Big Island Grown**, which carries all types of products made locally. Across the street is **Symbiosis**, for eco-friendly items. Check out **Vera's Treasures & Mall** for some good pre-owned finds at fair prices.

On the way to 'Akaka Falls in Honomu, stop at **Purple Eye** for a sarong. Visit **Glass From The Past** for an extensive antique bottle collection. **Woodshop Gallery & Cafe** has a great selection of Hawaiian wood products, rocking chair kits and sometimes raw woods.

HAMAKUA & WAIMEA'S BEST BETS

Best Garden—Hawai'i Tropical Botanical Garden
Best Waterfall—Umauma Falls
Best Place to Ride a Horse—Waipi'o
Best View (Easy)—Waipi'o Overlook
Best View (Hard)—From the zigzag trail on *other* side of Waipi'o Valley
Best Treats—Hamakua Fudge Shop in Honoka'a
Best Hole to Avoid—Douglas Pit
Best Picnic Table—Kolekole Beach Park

Here's one place where you don't want a foggy mountain breakdown.

Saddle Road runs between our largest volcanoes, Mauna Loa and Mauna Kea. The entire area is called the Saddle because of the saddle-shaped valley between the two mountains. It travels through some unpopulated and very surreal-looking country and is worth considering if you are driving from one side to the other.

The saddle crests at an impressive 6,578 feet. That's some saddle. The 52-mile-long road has a bad and outdated reputation. It was hastily built by the military in 1942 for strategic purposes. This was wartime, and they wanted a road connecting the two sides of the island, and they wanted it fast. They didn't design it with general traffic in mind; it was meant for military vehicles. Until 2013, driving on Saddle Road was prohibited in some rental car agreements, meaning your Collision Damage Waiver with them wouldn't cover you. Previous to that their fears had been quite well founded. Saddle was a winding, hilly road with blind turns that weren't banked and had been paved by *Sadists-R-Us*. But it's been improved and rerouted in areas and today is an easy drive. There are no lights, and the road is often licked by fog toward the center crest. (We came out here in the middle of the night to watch a comet some years back and *got chicken skin fo days*—i.e., it was spooky. The only sound was a lone birthing cow screaming in the blackness.)

So why drive Saddle Road? Two reasons. First, it's the only way to drive to the top of Mauna Kea. Second, it cuts between Mauna Kea and Mauna Loa and has some nice sights. The landscape is otherworldly in places and decidedly different. Even back when it was in horrible shape, we'd take our own personal car on it. (As we all know, *drive it like a rental* is like saying, *drive it like it's stolen*.) And it's a shorter distance than Hwy 19, known locally as *the upper road*. We like to take Saddle Road from the Kona side and return from Hilo on the upper road. In 50 miles the terrain goes from dry lava scrub land to rolling green hills and plains to young lava fields to dripping fern-covered forests. With this in mind, we'll describe it from west to east. There's no **gas** on this road; get it in Waikoloa Village or Waimea in the west, Hilo in the east.

Look at the foldout back cover map to familiarize yourself with the route and to put it in context. From the intersection of Saddle Road (200) and Hwy 190, you leave lava land behind and enter rolling plains of grasses. Keep an eye out for wild turkey (the bird, not the booze) and pheasant, which are plentiful here.

A As you ascend to the crest of this saddle, you'll get an idea of the scale of Mauna Kea on your left and Mauna Loa on your right. The military often drives this road in their HUMVEES and other camouflaged vehicles. If you stop and listen, you'll often hear the booms of artillery from the Pohakuloa Military Training Area. Sometimes you'll see their choppers swooping low like a scene out of *Apocalypse Now*. Tanks and Armored Personnel Carriers also use this road on occasion. (We respectfully suggest that you *always* give armored tanks the right of way.) They have even used B2 Stealth Bombers to drop unguided inert bombs from 18,000 feet. If you use the HISTORICAL IMAGERY feature on Google Earth, you'll even find a fake airfield and broken jets from bombing practice scattered on part of their lava field.

Mauna Kea Recreation Area is near the 34 mile marker. After you turn into

*Letters (**A**) correspond to paragraphs in text.*

the park, there are restrooms and a phone to your right. Cabins are available (See CAMPING on page 179.) Restrooms here are rustic at best, and they've literally torn the sinks out due to a lack of water.

You'll find the road up Mauna Kea (on your left) is marked by a large mound, called **Pu'u Huluhulu** (hairy hill). This pu'u is a good place to stretch if you want to walk the ⅔ mile round trip to the top. (If you have kids, this is a good place to let 'em burn off some of that extra energy.) It's an old cinder cone created long ago by Mauna Kea and has been surrounded by more recent lava flows from Mauna Loa. (You can tell by scars on the side that it was once mined for its cinders.) The main trail is on the far (east) side of Pu'u Huluhulu, just off the road to Mauna Loa, on your right. There are several trails on top of this forested mound, but it's kind of hard to get *too* lost. You can go around the top and connect to the trail you took coming up. The splendid view, as well as the birds, makes it a short but worthwhile diversion.

MAUNA KEA

B If someone asked you to climb from the base of Mauna Kea to the summit (which is more than 13,000 feet above sea level), you'd have to climb over 30,000 feet. (The base of Mauna Kea just happens to be 17,000 feet *below* sea level.) Those wimps who climb from the base of Mt. Everest to the summit only have to climb a mere 12,000 feet. (Its base just happens to start at 17,000 feet *above* sea level.) Everest, too, is located in a warm latitude, 28°, as far south as sweltering Orlando, Florida. But people still freeze to death in the summer on Everest because the summit's high altitude (29,035 feet) offsets the warm latitude.

The second of the five surviving volcanoes to create the island, Mauna Kea (meaning White Mountain) pokes its head 13,796 feet above the ocean. In its prime, half a million years ago, Mauna Kea was 3,500 feet higher. But it gets shorter with age. It shrinks every day, settling under its own weight, and bending the ocean floor beneath it. The ancient Hawaiians consid-

Mauna Kea

Summit

Ancient Adz Quarry
19°48.068
155°28.097

Unpaved Rd.

Mauna Kea Trail

Visitor Center
9,200 feet

Mana Road

Mauna Kea Rd.

Restrooms
& Telephones

Mauna Kea Recreation Area

14.7 Miles to Mauna Kea Summit

17.4 Miles to Mauna Loa Weather Observatory

35

28

25

200

22

Summit Close-up

Keck
Subaru
U of H Scope

Summit
●13,796'

Saddle Road　Pu'u Huluhulu
Crest of Saddle at 6,578 feet

Lake Wai-au
13,020
19°48.662
155°26.629

© 2014 Wizard Publications, Inc.

One of many telescopes perched high above a sea of clouds during Mauna Kea sunset.

ered it the home of Poli'ahu, the snow goddess. She and Madame Pele, next door on Mauna Loa, didn't always get along very well, and the saddle between Mauna Loa and Mauna Kea was said to be their battleground. The ancient Hawaiians were uncomfortable in this region, not wishing to get in the middle of this domestic disturbance.

Atop the mountain, the air is thin and incredibly clear. Scientists recognized this spot as possibly the best place in the world to observe stars and have been placing the world's finest telescopes up here for years. (The *twinkle, twinkle* of the little star is caused by air turbulence, and the air above Mauna Kea is some of the least turbulent in the world—windy, but not turbulent.) With little precipitation (except for the occasional blizzard), little in the way of city lights below (those that *do* exist cast a carefully chosen color to make life easier on astronomers), and relatively easy access, Mauna Kea is the pride of the astro-

nomical community. Two dozen of the finest telescopes in the world are sprinkled about the summit or are in the works. One area up there is called Millimeter Valley since its peepers are designed to look not in the optical wavelength, but rather at the high end of the radio band, in the much longer millimeter and sub-millimeter wavelength. This allows scientists to look through cosmic clouds and watch stars being born. Some of these telescopes can look at objects over 12 billion light years away, meaning that the light they are seeing left those objects long before the earth and sun were even born. The mighty Keck telescope has a 33-foot wide viewing surface. The moveable part weighs 300 tons but is so perfectly balanced that it can be moved *with one hand*.

Here's a thought for you: Look around at all the infrastructure necessary to look at the stars—the roads, the buildings, the computers, the people, the research, the scopes themselves. All of these things and the hundreds of millions of dollars they cost are here for a single purpose: to hold *one tenth of an ounce* of metal in a specific shape. That's how much aluminum coats the giant mirrors that gather all the starlight and where all the information comes from.

Tours of the **Subaru Telescope** are available 15 days a month. You have to reserve a week in advance from their web site. Call 935–6268 for a recorded weather update of Mauna Kea. Except during summit tours, visitors won't be able to visit the inside of any of the telescopes except Keck (see map), which has a visitors' gallery open weekdays 10 a.m. to 4 p.m., as well as restrooms. You'll get a glimpse through the window of the telescope itself there. (As cold as it gets outdoors, it feels even colder in the temperature-controlled rooms housing the telescopes.)

The view from atop Mauna Kea can only be described as majestic moonscape. The Apollo astronauts did considerable training up here because it was deemed uniquely moon-like. Looking down on the clouds *below* is mesmerizing. It's a cliché but true—you feel like you're on top of the world! Off in the distance, the still-active volcano of Mauna Loa seems bigger than life, especially from a place about 2 miles down the road from the summit. Ironically, Mauna Loa's massive size makes it appear smaller than Mauna Kea. *(Huh?!)* Because Mauna Loa rises so gently to its 13,677-foot height, you don't get the sense of size that you would if it were steeper, like Mauna Kea. But that very gentle slope hides a volume of rock far greater than Mauna Kea—10,000 *cubic miles* of stone. From atop Mauna Kea, the islands of Maui, Moloka'i and Kaho'olawe can be seen on clear days. From this area people ski down the mountain to link up with the road below. The actual summit is a quick (5–10 short-of-breath minutes) hike from the University of Hawaii Observatory. (You'll see the trail if you look over the railing.) Sunsets from up here when clouds cooperate are an unrivaled splen-

The only one of its kind—a tropical lake fed by permafrost.

dor of unequaled expansiveness. The summit appears utterly lifeless except for a few unlucky bugs blown up from below and a few flightless native insects that feed on them. No trees, no plants. Just a lifeless void. The mountain last erupted 4,500 years ago and is considered dormant. (If it erupts when you are up there, please disregard this last statement.) Sunset visitors can expect to be rousted 30 minutes after the sun goes down by officials. It's not *you* they hate, it's your headlights that annoy astronomers.

Also located near the top are two oddities. **Lake Wai-au**, at 13,020 feet, is one of the highest lakes in the United States and its existence appears to defy explanation. What could be feeding it? There are no rivers at the top of a mountain, and natural springs need a higher source to gravitationally feed them (like water in a siphon tube). Rain and snow are insufficient, though they do help some, and the lake is here year round. The answer is *permafrost*. During the last Ice Age (and until 13,000 years ago), Mauna Kea was covered by a 20-square-mile glacier that was up to 350 feet thick and extended 3,200 feet below the summit. It carved and scoured the mountain and left permafrost several feet below the surface. Each day, as the sun heats up the mountain, it melts a fraction of the permafrost, which then works its way into Lake Wai-au. Though shallow, the ancient Hawaiians thought the lake was bottomless—probably because they couldn't find anyone crazy enough to venture into it at this frigid altitude. Lake Wai-au can be accessed by a 15–30 minute walk from the road. (See map and turn right when the trail intersects another trail. The upper trail, near

the hairpin turn on Mauna Kea Road at the 7 mile marker, is the easier trail.) Many of the gulches you see on the side of Mauna Kea were created when the glacier melted, sending the snowmelt to scour the sides of the mountain.

The other oddity up here is **Keanakako'i**, an ancient Hawaiian adz quarry. (An adz is a stone cutter used for shaping wood.) When Mauna Kea erupted during the last ice age, the glacier cap cooled the lava very quickly. The result is the densest and hardest rock in all the islands (tougher than spring steel) and was the hardest substance in the state (except for the bread at a Kona restaurant we reviewed recently). What's impressive is that the ancient Hawaiians discovered this site (at 12,400 feet) and were able to successfully mine it for generations, trading it to other islanders for assorted goodies. The only trail to the adz quarry is near Lake Wai-au. Coming back up involves a grueling 800-foot ascent, a genuine 'okole kicker at this altitude.

DRIVING UP TO MAUNA KEA

From Saddle Road it's 14⁷⁄₁₀ miles to the summit. About 2 miles into Mauna Kea Road is a dirt road on your right called **Mana Road**. It leads 44 miles *around* Mauna Kea Mountain all the way to Waimea and passes through tranquil forest. There's rarely anyone on Mana Road, and you need 4WD (or a mountain bike and legs of steel) to take it. The **Onizuka Center for International Astronomy** is 6 miles up Mauna Kea Road at 9,200 feet. Ellison Onizuka was a native of Kona and part of the crew of the Space Shuttle Challenger in 1986 that *"slipped the surly bonds of Earth to touch the face of God."*

The Visitor Information Station has a few displays and small telescopes that

As the snow begins to melt, the summit of Mauna Kea becomes a land of many contrasts.

they break out at night for visitors. They also sell warmies (for those who came in shorts) and brake fluid (for brake-riders coming down the mountain), as well as water and some snacks like freeze-dried ice cream (really weird), sandwiches and instant noodles. Their staff is good. In the past, trying to get information out of them was like interrogating a Klingon POW. These days we find them friendly and helpful. There are restrooms available (the best in this region). About 50 people live up here (tending the 'scopes), and they have to bring in their water several times a week by truck.

While driving up this part of Mauna Kea Road, watch out for mindless, wayward cows occasionally wandering onto the road.

After the Visitor Center the road is unpaved for 5 miles before it becomes paved again for the last 3⁷⁄₁₀ miles. You are allowed access to the top of the mountain in any vehicle. 4WD is what astronomers are *hoping* you're driving because it causes less road wear, but countless regular cars drive it anyway. (We've taken underpowered, fully loaded economy cars up here and had them gasping for air the last couple of thousand feet—

but they'll make it.) 4WD is also nice because the unpaved portion of the somewhat steep road coming down can get a bit slippery at times, especially when wet. 4WD vehicles usually have a gear low enough to obviate this situation. We've found, however, that 4WD vehicles seem to fishtail *going up* more than 2WD cars do. The road is a bit washboardy, and they'll often close it for a short time after a snow until they can plow it. (Finding a good snowplow repairman in Hawai'i must be about as easy as finding a good surfboard shaper in Anchorage, Alaska.)

If you don't want to drive it, several companies will pick you up on the west side and take you to the summit for sunset, then come down a bit for some stargazing and hot chocolate sipping. They'll provide warm coats for you, and the total time is 7½ hours. See STARGAZING on page 223 for more.

Those who *really* want a challenge can opt to hike the trail from the Visitor Center to the top. (See map.) It's 15 miles round trip and a *very* tough day hike, even for the fittest. You need a very early start and should take precautions mentioned in the hiking section. Expect blinding headaches, extreme nausea and bewildered looks from anyone who ever finds out that you did it.

If you drive up, drink *plenty* of water before, during and after, as dehydration is a severe problem at that altitude. Children, pregnant women and those with respiratory problems should avoid the summit. Try to avoid soft drinks and (how do I put this delicately?) foods that produce gas. (You figure it out.) Bring a can of unopened Pringles with you and watch how it explodes when you open it up top. And consider chewing gum on the way down to help with your ears. Don't come up here within 24 hours of a SCUBA dive. As far as your nitrogen is concerned, you're flying. Altitude sickness can strike anyone, causing weakness, dizziness and nausea. Some claim that ibuprofen *before* the trip will help this, similar to the way aspirin is said to forestall hangovers, but we won't swear by it. (Well, we'll swear to the *hangover* part.) Go slow and don't exert yourself too much. Acclimating for a half hour or so at the 9,200-foot visitor center can help.

Then there's the cold. Between November and April, snow is not uncommon. Even summertime brings the occasional freak snowstorm. During the rest of the year, it's often bone-chilling up there. Dress warm. *(Like you packed your parka for your Hawaiian vacation!)* The wind can be exceptionally fierce. It's often warm and calm up there, but you shouldn't *count* on it being this way, especially during sunset. During the winter, you can snow ski short distances. See SNOW SKIING in ACTIVITIES. When it snows, local residents often rush up the mountain to frolic. We've seen people dashing down the hill below the summit on every conceivable mode of transportation: skis, snowboards,

sleds, boogie boards, surfboards, tarps— we've even seen people sliding down in *ocean kayaks,* complete with paddles!

According to King Kalakaua, the Hawaiians had their own version of the Ironman Triathlon. Here, the objective was to climb Mauna Kea during the winter, grab all the snow you could carry, bolt back down the mountain, and run all the way to the ocean. If you had enough snow for a snowball, you won. (If you didn't, you probably grabbed the winner's snowball and stuck it in his pants.) Ironically, this is still done. Only today people bring the snow back in pickup beds and throw a party when they get home. This may be the only place in the world where you can experience snow less than 30 miles from an 85° tropical resort area.

On your way down, a couple of miles below the Visitor Center, you *may* (clouds permitting) see the smoldering Pu'u 'O'o cone at Kilauea Volcano 30 miles to the southeast. Without question, the best views from Mauna Kea are while coming down, not going up.

MAUNA LOA

C Across the saddle from Mauna Kea is the more active Mauna Loa (long mountain). This is the most difficult volcano summit on the island to access. You've got two choices, and both are a *buggah.* (See HIKING.) However, off Saddle Road a quarter mile east of the road up Mauna Kea, there is a narrow, paved road leading 17⁹⁄₁₀ miles up to the **Mauna Loa Weather Observatory**, just above the 11,000-foot level. From there the view across the saddle to Mauna Kea is stunning, especially if there is snow on top. Otherwise, Mauna Loa Observatory Road offers little for you. Created in 1958, the observatory has the longest record of direct measurement of CO_2 in the world, and their findings are universally cited by climatologists to bolster arguments in favor of global warming. Built near the top of a semi-active volcano, it is protected by a first-of-its-kind lava barrier on the upslope side designed to redirect any lava flows long enough to get the scientists out during an eruption.

This part of Mauna Loa is littered with portions of lava tubes. After telephone pole #138 (then after the lava goes from rough a'a to smoother pahoehoe) there are numerous short sections of a discontiguous lava tube going up the hill for over ½ mile. Some are long enough to hike into where you'll get to utter pitch black. Stay on the pahoehoe. Also, you might want to check out the pit crater across the street from telephone pole #200. It's about 50 feet from the road and 50 feet deep where lava drained after overflowing.

APPROACHING HILO

D As you continue on Saddle Road, you'll descend toward Hilo. Look at the foldout back cover map to get an idea of where the lava has flowed during historic times. You'll be periodically passing through fields of it.

You're on the windward side now, and things will start to get greener. One mile after the 7 mile marker (the 6th was missing at press time) you'll have to turn left to stay on Kaumana Drive and Hwy 200; look for the sign. (Otherwise, the bypass—Hwy 2000—will take you to Hwy 11 if you remember to dog-leg to the right at the end of Hwy 2000 onto Puainako—see Hilo map on page 108.) As you approach Hilo, before Hwy 200's 4 mile marker, you'll see **Kaumana Cave** on your left. Created by the Mauna Loa lava flow of 1881

that traveled 25 miles and threatened Hilo, this lava tube skylight is saturated with green. Full-grown trees and ferns have taken over the cave and its entrance. It stands in stark contrast to other caves throughout the island. Elsewhere, a century-old lava tube would be little changed from when it was created. But here, in lush, wet Hilo, geologic time marches at a rapid pace. The cave looks old, worn and rickety. You can take the stairs to the bottom and peer in. Once down there, most people are immediately attracted to the large opening to the right, never even noticing the cave entrance to the left. Remember, this is simply an interruption in a 2-mile long lava tube. If you have a flashlight (make that two—it's so dark you can't tell whether your eyes are open or closed) and sufficient nerve, you can go cave exploring. (Called spelunking—in case that's the only word you forgot in your last crossword puzzle.) The cave to your right has more low overhangs between long stretches of tall ceilings, but the formations are more fascinating. To your left, after an initial low overhang, the cave is more cathedral-like. Tree roots occasionally poke through the ceiling. You could spend hours exploring this lava tube if you wanted.

This flow came within 1½ miles of Hilo Bay. Princess Ruth was sent from Honolulu to save Hilo. She stood in front of the lava flow beseeching Pele to stop the lava. That night she slept next to the advancing flow, and by morning it had stopped. Today several hundred homes are built on the 1881 flow and can easily be recognized by their rock gardens.

Rainbow Falls and Boiling Pots are off Waianuenue Road in this area. See HILO SIGHTS for more on these.

In addition to the popular beaches, lesser known gems such as Kikaua Beach are scattered along the west side of the island.

The Big Island has the reputation of being the island without beaches. That's because in the past, lack of roads and lack of knowledge caused most of its more glorious beaches to go unnoticed. Granted, the island has fewer sand beaches per mile of shoreline than any of the other islands. It's newer, and plentiful beaches are the blessings of older, more mature islands. However, what beaches we *do* have, especially on the west side, are among the very best in the state. The water off the west side of the Big Island is the clearest, cleanest and often calmest water in all the islands. There is not one permanent stream on the entire west side, so cloudy river runoff is not a problem. And the shape of the island, along with the prevailing current, often gives the west side relatively gentle water. Rough seas usually come from the northeast. Kona and Kohala's calmer waters can be dramatically seen from the air. During normal conditions, the inbound flier will notice that the transition from coarse, choppy channel waters to fine textured leeward waters is almost instantaneous, just south of the northernmost tip of the island. (By the way, flying a small airplane through that wind transition is utterly *nasty*.)

On the Big Island we have white sand, black sand, salt-and-pepper sand and even green sand beaches. As for beach quality, Hapuna Beach is consistently named the best beach *in the entire country* by travel magazines. Mauna Kea Beach is not far behind. Kahalu'u and Honaunau offer outrageous snorkeling. And secluded gems like Makalawena and Road to the Sea, along with unusual delights such as Kiholo Bay, Kapoho Tide-pools, and Green Sand Beach probably make beach-going on the Big Island the best in the state.

BEACH SAFETY

The biggest danger you will face at the beach is the surf. Though it is calmer on the west side of the Big Island, that's a relative term. Most mainlanders are unprepared for the strength of Hawai'i's surf. We're out in the middle of the biggest ocean in the world, and the surf has lots of room to build up. We have our calm days where the water is like glass. We often have days where the surf is moderate, calling for respect and diligence on the part of the swimmer. And we have the high surf days, perfect for sitting on the beach with a picnic or a mai-tai, watching the experienced and the audacious tempt the

Tell me a lawyer didn't write this beach sign!

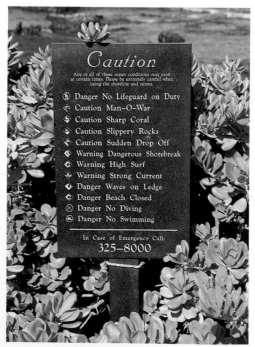

ocean's patience. Don't make the mistake of underestimating the ocean's power here. Hawai'i is the undisputed drowning capital of the United States, and we don't want you to join the statistics.

Other hazards include rip currents, which can form, cease and form again with no warning. Large "rogue waves" can come ashore with no warning. These usually occur when two or more waves fuse at sea, becoming a larger wave. Even calm seas are no guarantee of safety. Many people have been caught unaware by large waves during ostensibly "calm seas." We swam and snorkeled most of the beaches described in this book on at least two occasions (usually more than two). But beaches change. The underwater topography changes throughout the year. (White Sands Beach is a dramatic example.) Storms can take a very safe beach and rearrange the sand, turning it into a dangerous beach. Napo'opo'o Beach vanished after a storm in 1992 and never came back. Just because we describe a beach as being in a certain condition does not mean it will be in that same condition when you visit it.

Consequently, you should take the beach descriptions as a snapshot in calm times. If seas aren't calm, you probably shouldn't go in the water. If you observe a rip current, you probably shouldn't go in the water. If you aren't a comfortable swimmer, you should probably never go in the water, except at those beaches that have lifeguards. There is no way we can tell you that a certain beach will be swimmable on a certain day, and we claim no such prescience. There is no substitution for your own observations and judgment.

A few standard safety tips: Never turn your back on the ocean. Never swim alone. Never swim in the mouth of a river. Never swim in murky water. Never swim when the seas are not calm. Don't walk

Waters on the west side of the Big Island tend to be calmer than the rest of the state. But watch for nature's subtle signals that perhaps you should stay out of the water.

too close to the shorebreak; a large wave can come and knock you over and pull you in. Observe ocean conditions carefully. Don't let small children play in the water unsupervised. Fins give you far more power and speed and are a good safety device in addition to being more fun. If you're comfortable in a mask and snorkel, they provide considerable peace of mind, as well as opening up the underwater world. Lastly, don't let Hawai'i's idyllic environment cloud your judgment. Recognize the ocean for what it is—a powerful force that needs to be respected.

If you're going to spend any time at the shoreline or beach, water shoes are the best investment you'll ever make. These water-friendly wonders accompany us whenever we go to any beach. Walmart or Kmart in Kona sell cheap ones, perfect for your short duration usage. Even on sandy beaches, rocks or sea life seem magnetically attracted to the bottom of feet. With water shoes, you can frolic without the worry. (Though don't expect them to protect you from everything. Some beaches are backed by kiawe trees, and their thorns could probably penetrate an armored car.)

The ocean here rarely smells fishy since the difference between high and low tide is so small. (In other words, it doesn't

strand large amounts of smelly sea plants at low tide like other locations.)

Theft can be a problem when visiting beaches. Visitors like to lock their cars at all beaches, but piles of glass on the ground usually dissuade island residents from doing that at secluded beaches. We usually remove anything we can't bear to have stolen and leave the car with the windows rolled up but unlocked. That way, we're less likely to get our windows broken by a curious thief, though leaving it unlocked *may* leave your insurance company off the hook. Regardless, don't leave anything of value in your car. (Well... maybe the seats can stay.) While in the water, we use a waterproof box or bag for our wallet, phone and keys, and leave everything else on the beach. We don't take a camera to the beach unless we are willing to stay there on the sand and babysit it. This way, when we swim, snorkel or just walk, we don't have to constantly watch our things.

Consider a disposable underwater camera. Even if you don't go in the water, they will withstand the elements. Their quality is better than most people think. And waterproof digital cameras are getting pretty cheap as well.

Use sunscreen early and often. Don't pay any attention to the claims from sunscreen makers that their product is waterproof, rubproof, sand blast proof, powerwash proof, etc. Reapply it every couple of hours and after you get out of the ocean. The ocean water will hide sunburn symptoms until after you're toast. Then you can look forward to agony for the rest of your trip. (And yes, you *can* get burned while in the water.) Gel-based sunscreens work best in the water. Lotions work best on land.

People tend to get fatigued while walking in sand. The trick to making it easier is to walk with a very gentle, relaxed stride while lightly striking the sand almost flat-footed.

The Hawai'i Supreme Court ruled in 2006 that all beaches are public to "the upper reaches of the wash of the waves...at high tide during the season of the year in which the highest wash of the waves occurs." This means that if the ocean can touch it, you can be there. The trick, sometimes, can be access. You might have to cross private land to get to a public beach. We've pointed out a legal way to every beach on the island, and some of the maps have access routes in yellow to show you the way.

In general, surf is higher and stronger during the winter, calmer in the summer, but there are exceptions during all seasons. When we mention that a beach has facilities, it usually includes restrooms, showers, picnic tables and drinking water.

Lastly, remember that just because *you* may be on vacation doesn't mean that residents are. Consequently, beaches are more crowded on weekends.

To get **ocean safety information**, visit: www.hawaiibeachsafety.com or call 327-3570 on the west side of the island and 961-8689 on the east side.

Beaches that are *supposed* to have **lifeguards** are highlighted with this ❶ symbol. Those that had year-round lifeguards at press time were:

West—Hapuna, Kahalu'u, White Sands
Puna—Ahalanui (north of Isaac Hale), Isaac Hale
Hilo—Honoli'i, Richardson's

Those with lifeguards on weekends and holidays:
West—Spencer
Hilo—Onekahakaha, Carlsmith

Those with lifeguards on weekdays only:
South—Punalu'u

We'll start our descriptions at the end of the road at the top of the island and work our way counter-clockwise. The first few beaches have marginal swimming.

KOHALA BEACHES

❖ Pololu Beach
Located at the end of Highway 270 on the northern end of the island, this beach is very pretty. High surf and currents usually make this a poor swimming or snorkeling beach. Access is via a 15–20 minute trail from the Pololu Valley Overlook 400 feet up. No facilities.

❖ Keokea Beach Park
Although the swimming is usually poor, the exception is a small cove created by a manmade boulder breakwater. It was constructed as a community project by locals with the help from some heavy equipment donated by a long-gone sugar company. Not worth driving to unless you're in the neighborhood. Access road near the 27 mile marker on Highway 270 in North Kohala. Full facilities.

❖ Kapanai'a Bay
Tell anyone outside North Kohala that there is a beach below Kapa'au, and they'll look at you like you're crazy. Kapanai'a Bay is one of the best-kept secrets in North Kohala. This small pebble-and-sand beach is backed by trees and was carved out of the cliffs by a small brook.

Even during moderate surf, you may see keiki boogie boarding in the back part of the bay. Surfers venture farther out where the waves are completely unobstructed. While there's not much sand and the water is a bit murky, the bay is very picturesque and a wonderful place for a picnic. The catch is that the access road requires a 4WD vehicle and the nerve to punish it. See map on page 46.

❖ Kapa'a Beach Park

No sand at this beach, just rocks and a little coral rubble. The attractive assets here are the exceptionally clear water for snorkeling and SCUBA, usually abundant fish (sometimes large pelagic fish), coupled with somewhat protected waters *except* during periods of high surf (which can bring rips and surges). Be careful of surge here. Clear water makes it a good place to take underwater fish pictures. Not much coral but plenty of sea life. Rarely visited during the week, but easy to access just north of the 16 mile marker on Highway 270. Facilities include possibly dilapidated

restrooms, as well as a BBQ and picnic tables. Excellent view of Maui and a nice place to watch the sunset. Bees and wasps are sometimes a problem here.

❖ Mahukona Beach Park

When the seas are calm, it's *really* calm here. Not a beach, but an old abandoned sugar company harbor, Mahukona boasts crystal clear water and ridiculously easy access for snorkeling or swimming. You can practically drive up, open your door and fall in. (But use the ladder at the entrance to the right, OK?) The underwater relief is interesting. There's usually a large variety of fish, as well as abandoned sugar equipment (giant chains, wheels, etc.) and sparse remains of an old shipwreck. Swimming north along the shoreline brings more coral and more fish. If the surf's up, don't go. When it's calm, check for surginess. During the week you *may*

Normally placid, Spencer Beach Park is a popular place for families with keiki (kids).

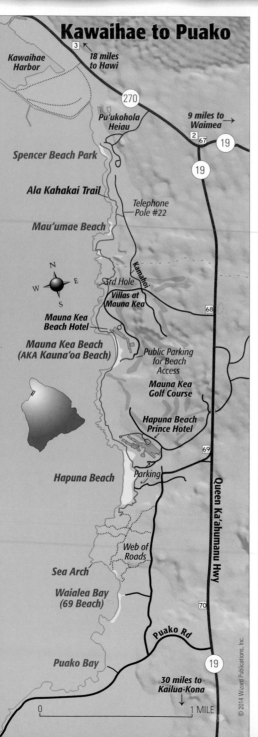

Kawaihae to Puako

Kawaihae Harbor

3

18 miles to Hawi

270

Pu'ukohola Heiau

9 miles to Waimea

2 67 19

Spencer Beach Park

19

Ala Kahakai Trail

Telephone Pole #22

Mau'umae Beach

N W E S

Kamahoi

3rd Hole

Villas at Mauna Kea

68

Mauna Kea Beach Hotel

Mauna Kea Beach (AKA Kauna'oa Beach)

Public Parking for Beach Access

Mauna Kea Golf Course

Hapuna Beach Prince Hotel

69

Hapuna Beach

Parking

Queen Ka'ahumanu Hwy

Web of Roads

Sea Arch

Waialea Bay (69 Beach)

70

Puako Rd

Puako Bay

19

30 miles to Kailua-Kona

0   1 MILE

© 2014 Wizard Publications, Inc.

have it all to yourself. Facilities, except drinking water. (Don't drink the shower water!) The dirt road from the other side of the harbor (to the left of the old, giant former sugar building) heading north leads to the navigational heiau shown on page 14. See map on page 46. Afternoon sometimes brings annoying flies that might drive you bonkers.

❖ Lapakahi

We feel kind of funny putting this in the beaches section. Located in Lapakahi State Historical Park near the 14 mile marker on Highway 270, this is a reserve and there is no real beach here. (See page 51.) But the *snorkeling* is exceptional. The water is clean and clear in **Koai'e Cove** between site 11 and site 7 near the coconut grove. Not much coral but usually *lots* of fish. Stay inside the cove; the waters get unfriendly outside of its protection. Speaking of unfriendly, don't expect to be overwhelmed with aloha from park personnel. They seem to resent snorkelers here. And don't bring towels or chairs, or you'll get stink eye.

❖ Kaiholena (Sapphire) Cove

There's an unpaved road between the 11 and 12 mile markers that leads to a parking area, which is an easy 750-foot walk to a beautiful cove that has inviting waters, lots of fish and sometimes fairly easy entry. The area itself is hot, harsh and prone to a particularly annoying small fly, especially in the mid to late summer, that may not leave you alone on the land. But the waters here are incredible. Stay in the cove as it gets rougher and more exposed outside. Morning is best, but even afternoons can bring great snorkeling memories.

➕ Spencer Beach Park

A great family beach. Located just south of Kawaihae Harbor, the beach is protected by a long offshore reef and the extensive landfill of the harbor to the north. The beach slope is very gentle, and the swimming is usually quite good. Keiki (kids) enjoy the usually calm waters of Spencer. Though the water is a bit cloudy due to its proximity to the harbor, this shouldn't deter you from enjoying the ocean here. If you snorkel, you will probably see miniature underwater volcanoes from small amounts of cold freshwater seeping from the floor. The amenities include several showers, restrooms, a pavilion, lifeguard, picnic tables, barbeques, a lawn area, lots of shade and basketball/volleyball courts. Camping is permitted by county permit (see CAMPING). As you approach the park from the access road between the 2 and 3 mile marker on Hwy 270, you can go to the right or left side of the park. Whether by design or not, the right (northern) side seems to be used mostly by locals and the left side by visitors. Expect this park to be a little messier than other, more pristine beaches.

Just north of here is a small beach in front of the Pu'ukohola Heiau called **Pelekane Beach**. No swimming or sunbathing is allowed there out of deference to the sacred heiau complex.

The **Ala Kahakai Trail** between **Spencer** and **Hapuna Beach** hugs the shoreline. It crosses hole #3 on the golf course but otherwise is easy to follow and passes some pretty shoreline.

❖ Mau'umae Beach

Pretty, secluded, uncrowded during the week and decent swimming when calm. Nice place for a picnic, and you may have it to yourself during the week. Snorkeling is only fair due to slightly cloudy water. Access is through the Mauna Kea Resort entrance, right on Kamahoi, park at pole #22. 10-car maximum is rarely a problem (see map). Less than 5-minute trail walk from your car. No facilities. Usually pronounced Mow-

MY. This is one of the most underrated and unknown beaches in this part of the island. Winter usually thins out the sand a bit. Sometimes frequented by nudists.

❖ Mauna Kea Beach (AKA Kauna'oa Beach)

A REAL GEM

This is a great beach! Probably the most classically perfect beach on the island. This gorgeous crescent of sand over ¼-mile long offers *very fine swimming* and boogie boarding during calm seas. On the left side of the beach is a bunch of rocks, creating a linear reef that offers outstanding snorkeling. Don't venture too far out unless calm (the outer portion of this reef is more surgy and unpredictable). The northern (right) side of the beach also offers interesting snorkeling but is more exposed and should only be snorkeled by strong swimmers. There is a big light there that attracts plankton at night, which in turn sometimes attracts large manta rays. Try to resist the urge to swim over to them in the shallow water near the light; it just scares the buggas away. This beach and Hapuna are the two best frolicking beaches on the island, if not the state. Mauna Kea is usually less windy than Hapuna. Full facilities. Only 40 cars allowed in the Mauna Kea Resort parking lot at a time, which is usually a problem, so try to arrive before 10 a.m. or take the 1-mile shoreline trail from the north end of Hapuna Beach. Located 32 miles north of Kona in the Kohala resort area off the 68 mile marker. See map on page 152.

➕ Hapuna Beach

A REAL GEM

If you close your eyes and picture a perfect beach, there's a good chance you'll see Hapuna in your mind's eye. Half a mile long and 200 feet wide

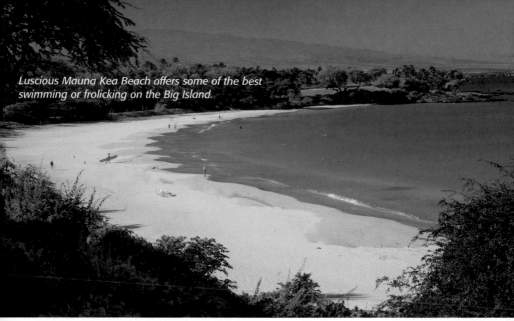

Luscious Mauna Kea Beach offers some of the best swimming or frolicking on the Big Island.

during the summer, beautiful Hapuna is the ultimate frolicking beach. You know how frenzied dogs can get when they go to the beach? That's how most people act when they come to Hapuna or Mauna Kea Beach. It's a beach to savor. Fine golden sand slopes gradually into the ocean. Clean, clear water and excellent swimming conditions during calm seas, full facilities, easy access and gorgeous scenery. The **boogie boarding** here, when the surf's not too high, is exceptional. These are some of the elements that account for the fact that *Condé Nast Traveler* magazine has often voted this beach the best in the entire nation. During the week it usually isn't too crowded, but weekends and holidays bring lots of locals who know a great beach when they see one. Most people who live here bring their guests to Hapuna at least once to gloat. The north lifeguard tower is near the sign saying that there's no lifeguard on duty. Swimming is not safe during periods of high surf, which will kick the living daylights out of you. Also note that the wind sometimes kicks up in the afternoon. We've noticed that the southernmost (left) part of the beach is usually more protected during strong winds, but the north end

is usually less crowded. The only shade *on* the beach is a tree at the southern end. (Though there are shaded pavilions behind the beach.)

For more advanced snorkelers on calm days, the area directly south of the sand beach offers superb snorkeling, and it's usually empty during the week because no one knows about it. The waters are usually teeming with fish, and coral is abundant. The sea is unprotected here, so don't go in if it isn't calm, or you'll get beaten up. Check for currents. If it starts to get rough, get out. We often start at the southern end of the beach and snorkel along the rocky coastline all the way to a little black gravel cove half a mile down the coast near a sea arch. Then we walk back along the shore in our water shoes via a poor trail or use the dirt road (don't do it bare-footed). Be careful of the wicked kiawe thorns—they can penetrate nearly any shoe and probably most bullet-proof vests. If you have some energy left, keep snorkeling past the little gravel cove to Waialea (69) Beach. The area just past the cove is absolutely heavenly. The north end of the beach can also be awesome.

Hapuna is located 30 miles north of Kailua-Kona in the northern part of the

Kohala mega-resort area near the 69 mile marker off Highway 19. The restrooms by the parking lot usually look like they're from the third world. Use the ones behind the north lifeguard station. An unimpressive concessionaire near the parking lot has food and beach supplies. Parking is $5.

❖ Waialea (Beach 69)

A REAL GEM *Sigh!* Just another kickin' Kohala beach. This beach slopes gently into the water, giving it nice swimming conditions most of the year when the sea is calm. Not as long or as well known as Hapuna or Mauna Kea, this beach is popular with *akamai* (savvy) residents who sometimes bring their families for a day at the beach on weekends. To the north (right) of the main beach is a secluded little cove, which people sometimes claim for the day, sometimes sans clothing. The snorkeling around the northern part of the beach can be excellent. There's a sea arch at the northern tip, but refrain from walking on it; it looks like it's getting ready to go. Located 30 miles north of Kona near the Kohala resort area off Puako Road. (See map on page 152.) The short road is near telephone pole #71 (it used to be pole #69—hence the name). Facilities include toilets and showers. High surf occasionally strip mines the beach of its sand, which can take months to naturally replenish itself. Parking is $5. Open 7 a.m. to 7:30 p.m.

❖ Puako

Great snorkeling and SCUBA (see page 218 for directions to best spots, and photo of the reef), but the swimming is marginal and entry can be tough at low tide. The reef at Puako is *very* extensive. The somewhat cloudy water on entry usually gives way to very clear water at the reef's edge. You stand an excellent chance of sharing the water with multiple turtles. (Oh, yeah, what's a multiple turtle?) The tops of the reefs are not the most interesting part (and can subject you to the prospect of being raked over them). The best fish and scenic action are at the outer edges of the reef. Check for currents and give the ocean respect. People occasionally bring their dogs to this beach (which end up chasing the catfish, no doubt). Wind often creates chop on the water here, but that doesn't usually affect the underwater experience much. There are nine legal public accesses along the bay from the boat launch. Some may be *conveniently* unmarked. A check of the county tax map and a site check shows us that they are by telephone poles #101, 106, 110/111, 115, 120, 123, 127/128, 131/132 & 137, plus the dirt road at 143.

❖ Mauna Lani

The Mauna Lani Bay Hotel and the Fairmont Orchid both have small, manmade (or enhanced) beaches, such as Pauoa Bay, which has lots of fish. The Mauna Lani Bay Hotel beach to the south is usually *very* protected. Access is via the public parking lot shown on the map on page 53. You'll have to walk for about 15 minutes, but the trip through the fishpond area is worth it.

❖ Honoka'ope Beach

This small salt-and-pepper beach is located between the Hilton Waikoloa and the Mauna Lani. Go south from the Mauna Lani roundabout and turn left on Honoka'ope Place. Open 8 a.m. to 5 p.m.; the lot holds 20 cars. It's a 2-minute walk from your vehicle. Like other beaches in this area, it can get windy in the afternoon. If you're seeking a hike, the ancient Ala Kahakai shoreline lava trail takes 30–60 minutes to reach the beach. (See map on page 53.) This trail segment, which starts near the Mauna Lani fish-ponds and ends here, goes through some fabulous lava cliff scenery. When surf's up, waves explode onto the twisted, gnarled lava fragments in the ocean. Facilities.

At the beach the swimming and snorkeling are fair if it's calm, ugly if it's rough. (Visibility is often poor here.) If the surf's right (not too big, not too small), you can float face down with a mask and snorkel at the surf's edge. As the waves rake you back and forth, listen as the black pebbles mixed with the sand make a great sound as they, too, are raked back and forth.

❖ 'Anaeho'omalu Bay

A REAL GEM

Another nice Kohala beach. (Even those born and raised here usually call this 6-syllable tongue-twister *A Bay*.) This long, curving salt-and-pepper sand beach is popular with both locals and visitors. The swimming is best in the sandy center, whereas the snorkeling (though not great) is best on the right side past the sandy area. The water is not as clear as what you'll find at other nearby beaches, but it's so tranquil here, you won't care. Protected by an offshore reef, this bay is usually safe except during very high surf. Windsurfing is popular here. Say *meow* to the wild cats that live near the restrooms.

'Anaeho'omalu is well known throughout the islands for its two large fishponds. These exceptionally picturesque and placid pools were used by ancient Hawaiians for raising mullet. Hawaiian royalty were the beneficiaries of these ponds—commoners weren't allowed to partake. The ponds are ringed by palm trees, making sunset photos from behind the trees a sure-fire winner.

There's a pleasant paved path on the mauka side of the fishpond that's worth a stroll. Numerous signs along the way give information about the fishponds and the area in general. Toward the center of the path are the remains of an ancient dwelling, probably a combination of sleep-

While not as flashy as some of the other beaches in the area, Honoka'ope Beach is a good place to listen to what's going on under the water.

ing and eating quarters as well as a shrine. The pond itself contains brackish water; fresh water flows from a natural spring and mixes with ocean tide water. The ancient Hawaiians covered the opening to the fishpond with a grate, which allowed small fry to enter from the ocean. Once inside, they gorged themselves on algae and small shrimp and became too fat to get back through the grate, at which time they were sitting ducks (so to speak) for the Hawaiian pond keepers.

On the right (northern) side of the beach is a hut that rents snorkel gear, kayaks, boogie boards, windsurfers, etc. (at confiscatory rates). They also have guided snorkel and SCUBA tours. If you're hungry, the restaurant at the Waikoloa Beach Marriott behind the beach has pricey but available burgers and hot dogs.

There's a marvelous shoreline trail north between the two Waikoloa hotels that leads through sand, lava and large amounts of brilliant white coral rubble. All along the trail you'll find various tidepools tucked against the shoreline. Turtles tend to hang out at one particular tide pool just a few feet from shore. At the north end of this trail is the Hilton Waikoloa. What a way to see this place for the first time! A sunset stroll along this path is unforgettable. Footwear is a must. There is an alternative place to park along this stretch—see map on page 53.

A few minutes walk south of A Bay on a narrow ribbon of sand leads to **Kapalaoa Beach**, a series of sand pockets. There is shade and a pleasant cove for snorkeling at the last pocket. If the surf's not high, the cove is amazingly protected. The short walk to this beach goes by numerous Hawaiian petroglyphs, some ancient and some modern. The more ambitious will want to take the lava trail farther south for about half an hour until you reach a lone palm tree in the lava, less than a hundred feet from the shore.

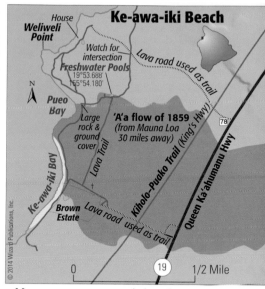

Here, you are rewarded with an outstanding spring-fed brackish pool with lots of charm. It is very deep in spots and is great for dipping after a hike. You will rarely see anybody else here as it is only accessible by foot, and it's a favorite stopping place of ours. The lava trails in this area offer good hiking, but they can get a bit hot in the middle of the day. The trail leads mostly along the shoreline for miles, all the way to Ke-awa-iki below.

To get here from the Hwy, take Waikoloa Beach Road, turn left before the Marriott and park in the lot before the end of the road.

❖ Ke-awa-iki Beach

This black sand-and-gravel-lined bay is never crowded due to the access—to get there you have to walk on a lava road half the time, and a rougher 'a'a trail to the right of the fence the other half. Few on the island even know it's there. (It takes about 15 minutes to walk to it.) The water off the left (south) is clear and offers good snorkeling when calm, but be wary of currents. There's also some shade there (and sometimes a swing from one of the trees).

The best snorkeling is usually in the center of the bay. If you keep walking past the southern edge of the bay, there are lots of tide-pools to explore on an older, smooth pahoehoe lava shelf at low tide. (This is a good place to be wearing water shoes.) Past that are numerous salt deposits from evaporated seawater. These deposits attract goats from the dry scrub inland who warily come and lick the salt off the rocks. Past the right (northern) side of Ke-awa-iki Bay is **Pueo Bay**, lined with black pebbles and semi-protected with nice swimming on calm days. There are off-shore freshwater springs here, causing areas of perturbations in the water, visible as waves of underwater distortion. You will almost certainly have this bay to yourself. No shade here because it's backed by an 'a'a field. If you feel like an extended stroll, you can walk past Weliweli Point and take a lava road inland to circle back to the highway. Mauka of Pueo Bay are some beautiful golden pools, described under HIKING on page 201.

Both of these beaches were created in 1859 when 'a'a from Mauna Loa drooled down the mountain and exploded when it hit the ocean, creating black sand. The eruption only covered half the bay and some white sand is still sprinkled at the southern end because there hasn't been enough time to evenly distribute the newer black sand. The entire area has a desolate but pretty character to it and is one of the least known beaches on the west side of the island. The only pockmark is the Brown Estate lining the center part of the beach with its barbed wire fence and its unwelcome feeling. Francis I'i Brown was an influential and beloved Hawaiian businessman in the early 1900s, and in turning his estate into a historical landmark, they seem to have taken away all its charm. They have tours of it for a few hours on the third Tuesday of every month. (Gee, *that's* convenient!)

Located 20 miles north of Kailua-Kona just after the 79 mile marker.

❖ Kiholo Bay

A REAL GEM

More of a region than a beach, and there are a few surprises. Access to much of it requires a little hiking. See HIKING on page 199. It's certainly worth it.

NEAR KONA BEACHES

❖ Ka'upulehu Beach
Most of this long sand beach is fronted by a lava bench, making the swimming poor, but there is a pocket of sand in front of the Kona Village that allows easier access to the water as well as two protected coves (man-made) in front of the Four Seasons. You can access this beach from either of these two resorts. From the Four Seasons it's only 1/10-mile walk, but there are only 10 Beach Access stalls lumped in with employee parking, and the stalls tend to be filled with cars that *don't* look like rentals. From Kona Village there are plenty of stalls, but it's a 1/2-mile walk from your car to the beach. (Not "1 mile" as we've been told from the guard shack.)

❖ Kuki'o Beach
Near the Four Seasons Resort between Kona and the Kohala Resort area, this is yet another pretty Kohala beach. This long, fringing crescent of white sand is backed in parts by palm, ironwood and kiawe trees offering inviting shade. At the southern end of the bay is a small but very protected sandy cove. The swimming in the bay itself is only fair during calm seas, and the snorkeling offers somewhat murky water. **Turtles** commonly beach themselves here. There is public access from the resort area (see map on next page). While Kuki'o Bay might sound like a pretty name, in

Hawaiian it means to *stand and defecate* (traditional definition) or *settled dregs* (modern definition). You probably won't be seeing *that* on the back of a postcard. The reason behind the *lovely* name has been lost to the generations, but it's probably safe to say that whoever named it was having a bad hair day.

❖ Kikaua Beach

A REAL GEM

One of the things that makes the Big Island so different is its ever-changing nature. Active volcanoes sometimes create new beaches overnight. But in this case, we have modern man—developers, no less—to thank for this one. Kikaua Point was once an isolated area with a pretty, but rocky, cove defining it. A few years ago a private golf and beach club was built behind this point, and it seems obvious that a lot of sand was been transported to this cove, whether by man or by nature we can't say. But the result is a dreamy, softly padded sandy bottom and a protected cove that offers easy swimming and wading most of the time. The 27 parking spaces fill up on weekends, but weekdays are usually not bad. To get there, take the Kuki'o Nui Road just south of the 87 mile marker. Although this is private property, just tell the nice guards at the gate that you're exercising your beach access rights. It's a 5-minute walk from your car. Full facilities.

❖ Manini'owali/Kua Bay

A REAL GEM

This is one of our favorite beaches. (Most on the island know it as **Kua Bay**, but the state has been pushing Manini'owali Beach as its name.) Off the beaten path, beautiful fine white sand, clear, clean water, gentle slope and a picturesque setting. When the ocean is calm, the swimming is fabulous. The snorkeling off to the right (north) is interesting

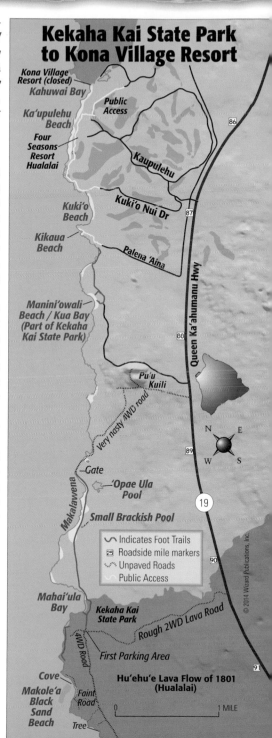

Kekaha Kai State Park to Kona Village Resort

Kona Village Resort (closed)
Kahuwai Bay
Ka'upulehu Beach
Four Seasons Resort Hualalai
Public Access
Kaupulehu
86
Kuki'o Beach
Kuki'o Nui Dr
87
Kikaua Beach
Palena 'Aina
Manini'owali Beach / Kua Bay (Part of Kekaha Kai State Park)
80
Queen Ka'ahumanu Hwy
Pu'u Kuili
Very nasty 4WD road
N E W S
89
—Gate
'Opae Ula Pool
Makalawena
Small Brackish Pool
19

⌇ Indicates Foot Trails
25 Roadside mile markers
⋰ Unpaved Roads
⌇ Public Access

90

Mahai'ula Bay
Kekaha Kai State Park
Rough 2WD Lava Road
4WD Road
First Parking Area
21
Cove
Makole'a Black Sand Beach
Faint Road
Hu'ehu'e Lava Flow of 1801 (Hualalai)
0   1 MILE
Tree

© 2014 Wizard Publications, Inc.

The clean, clear waters of Manini'owali/Kua Bay.

not for its coral, but for the underwater relief. **Boogie boarding** is excellent during moderate surf, but the waves can be strong and deserve respect. There is sand here most of the time, but it is most abundant during the summer months. During the winter, high surf sometimes shifts the sand offshore for a time, leaving the area rocky and undesirable. Many residents consider this one of the best swimming beaches near Kona when calm, and on weekends they sometimes make their presence known. Crowds are less common during the week. From Hwy 19 take the paved access road between the 88 and 89 mile markers. Open 9 a.m. to 7 p.m. Note that the waves here have a lot of power, so if the surf's up, don't go in. No shade *at the beach*, but restrooms and barely-shaded picnic tables are available behind it.

❖ **Makalawena**

A REAL GEM To many, this is the choicest beach on the island…if you don't mind walking to it. In fact, Makalawena is as idyllic a beach as you will find anywhere in the islands. Gobs of superfine, clean white sand, plentiful shade and no crowds. The setting is utterly beautiful. Consisting of a number of coves and rocky points united by a long, curving stretch of beach, the best swimming is in the largest inlet backed by high sand dunes. **Boogie boarding** can be great here. There's a freshwater pond (see map on previous page). A herd of wild goats visits this area often, so keep an eye out for them.

Backed by private (Bishop Estate) land, you get there over the trail from the red houses behind Mahai'ula Beach (about a 20-minute walk). It's a lava trail through an 'a'a field, and the footing is fairly annoying. Watch for bees en route. As you walk this trail, try to imagine how ridiculously difficult it would be to walk through the field itself without the trail. Then imagine doing it *barefoot,* as the ancient Hawaiians did. As you approach Makalawena from the Kekaha Kai side, the 'a'a trail suddenly gives way to sand dunes. But if you climb the dunes to the left, rather than finding ocean, you find more 'a'a, indicating that this had been shoreline until a lava flow of 'a'a came along and added more real estate, cutting off the dunes from the sea.

If you have a 4WD (and your fillings are tight), you can take the nasty and intimidating road from the highway between the 88 and 89 mile marker. Locals do in their stock pick-ups and JEEPs all the time without even blinking, but readers constantly write to us saying it's impassable in their rental JEEPs. It'll take you just north of the beach before a gate forces you to walk like the rest of us dogs. By the way, because it's so isolated, people sometimes travel light to this beach, omitting such extraneous things as their bathing suits. (Yeah, *that* must be the reason.)

❖ Kekaha Kai State Park;
Also Mahai'ula/Ka'elehuluhulu

A REAL GEM

This beach is outside of Kona town and pretty. It's usually not too crowded. **Mahai'ula Beach** (which you access after a 5-minute walk to the north from the first parking area) offers good swimming and interesting strolling. Just around the southern corner is a pocket of sand called **Ka'elehuluhulu Beach** (park at the second parking area at end of the lava road), not as good as the northern beach. The entire area was once owned by a prominent part-Hawaiian family called the Magoons. They sold the land to a Japanese investor who had visions of a resort. When the state refused permis-

sion, the investor sold it to the state, which turned it into a park. The abandoned Magoon house is still located at the northern end of Mahai'ula Beach. This area abounds with freshwater springs that bubble to the surface, occasionally forming ponds. At the farthest northern part of the beach near some palm trees and a rock wall, you may see strange indentations in the sand at low tide. Here, freshwater gurgles right out of the sand and into the ocean. The snorkeling is only fair because the water can be a bit cloudy, especially during spring, and wild goats are common here. This is a good beach to get away from it all, yet still have fairly easy access. There's plenty of shade at the backshore. Access is via a bumpy, but *usually* driveable, semi-paved 1½-mile road halfway between the 90 and 91 mile markers on Queen Ka'ahumanu Highway north of Kailua-Kona. The only negative is the occasional plane overhead as it lands at Kona Airport. Facilities include picnic tables and toilets. Bring your own

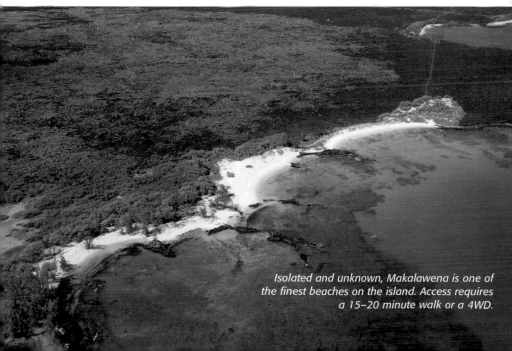

Isolated and unknown, Makalawena is one of the finest beaches on the island. Access requires a 15–20 minute walk or a 4WD.

water. The gate to the beach is open 9 a.m. Look at the signs to see what time they close it. Note that the closing of the gate is one thing state workers are *guaranteed* to do promptly.

Legend states that before 1801 there was a 3-mile-long fishpond here. That year an old lady came to the village and asked for fish. The village overseer refused, saying that it *all* belonged to the chief. On her way out she was stopped by one villager who gave her food. After eating, she told the kind stranger to place kapu (forbidden) sticks outside his house. That night lava from Hualalai roared down the mountain to the village, destroying the great fishpond but sparing the man who fed her. The villagers realized that the old woman was the volcano goddess Pele, avenging the selfishness of the chief.

Check out some of the lava on the road leading to this beach (you'll certainly be driving slowly enough). There are lots of interesting formations where different flows meet. It has patches of gold/rust colored lava, streaks of blue, red and other colors indicating the presence of numerous elements and gases present during cooling.

❖ Makole'a Beach

A REAL GEM

Ask a hundred residents of Kona about a black sand beach just north of town named Makole'a Beach, and you'll get a hundred blank stares. Aside from a handful of shoreline fishermen, few seemed to have known about this beach—until we stumbled upon it for a previous edition. Created during the 1801 lava flow of Hualalai, this small pocket of jet black sand is the only black sand beach on this part of the island.

To get there you have two options. After driving to Kekaha Kai State Park (see page 161), those with 4WD can take a left at the first parking lot and drive the lava road heading south. Look at the sign to see what time they close and lock the gate and *believe* in their promptness. Just under $7/10$ mile is a faint car path marked by some coral that leads 1,100 feet over lava to the sea. (Though driveable, you can walk this last part if the lava there dis-

Did you spring for 4WD? If so, Makole'a Black Sand Beach near Kona is all yours today.

The quiet tide-pools of Wawaloli Beach at the Natural Energy Lab are an excellent place to go when the surf's pounding.

suades you.) The other way is to park at the beach at Kekaha Kai State Park and walk along the shoreline for 15–20 minutes. At one point the sandy trail is interrupted. Best to walk on the smooth pahoehoe lava behind the beach boulders for this part. Just before the black sand beach is a small cove protected at low- to mid-tide during calm seas. It's a perfect place to take a quick dip. The snorkeling and SCUBA diving are great at the black sand beach. Though the visibility is only fair (it's better when you get away from the beach), there is a beautiful field of coral to the north (right) of the beach and to the south farther out. Enter at the sandy part in the center, and beware of unchecked waves. If you walked here, consider cutting across the lava field on your return for different scenery.

This beach, while certainly not on par with Mauna Kea or Kua Bay, deserves the GEM rating because it's the *only real black sand beach* anywhere near Kona, it's not overly difficult to access, and you are likely to have it all to yourself on weekdays. (Some fishermen use it on weekends and sometimes leave their beer bottles.) It's that rare treat—an undiscovered black sand beach.

❖ Wawaloli Beach

A REAL GEM

This is our favorite tide-pool area on the west side of the island (shown above). The instantly accessible sand beach is cut off from the ocean by a large tide-pool that offers warm swimming when the surf is too high elsewhere. There are restrooms and showers here, making it popular with local families who bring their keiki (kids) to play in the mostly protected area. The largest pool (mostly sand-lined) is best near high tide most of the year, only best at low tide if the surf's cranking. The other, less protected tide-pool is better at low tide. A water channel in the lava closer to the restrooms can be fun to wander in. In late afternoon you might want to pick up a pizza on your way out, bring the kids, if you have 'em, and watch the sunset. Take the road to the Natural Energy Lab (near the 94 mile marker on the main highway north of Kailua-Kona), and park just as it veers to the right along the shoreline. Some equipment to the south is an eyesore, but try to ignore it, and airplanes sometimes shatter the quiet.

Near here is a 4WD road that leads a mile south to **Pine Trees** (Hawaiian name

Kohanaiki), one of the island's premier surf spots. It's so named because of the mangrove in a brackish pool. Surfer dudes thought they were pine trees. The road is fairly poor and might be gated off. If so, you can access Pine Trees from the paved road south of the 95 mile marker of Hwy 19.

❖ Kaloko-Honokohau

Honokohau is an area rich in archaeological treasures. This part of the coast was inhabited for centuries and is filled with relics. Consequently, it was made a national park in 1978 in an effort to preserve what remains (entrance is free). At first it might seem surprising that people thrived here. Barren and rocky with particularly harsh 'a'a fields in many areas, the draw here was the freshwater springs. The Hawaiians took advantage of the water to create large fishponds to raise mullet and other fish.

Located just south of the airport (see map on this page), you can access the park between 8:30 a.m. and 4 p.m. from a parking lot near the 97 mile marker on Hwy 19 just north of Kailua-Kona or a

Kaloko-Honokohau

Kaloko Fishpond
2WD OK
Kaloko-Honokohau
Nat'l Hist. Park
Entire area rich in
Hawaiian ruins.
N
Old Mamalahoa Trail
Queen Ka'ahumanu Hwy
96
Hina-Lani
Olowalu
Kaloko Industrial Park
Kauhola
Kanalani
Kamanu
Maiau
Costco
(Cheapest gas in town if you're a Costco member.)
97
Queen's Bath
Rock Mounds
'Aimakapa Fishpond
Honokohau Bay
'A'opio Beach
Small Boat Harbor
(where most charters leave)
'Alula Beach
Arch
Holua
(Ancient Hawaiian Slide)
Visitor Center
(Parking)
Parking
19
Kealakehe
Parking
Two Miles to
Kailua-Kona
© 2014 Wizard Publications, Inc.

gravel road between the 96 and 97 mile markers that leads to **Kaloko Fishpond**. You can also access the park from **Honokohau Harbor**, off the paved road between the 97 and 98 mile markers. From the harbor, a brief walk north will take you to **'Ai'opio Beach**. There are scads of turtles munching on grasses in the cloudy cove water. This was an ocean fish trap in ancient days, where fish entered at high tide and were easily captured. A protected area here is perfect for keiki (kids). An impressive heiau called Hale o Mono rests at the south end. Park at the north end of the harbor (past the restaurant) and take the trail for a minute or two. Turn toward the ocean before you reach the restrooms. This is a nice beach for relaxing. Farther north is **Honokohau Beach**. You may read elsewhere that this is a nude beach, but it is no longer permitted and they cite violators. This long stretch of salt-and-pepper sand offers reasonable swimming at the center. One nearby highlight is known as **Queen's Bath**. (Even locals get confused by Queen's Bath. There are several of these scattered throughout the islands. Essentially, any place that was considered an outstanding place to bathe was called Queen's Bath.) This 15-by-20 foot natural lava pool of brackish water was lovingly enhanced by the Hawaiians to make it a fine place to congregate and splash in relatively fresh (and very cool) water. They lined the pool, located in the middle of a harsh 'a'a field, with smoother stones, built areas to sit, and generally made it a pleasant place to visit. These days, it is only sporadically visited by hikers and beach-goers from the nearby beach. To get there from Honokohau Beach, walk north along the beach. At 200 yards past the *end* of the beach you'll come to a rock wall. Look mauka (toward the mountain), and you will see numerous large piles of rocks. These are also ancient in origin—the largest is 10 feet high and 15 feet thick—and are part of 12 rock piles placed in a rectangle around the Queen's Bath, possibly used for lookouts. The trail to them from the south end of the wall is along the dividing line between the lava and yellow clumps of grass. Go toward, then between, the two largest mounds. The pool is about 100 feet north of the largest mound near the only large green shrub in the area. Enjoy!

At the south end of the Honokohau Harbor is **'Alula Beach**, a small, pleasant crescent of sand, which is fairly protected during calm seas—a good sunning beach. A short walk south of here leads to a large, impressive sea arch.

❖ Old Kona Airport Beach Park

A REAL GEM

This beach park is located at (do we *really* need to say it?) the Old Kona Airport, closed in 1970 because it was unable to accommodate larger aircraft. You park anywhere on the runway (you may taxi as long as you like) and enjoy the patchy beach and full facilities. On the south end are ball fields where Little League parents battle for supremacy. The long beach is an easy one to access, and the sunsets from here are nice. Though you won't be overwhelmed by an abundance of thick sand, it's rarely crowded *during the week.*

The far end of the runway has a small cove with good snorkeling. Fish counts here can be incredible. Located ½ mile west is the finer **Papawai** or **Pawai Bay**. The **snorkeling** on the way to Papawai Bay is very exciting, especially for the experienced snorkeler. There's a little of everything with crystal clear water, lots of life, caverns, sea arches, drop-offs, small caves and some pinnacles along the shoreline. Here you may see the elusive and extraordinary frog fish (an angler fish) on the coral and Spanish

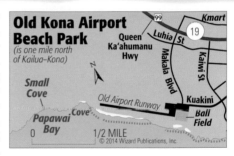

dancers (a contorting nudibranch). During tricky surge, novices should stay away from the more interesting shore. (See ADVENTURES on page 231.) The shady backshore of Papawai Bay has plush camping facilities that are private and belong to the Queen Lili'uokalani Trust, used for Hawaiian children.

❖ Kailua Bay

Located in the heart of downtown Kailua-Kona. (See map on page 61.) Usually areas around piers have nasty water. This one is surprisingly clean due to the daily flushing action of the sea. There are a surprising number of fish in Kailua Bay. We've seen super-schools numbering in the many thousands off Hulihe'e Palace. On calm days we like to snorkel from the pier to the sand pocket across from Kona Islander Inn or the boulder beach across from Lulu's. If you are looking for *exceptionally* calm water and a sandy beach, the very small **Kamakahonu Beach** to the right of the Kailua Pier (in front of the King Kamehameha Hotel) is perhaps the gentlest and safest water on the island (with the *possible* exception of your hotel bathtub). Children love frolicking in the water here, though freshwater springs sometimes make it cold. This is where King Kamehameha chose to spend the last years of his extraordinary life, so you gotta figure it has something going for it. His personal 'Ahu'ena Heiau is right in front of you. The sand at the beach

Good reef protected by a boulder breakwater have made Kahalu'u the most popular snorkel site in Kona.

doesn't extend very far into the water, but it is shallow the whole way. If you swim out from the beach, you'll notice a private ocean entrance to the right. It leads to a house owned by billionaire Paul Allen, the less famous co-founder of Microsoft. He bought this gloriously located house in the 1990s for $11 million. (Don't worry, it was probably a mere rounding error in his checkbook.) That was 10 years before the land boom-turned-bust. A recently discovered map hints that this might be the location of Kamehameha's tomb, but if so, it was probably destroyed when the shoreline was rearranged in the 1950s.

There is a concessionaire at Kamakahonu renting various beach accouterments at the usual confiscatory prices—but it's convenient. Large schools of fish sometimes congregate on the other side of the heiau. It's about 300 yards from the public parking lot to the beach, so you may want to drop off your stuff (and a person) at the pier first.

To the left (south) of the pier is another pocket of sand, sometimes called **Dig Me Beach**. (They sometimes do SCUBA intros there.) It's a bit less protected but still relatively calm. Boogie boarders like to ride the normally small but long lasting swells. The grueling Ironman Triathlon (see page 60) starts here. They swim 2⁴⁄₁₀ miles before starting their 112-mile bike ride and 26-mile marathon run—*all in the same day!* (Makes you sore just thinking about it, huh?) If it's rained recently, snorkelers should look for little calderas of what looks like boiling sand, like mini volcanoes. They're caused by small amounts of cold freshwater bubbling to the surface.

South of the Royal Kona Resort is a small sand pocket called **Honl's** that has good boogie boarding if you have fins.

❖ Pahoehoe Beach Park

Though there's little sand here to speak of, this is a nice place to have a picnic and enjoy the surf and sunset from the benches. We've never seen it crowded. Backed by pretty trees and a lawn, there is a small gravel entrance to the water, but swimmers are discouraged from entering unless equipped with snorkeling gear. Even then, advanced snorkelers only need apply. That's because there are numerous holes, arches and pockets on the lava shelf offshore, making exploration very exciting. But surf can sometimes rake you over and even under the reef, making it *too* exciting. Lots of fish here, as well. Located north of the 4 mile mark on Alii Drive in Kailua (just north of White Sands Beach).

➊ La'aloa Bay Beach Park

Also known as **White Sands**, **Magic Sands** and **Disappearing Sands**. Located just north of the 4 mile mark on Alii Drive in Kailua, this small beach has particularly nomadic sand that retreats at the first sign of a surf assault, settling in a repository just offshore. Once the surf subsides, the sand slowly drifts back onto the shoreline until the next high surf. This occasional flushing of the sand tends to keep it clean and white. Those who live here can tell you of countless instances where the entire beach washes away in less than a day. Much of the time there is a shallow sandbar just offshore, making the swimming and boogie boarding quite good. (The best wave break is on the left [south] side of the beach.) Watch for undertow and some rocks at the end of the ride. When the sand's thick, the frolicking is good. (But water shoes are recommended in case you step on a rock.) When there's no sand or it's in the process of disappearing (i.e., when the surf's high), there is a strong rip current, making water activities hazardous. This small beach tends to be pretty crowded. Lifeguard and facilities are here along with some shade trees. On calm days, the snorkeler will want to check out the area to the right (north), in front of Kona Magic Sands condominiums. Especially large schools of fish sometimes hang out there. We've also seen more moray eels here than at any other place on the island. *(If an eel bites your hand, and you bleed in the sand… that's a'moray.)*

Just south of here right at the **4 mile mark** is a **small cove** where the SCUBA diving is excellent, offering short, easy access and good underwater relief and caves. The snorkeling is not bad either. Just offshore from this location we often see a pod of dolphins patrolling the waters. Why they hang out there, we don't know, but whatever the reason, keep an eye out for them.

➊ Kahalu'u Beach Park

A REAL GEM

This is one of the nicer snorkeling spots on the Big Island. It is teeming with fish and offers more variety of sea life than any other easily accessible spot in Kona. Among the many fish present are wrasses, parrotfish, convict tang, porcupinefish, needlefish and puffers, as well as the occasional lobster, eel, and octopus. Outside the reef you may occasionally see deep sea life, such as tuna, marlin and dolphin jumping about. When you first enter the water you might think, "What's all the hubbub about?" Well…it's about 100 feet offshore. The perimeter of this small, sheltered bay has numerous freshwater springs, making the near-shore water cold and cloudy. But once you swim out toward the middle, it gets warmer and clearer, and life is abundant. One reason is the Menehune breakwater offshore. Built in ancient times, it has been partially disassembled by countless waves, creating an excellent fish environment. There's usually a truck at the beach where you can rent snorkel gear. Almost across the street is the Kona Surf School that will rent snorkel gear "only if the surf business is too slow." They also have boogie boards (but the boogie boarding here is not good—just surfing), and you can usually take surfing lessons at the beach. There is a full range of facilities. There's also a lunch truck with hot dogs, ice cream and bad shave ice. A family of turtles calls Kahalu'u home, and they usually won't dart away from you if you don't harass them. (We've noticed that near high tide, they often work the grasses that are otherwise exposed on the left/southern side of the bay.) Your odds of swimming with turtles are probably greater here than anywhere else on the island, with the possible exception of remote Punalu'u Beach. The best way to keep a turtle from fleeing is to act disinterested—like you don't give a flying fish. (*Ooo*, sorry.) If you scope him out, he'll run off. If you pretend to eat the same grasses he eats, you aren't

a threat. The more intrepid might venture around the breakwater on very calm days where life is also abundant. Exceptionally large mixed schools of fish sometimes congregate just outside the reef, but you expose yourself to the possibility of being strained through the reef—better stay inside unless it is real calm or you are real confident.

Crowds accumulate at Kahalu'u, but it's *usually* less crowded than White Sands Beach. During periods of high surf, large waves can wash over the reef and form a rip current flowing out the reef opening at the north end of the bay, making it unsafe.

Though this has traditionally been a popular place to feed fish, conservationists are making a concerted effort to end the practice here. See SNORKEL-ING for more.

To the left is a **tide-pool**. The water there is sometimes as warm as bathwater as it gets heated by the sun, a natural black-bottom pool. Cruise around in the shallows and look for eels, which like to be fed by people at the railings of the hotel.

Eight hundred feet to the left (south) of Kahalu'u is **Makole'a Beach**. (Not to be confused with the beach described on page 162 with the same name.) There are several heiau along this beach that are under restoration. The salt-and-pepper sand and gravel beach is usually empty and has a lonely, forgotten feel. The swimming is poor since you are facing large tide-pools. Look for the gory petroglyphs mentioned on page 65.

❖ Napo'opo'o Beach

Well, it *used* to be a beach. It disappeared when Hurricane 'Iniki sideswiped the island *way* back in 1992, and the surf wiped the beach clean, depositing boulders there. You'll find little more than a small patch of sand. This beach will prob-

Kahalu'u Beach Park

Excellent surf break ↗

N

Alii Drive

Menehune Breakwater

Strong rip current when surf's high

Best snorkeling is in this area

Kahalu'u Beach Park   5   Makolea
Parking

Between low & high tide on calm days, **Tide-pool Area** → is excellent for the timid snorkeler. Do not walk on the fragile coral.

0   1000 Feet

Petroglyphs ⊙ Ke'eku Heiau
(at low tide)

© 2014 Wizard Publications, Inc.

ably never return to its former glory—part of the ever-changing nature of the Big Island. Across the bay is the Captain Cook Monument, described on page 69. Slightly south is **Manini Beach** (shown on map on page 66). Coral rubble sprinkled with 'a'a lava, and poor swimming make this another must-miss beach.

❖ Ke'ei Beach

Between Kealakekua and Honaunau (see map on page 66), this pretty but small stretch of sand is backed by numerous coconut trees. Though picturesque, poor swimming and difficult parking mean that it is used almost solely by the small, adjacent community. This area seems to have been a magnet for historical events. Local legend (bolstered by old Spanish records) states that foreigners washed ashore here during the 1520s. Several big battles took place nearby, including the one where Kamehameha became king. (See page 71.)

❖ Pu'uhonua o Honaunau

A REAL GEM

This is a popular place to visit for reasons other than its water. It was the Place of Refuge in ancient times. See detailed description on page 72. For ocean lovers, the snorkeling and SCUBA just north of the boat launch (at a place commonly called **Two Step** because of its easy entry) are incredible, perhaps as good as the more difficult to-reach Captain Cook Monument at Kealakekua Bay, making it some of the best in the state when conditions are good, though it's deeper. It's outside the park so you don't have to pay. There are also picnic tables near the shoreline at the southern half of the park that make for absolutely splendid sunset picnics. We've made good use of the BBQs there and can recommend them highly. No showers.

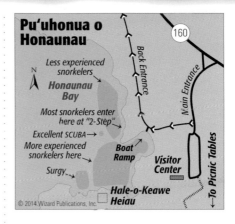

Pu'uhonua o Honaunau

Less experienced snorkelers

N

Honaunau Bay

Most snorkelers enter here at "2-Step".

Excellent SCUBA→

More experienced snorkelers here

Surgy

Back Entrance

Main Entrance

160

Boat Ramp

Visitor Center

To Picnic Tables

Hale-o-Keawe Heiau

© 2014 Wizard Publications, Inc.

SOUTH ISLAND BEACHES

❖ Ho'okena Beach Park

South of Kona between the 101 and 102 mile markers is a paved road leading 2³⁄₁₀ miles to Ho'okena Beach Park. Unlike other beach parks, the local community gathered together and petitioned the county to turn park operations over to them, and they have transformed this into a _(usually)_ family-friendly gathering place for locals and visitors alike. You can tent camp (328–7321) for $20 per person per night, rent kayaks, snorkel gear or boogie boards, purchase food and the facilities include showers, restrooms, picnic tables and shade. This pocket of fine salt-and-pepper sand is hot on your feet. Keiki (kids) ride the waves on calm days and splash about in a few tide-pools adjacent to the sandy beach. Decent snorkeling is to the left. Dolphins often enter the bay. If you walk 250 yards along the shoreline to the north, you'll come to a small inlet, the size of a swimming pool, that is _sometimes_ protected from the stronger ocean. Keep walking north to the end of the houses, and you find one of the nicest sea arches on this whole coastline. Make sure you stay at the shoreline. Walking on the other side of the houses might bring unwanted attention from neighborhood dogs.

❖ Pebble Beach

Located down a *very* steep road. (You lose 1,050 feet of elevation in 6,000 feet of driving—that's almost as steep as the notorious road into Waipi'o Valley.) It's at the bottom of Kona Paradise (off Hwy 11 between the 96 and 97 mile markers 20 miles south of Kona) and is one of the most violent beaches we know of. Even when calm, it will kick your 'okole. We've seen fish tossed out of the water on calm days. *(Seriously!)* The "beach" is actually countless large water-worn pebbles, which make a great sound when the surf's up. If you've got the nerve, it's fun to let the surge pull you up and down the steep beach (but stay away from the shore break).

A 5-minute walk to your right leads to a small cove with smaller pebbles and black and green sand beneath them. Not good swimming but secluded and private. Unlike the Pebble Beach rumble, this one fizzes like a glass of soda.

❖ Miloli'i Beach Park

Located 30 miles south of Kailua-Kona, this is considered a very local beach, meaning that *on weekends* it's best to leave it to them. There is a very tight local community here, and, though Hawai'i is as friendly a place as you will find, you may get a little stink eye if you visit during "their time"— like crashing someone's family barbeque. This community beach sports a pavilion used by local bands playing outstanding Hawaiian music on weekends and holidays. There's not much sand, but the surfing is good, and the facilities are well-developed. (The sand was removed by a storm in the 1970s. The same storm also removed many houses. Some homeowners made the mistake of bulldozing their crumpled houses and were not allowed to rebuild. Shrewd owners knew that to stay that close to the water, they were required to keep and repair the *original* structure.)

Take the winding, one-lane paved road just south of the 89 mile marker. Drive slowly at the end of the road, and watch for local kids.

❖ Honomalino Bay

Ask most people who live here where Honomalino is, and they'll probably tell you it's on Maui. This beach is a moving target. Formerly a lovely black-and-white sand beach 150 yards or so long, backed by scads of coconut trees, decent swimming when calm (which is often), and it's usually deserted. It's a 20-minute walk from your car. But the Japanese tsunami of 2011 badly damaged this bay, killing trees and vegetation and generally roughing it up, washing away our GEM rating in the process. Our photo was taken *pre-tsunami* because hopefully it will look like this again. It's recovering, but hard to say how long it will take. Also, though one of the larger *south* Kona beaches, it eroded considerably during the 20th century (as black sand beaches naturally tend to do— see explanation on page 174) and will probably be mostly a memory a hundred years or so from now.

To get there, start at Miloli'i Beach Park (see previous beach). Go to the end of the road, and you'll see bathrooms and a yellow church. The public access is between them. (A left fork is private property; the right fork is yours.) If tide is up, you may get your feet wet. About 3–4 minutes into the trail after some tide-pools and a palm-backed spit of sand, follow the fenceline on your left up and over the black rock at the back of the beach and continue south for 15 minutes. There may be a few fallen trees to hop over. The snorkeling on the right side of the bay in the cluster of rocks is interesting when calm. There is a small cave there where a 6-foot white-tipped reef shark often rests. Don't worry, he's not a man eater—yet. (One has been there a long time, so maybe it's his family estate.) If you plunge your hand into the sand at the water's edge at the south end of the beach, the sand's cold. That's freshwater (called a basal spring) percolating into the sand from below.

One of Honomalino's little-known joys is the pod of **dolphins** that sometimes cruises the sand-lined bay in the morning. Scientists think that, while resting, dolphins are able to turn off half their brain (including the half that runs their echolocation abilities). They do a sort of snooze and cruise, counting on the fact that the shallow water and light bottom will alert them to predators in the absence of their sonars. This means that, in the morning, dolphins are literally operating on half a brain. (Come to think of it, so am I before my coffee.)

❖ Road to the Sea

A REAL GEM

This is one of Ka'u district's best-kept secrets. In BASICS we mentioned that having a 4WD can come in handy. Here's a perfect example why. First, if you don't have a 4WD, you won't make it. Even some SUVs might have issues, depending on the level of cruelty you normally inflict on rental cars. We've had some readers scold us, calling the road impassable. Others blast all the way through without difficulty. The access road is ⅔ mile past (south of) the 80 mile marker on Hwy 11. The first of two beaches is at the end of this 6-mile long dirt road. Remember, you're far from Kona. If you get stuck, the first thing the tow truck driver will ask is, "Do you own your own home?" County maps show this as a *public* access, though we've seen handmade KEEP OUT signs in years past.

Anyway, these two beautiful black-and-green sand beaches are nearly always deserted, especially during the week. The first beach is at the end of the road. Swimming *during calm seas* is fair, and the beach is inviting; enter it from the left (south) side. Harmless plankton-eating whale sharks are

Honomalino Beach on a crowded day.

Sure, you can 4WD right up to the second Road to the Sea beach. But only if you're willing to beat your vehicle like a rented mule (as the driver above apparently did). Best to walk the last mile.

sometimes seen in the area. To the right of the end of the road is a *deep* tide-pool—7 to 9 feet in spots. It makes a *great* wading pool, and there's even some coral in it—unusual for a tide-pool.

The second beach is reached via a 1-mile long *rough* 4WD road ⅓ mile back up from the *very* end of the road. Don't take the first Fool's Road to the left (which only leads to sorrow). Take the one with the yellow gate. If you find it too rough for your driving tastes (which you probably will), walk the mile to the second beach. It's worth it. The road leads to a much longer and finer black-and-green sand beach. (See Green Sand Beach below for an explanation of green sand.) At the end to the right is a freshwater pool. This one is saltier than most, but is great for dipping. There is some shade at the back part of the beach. Stay close to shore; the water can get tricky farther out.

This is a great beach to get away from it all, and you *may* have it all to yourself except during times it gets claimed for weeks at a time by…campers.

The entire area out here is lifeless, arid and desolate. It was utterly assaulted by savage lava flows 250 years ago and on paper isn't worth a hill of beans. Yet despite this (or perhaps because of it), it is alluring. The lava field looks young and raw, and the beaches are desirable. If you have 4WD, it is a recommended trip. Located 40 miles south of Kona; see map.

By the way, shade is provided courtesy of the way winds wrap around Mauna Loa. Almost every day during normal tradewinds between 10 a.m. and 11 a.m., a shearline cloud forms about 5,000 feet above the beach, creating shade for the rest of the day.

❖ Green Sand (Papalokea) Beach

A REAL GEM

(Literally!)

So you say you've seen white sand beaches. You've seen plenty of golden sand beaches. Maybe you've even seen a black sand beach. But when is the last time you frolicked on a *green* sand beach? This unusual beach owes its name and color to a large deposit of a semi-precious gem called olivine liberally mixed with black sand. After ancient volcanic eruptions created Pu'u o Mahana, a small littoral cone containing gobs of the stuff, the ocean went to work dismantling it. It has already broken through one side, and when the surf is up, each wave rakes at the back side, revealing more and more olivine. Though most of the gemstones are in the form of sand particles, people occasionally find large nuggets. (Actually, your best chance of finding a nugget is at the rarely visited adjacent cove on the far side of Green Sand Beach. Access is from the far [northeast] side). See map of South Point on page 79.

Located near South Point, which (this will stun you) is at the southernmost point on the island, access to the beach requires a 2¼-mile (each way) walk or 4WD from Kaulana Boat Launch. (The four-wheeling is sometimes pretty rough, depending on road conditions during your visit.) There are more dirt roads than we showed on the map because people are constantly creating new ones. They all go to the beach and beyond. You'd have to try real hard to get lost since you always stay within sight of the shore. Drivers will want to take the high road (near the fenceline) whereas walkers will want to stay closer to the shore, where you might find cool pockets of stranded white and green sand before reaching the actual Green Sand Beach. Keep an eye out for the remains of several Hawaiian structures dotting the area. During extended dry times the government often prohibits 4WD vehicles in the name of fire safety, though local residents seem to ignore the prohibition and will often charge a fee to drive you out. Hey, beats walking it.

Once at the cone, most people take a "path" on the closest (southwest) side (see map), which requires a short hop off a rock at one point. Unfortunately, the path is more evident from the beach than from the top and might be tough to spot. Others walk down a path from about the middle of the cone, which can be slippery due to sand particles on the hard surface. A helpful ladder in one section was there during our last visit. Don't try to walk from the highest part of the cone; it's treacherous. Use your best judgment. Everyone from small keiki to the elderly goes to the beach, but you are on your own in evaluating it. Check to see that the waves are not inundating the entire beach before you go down. The ocean is unprotected, so the waves are at full strength. Many books tell you that you will drown if you even *think* about swimming there. We swam there plenty of times, and if the surf's not up, it's not bad. The sand bottom is thick and there are few exposed rocks. We have yet to encounter nasty currents *in the bay,* but we're not stupid enough to venture out of the bay where the prevailing current will give you a splendid tour of Antarctica. Again, use your best judgment. There is a shorebreak, and the undertow can be harsh. You might see plenty of local kids (or us) playing in the surf, but this is not Waikiki. And if the surf is high, definitely stay out. Those same large waves that expose the

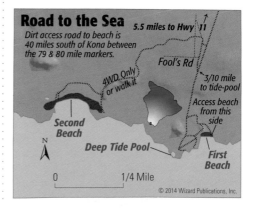

Road to the Sea   5.5 miles to Hwy 11

Dirt access road to beach is 40 miles south of Kona between the 79 & 80 mile markers.

Fool's Rd

4WD Only or walk it

3/10 mile to tide-pool

Access beach from this side

Second Beach

N

Deep Tide Pool

First Beach

0   1/4 Mile

© 2014 Wizard Publications, Inc.

olivine could pull you in. There's no shade here, and the wind, which has beautifully sculpted the eastern side of the bay, is also the same wind that might get on your nerves if it is blowing hard, particularly in the late afternoon. Go earlier if you can. No facilities. Please resist the urge to take any of the sand with you. We've seen people taking large amounts, and the supply is finite.

The spooky snorkeling at **South Point** itself is described on page 81.

❖ Whittington Park

Located off the road between the 61 and 62 mile marker on the southern part of the island. Very pretty from a distance. Formerly run down, but they've spiffed it up recently. Think of it as a pit stop with restrooms and picnic tables.

➊ Punalu'u Black Sand Beach

A REAL GEM

This is the most easily accessible black sand beach on the island (now that Kaimu Beach is under 75 feet of lava). Backed by palm trees and a freshwater pond, the sand is *genuine* black sand—the kind created when a chunky 'a'a lava flow meets the ocean and shatters into small pieces on contact with the water. These small chunks are quickly pulverized by the ocean, forming a delicious black sand. This differs from older black sand beaches where the sand is made up of lava chipped from a river bed by coursing water. Genuine black sand beaches are relatively fleeting since the source of the sand ends as soon as the lava flow stops. This contrasts with white and golden sand beaches, which have organic sources (coral or shells) that continue to build up sand over time. (In fact, one large, coral-munching parrotfish can produce three *tons* of white sand per year by himself!) That's why you don't see genuine black sand on old islands—the black sand erodes into the ocean over time and cannot be recovered.

The swimming is a bit different here than at many other island beaches. Cold freshwater springs bubble up from just offshore. Consequently, the top 8–12 inches of the water is guaranteed to freeze your 'okole off. You can usually see the floating freshwater while swimming and will be tempted to swim below to get a semblance of warmth. The visibility here is only fair, and you need to be conscious of rip currents. Generally, you want to stay fairly close to shore and be aware of currents during all but the calmest seas. Past the boat launch on the left (north) side of the beach, the rips can be a problem.

So why swim here at all? Well, one of this beach's lesser-known treats is its **turtles**. The waters can get almost crowded with them. We've been here when you could see small groups of turtles every couple of minutes. They munch on limu that clings to rocks on the sea floor. Please remember not to disturb or play with them. In addition to the possible harm, it might cause them to find a less accessible beach to frolic.

Near the southern tip of the island between the 56 and 55 mile markers on Hwy 11. The facilities at the south end parking lot get heavy use from the local community as well as tour buses. The less-used north lot is more convenient.

EAST SIDE BEACHES

Past Punalu'u your choices for beaches diminish along with their caliber. Put simply, the east shore, which is exposed to more hazardous surf and lots of river runoff, has fewer and mostly poorer beaches. Therefore, we are breaking them up into regions and deviating from our previous rules by describing many in the tours of the various regions.

❖ Puna Beaches

Located near the extreme eastern part of the island, **Kehena Black Sand Beach, ✛ Isaac Hale Beach Park, ✛ Ahalanui Warm Springs**, and **Kapoho Tide-pools** are described in HILO & PUNA SIGHTS because you won't encounter them unless you are touring that area anyway.

❖ Hilo Beach Parks

To the east on Kalanianaole (where highways 11 and 19 meet) are Hilo's most popular beach parks starting with **Keaukaha**. During summer months it's a tent and tarp city with long-term campers. The rest of the year it's simply a great park to avoid. **✛ Onekahakaha Beach Park** has a boulder-enclosed pool that is popular with local keiki (kids). The sand-lined pool is utterly protected except during very high seas. The pool to the left is rockier and has lots of urchins on the floor. Past Onekahakaha is **(James) Kealoha Beach Park**. Though picturesque, the swimming is poor, and you're likely to share it with young toughs drinking too much and giving you stink eye. Best to move on to **✛ Carlsmith Beach Park** just across the bay. There are full facilities and a nice lawn area. The swimming is marginal around the lifeguard tower. Go to the far right side where the water is more protected, and keep an eye out for turtles. Instead of the parking lot, if you drive past the Mauna Loa Shores condo to an unmarked lot, you can access the park from a short but *very* cool jungle trail. (Bring bug spray for it.) Farther east is **Wai'olena and Wai'uli Beach Parks**. This last area contains **✛ Richardson's Ocean Center** at the far end and is particularly attractive with freshwater pools sprinkled about. The county Aquatics Division is located here. This is an excellent place for a picnic, though sometimes the (James) Kealoha crowd spills over to here. There's a small black sand cove where you can enter the water. It'll be cold from freshwater intruding into the area. Some of Hilo's better snorkeling is here. Dolphins often frequent the area, and turtles usually congregate a little farther down the coast toward Hilo. Check with lifeguards because this area is subject to strong surf.

Other beach parks north of Hilo are **✛ Honoli'i, Kolekole Beach, Hakalau Bay, Waikaumalo Park**, and **Laupahoehoe Point**. Farther north is the difficult to access but beautiful black sand beach of **Waipi'o Bay**. All are described in the HAMAKUA & WAIMEA SIGHTS chapter.

| Kua Bay White Sand | Green Sand Beach | New Black Sand Beach | White Powder Sand from Florida |

The Big Island is a snorkeler's paradise. This is at the Captain Cook Monument in Kealakekua Bay.

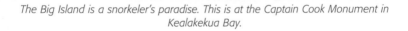

Take a deep breath and do some stretching before you read this chapter, because the Big Island has so much to see and do that you're likely to pull something just reading about it all. Among the more popular activities are fishing, golfing, snorkeling, SCUBA, hiking, horseback riding, kayaking, helicopter tours, boat trips, submarine rides and whale watching. Whatever you're into—even snow skiing!—you're likely to find it here on the Big Island.

Activities can be booked directly with the individual activity providers or through activity companies. *Sometimes* you can get better deals through activity companies or online. Many resorts have activity directors and booths, sometimes run by the activity providers themselves, so be aware that their "recommendations" are sometimes biased. Many of the booths spread around the island are actually forums for selling timeshares. That's not a dig at timeshares; it's just that you need to know the real purpose of some of these booths. They can be very aggressive. (Don't get skewered by one of the long metal hooks.) Free breakfasts and "island orientations" are often similar to activity booths. So if you are steered to XYZ helicopter company and assured that they are the best, that's fine, but consider the source. We walk up to these booths frequently. Some are reputable and honest, and some are outrageous. We have no stake in *any* company we recommend; we just want to steer you in the best direction we can.

And speaking of our smartphone app (OK, we weren't speaking of it—this is just our clumsy way of talking about it here), we've GPSed all the companies in this and every other section. Not necessarily their home office (which Google might take you to) but the actual location where you are expected to meet them, as well as all of our trails, all the roads, etc. You can even see where you are on our maps at all times. Can't do that in a book or eBook. But our *Big Island Revealed* smartphone app does just that, even when you're out of cell phone range. It does a bunch of other cool stuff, too.

These are those 4-wheeled things that look like Tonka Toys on steroids with knobby tires. They are often used by ranchers these days to chase cows, and they're quite a bit of fun to ride. **ATV Outfitters** (889–6000) is our favorite. They'll take you around private land near the northern tip of the island on ATVs. For $129 you cruise along for 1½ hours, taking in the coastal scenery. They'll provide beverages and long pants (if you left them at home) for a fee. The ATVs are easy to operate with automatic transmissions. (Riding wimps will do fine on these.) You need to weigh between 90–300 pounds. They also have a 2-hour waterfall ride for $179 that's even more fun. It goes from coastline up to the 2,500-foot level. Lastly is their 22-mile, 3-hour deluxe tour for $249. All in all, these trips are lots of fun, and the coastal scenery they show you is great. If you have two people on one ATV, ask for the side-by-side model, unless you want to ride super slow or are interested in bouncing your spouse off the ATV.

Also available but less interesting is **Kahua Ranch** (882–4646) that has 1½-hour tours for $150.

Ride the Rim (775–1450) is a great and incredibly misleading name for an ATV company. The impression left by their brochure is that you'll be cruising along the rim of beautiful Waipi'o Valley. I guess it's easier to market than **Buy the Farm**, which is what you're *really* doing—buying a dirt road tour of a eucalyptus tree farm with only *two* views of Waipi'o Valley, if the clouds are cooperating, and one small, pretty falls and pool. Nearly all of the 15-mile circuit is among the skinny trees as you scoot along at 16–18 MPH for about two hours. Nice folks and all, but there are *way* better things you can do with your $179 per person.

On a ranch mauka of the highway near Kona there's **Kona Eco Adventures** (889–5111). The terrain is not very interesting, and the single file trip is on a conservation road with a 15 MPH speed limit, so you certainly won't be cutting loose. It's cooler at this higher elevation and this is a working ranch. Less than 2 hours long for $145.

With a moniker like the Big Island, you would expect an endless variety of biking choices. Sure enough, many of the highways, such as Queen K where they run the Ironman, have nice bike lanes so you can cruise long distances. But be prepared for strong crosswinds in Kohala. If it's **mountain biking** that you prefer, and you are willing to transport a mountain bike somewhere, these three rides can be fun:

South Point—See map on page 79 and the description of the area. You can ride from South Point past Green Sand Beach on the 4WD roads—lots of fun.

The wind is usually with you coming back. This is wide-open country with good mountain bike roads.

Volcano—There's a dirt "escape" road that leads through beautiful rain forest from Thurston Lava Tube to Chain of Craters Road and the Mauna Ulu Trailhead. (See maps on pages 92 and 197.) The 4-mile road is well maintained and very scenic, with green assaulting your eyes from both directions. Return on the escape road, or take Chain of Craters road back up (right) 1½ miles, then take Hilina Pali Road (before Chain of Crater's 3 mile marker) as far down as you want to go before returning.

Mana Road—This road leads through Parker Ranch in Waimea and winds around Mauna Kea to near Saddle Road. It starts near the 55 mile marker on the main highway in Waimea. See maps on pages 124 and 135, as well as back foldout map to get an idea of the route. It's a 44-mile dirt road to Mauna Kea Road near Saddle Road. Unless you are motivated and arrange for transportation from Saddle Road, you'll probably just want to take it as far as you like, then turn around and come back. The first 18 miles are relatively easy and pass through *fairly* flat, sometimes foggy, quiet plains of grass and cows. Past 18 miles, it gets hillier and bumpier and enters a beautiful forest reserve. Be sure to close any gates you pass (all 4 of them) that are already closed. Cleverly worded or placed signs sometimes *imply* that you may not traverse the road. Actually, it's a public right of way. At 10⁴⁄₁₀ miles is a fork—take the right one.

A boogie boarder rides his first...and last wave of the day.

Kona and Hilo—If you are staying in Kona and want to ride on the street, cruise down Alii Drive along the coast. If you're staying in Hilo, Stainback Highway (described on page 111) is a great road to sail down on a mountain bike. You could then take North Kulani to Hwy 11 where the shoulders coming back to Hilo are usually wide.

Guided Tours

Several companies offer a variety of guided tours. **Velissimo Cycling Destinations** (327–0087) has tours for $125–$145, plus some week-long trips including lodging for up to $3,500. And **Bike Volcano** (934–9199) does tours of Volcanoes National Park for $134. Their advertising photos—showing Pu'u 'O'o from the air and surface flows of fountaining lava—are a bit over the top for a *bike* tour.

Bike Shops

In Kona, the best bike shop we know is **Bike Works** (326–2453), visible from the highway, off Kaiwi Street. Excellent selection of bikes and bike accessories. Full suspension mountain bikes (the best you'll find on the island) rent for $60 per day; front suspensions are $40. (Prices drop if you rent for longer.) **Kona Beach & Sports** (329–2294) rents cruisers for $25. In Kohala, **Bike Works Beach & Sports** (886–5000) in the Queen's MarketPlace has Specialized road bikes for $60–$75, hybrids and cruisers are $25 per day. **Mountain Road Cycles** (885–7943) is in Waimea on Hwy 19 near Kamamalu. Mountain and road bikes are $40–$80 per day. If you're a serious biker and want to bring your own from home, **Hilo Bike Hub** (961–4452) will receive and assemble it, then pack it back up for you for about $85. Adjustments are extra, as are shipping cartons. **Bike Works** has a similar service.

BOAT TOURS
See OCEAN TOURS on page 210.

Boogie boarding (riders are derisively referred to as *spongers* by surfers) is where you ride a wave on what is essentially a sawed-off surfboard. It can be a real blast. You need short, stubby fins to catch bigger waves (which break in deeper water), but small waves can be snared by simply standing in shallow water and lurching forward as the wave is breaking. If you've never done it before, stay away from big waves; they can drill you. Surf is usually highest in winter months. Smooth-bottom boards work best. Men who don't do this often should—*this is important*—wear shirts, otherwise you can rub your *da kines* raw. (Women will already have their *da kines* covered, except at Kehena Beach.)

The section on BEACHES describes whether a beach is good for boogie boarding. Our favorite is **Hapuna** in Kohala. Conditions are usually excellent. We also like Mauna Kea, Manini'owali/Kua Bay and White Sands Beach or Honl's (fins necessary for this one). You won't have any trouble finding places to rent boards, so we won't bother mentioning them individually. Just keep an eye out for signs. Expect to pay $5–$8 per day, $15–$20 per week. You can buy them at Costco, Walmart, etc., for $40+.

CAMPING

There's a drive-up campground at the **Kilauea Volcano** called **Namakani Paio**, just outside the park entrance at 4,000 feet. (See map on page 92.) They have 10

Campsites–County Sites in Black, State Sites in Red, National Park Sites in Yellow

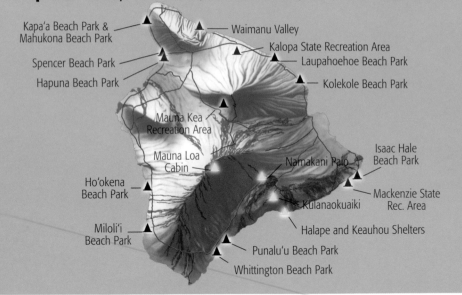

Kapa'a Beach Park & Mahukona Beach Park
Waimanu Valley
Spencer Beach Park
Kalopa State Recreation Area
Laupahoehoe Beach Park
Hapuna Beach Park
Kolekole Beach Park
Mauna Kea Recreation Area
Mauna Loa Cabin
Namakani Paio
Isaac Hale Beach Park
Ho'okena Beach Park
Kulanaokuaiki
Mackenzie State Rec. Area
Miloli'i Beach Park
Halape and Keauhou Shelters
Punalu'u Beach Park
Whittington Beach Park

simple cabins for $80 each. Each has a couple of beds, community showers (good thing it's not the other way around) and a BBQ. Call 866–536–7972 for reservations. Tents are also permitted for $15, and there's almost always plenty of space. No reservations. There's a campsite (pit toilet only) in the park called **Kulanaokuaiki** on Hilina Pali Road.

Also in the park are several campsites that require long hikes. (Halape is awesome.) Contact the park directly at 985–6178 to see which ones are open. You can pick up your permits when you get there, and there's usually not a problem getting them.

Off Saddle Road at a chilly 6,500 feet, cabins are available in **Mauna Kea Recreation Area**. Call 961–8311 for information. They're $80 per night for up to six people, and have two bedrooms (no linens/ towels), range, refrigerator, toilet, but no cookware or running water. Some are heated. They close them for long periods during droughts. Available weekends only.

Kalopa State Recreation Area has decent cabins for $90 and covered campsites for tents. The limited hiking is

good, and the park is in beautiful shape.

Many of the beach parks around the island are available for camping with a county permit. Ho'okena (page 169) stands out. They are shown on the map on this page. They even have packages for people with no camping gear. Hapuna has A-frame cabins available from the state, but they're pretty bleak and $50 per night. There were other sites at press time that were too disgusting to recommend, so we left them off the map. Tent camping at state parks is $18 per family per night. Some beach parks, such as Punalu'u and Miloli'i, might not be as peaceful as you'd like. **MacKenzie** in Puna can be nice. If you show up at a county site with no permit, you *might* be able to get a courtesy permit from a county worker—if there's room—but you'll have to go get an after-the-fact genuine permit the next day.

Waimanu Valley is utterly remote and stunningly beautiful. It'll take most of a day to go down into Waipi'o Valley, up the trail on the cliff, then down into Waimanu. See ADVENTURES on page 238. For other **state campsites**, call Division of Forestry and Wildlife at 974–4221 or State Parks

(961–9540). For **county campsites**, call Parks and Recreation at 961–8311.

OK, so technically we should have put this under *spelunking*, but we had a sneaking suspicion that it might get overlooked there.

The Big Island is the land of lava tubes. The other islands had them, too, but most collapsed over time. Lava tubes are a characteristic of young, growing islands. And they don't get any younger than the Big Island.

In the ADVENTURES chapter and HIKING section we've identified some lava tubes that you can hike through *on your own*. If that prospect seems too much trouble or too risky for you, there are guided lava tube hikes that you may want to consider. They are in the southern or eastern part of the island since it's the most geologically active. We list them in order of our preference. Contemplate bringing your own bright light since the one provided might not be that great.

Kazumura Cave Tours (967–7208) takes you along part of Kazumura Cave near Glenwood, the longest lava tube known in the world. The guide's knowledge of geology is the best of the bunch, and he reminds us of our favorite teacher from high school. The walking is pretty easy (with a few ladders), and you'll learn a lot. $30 per person. Their 4-hour tour—more physical with some rock scrambling—is $50 and well worth it. Closed Sundays. You have to wear long pants and closed shoes, or you'll be turned away by the guide's mother.

Kula Kai Caverns (929–9725) in Ka'u is a different experience. They have a short 30-minute tour for $20, which we *don't* recommend. That portion of the cave is lighted but lacks the punch of the longer tour. For $95, they take you to a harder-to-reach portion where you get to walk in the footsteps of the ancients. In days of old, living in Ka'u was hard, and finding freshwater was even harder. Hawaiians used to place hollowed-out gourds to catch water from the dripping ceilings, and some of their remains, including burned out torches, gourds and spent kukui nuts (for lamp oil) are still evident. There is nothing else like this in Hawai'i, and the owners are serious cavers who have a passion for conservation. They have other tours for different prices.

Volcano Cave Adventures (960–5664) has an unusual cave from a Mauna Loa flow in Glenwood. Though their geology knowledge is poor, the tube is a bit more interesting. It's unusual in that there's lots of mud and some water flowing through it. The footing is much more awkward here (and the lights are weak, too), but it's fun and they're friendly, if a bit unorganized. $25 per person—2-person minimum. Available when the owner isn't too busy. Try to call him after 5 p.m.

Our last choice would be **Kilauea Caverns of Fire** (217–2363). It's 10 miles south of Hilo. Their stretch of lava tube is less interesting than the others, and their command of the geology is highly suspect. They really need to work on their light situation. (On our most recent visit, our dim flashlight was the only one working when the guide's light got used up.) It's $29 for the 1-hour tour. The $89 3-hour "adventure tour" is even less recommended.

If you had to pick the one sport Kona is most famous for, it would probably be its big game fishing. The waters off the Kona coast drop to great depths quickly and are teeming with big game fish. When there's a strike, the adrenaline level of everyone on board shoots through the roof. Most talked about are the marlin *(very hard fighters known for multiple runs),* including blue, stripers and the occasional black. These goliaths can tip the scales at over 1,000 pounds. (Virtually all marlin above 300 pounds are female.) Also in abundance are ono, also called wahoo (one of the fastest fish in the ocean and indescribably delicious—they strike very hard but tire quicker), mahimahi (vigorous fighters—excellent on light tackle), ahi (delicious yellowfin tuna) and spearfish. With calm sunny conditions 300 days per year, quick access to the fishing areas, and strong competition among over 100 fishing companies, Kona has become a magnet for first-timers wishing to try their hand at catching the big one.

A Few Things You Should Know

Fish are plentiful year-round but more numerous in the summer, a bit less so in the winter.

The largest blue marlin ever caught in the state was a hull-popping 1,805 lbs.

Most boats leave out of Honokohau Harbor, just north of Kona. A surprising number of the thousand pounders (granders) have been caught just outside the harbor. This is probably because the harbor is flushed every day by freshwater springs, making the water clean and clear. This natural flushing expels the contents of the harbor on a daily basis. Perhaps passing fish like to hang around the harbor entrance to scoop up the results of that day's fish cleaning.

Most boats troll nonstop. Licenses aren't required. You will probably have to bring your own food and beverages.

Most boats here don't target a particular fish—they just troll for whatever they can get.

Most passengers on Kona fishing boats are novices, so don't feel self-conscious if you have no idea what you are doing. Deck hands will handle all of the arrangements; just sit back and relax.

You should know in advance that in Hawai'i, the fish belongs to the boat. What happens to the fish is entirely up to the captain, and they usually keep it. You may catch a 1,000-pound marlin and be told that you can't have as much as a steak from it. If this bothers you, you're out of luck. If the ono or another small fish are striking a lot and there is a glut of them, you might be allowed to keep it—or half of it. You *may* be able to make arrangements in advance to the contrary, but I doubt it.

You will either go on a shared charter (with other folks) or do a private charter. Nearly all charter boats are licensed for six people. Since boats range from 26–60 feet, how big a boat you charter will determine how roomy you feel. The fewer people on your boat, the greater the chance that *you* will be the one reeling in the fish since you share the lines with fewer people.

There are half-day (morning or afternoon) charters available, full-day, and overnighters. If this is your first time, do a half day to see if boat travel agrees with you. Mornings offer best conditions. Shared charters are getting harder to find. Sea Wife II has them for $109. Camelot has them for $125, and they distinguish themselves by promising that you can keep part of the catch if you like. You can do a private half-day charter for $400–$600. Full-day private charters go for $700–$1,000 or more for the big boats. *Usually,* the bigger the boat, the higher the price. Individual boat rates can change often depending on the season, fishing conditions and whims of the owners. Consequently, we'll forgo listing individual boat rates since this information is so perishable and instead list a few companies that we recommend. Call them directly to get current rates.

If you're easy-queasy, take an anti-seasickness medication. There are people who never get sick regardless of conditions, and those who turn green just watching *Deadliest Catch* on the DVR. Nothing can ruin an ocean outing quicker than being hunched over the stern feeding the fish. Scopolamine patches prescribed by doctors can have side effects, including (occasionally) blurred vision that can last a week. Dramamine or Bonine taken the night before and the morning of a trip also seems to work well for many, though some drowsiness may occur. Ginger is a mild preventative. Try powdered ginger, ginger pills or even *real* ginger ale—can't hurt, right?

Tipping: 15–20% split between the captain and deck hand is customary if you are pleased with their performance. If the captain is a jerk and the deck hand throws up on you, you're not obligated to give 'em diddly.

If you want to catch and release, or tag and release, make sure in advance that your boat will accommodate you. Most will, but some don't. If you do, use lures—live bait usually results in the fish coughing up its stomach, which kills it.

You might want to go down to the fuel dock at Honokohau Harbor around 11 a.m. or 3:30 p.m. for fish weigh-ins to see what's being caught and by whom. The boats hoist flags on their way back, each one representing a different species of fish caught on that trip.

If you fish from Kawaihae, expect ono and mahimahi rather than bigger stuff.

Popular boats can get booked up in advance. Making arrangements before you arrive can maximize your chances of getting a good boat.

Captains and deckhands come and go. Below are some boats that we've had good experiences with or that have good reputations as of press time. If you have a contrary experience with any one of them or have an experience with any company that you'd like to share with us, please contact us at the address listed on page 4 so we can stay on top of these boats. The number after each name is the boat length.

For the big stuff, try:

Camelot (34').....................936–9515
Strong Persuader (43').......896–3111
Ihu Nui (40' & 45')............960–1424
Sea Genie II (39').............325–5355
Sea Strike (31')..................895–1972
Sea Wife II (38')................329–1806

For light tackle, try:

Reel Action (25').................325–6811

To cut through the maze of companies, a reputable charter service company can be invaluable. Unfortunately, these come and go with amazing rapidity. **Charter Services Hawai'i** at 334–1881 has helpful personnel who gave the facts without the nonsense. Also, many company reservations default to a booking company called **Charter Locker** (326–2553).

As a rule, we are always leery of activity booths—some are helpful and knowledgeable, but some are scoundrels. However, at Honokohau Harbor, you might want to call 329–5735. They are right at the harbor, they have *lots* of boats to choose from and usually have the skinny on what's going on there.

Kona's famous **International Billfish Tournament** is held each year in July or August. Fishermen from all over the world come to compete for top prize. As a result, boats tend to fill up faster during this time.

Whether you catch fish or not, it's great being out on the Kona Coast.

Shoreline Fishing

The entire shoreline is available to you. If you want, you can find a secluded spot off any ugly-looking lava road on the island. Otherwise, on Hilo side, Hilo Bay, especially near the mouth of the Wailuku River, is good. South Point is excellent. In Kailua-Kona, the seawall in front of Hulihe'e Palace is a great place and easy to access. As snorkelers, we've seen schools numbering in the many thousands congregate off this area.

And remember: You never say, "I'm going fishing." Say, "I am going to the woods." Hawaiian legend holds that the fish will hear and avoid you if you warn them.

The Big Island is rapidly becoming known as *the* island to visit if you want to golf till you drop. This actually presented a problem for us in evaluating the individual courses. It would have been easy to froth at the mouth over most of them because compared to courses elsewhere, most are outstanding. But that would have missed the point. So with elevated expectations in mind, we have reviewed the courses *relative to each other*. This is important because if we get less than excited about a particular course, it doesn't mean it's a dump. It just means that you can do better elsewhere on the island.

Prices at the top courses are higher than many are used to. If you stay at a resort near the course, you'll probably be eligible for much cheaper rates.

A Few Tips

Wind is often a factor at Kohala courses and is usually stronger in the afternoon. Sunshine is *almost* guaranteed in Kohala.

Conditions are usually best in the mornings at all courses around the island.

Greens tend to break to the ocean, even when they look uphill.

If you're looking to master this game (yeah, good luck with *that*), there's a good golf academy called **Darrin Gee's Spirit of Golf** (887–6800).

Some courses offer big discounts after noon or 3 p.m. Check with individual courses for these or other discounts.

All the courses rent clubs, but only Mauna Kea, Mauna Lani and Hapuna rent shoes (for $15).

Mauna Kea Golf Course (882–5400)

According to local lore, in the early 1960s, Laurence Rockefeller flew Robert Trent Jones, Sr., to an isolated, barren, mostly unknown place on the Big Island called Kohala. He took him out to an 'a'a lava field, pointed to the rock and asked, "Can you build me a golf course out of that?" Jones supposedly knelt down, picked up two pieces of 'a'a and ground them together. They crumbled. He then said, "Mr. Rockefeller—you've got yourself a golf course."

Opened in 1964, Mauna Kea is still the course by which all others are compared. Fairly open and forgiving rolling terrain, this course epitomizes what a Big Island course can be. The layout is brilliant, the location is dazzling, and the course is just plain fun. Number 3 is a signature hole that hugs the shoreline— a very difficult hole. The view from the black Ts alone is worth the risk of losing your ball. Number 9 shoots downhill toward the hotel. Hole 11, a par three, drops precipitously downhill—consider yourself lucky if you par. Hole 17 is 538 beautiful curving yards. If you were on island visiting us, this might be the course we'd take you to. (Of course, we'd probably make *you* pay.) The rolling scenery and the time-tested play seem ageless.

Course	Par	Yards	Fees
Big Island Country Club	72	6,528	$95*
Hamakua Country Club (X2)	66	4,920	$15
Hapuna Golf Course	72	6,029	$150*
Hilo Municipal Golf Course	71	6,006	$35–$40
Hualalai Golf Club	72	6,032	$275*
Makalei Golf Club	72	6,161	$99*
Mauna Kea	72	6,358	$275*
Mauna Lani North	72	6,057	$225*
Mauna Lani South	72	6,025	$225*
Naniloa Golf Club (X2)	70	5,615	$15
SeaMountain at Punalu'u	72	6,045	$50*
Volcano Golf & Country Club	72	6,190	$55*
Waikoloa Beach	70	5,958	$180*
Waikoloa Kings'	72	6,010	$180*
Waikoloa Village	72	6,230	$98*

*Indicates golf cart included in price. Yards are from the men's regular tees.

Located at the Mauna Kea Resort just south of Kawaihae—the turnoff is near the 68 mile marker on Highway 19. Fees are $275 for standard, $235 for resort guests. Carts are included; walking is not allowed.

Hapuna Golf Course (880–3000)

This is the other course at the Mauna Kea/Hapuna Prince resort complex. Designed by Arnold Palmer and Ed Seay and opened in 1992, it features narrower fairways, so bring more balls than you would at Mauna Kea. The course is well marked, well organized and well kept. Don't expect to be overwhelmed with hazards, however. The narrowness is your challenge. The course is ensconced in an older lava field filled with scrub, rather than the starker, yet more attractive newer lava fields, such as the Mauna Lani's South Course.

Hapuna is a very pleasant and well-run course, though not overly remarkable. (Services, however, are excellent.) Standard fees are $150, resort guests pay $130. Carts are included and mandatory.

Mauna Lani Resort (885–6655)

Called the Francis H. I'i Brown South Course and the North Course, these two courses are the result of the 1991 splitting of the 1980 course. North and South each got nine and added nine. Of the two courses, the **South Course** is by far the most popular. It is closer to the ocean and is nicely incorporated into the stark lava. Fingers of 'a'a seem to reach out and grab your ball, so the accuracy-challenged will want to bring more than usual. 'A'a is a notorious ball eater and shoe wrecker. The course is well maintained, and some of the holes are highly memorable. Number 13 is quintessential Hawai'i. Driving toward and along the ocean, make sure you drive *your cart* on the left side for incomparable ocean views. Look back toward hole 7 and Honoka'ope Beach—a stunning hole by anyone's definition. At 15 you can count yourself among the elite if you can make par. It shoots over a respectable ocean cove onto greens guarded by cleverly placed traps. Par 3...we'll see.

Whereas the South Course is more open and expansive, the less used **North Course** has more trees and a more "traditional" use of lava boundaries. There are several lava tubes sprinkled about, and the kiawe trees often define the fairway. (Remember to be careful of their penetrating thorns when looking for an errant ball.) Make sure you hit solid on number 4—the scrub-filled lava gorge is laden with muffed drives. Number 17 is a short 119 yards from the tournament tees, but the narrow channel and well-placed traps call for lots of concentration.

Mauna Lani courses are the best-maintained courses on the island. If you can only play one, make it the South. Otherwise, you'll find that playing both will offer very different and enjoyable games. Our biggest gripe is that both courses are poorly marked, and the free map is not very accurate. Standard fees for South & North courses at $225. Resort guests pay $170. Discounted during certain times. Between the 73 & 74 mile markers on Highway 19 in Kohala. See map on page 53. Carts are included.

Waikoloa Resort

You have your choice of the **Waikoloa Kings'** or the **Waikoloa Beach**.

Waikoloa Kings' (886–7888) is a links-style course that is better but the tougher of the two. Features include deep bunkers, clever use of lava terrain and confiscatory lava boundaries. You stand little chance of retrieving your ball in this 'a'a from hell. They made good use of lava balls (you'll know them when you see them). Golf balls seem magnetically attracted to them.

Hole 5 is deceiving. There are two enormous lava balls nestled in a sand trap larger than many Kohala beaches. The cup is 327 yards away, and if there is a wind at your back and you are in a hard-driving mood, you might make it over the lava—or you might want lay up...anything to avoid being *behind* them. From most of the course on a clear day, you can see five volcanoes—Kohala, Mauna Kea, Hualalai, Mauna Loa and Haleakala on Maui. Palms and plumeria are scattered about among the trees. Though challenging, this is a course to be savored.

Waikoloa Beach (886–7888) gets far more golfers than Kings'. That's probably because it is in a location that affords more visibility and because it is closer to the ocean. Kings' is not seen from as many hotel rooms. Waikoloa Beach is a par 70, and its resort style layout is a bit more forgiving. It has less personality than the Kings' but is a fine course nonetheless. Check out the petroglyphs on your left on your way to number 4.

Both courses have lost a step when it comes to maintenance and are not in the same league as Mauna Lani or Mauna Kea. These two courses can get more crowded than other Kohala courses because they actively seek local players. Standard fees are $180, resort guests pay $145, kama'aina rate is $75. Near 76 mile marker in Kohala. See map on page 53. Rental clubs are pretty nice.

Hualalai Golf Club (325–8480)

Opened in 1996, this course is private, meaning that only those staying at the Four Seasons Resort or at the adjacent residential community can play. This Jack Nicklaus course is more player-friendly than most of his designs. There's a constant 5% grade toward the ocean, so there's lots of ocean views from the lushly manicured fairways. Very fast greens and a bit less wind than most Kohala resorts. Rates are $275.

Waikoloa Village (883–9621)

Up mauka of the Kohala resort area, three words come to mind here—cheap-

Over the water and onto the green. Mauna Kea's hole #3 is vintage Hawaiian golf.

er, windy and walking. At $98 for standard rates, it's cheaper than the big boys in Kohala. This course is popular with locals for the $50 Big Island kama'aina fares (cheaper with specials). As for the wind, you may see a bird on this course lay the same egg three times. Play *early* if you want to avoid the wind. Lastly, you can walk the course if you so choose, unlike most Kohala courses.

There are more trees here than many other courses. Some like to compare it to a very good municipal course, which sounds fair. It is adequately maintained (though poorly marked—you may even get lost on occasion). Overall, you get what you pay for here. Look for lots of wild goats and turkeys here.

Makalei Golf Club (325–6625)

This is one of the lesser-known Big Island courses. Located 2,100–2,900 feet upslope, it's cooler and less windy up here than at the Kohala courses.

There are beautiful views down the coast, and bougainvilleas dot the cart paths. The course is carved nicely into the forest. Wailing peacocks are scattered about, as well as pheasant and turkeys. Number 4 has a low rock wall to act as a speed bump for low shots. Hole 10 wanders 580 yards with impressive views of the coastline below. Makalei is a fun course. You won't get pounding Pacific surf, but you will get a moderately challenging course that's well maintained and easy to recommend. Designed by Dick Nugent. (Any relation to Ted?) $99 for standard fees. Seven miles north of Kona on Hwy 190. Carts are included and mandatory.

Big Island Country Club (325–5044)

Being on a slope up at 2,200 feet elevation, you would expect more expansive views. But the pleasing rolling terrain keeps you a bit boxed in. What you will get, however, are lots of close encounters with birds. The amount of wild turkey, nene, pheasant and small colorful birds is impressive. They even have roaming sheep. As for the golf, fairways are in decent shape but can be a bit narrow, and the course is not well marked. Slicers beware on number eight—the water is elbowing you the whole way. And at number nine you should observe the commandment, *Thou shall not kill*. Use a 3 wood. Number 17 is their signature hole. Over the water and onto the small island. Easy to over-club. 17 is where it should've ended. Because 18 is just...Well, it's annoying. You'll see what I mean. Good luck parring that one. Since this area usually clouds over around lunchtime, afternoon games are often cooler, though sometimes windier than mornings. Overall, a pleasant course, though lacking the views and exotic nature of some of the Kohala courses. It's priced fairly reasonably. $95, after noon it's $79. Carts are included. Twenty miles north of Kona on Hwy 190.

SeaMountain—Punalu'u (928–6222)

The layout and promise were excellent here, but the course appears to be a victim of the fortunes (or lack thereof) of the developer. As a result, it's getting pretty mangy in spots, and we haven't seen much evidence that the current owners are keen to make it a grand course. The lack of water as well as lack of maintenance create a fairly sad golf experience. But the price is cheap, and you won't have to fight the crowds. Located near Punalu'u Beach on the southeast side of the island, 56 miles from Hilo and 65 miles from Kona. Fees are $50 for everyone. Carts are included.

Volcano Golf & Country Club (967–7331)

Who would ever think that you could have a lush course just 1 mile from the main crater of the most active volcano on earth? Bring your warmies—the 4,000-foot altitude brings a chill to the air. The

Not all golf courses are created equal. Some, such as SeaMountain, aren't exactly worth the long drive to get there.

play is straightforward with few hazards. They seem to have lost that loving feeling—the clubhouse, restaurant and grounds all show signs of neglect. Unlike other courses, the afternoons here *may* be better in the summer. Mist and fog sometimes make it interesting, but wind is usually low. Remember to club down since the ball travels farther up here. This is a nice course offering a moderate challenge and a peaceful setting. Standard fees are $56.

Naniloa Golf Club (935–3000)

Much of the infrastructure is run down and dilapidated, but the course, aided by the fertile Hilo climate, is in fairly nice shape. This is a nine-hole course, but at least it's lightly used. Overall, forgettable. Standard fees are $15 to do the nine holes twice. Carts are $15 per 18 holes.

Hilo Municipal (959–7711)

Fairly flat layout and no sand traps (too much rain) are the hallmarks of this course. The play is not overly hard, and the setting is quite pretty. It gets soggy after a heavy rain, so consider this beforehand. This course is usually pretty crowded and about half the players walk, so weekends should be avoided for the delays. Standard fees are $35–$40. Carts extra.

Hamakua Country Club (775–7244)

Built as a community course in the formerly sugar-rich area of Hamakua, this *small* 9-hole course is popular with locals who come to play and talk story in the "clubhouse." Greens fees are $15. (You're on the honor system—just drop your money in the box in the clubhouse and grab a hand-drawn scorecard.) The holes are very close together and amazingly well tended. The community takes obvious pride in caring for it. You won't find a lot of challenges (and you won't

find club rentals or power carts, will find a gentle course set in a friendly community.

From the main highway (19) east Waimea, turn just before (west of) the gas station between the 42 and 43 mile markers on Opuhe Road, and take the frontage road 100 yards to the "clubhouse."

Unlike most activities that I can review *anonymously*, powered hang gliders (known as trikes) are aircraft that I fly myself, and I'm familiar with pilots of these aircraft since we're all members of the small flying community. So this is one of those rare cases when it's not possible for me to review the company without them knowing who I am.

Don't confuse this with hang gliding. This craft has an engine, it's bigger and more stable, and some even have a powered parachute attached to the craft... just in case (a safety feature that only a handful of traditional airplanes have). Trikes take off and land on regular runways, and the ease and grace of the craft are glorious. (Rent the movie *Fly Away Home* if you want to see what they're like.) It's as close to flying like a bird as any form of flight I know. Although I also fly traditional aircraft between the islands, I came to love trikes for the pure joy of flying, and in my opinion, they are the safest form of microlight flight available. (I'm not a daredevil and wouldn't fly them myself if I felt unsafe in them, though any time you're in the air, you're potentially at risk, even on the airlines.)

Advanced Recreation (775–9393) gives lessons in a powered hang glider. Pilot Jeff Hoff is an accomplished pilot

This ain't no sightseeing tour. You'll actually be flying this powered hang glider.

who has been flying for many years, both microlights and fixed-wing airplanes. It's $125 for a 30-minute instruction flight in the back seat. After that it's $175 per hour. You can cruise along the lightly populated shoreline heading north, or opt for a longer flight where you'll see the dramatic Hamakua Coast. No credit cards.

HELICOPTERS

If you've been on a helicopter or airplane flight on another island, especially Kaua'i, you've been treated to wall-to-wall, tongue-wagging sights. The Big Island, however, has lots of fantastic areas spread about with less interesting areas connecting them. The northeast side is a lush wonderland, the southeast side is where the active volcano is, and the west side is dominated by lava. That's why limited tours are so different on each side of the island.

Here, more than most islands, your tour is affected by the passion (or lack thereof) of the pilot. A boring pilot will sound something like this: "On your left is such and such valley, and on your right is such and such hill, and in front is the such and such lava flow." *So what?!* What you really want is a knowledgeable pilot with a command of the island who also knows to speak only when it improves the silence. We prefer companies that let you ask the pilot questions through a microphone, as opposed to those where the pilots tells you "everything you need to know."

Years ago helicopters were allowed to skim the ground. Now, air tour operators are restricted to flying 500 feet or higher over unpopulated areas. That doesn't mean that you won't walk off the aircraft with drool running down your shirt from the mesmerizing experience. It can still happen; you just aren't *assured* of it. When the music, helicopter, pilot and sights all come together, it'll still blow you away. We've flown with pilots who have an undisguised passion for the island and those who may as well be driving a flying bus. Unfortunately, most companies don't use the same pilots all the time, so it's sometimes hard to steer you toward the good ones.

In general, we recommend that helicopter tours be taken from Hilo. Tours that leave from Kona bound for the volcano spend too much time over less interesting areas, and you'll pay through the nose. The exception is Blue Hawaiian's trip from Waikoloa to the Hamakua coast (described below).

A-Star helicopters are the most popular. They hold six passengers, with four in back and two beside the pilot up front. The middle seats in the back are so-so; the others are good. Think of the A-Star as a pleasant tour bus. Blue Hawaiian and Sunshine use **Eco-Stars**, a much larger, quieter and cushier cousin to the A-Star. Windows are larger, so you'll have better views, and it's noticeably roomier inside. The downside is the price. Since these birds are so expensive (more than $3 million a pop), you may pay a hefty premium of around 20% more for the comfort. **Hughes 500Ds** have two passengers in the somewhat cramped back and two *outstanding* front seats next to the pilot. This copter feels like a sports car, and the side views from the back are excellent. Windows come off if you want. They are less popular because they are less profitable for the operators. Some companies, like Tropical, have them but use them more often for non-tour business. **Bell Jet**

Rangers are less comfortable with three in back and one passenger up front. The back middle seat is a poor seat indeed. We like the Hughes, Eco-Stars and A-Stars. We're lukewarm on Bell Jets.

Afternoon tours are sometimes bumpier. I can tell you that as a pilot myself, I do most of my flying on the Big Island in the morning when conditions are usually best. You may want to also.

If you want to get around the altitude restrictions, think about *chartering* the aircraft. It's worth considering if you have a group, or if you strike up a friendship with other travelers. It might not cost any more than a regular tour, and *you* get to call the shots. (Leave the doors off if you want on the Hughes.) Make sure you rent one that has two-way communication with the pilot.

The Companies

Blue Hawaiian (961–5600) uses nice A-Stars and Eco-Stars out of Waikoloa, near the Kohala resort area, and out of Hilo. They use the expensive Bose Acoustic Noise-Canceling headphones and have DVDs of your trip for an extra $25. (Pretty poor quality, though.) The two-hour volcano and Hamakua Coast tour (called the Big Island Spectacular), which leaves from Waikoloa and briefly lands in Hilo, is $562 and uses roomy **Eco-Stars**. (It's $112 cheaper on their A-Star.) They also have a Waikoloa to Hamakua Coast trip for $294. No volcano, just lots of beautiful valleys you

Company	Phone #	Departure	Helicopter Type	2-Way*
Blue Hawaiian	961–5600	Waikoloa, Hilo	A-Star, Eco-Star	Yes
Tropical Helicopters	961–6810	Hilo, Kona	Bell Jet, Hughes	Yes
Sunshine	882–1223	Hapuna	Eco-Star	No
Safari Helicopters	969–1259	Hilo	A-Star	Yes
Mauna Loa Helicopters	334–0234	Kona	Robinson R22, R44	Yes

Companies toward the top are recommended more than the ones toward the bottom.
* Indicates whether craft has a microphone for you to talk to the pilot.

Air tours give you a perspective on the volcano that you can't get any other way.

won't see on a volcano flight. They also have a trip that visit's Maui's Haleakala. Overall, the most tightly-run outfit of the bunch. Their online discounts can be pretty decent.

Tropical Helicopters (961–6810) is our second choice. (They also go by the name **Paradise Helicopters**.) They use a Hughes from Hilo. They have a 35-minute quickie trip to the volcano from Hilo for $160, as well as a more comprehensive (and really fun) volcano experience from Hilo *with no doors* for $217. Less recommended trips from Kona in their Bell are also available.

Sunshine (882–1223) uses Eco-Stars (which they call Whisper-Stars), but it's hard to justify their prices—$560–$635 for the trip from Kohala at the Hapuna Heliport. If you can't get a deep discount, head elsewhere.

Safari (969–1259) leaves from Hilo. We've always been a bit lukewarm toward their product and still are. Their prices seem unjustifiably steep. Their

55-minute A-Star volcano tour is $239; the 40-minute is $207. Online rates, however, can be dramatically cheaper.

Mauna Loa Helicopters (334–0234) is a little different. *You* fly the beast. It's a 2-person chopper and they give lessons, or you can charter it or their 4-passenger chopper *relatively* cheap.

Airplanes

Because of its size and relative flatness, the Big Island makes airplane tours an acceptable alternative. Some, like Big Island Air, use large tour planes. The volcano experience is certainly diminished from a plane (since you rush by things), but if you insist on leaving from Kona, the price is tempting.

Iolani Air Tour (329–0018) uses small (four- and six-person) airplanes out of Kona and Hilo for aerial sightseeing. Flights are cheaper and shorter from Hilo ($179 for 50–60 minutes) than Kona (2½ hours for $299). The more expensive Kona flight is round-the-island, so you'll get to see the awesome valleys of the Hamakua Coast. Overall, a good company.

Big Island Air (329–4868) flies large (nine-passenger) planes from Kona on round-the-island tours (well...*mostly*

around) for an overpriced $449. They do a pretty good job, the routes are interesting, and the pilot does his narrating well. As with Iolani, it's bumpy at times, so consider motion sickness medicine. (Morning is definitely best.)

Renting an Airplane

Iolani Air Tour rents 172s for $179 per hour wet plus $234 for the hour-long instructor check ride.

The Big Island has plenty of hiking to keep you happy. You can wander through a lush rain forest, walk on a volcano crater floor, puff up a frigid, snow-covered mountain, hike along an empty tropical beach, teeter on the edge of steep canyons, or saunter along an old Hawaiian lava trail. The possibilities and diversity are incredible.

Footwear—We do much of our hiking here in hiking sandals or light trail shoes. For really muddy conditions we occasionally use boots lined with Gore-Tex. And for stream hiking, nothing beats tabis. These look like green fuzzy mittens for your feet and stick to wet, mossy rocks better than any other kind of footwear. (Because they're not very stiff, tabis may leave the bottoms of your feet feeling a bit sore.) You'll find tabis for about $25 at Walmart in Kona, Walmart or Longs in Hilo, KTA in Waimea.

If you're looking for the topographic maps of the island (it takes 74 to cover the island!), **Basically Books** (961–0144) in Hilo or **Hawai'i Forest & Trail** (331–8505) in Honokohau (on the highway north of Kona behind Tesoro) are your best bets. The latter also has hiking sticks and other supplies.

We hike a lot and have become big fans of hiking sticks. We'll use two on some long hikes and find that they greatly ease the hikes and give us better bal-

Hamakua Coast by air is the only way you'll be able to see its waterfalls.

ance. They have saved us several times from falling on nasty lava. Some have straps on the handles and are telescopic.

Lastly, it's nice to be able to visually see *where* you are on a trail and know you're going in the right direction. But many of the trails on the island do not show up on a typical GPS or Google maps. *Well,* it just so happens that we GPSd every trail in our books, and they are in our geo-aware smartphone apps available on iTunes and Google Play.

KILAUEA VOLCANO HIKES

Much of the best hiking on the island is found in and around Hawai'i Volcanoes National Park. In VOLCANO SIGHTS we've described lots of strolls of 30 minutes or less. They include **Bird Park** (a nice 30-minute walk through the forest), **Devastation Trail** (see how the volcano wiped out part of a forest with flying, frothed lava and how it is coming back), **Pu'u Loa Petroglyph Trail** (less than 2 miles round trip, it heads to a massive field of ancient rock carvings—this one takes a bit more than 30 minutes), **Thurston Lava Tube** (see what lava sees as it travels underground) and a few others. We've also described a trek to the edge of the smoldering **Mauna Ulu Crater** in ADVENTURES.

© 2014 Wizard Publications, Inc.

Kilauea Iki (3 mi loop trip)

This is a great hike! If you are only able to do one hike while you are on the Big Island, this is one we'd recommend. It goes from ancient rain forest to a newly lava-paved crater and back through rain forest. At a little over 3 miles, it can take anywhere from two hours if you hoof it without distractions, to four hours if you stop and gawk as much as we do and enjoy lunch on the crater floor. It is a *reasonably* easy hike (well...maybe moderate) with only about 15 minutes of gentle but constant incline toward the end when you ascend about 450 feet. Before hiking, read some background on this crater and its attention-grabbing past in VOLCANO SIGHTS.

We like to start this hike at the Kilauea Iki Overlook and go counterclockwise, through the forest first. The trip is gentler this way and is preferable to going into the crater first. (You could also start from the Visitor Center and get there via the Earthquake Trail and Byron Ledge Trail—see page 196.) You will go through a gorgeous, ancient fern and 'ohi'a forest as the trail skirts the edge of Kilauea Iki Crater. Take your time here, and enjoy the beauty and grace of the forest and birds. All along are short spur trails offering magnificent views of the crater. Judging size and distance is surprisingly difficult here until you see people walking on the crater floor. The abrupt contrast between the ancient fern forest and the newly created maw of the crater floor couldn't be greater. Though the forest is lush and cool, the 4,000-foot altitude seems to prevent mosquito problems here (though it's always a good idea to bring a repellent, just in case). Before the trail veers away from the crater for a bit, take a look across at Pu'u Pua'i, and you will appreciate the scale of the eruptive event. Just keep to the left whenever you encounter a trail intersection. The descent into the crater is

First through lush rain forest, then across the eerie crater floor, the Kilauea Iki hike is smashing!

somewhat steep, but there are steps carved into the trail in spots and a few railings to help ease the way.

In a heartbeat you go from lush forest to barren lava. The trail bears to your left for a bit, then goes right. Cairns (piles of rock) mark the path across the floor. The lava here is more jagged since it contains remnants of lava spatters rather than the smooth lava farther ahead. Keep an eye out for a small sign pointing to the actual vent, where lava fragments are accumulating. Where you see steam escape from cracks, you will notice minerals leaching from the rock. The steam seems inoffensive compared to the nasty stuff that comes out of parts of Halemaʻumaʻu. We like to have lunch near a steam vent about ⅓ of the way across the crater floor.

The crater floor is quiet and peaceful. You may be hot, cold, wet or dry here, depending on the weather. (Gee, *that's* a useful piece of insight.) Sounds bounce around the crater in an unpredictable way. You may hear the crunching of footsteps when no one is nearby. Plants and trees are already starting to make themselves at home in cracks on the lava floor. It's amazing to stand in this near-

dead crater and to see and hear the profusion of life all around you just beyond this hostile field of Pele's destruction.

After you ascend the crater wall, keep to your left along the edge of the crater, and you are back at the overlook. Outstanding!

Napau Crater Trail (2 or 13 mi round trip)

Another nice hike is the Napau Crater Trail to **Puʻu Huluhulu**. The trail (occasionally called the Mauna Ulu Trail) is the only place in the park where you can see Puʻu ʻOʻo, the heart of the current eruption. (There is an easier view of Puʻu ʻOʻo outside the park—see page 121.) This is a *long* day hike if you do the whole thing. Mauna Ulu (meaning growing mountain) erupted between 1969 and 1974, adding more than 200 acres of new land to Hawaiʻi's coastline, and its effects are dramatically seen on this trail. It was Kilauea's second longest flank eruption in recorded history. This trail starts on an old segment of Chain of Craters Road. (Twelve miles of this road were buried by the Mauna Ulu flow, and we've shown it on the map on the inside back cover as a stippled line.) This fairly easy trek wanders over the young Mauna Ulu flow, as well as through old forest. You'll notice stone sentries along the way, strangely shaped columns of rock. These are called **lava trees**. When lava from the Mauna Ulu flow coursed its way through here, it occasionally encountered exceptionally wet trees. These resisted the flow and the temperatures long enough for the lava to harden around the tree. When the lava level lowered, these piles remained. You will often see a circle in the middle of lava trees, the outline of the now-dead tree. Sometimes, there are half-circle outlines of the tree. These are on the upstream side of the lava, showing you which way the lava flowed.

At about 30 minutes, you come to Pu'u Huluhulu (shaggy hill), a heavily forested mound. There is a five-minute spur trail leading up to the top. From there you get an awesome view of Mauna Ulu, a third of a mile in front of you. You may see Pu'u 'O'o smoldering off in the distance (quite a bit to the left of Mauna Ulu, partially obscured by the Kane Nui o Hamo Lava Shield—see map). Be sure to look down into the pristine, fern-filled rain forest below you in the crater. It's utterly untouched, looking much like it did a thousand years ago. Unfortunately, during our last visit, the park had let the vegetation grow, blocking your view of the crater floor. Looking off in the distance, you can see how the Mauna Ulu flow cut into the heart of the forest, going from green to black in a single footstep.

The view of Mauna Ulu is gorgeous. Looking over at it, you might be tempted to walk over to the top and peer into **Mauna Ulu Crater**. If so, check your insurance and see ADVENTURES.

Most people turn around from here. Past this point the trail footing gets more difficult and goes to the massive Makaopuhi Crater, then to Napau Crater, where camping is allowed. (Technically, you need a permit to go that far.) That's 6⅔ miles one way. Just before Napau, you will pass the remains of an old pulu factory. Pulu is the soft, down-like fuzz that covers the stems of some ferns. Someone thought it would make a great stuffing for pillows and mattresses, so they built a factory out here. Unfortunately, pulu turns to dust after a few years. Consequently, so did their business.

Another 2 miles past Napau is **Pu'u 'O'o**, and this is the best part of the trail. The menacing volcano looms ahead of you the whole way, reminding you why you've started this 17-mile round trip hike. The trail goes nearly to the base of the active volcano, and if the trade winds are blowing in your face, you may have to contend with volcanic fumes for the last part of the trail. This is probably why this last 2 miles was closed at press time—to keep you and your lungs safe.

On the way back, you might choose to detour south onto the Naulu Trail. Parts of the trail are along the old road, so you go from lava to road segments spared from an eruption, eventually through a beautiful forest before the trail encounters Chain of Craters Road. (You'd have to hitch a ride 6 miles back up to your car.)

Earthquake Trail/Byron Ledge
(3½ mi loop)

There is a cluster of trails around and below Volcano House. One of our favorite combinations is described below. It sounds more complicated than it is—use the map on page 92. All told, it takes 90–120 minutes and is moderately difficult (if that). You descend, then ascend about 400 feet. This is a good hike to take on a clear day because the views of the crater can be spectacular.

From the Visitor Center, you can walk around the right side of Volcano House, eventually heading to your left as you pass in front of Volcano House. Parts of the old trail and Crater Rim Road *fell into the crater* after an earthquake in 1983. This part of the road has become part of the Crater Rim Trail. It is eerie to see the road split in half, with guard-rails dangling into nothingness. Large, gaping chasms in the old road dispel any notions you may have that ground is inherently stable. Parts of the trail detours from the old road for safety reasons, but it is fascinating to try to safely glimpse as much of the crumbling road as you can, even if through the bushes at times. The best part shows the guard-rail and split road. Watch for this part as it's off the main trail. When the road forks, you'll usually take the right fork whenever you can. See map. The trail will eventually leave the road and descend through 'ohi'a forest. You'll turn right onto Kilauea Iki Trail, then right onto Byron Ledge Trail and continue to the Kilauea Crater floor. (The map and trail intersection signs make it much clearer.) On the crater floor, you'll get an idea of the texture of a skimmed-over lava lake. You are only on the crater floor for a few minutes before you head back up. It's not overly steep. On the way back up, you will pass the remains of a landslide. Look up from the big rock. You are at eye level and can almost feel the slide coming at you.

At the intersection with the **Sandalwood ('Iliahi) Trail**, you have the choice of continuing up to the right (which is a little steeper) or taking the Sandalwood Trail. We recommend the latter. It straddles the crater for a while, featuring great views and several steam vents. Then take the Sulphur Banks Trail back to the Visitor Center.

You might want to add the **Kilauea Iki Trail** to this hike. You can access it early on from the Byron Ledge Trail. See map and description of Kilauea Iki earlier.

Also in the Park

Consider the **Crater Rim Trail**. It circles the entire Kilauea Caldera, but the portion between Jagger Museum and Chain of Craters Road is closed. Segments such as the one between Volcano House and the Jagger Museum are dramatic. And the part from the Escape Road to Chain of Craters Road passes through an exquisite fern canopy.

From the end of Chain of Craters Road, there may or may not be a trail to an **active lava flow**. See ADVENTURES for more on that.

There are long overnight trails (with camping) at **Halape**, **Keauhou** and **Ka'aha**. (Halape is *incredible*.) Hikes are down the mountain or along the coast and go for many miles. Contact the Park Service at 985–6178 for more information.

Mauna Loa Summit (13 or 38 mi round trip)

Getting to the top of Mauna Loa is tough, no matter which way you slice it.

Forests ruled by ferns and 'ohi'a trees make volcano hiking a time of wonder and magic.

It's 13,677 feet high, and there are no roads to the summit. You can do it the hard way or the *very* hard way—it's your choice. The first is a 3- to 5-day hike from the Kilauea side up the Mauna Loa Trail. The trail starts at the end of the Mauna Loa Scenic Road. This hike has been known to humble even the most conditioned athlete. Though the gradient rarely exceeds 12°, it's 38 miles round trip through lava with mediocre footing, constant exposure to the sun and wind, and you gain 6,500 feet. Red Hill Cabin is 7½ miles into the hike at 10,035 feet, and Mauna Loa Summit Cabin is near the crater rim at 13,250 feet—another 11½ miles. This trail is in Hawai'i Volcanoes National Park, and you need a permit from them to camp. There's no cooking gear at the cabin and no trash cans anywhere on the trail, so pack it out.

The other way up is a *tough* 13-mile round-trip day hike from the **Mauna Loa Weather Observatory** off Saddle Road. (See page 145 for directions.) You start at 11,000 feet, so you won't have a chance to get acclimated—count on altitude sickness from starting so high. (Savvy hikers often car-camp at the weather observatory the night before to acclimate.) This trail is steeper than the Mauna Loa Trail and over rougher terrain, but you can do it in a day if you're into punishment, and the views across the saddle will be superb. Make sure you get an early start.

It's always cold up there, and snow can come at any time of the year without warning. Altitude sickness is common, even among the fittest. For either of these hikes, thorough preparation is the key. Just because you are in the tropics doesn't mean you can take this mountain lightly. The *base* may be in the tropics, but the *summit* is in Alaska. And make note: The park can tell you if there's water at the cabins, but don't you dare *rely* on it. We've hiked to the top dreaming of (and *counting* on) water at Mauna Loa Summit Cabin, only to turn tail and hoof it back down after finding nothing but dry tanks and utter disappointment up there.

KOHALA AREA HIKES
Puako/Malama Petroglyph Trail
(1¼ mi round trip)

Located near the Mauna Lani Resort area in Kohala, this 10- to 15-minute-long trail (each way) through a kiawe forest has a few petroglyphs sprinkled along the way. (Kiawe thorns are evil, wicked and hateful; be careful not to let them penetrate your shoe.) The real payoff is at the end (just past a dirt road intersection) with hundreds and hundreds of lava carvings adjacent to each other in this field in the middle of nowhere. The reasons for the Hawaiians' selection of this site has been lost to the ages. Perhaps the most obvious reason is that the slabs in this area make nice canvases. Regardless, some Hawaiians say that if you close your eyes and listen to the breeze, you can hear the sound of rock scraping against rock.

Kiholo Bay (2–3 mi round trip)

This is a fabulous place. You can catch a nice glimpse of the bay from the scenic turnout near the 82 mile marker on Highway 19. (See map on page 200.) Between the 82 and 83 mile markers a smooth gravel road leads almost to the shore. (The last short patch is rough, and some 2WD drivers may

want to park the car and walk to the water.) From there you could walk 300 yards to the right along the shoreline to Queen's Bath. (See map on page 200.)

There's also a trail from the main highway just south of the 81 mile marker. If you take the latter trail, park at the north end of the guard-rail and take the trail toward the ocean. The trail from the highway to Kiholo Bay takes 15–20 minutes. When the trail becomes a gravel road, it will eventually curve to the left. (At that intersection there's a gate to your right, but it's private. The public access is a bit farther along the road. The map makes this clearer.)

Kiholo Bay is a beautiful and uniquely shaped ocean inlet. It has several points of interest that make it great for exploring. First, the lagoon offers waters that are usually dead calm (but cold and fairly cloudy due to freshwater springs leaking into the bay, kicking up fine silt). Turtles *abound* here, grazing on limu in the bay. The fishponds inland, called Wainanali'i Pond, are on private property. Turtles swim through the manmade channel to the fishponds at night, perhaps to sleep unmolested. Walking around this part of the bay offers magnificent scenery. You can usually look right into the lagoon water and see the fish.

This whole area was once a gigantic freshwater/brackish fishpond, built by Kamehameha the Great in 1810 after another fishpond (where the airport is now) was destroyed by lava from the 1801 Hualalai flow. Enormous stone walls up to 6 feet tall and 20 feet wide were laboriously erected, creating a deep pool 2 miles in circumference where all manner of deep sea fish were stocked. It was said that half the population worked to complete it, and it was considered one of the "artificial wonders of Hawai'i" at the time. The lagoon now composing the farthest reaches of Kiholo Bay was once part of that pond, and the water-worn stones were part of the wall. The Mauna Loa lava flow of 1859 traveled *30 miles* to fill in most of the pond and breach the southern wall, creating the lagoon. Freshwater, which initially fed the pond, still intrudes into the bay from springs. Since the water in the back part of the bay is usually as calm as a swimming pool, the snorkeling there, though the visibility is poor, can be surreal. If nobody has been there to disturb the water (except for the ubiquitous turtles), the swimmer or snorkeler might encounter what appears to be a pane of glass suspended horizontally in the water about a foot down. That's the lighter freshwater floating on top of the heavier seawater. Left undisturbed, the dividing line between the two can be straight, razor thin and very visible. If you swim slowly with your hand extended vertically in the middle of the joining of these two layers, the top of your hand will be cold (from the freshwater) and the bottom will be warm (from the seawater).

Walking along the gravel shoreline from the bay heading southwest, you pass several houses. One is called the **Bali House**. It was built by the guy you see on TV who runs Paul Mitchell hair care products. He paid 200 Balinese workers $1.50 a day for two years to create the intricate carvings and assem-

ble the house. All was then disassembled and shipped to Kiholo Bay, where American and Balinese workers reassembled it. To the shock of many, they used large green logs from the *Borneo rain forest,* which shrank and split in less-humid Hawai'i, and much effort went into responding to the shrinking structure. While being built, the owner was amazingly gracious about letting people tour the house, so many on the island have gotten to see the inside. The Bali House is about midway between the row of houses on the beach, and you *will* know it when you see it.

Continuing south, you'll pass a big yellow house with security cameras, tennis courts and guards. (It was built by the guy who invented the pacemaker.) About 300 yards southwest of the house, only 80 feet from the ocean *and on state land* is a delight known as **Queen's Bath** (Keanalele Waterhole). It's just off the mauka (mountain) side of the gravel road and easy to miss. There you are, spitting distance from the ocean, in a fabulous crystal clear, spring-fed lava tube bath, open to the sky in two spots. (See photo on page 32.) It is attached to a dry lava tube cave, shown on the map. (By the way, the dry part of the lava tube has numerous petroglyphs carved into it and can be fascinating to visit, if you are careful and keep your eyes peeled.) Though filled with freshwater, its level rises and falls each day with the tides. (It goes back farther than it looks—a waterproof flashlight can make exploring it fun.) You can't help but think it doesn't get much better than this. Once you've refreshed yourself in the exquisitely cool water, you can make your way back to your car. (Our thermometer says it's 71°, but it sure *feels* colder.) By the way, if you have a lot of suntan lotion on, please consider rinsing in the ocean first, perhaps in the bay, to avoid leaving an oil slick in the bath.

Kiholo Bay

Queen's Bath 19°51.131' 155°55.782'

Black Sand & Gravel Cove

Luahinewai

4WD Gravel Rd

Gate from here

Restroom

Public Access Rd (Open 7am -7pm)

Hualalai Flow of 1800

Kiholo Bay

Mauna Loa Flow of 1859

Coconut Grove Gate

Bali House

Big Yellow House

Lava Tube Cave

Scenic Turnout

Quickest way to the Bay

Queen Ka'ahumanu

Guard-rail

81

19

82

N

0   1/2 Mile

© 2014 Wizard Publications, Inc.

Kiholo Bay is a fabulous place to wander around.

There occasionally may be some yellowjackets flying around the area. Try not to make them mad.

Luahinewai (2 mi round trip)

If you had a vast sea of blackened lava and found a beautiful, coconut tree-lined pond just 200 feet from a secluded black sand and gravel cove 1,000 feet long, what would you do? If you said *build a mansion,* you're out of luck. Somebody beat you to it. But hey, you can still hike to it. And although the owners of this enviously located estate comically watch over what they imply is their private pond (using a high-powered camera lens, no less), you'll still get a peek at the pond and possibly have this long cove to yourself. (By the way, we seem to recall a former governor being quoted that the public has access to the pond, called Luahinewai, but we don't know if that's true.)

Anyway, the short hike of about 20–25 minutes each way is worth it. It's along the lava coastline and is pretty. Take the road toward Kiholo Bay mentioned on page 199, and toward the end take the left fork and park near the Porta-Potties.

That round house you see is the old, unoccupied Loretta Lynn home. Pick up the trail to the left and follow it toward Luahinewai, marked by lots of coconut trees.

The Golden Pools of Ke-awa-iki (4 mi round trip)

How about a hike that leads to a deserted beach with white sand on one end and black sand on the other? A trail that leads over harsh 'a'a, along the beach, past a jewel-like freshwater pool and back to your car in 4 miles. We've taken friends on this hike, and they love it. It displays the raw nature of the Kohala coast, has a variety of sights you'll never forget and rewards you with a cool dip if you get warm. (See photo on page 202.)

Slightly north of the 79 mile marker on Queen K (Hwy 19) there are boulders blocking a road on the fresh (150-year-old) lava leading to the sea. (See close-up map on page 157.) Take the road-turned-trail toward the ocean and go around the right side of the fence.

The beach was created when lava from the 1859 Mauna Loa eruption flowed 30 miles, landing at the north end of the beach. The black sand created hasn't had a chance to mix with the previous white beach sand at the southern end, resulting in a nice blend from black to white along the stretch. Just past the south end there are tide-pools to explore if you have water shoes.

Continuing north (right) you'll come to Pueo Bay. Large amounts of freshwater enter this tiny bay from underground, creating some strange snorkeling conditions. From Pueo Bay you can either take the trail toward the highway (to the right of a very large lava rock) to the pools, or take the other trail to Weliweli Point and link up with another trail. Look for the latter to Weliweli marked with pieces of coral. (The map makes these trails easier to visualize.) The pools (there are two of them) can be seen from far away because they are marked by hala trees. (The ends of their branches look like palm tree-inspired pompoms.) Once at the pools, take a moment to savor the scene. Here in the middle of all this raw harshness is a magnifi-

cent oasis—freshwater (no hint of seawater at all) lined with golden-coated lava. (The gold comes from a growth on the rocks and makes the ponds too fragile to swim in.) If you want a quick, cool dip, walk just beyond the golden pools to the pool under the hala trees. It's sand- and gravel-lined and makes a good place to cool off your legs before taking the trail back to your car.

Pu'u Wa'awa'a (6½ mi round trip)

About 100,000 years ago, an explosion under Hualalai Volcano created the largest cinder cone on the island—Pu'u Wa'awa'a. Meaning "many furrowed hill," it is known by locals as the "Jello Mold." Big hill—gotta climb it, right? Luckily there's a trail to the top, but the cone is bigger than it looks, and you can easily be humbled by the steep grade. The 3²⁄₁₀ mile trail ascends 1,800 feet from your car to the summit and will literally take your breath away. Equally breathtaking is the view from atop the pu'u. On a clear

Inland of Ke-awa-iki you'll find a golden jewel ensconsed in a harsh lava desert.

day, expect to see Hualalai, Mauna Loa, Mauna Kea, Kohala and possibly Haleakala on Maui. Your best chance for clear skies is early in the morning, and a picnic lunch up top can be spectacular if the weather cooperates.

The road to the trailhead is ⁹⁄₁₀ mile past the 22 mile marker on Hwy 190. (See map on page 45.) A white pipe fence funnels you to a gate that's unlocked 6 a.m.–6 p.m., Mon.–Fri. This is an active cattle ranch, so be sure to close the gate behind you and watch where you step. Go left at the fork and park at the hunter check-in station. There's a box here for hikers with a sign-in sheet and pamphlets describing the hike. You have two options. Walk the road all the way up or detour on the 'Ohi'a Trail adding a nature lesson and ⁴⁄₁₀ miles. While not very inspiring, it's a bit more scenic and less steep than the pavement. You'll go left when it reaches a gravel road called Miki's Road. After a long climb, you come out of the forest at the base of Pu'u Wa'awa'a.

Continue on the road until it reaches a rusty gate. Take the grassy path to the right. It will meander along the side of the hill, passing through a pedestrian gate, until it reaches the backside. Horses are often grazing around here, and you'll walk through a century-old corral. The grassy road curls into the crater and up the steepest climb yet to the rim. If you use the Porta-Potty, you should know that we've seen it knocked over by the wind, so get 'er done quick.

Follow the grassy road to the left on the rim. This takes you to the highest point and offers a commanding view of the island. The grass is really soft up here, so take a seat and revel in your accomplishment. Hiking back down is hard on the knees. Add the sweat you expended on the way up, and you have a strenuous 7 miles round trip. Give

yourself four hours for this hike, and start early for best viewing conditions.

KONA AREA HIKE
Arch City Coastline (2¼ mi loop)

We usually like to offer you certain distractions that are easy to get to with a pleasant reward, like a beautiful sea arch along a rocky coast. But this place takes the cake with over a dozen arches in a mile of shoreline. The coast is so riddled with holes that you'll also find hissing blowholes, surging cracks and picturesque coves along the way. It's located just north of Honaunau Bay near Pu'uhonua o Honaunau National Historical Park in South Kona.

Just before the entrance to the park is a one-way street that passes by Honaunau Bay. After you pass the people and driveways, you'll see a gravel trail through the brush on your left before the one-way road ends. (You may have to park at the bend at the end.) Take the trail to the shore, turn right and follow the coast.

You won't see arches at first, but there are holes where the ocean surges in and out and some sniffing and snorting cracks in the rock if the surf's up. There is no defined trail on the shore, and the terrain undulates with footing that is never level, making this hike moderately strenuous. Since you're looking down at your feet a lot, stop often to look around. The lava shoreline here has more character than most if you take your time.

For the next mile (it'll seem like more since the going is slow), 20-foot tall cliffs dominate the shoreline. In some places the vegetation gets close to the cliff's edge. Use common sense out here. If rocks are wet, that means waves have splashed or crashed on them recently, and you don't want to be there when it happens again. Keep an eye out for a green semi-precious gem called olivine encrusted in the rocks.

Over a dozen arches in a mile of shoreline make Arch City the most puka-strewn piece of shoreline we've ever found in Hawai'i.

After a giant lava mound there's a very picturesque arch, perfect for photographing from the land. (Our shot is of a different arch that was taken from the water.) Five to ten minutes later, look for a black lava rock wall on your right next to a lava road that ascends into the brush. You've seen the archiest part of the coastline. (Yeah, I know that's not a real word—but it fits, doesn't it?) You can walk this road ⅓ mile back to Hwy 160,

turn right and head back to the one-way road and your car, or (if you miss it) just go back the way you came. The gravel road climbs up through the Moku'ohai Battlefield where Kamehameha defeated Kiwala'o to become ruler of the Big Island (more about that on page 71). The loop is less than 2¼ miles and should take around 2–3 hours, longer if you follow the shore back. Bring water and take advantage of the easy swimming at Honaunau Bay when you finish.

HILO & PUNA HIKES
Wai'ale Falls (½ mi round trip)

Many people come to Hawai'i looking for an idyllic pool or waterfall to frolic in. Well, here it is, and it's only a 10-minute hike to get there.

Wai'ale Falls itself is a pretty and fairly high-volume waterfall. Above the falls lie several beautiful pools and some small falls that can be a delight to play in (if the flow's not too high).

You start on Waianuenue Avenue past Boiling Pots. You'll see the falls (700 feet away) from the bridge that crosses the river. (See map on page 108.) The trailhead is just past the bridge. The trail itself is plagued with mosquitoes, but once at the water we've haven't found them to be a big problem. Bring bug juice just in case. Follow the narrow trail up through the strawberry guava lining the north bank of the Wailuku River. There are several offshoots that allow you to visit the large pool below the falls (if you wish) and some false trails that can be confusing. The trail ends at the *top* of those falls. Remember that spot for your return.

At the top, pools and small falls await. The footing is much less slippery than many other stream banks around the islands, thanks to the consolidated lava here.

INSTRUCTIONS FOR WATERFALL USE: Prance, frolic and have fun. Repeat if necessary.

Stay out of pools that have a fast moving exit. Other pools lie farther upstream. And, of course, always be aware that a flash flood can occur anywhere in nature. So if you see a large wall of water coming your way…well, you're already screwed, so what does it matter?

Leleiwi Tide-pool (⁶⁄₁₀ mi round trip)

At the end of Kalanianaole Avenue in Hilo, past all the beach parks, you'll find a large gravel cul-de-sac near the shore. Beyond this is a unique coastline that hides a gem of a tide pool. The Leleiwi Tide-pool (in undeveloped Lehia Park) has a sandy bottom with an easy entry and is perfect for a dip. Plus it has a surreal backdrop of pine trees growing on large tilted slabs of volcanic rock with everything covered in pine needles. Although it's only ¼ mile away from the end of the road, it will take you 20 minutes or more to get there.

What makes this hike different is that if you time it right, you're walking in the water most of the way. (That's good, not bad.) A couple hours before high tide the water is snaking its way inland. Wear water shoes and hike up your shorts when necessary, then embrace the tide. You could mess around trying to stay dry in the jungle, but that misses the point. The tide-pools and the tide itself are the real jewels here.

Don't leave anything valuable in your car here—we've seen the place empty and we've seen shady characters. From the parking area at the end of the road, walk ahead slightly toward the ocean.

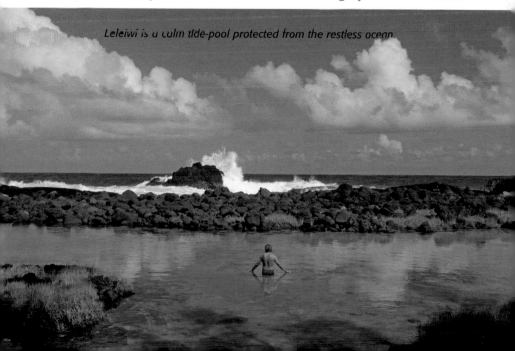

Leleiwi is a calm tide-pool protected from the restless ocean.

Almost immediately you'll encounter a tide-caused stream. Get your feet wet and slowly slosh your way along the tide-pool. Take your time—Leleiwi ain't far. The water is usually clean, and you might see disturbances where freshwater is percolating from the ground, mixing with seawater. Try to notice if you can see the tidal changes or the slight currents in the shallow pools.

Once at Leleiwi (look at the photo to orient yourself), you can take a cool dip in the sand-lined pool. Waves crash violently on the outer rocks that protect the pool, but inside, the waters should be perfectly still. You may see local families already swimming here, but the main pool is big enough to share. Bring a lunch and enjoy an afternoon of pristine relaxation here. There's no need to venture past the pools since it's only stark lava shoreline.

Ironically, this serene area, *Leleiwi Point*, refers to an altar on which the bodies of human sacrifices were left on display.

OTHER BEACH HIKES

For other beach hikes, often to secluded spots, check out **Honomalino**, **Makalawena**, **Green Sand**, **'Anaeho-'omalu** (going south to the freshwater pool), and **Road to the Sea** (the second beach), all described under BEACHES. Also consider the trail between **Spencer Beach Park** and **Hapuna**. It's along the shoreline and is vague only where it crosses the golf course at hole #3.

HIKES DESCRIBED ELSEWHERE

The hike to **Captain Cook Monument** is listed on page 71; the cold hike to **Lake Wai-au** on top of Mauna Kea is shown on the map on page 140. The awesome hikes through a *pristine* rain forest to the erupting **Pu'u 'O'o Volcano Vent**, **current lava flows** and a **lava tube** hike are all in ADVENTURES.

HORSEBACK RIDING

If you want to let someone else do the walking, consider horseback riding. The Big Island has quite a tradition when it comes to horses, and we've noticed that, of all the Hawaiian islands, companies here tend to be of a higher caliber. There are lots of companies offering wildly different kinds of rides. It just depends on the type of riding and terrain you want to see.

Most stables provide a small saddle bag and rain gear, require reservations, suggest long pants and closed-toe shoes and need a minimum number of riders before they'll go. Dress in layers, bring a hat, sunscreen and lip balm. Most have 230-pound weight limits.

Na'alapa Stables–Waipi'o (775–0419) has excellent rides in Waipi'o Valley. You can take a 4WD van tour or take a horse-drawn carriage in the valley, but riding through it on horseback is what riding dreams and movies are made of. If you have ever imagined fording a stream on horseback, here's your chance. You take 4WD van to their corral down in the valley. It's muddy and messy, so boots or trashable sneakers are recommended.

The nose-to-tail walking ride follows mostly shaded, single-lane dirt roads that meander along ancient taro fields and streams with some stretches actually going up or downstream for nice lengths of time. Morning or afternoon 2½-hour rides are $89. These same folks have another stable, **Na'alapa Stables–Kahua Ranch**, on the uphill side of Kohala Mountain Rd. where they run a 1½–hour ride for $68 and a 2½-hour for $89. Not as compelling.

Waipi'o on Horseback (775–7291) has a similar Waipi'o tour, but they're hard to book and not very accommodating. If you're a single rider and others who were supposed to go cancel, they'll buck you off as well. $85.

Waipi'o Ridge Stables (775–1007) has a different product. Instead of going *into* Waipi'o Valley, they walk part of the upper edge above Hwy 240. (See map on page 132.) Despite the name, most of the trip is through a tree farm, but the views from some of the overlooks are great. $85 for 2½ hours. Longer rides also available that go to the top of Hi'ilawe Falls. Eight to ten people max for $165. It's nose-to-tail, no running. Guides are good. Morning trips have less chance of clouding over and ruining your views.

Paniolo Adventures (889–5354) has nice quality, well cared-for horses and gear. Their 2½-hour trips are $99 and take you across a wide-open working ranch featuring beautiful views. This is not one of those nose-to-tail rides. You go across open country, and you can canter if you like. (That means to go faster than a trot, for all you city slickers.) The guides aren't patronizing; they genuinely seem to want you to experience the peace of the Hawaiian countryside. Rides have between 2 and 14 people and aren't at all gimmicky. This is a working ranch, and if it's calving season, you might get to see a calf being born. They also have 3-hour picnic rides for $124. Lunch is included in the price. Thick dusters and the like are available for free, but it's a good idea to bring a sweatshirt and long pants. Located ²⁄₁₀ mile north of the 13 mile mark on Hwy 250 in Kohala. Easy to recommend. They also have a 4-hour "Wrangler Ride" for experienced horsemen where they'll give you free rein to trot and canter for $175.

Dahana Ranch (885–0057) has 1½-hour tours of their 2,500-acre ranch off the Old Mamalahoa Highway (ask for directions) in southern Waimea for $80.

You see lush, rolling pastures from open country, not from a trail. Bring warm clothes; it's sometimes misty or rainy in this part of Waimea. (You might want to call them for a weather check.) They also have a range station ride for $150. This is not the kind where you sit there while they do all the work. For at least 2½ hours, your group will do all the hard work from horseback while they bark out orders, and you'll probably have a great time doing it. Four people are necessary for this. (Call them to see if any others have signed up.) Dahana Ranch has a 300-pound weight limit, and kids 3 and up are welcome (except on the round-up ride). Well run by good folks.

Lastly, **Cowboys of Hawai'i** (885–5006) operates out of Parker Ranch in Waimea. The good news is they'll let you run your horse a bit if you're so inclined. The bad news is you simply putz around a boring field next to the Kamuela-Kohala Airport for two hours. Hard to get happy over this one for $79.

Mule-Drawn Wagons

You can tour Waipi'o Valley for an hour with **Waipi'o Valley Wagon Tours** (775–9518) for $60. This carriage tour works pretty well for us.

Call them Jet Skis, Wave Runners (which are brand names) or personal watercraft—whatever your name for them, these motorcycles of the sea can be rented in Kona. **Kona Jet Ski** (329–2754) has fairly powerful 1,052cc jet skis. They seem to get most of their business from the cruise ships, and customer service improves when ships *aren't* in port. Early morning is usually very smooth, late afternoon choppy. Late morning seems a good balance to give the water some texture. It's $99 for 45 minutes on their small track, about the size of a Home Depot. The half hour will tucker out most people, especially if you're like me and you drive it like it's stolen. Experiment with different ways to hold your feet while you sit. Extra riders are allowed for $25, but we recommend one person per craft. *Do* spring for the goggle rentals; your eyes will be grateful. Doubling up seems to increase the risk of the passenger falling off, from what we observed. Some people seem to feel that these craft are hazardous to the ocean; others say modern jet skis are no different than regular boats. We honestly don't know which is the case; we're just saying what it's like to rent one. They leave from Kailua Pier. Unlike Jet Ski operations on Maui, these guys are allowed to operate during whale season.

On the Big Island, kayaking is mostly an ocean affair. Although other islands, such as Kaua'i, have rivers to kayak, the Big Island lacks navigable rivers. But there are several areas on the normally calm Kona coast where ocean kayaking is excellent. Our favorite is across **Kealakekua Bay** to the **Captain Cook Monument**. (See page 69 for complete description of the bay.) The 1-mile (each way) trip often features fairly calm waters, spinner dolphins and outrageous snorkeling at the monument. Other kayak trips are from Kailua Pier to the north or south, or from Kohala beaches such as 'Anaeho-'omalu. Old Kona Airport or Honokohau Harbor to Makalawena is a long, pleasant voyage. (See BEACHES for descriptions and locations of landings.) The area south of Keauhou Bay has numerous cavities (called "sea caves" by the more optimistic companies) that can be fun to paddle by.

Kealakekua Bay has been the source of *lots* of drama and government regulation in recent years, and the state has been slow on making their final decisions. At press time there were a few companies with permits to rent you a kayak to go on your own, and a few that could do guided trips. But check our web site for updates since this is a moving target.

Remember that the ocean, even in Kona, can be treacherous and unforgiving, especially during periods of high surf. We don't want to rain on anybody's parade, but if you don't give the ocean the respect it deserves, it can humble you quickly. Only paddle when it's calm, and always be wary near the shore where a rogue wave can beach (or rock) you.

Renting a Kayak for Kealakekua Bay

As mentioned, if you want to rent a kayak to paddle Kealakekua Bay, these companies can rent to you. You won't be able to *land* your kayak, you'll have to drag it around by rope as you snorkel. Since permits are limited, it's a good idea to reserve in advance. You will *probably* launch your kayak at an old boat launch called **Little Grandma's Beach**. Prices are higher for this location because the permits are like gold.

Bayside Adventures (896–0610) charges $40 for singles, $60 for doubles and they operate down at the bay. No lugging kayaks from afar. For an extra $50 they'll send a guide with you. Up off the highway there's **Ehu & Kai** (328–8775). They're friendly and knowledgeable. $45 for a single, $65 for a double. Also consider **Hawai'i Pack & Paddle** (328–8911) it's $50 for a single, $60 for a double.

There are other companies that have permits to rent them to you for Kealakekua, but were choosing not to—long story. There might also be others renting down at the bay, but they may or may not have permits.

Kayak Rentals Elsewhere

Aloha Kayak Co. (322–2868) in Kealakekua on Napoopoo Rd. closer to the bay has good gear. $35 for singles, $60 for doubles.

Kona Boys Kayaks (328–1234) prices are a bit too high. It's $54 for a single, $74 for a double. Past the 113 mile marker on Hwy 11. Both Kona Boys and Aloha Kayak Co. are inconvenient locations for renting.

Kahalu'u Bay Surf & Sea (322–4338) has $39 doubles across from Kahalu'u Beach Park on Alii Drive.

At Keauhou Bay, **Ocean Safaris** (326–4699) has singles for $25, doubles for $40.

One excellent shop that caters mainly to locals is near Costco called **P & P Kayaks** (880–1400) Super knowledgeable and friendly.

Kona Boys has a more convenient concession to the right of the pier in Kona that rents kayaks by the (expensive) hour for use in that area. Kohala companies rent them by the minute (OK, OK…by the hour). Among them are **Ocean Sports** (886–6666), which rents them at 'Anaeho'omalu Beach. You'll have to cash in your IRA for the Kohala rentals.

It's virtually impossible to rent a kayak with a **rudder** here. While rudders make it easier to stay on track in any ocean water, their absence is particularly felt in Kohala where winds will tend to annoyingly weathercock you sideways.

Guided Tours

If you want a guided trip and want to *land* at the Captain Cook Monument for snorkeling, **Adventures in Paradise** (447–0080), **Aloha Kayak Co.** (322–2868) and **Kona Boys Kayaks** (328–1234) have the proper permits and charge $100, $129 and $169 respectively. Expect about 5 hours. You'll get

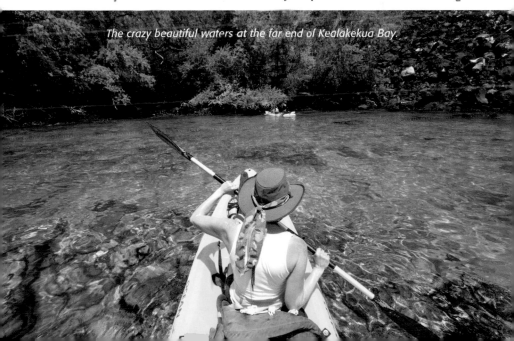
The crazy beautiful waters at the far end of Kealakekua Bay.

90 minutes or so at the monument for snorkeling and eating.

Other guided kayak trips in Kona are less desirable.

In Kohala, **Kohala Kayak** (882–4678) leaves out of Puako Ramp, heading north or south for snorkeling. They have some pretty cool gear, including pedal kayaks, sails and outriggers (to prevent tipping), and they're relatively inexpensive at around $70. (The prices seem to vary for some reason.)

If ocean kayaking is not your thing, **Kohala Ditch Adventures** (889–6000) past Hawi on the northern tip of the island has a unique way to kayak—in the Kohala Ditch. This narrow ditch spends much of its time in mountain tunnels. Along the way you learn about how this engineering feat was accomplished. Four people per kayak. No whitewater here—remember the ditch designers wanted to lose altitude as slowly as possible. So if you're visualizing something like the logger ride at Disneyland where you rush down a steep grade and splash at the bottom, you'll be disappointed. You drift along slowly, but you may get wet when passing under intersecting streams. Views are marginal since you're sunken into the ditch but most of it is in dark tunnels. Do it for the novelty and a relaxing cruise, not for a thrill ride. $139 for 60–90 minutes in the water along with a bumpy 30-minute ride in their 6WD vehicles. Wear water-friendly shoes and bring a towel.

Hawaiian Paddling Canoe Trips

We'd love to point you to a good paddling canoe trip, but we haven't found one we liked. **Eka Canoe Adventures** (756–3335) takes people in a twin-hulled canoe with a Hawaiian sail, but they *motor* most of the time, which kills the experience. **Ehu & Kai** (328–8775) will take you out, but they need 6 people to go for $85 per person.

Ocean Tours

Aspen has its ski slopes, Washington has its monuments, Orlando has Disney World, and the Big Island has the Kona Coast waters. Quite simply, if you visit the Big Island and don't ply the Kona waters, you haven't *really* been to the Big Island.

The waters off the Kona Coast are the finest in all the islands. Calmer, clearer and teeming with fish, Big Island waters make residents of other islands turn *blue* with envy. A popular way to see these waters is on an ocean tour. If you take one of the many tours along the coast, you *may* see turtles. You are *likely* to see dolphins, flying fish off the bow and whales during whale season. You *will* see smiles from fellow passengers.

You're less likely to get **seasick** on Kona's calm waters than anywhere else we can think of. Nonetheless, if you take seasickness medication, do it *before* you leave. (The night before and morning of are best. It's useless to take it once you're on the boat.) Also, avoid any alcohol the night before. No greasy foods before or during the trip. And some think that citrus is a no-no. Ginger is a very good preventative/treatment. Below deck is a bad place to be if you're worried about getting seasick. Without a reference point, you're much more likely to let 'er rip down there. Scopolamine patches work but have side effects, including (occasionally) blurred vision that can last a week. (Been there, done that, on a 10-day California–Hawai'i trip.)

Boats are usually less crowded on weekends since that's when visitors usually arrive and depart the island. And remember, most single-hull power boats are smoothest in the back.

Kealakekua Bay

The Captain Cook Monument in Kealakekua Bay is a favorite destination. Snorkeling near the monument is perhaps the best you will find anywhere in the state. If you've never snorkeled before, this is the place to start. Experienced snorkelers will be dazzled. A large number of spinner dolphins reside in the bay, and you're likely to see them— perhaps even swim with them, if you're *real* lucky. (They are called spinners because they are the only untrained dolphins that routinely leap clear of the water and spin on their longitudinal axis.) Companies sometimes offer morning or afternoon tours. Take the morning; it's calmer and the water is usually clearer.

The Big Boats

Fair Wind II (345–0268) uses a 60-foot power catamaran to bring 100 or so people. They leave from Keauhou Bay, 7½ miles north and stay tied to their mooring for a couple hours of snorkeling, BBQ burgers and general frolicking. People seem to really enjoy this trip and make good use of the short water-slides into the water, the high dive platform and the cash bar. Restrooms, hose to rinse salt off, shade, wheelchair accessible. Easy entry and exit from water. Continental breakfast on board. It's not as crowded on board as it looks from a distance. Unfortunately, since they troll along the way, the boat travels too far from the coast to see much of the coastal features. The sail is for decoration— you will be motoring at 10 MPH the whole way—but the boat is pretty smooth. This is a good tour, especially for those who are wary about ocean travel. $129 for the 4½-hour morning tour, $79 for the 3½-hour afternoon tour. Note that sodas are free *only during lunch*; they charge the rest of the time. Also, no dessert after your burgers. They only serve alcohol the *last* hour of the trip. Part of the year they also have a sunset cruise.

Hula Kai is from the same company that runs Fair Wind II, and it also leaves from Keauhou Bay. But this power cat smokes along at 25 knots, visits two snorkel spots and travels farther south than Kealakekua. Their usual second spot has a cool sea cave, conditions permitting. (Some readers say they've been chased out of the cave, claiming problems with the land owner, but that hasn't happened when we've been there.) They market this as a more upscale trip with a bit more personal attention, smaller crowds, no one under 7, and slightly better food. Though the seating is more regimented than Fair Wind II, there isn't a bad seat on the boat (though not all seats have shade), and they're very comfortable. Cash bar limited to beer and wine. Overall, a very nice 5-hour morning for $149.

Sea Paradise (322–2500) has a 50-foot sailing catamaran that leaves from Keauhou Bay. They attempt to sail on every trip if there's wind. With juices and muffins in the morning, sandwiches and BYOB at lunch, a friendly staff and good boat, this is an easy trip to recommend. $125 for this less-crowded alternative to the Fair Winds.

The Small Kine Boats

Sea Quest (329–7238) is totally different. They take 6, 12 or 14 passengers on their rigid-hull inflatables (which is a good design because it absorbs bumps better than a regular rubber raft) to the Captain Cook Monument and beyond to **Honaunau** (Place of Refuge) for snorkeling. It's bumpier than the Fair Wind II, and there's no shade except in the 14-passenger boat. (But bumpier means more thrilling.) You won't have all that wandering room that you have on the Fair Wind II, and it's snacks instead of a meal. But these guys go near the coastline and do the best job of narrating what you are seeing. Along the way they poke the boat into several "sea caves" along Arch City (see hike on page 203), and show you how they are formed. We like them better than Captain Zodiac below because they snorkel in two spots; and take their time on the way back. (They can afford to because they depart from Keauhou Bay, 10 miles closer to the monument than Captain Zodiac.) $96 for the more recommended 4-hour morning trip, $76 for the 3-hour afternoon trip, which omits Honaunau. And it's $114 if you want 3 snorkel spots (and shade) over 5 hours.

Dolphin Discoveries (322–8000) has a very similar product for similar prices. They do a pretty good job, as well. Their boats have a touch of shade—seems to be more for the captain, really.

Captain Zodiac (329–3199) leaves from Honokohau Harbor. Though the crew does well, they suffer from their location. Honokohau adds 20 miles (round trip) of relatively uninteresting Kona shoreline compared to rafts that leave from Keauhou Bay. Perhaps this is why they only snorkel at one spot. The good news is that one and a half of the four hours is spent at the monument area with snacks and light deli provided. $110 per person. This is an adequate tour, but we recommend Sea Quest or the Fair Wind over Captain Zodiac. They also have a contract with the cruise ships, so on cruise ship days, boats are packed to the max.

Other Boat Destinations

Body Glove (326–7122) leaves from Kailua Pier and usually cruises to Red Hill 10 miles to the south (which has fairly good snorkeling, but not as good as Kealakekua Bay). The Kanoa II is a 65–foot catamaran that carries 130 passengers (it's roomy enough with less than 80). They have continental breakfast at boarding and BBQ lunch at the site. In addition to snorkeling, they have SNUBA (for an extra fee). Good boats, crew and location make this a good deal, and we recommend it wholeheartedly when they're not at max capacity. (When they're full, expect lines getting in and out of the water.) Lots of shade, waterslide, restrooms and a full bar on board. Noodles and see–thru boogie boards for the timid. Their 4½-hour morning tour is $128. What they do best is their dinner cruise, described on page 281.

Kamanu Charters (329–2021) leaves Honokohau Harbor in their 36-foot *sailing* catamaran and heads 2¼ miles south to Pawai Bay. $95, 24 passengers at most, good snorkeling, sandwiches along with beer and wine provided. Only a little shade for this 3-hour tour (like Gilligan's Island?). Though an acceptable trip, unless you *have* to sail, you're better off on the Body Glove—better boat, longer trip. They also have a dolphin swim tour for $139; $99 online.

Kailua Bay Charter (324–1749) has quickie tours (under an hour) of Kailua Bay with a glass-bottom boat for $40. No food, just a quick jaunt through the water. Leaves from Kailua Pier. Not overly compelling.

Night Snorkel with Manta Rays

See page 221.

In Kohala

Ocean Sports (886–6666) has several boats but generally picks up their customers from the beach at 'Anaeho'omalu Bay in Waikoloa. Morning snorkel trips from their 58-foot cata-

With water this clear, it's easy to see why ocean tours are so popular.

maran **Sea Smoke** go south to the Ke-awa-iki Beach area or north to the Mauna Lani area. The 3½-hour trip includes fruit and juice in the morning, deli lunch and open bar that includes two local beers on tap. They'll usually sail for half the trip, and overall, the crew does a good job. (Avoid the pricey parking at the Marriott in favor of the free public beach parking.) Usually 30–40 people. $147.

Lava Viewing Tours

If the volcano is cooperating, two companies offer sunrise and sunset tours just offshore of the active lava flows. (Don't go midday; the visuals aren't as compelling.) **Lava Ocean Adventures** (966–4200) and **Lava Roy's** (883–1122) are the main players, though some fishing boats offer this tour at times. We've called them during periods when we *knew* there were *no* shoreline lava flows occurring and they weren't as…specific about our chances of seeing lava as we would like. Try to pin them down.

Lava Ocean Adventures has four boats, but you'll likely be in the 30- or 40-foot catamaran (which is more comfortable than Lava Roy's 8-person, rigid hull inflatable). In all, we lean a bit more toward Lava Ocean, though it's $175 vs. $150 for Lava Roy's. Either way, the ride back is usually rough, so ask for a cushion for Lava Ocean's benches. During sunrise tours you'll get close to the flowing lava in the dark or dim light, which is a magical experience. If you don't want to (or can't) hike out to the lava, this is a great way to see it.

For **Dinner Cruises**, see ISLAND DINING on page 281. **Submarine**, see page 224.

Parasailing is where you get pulled by a boat while attached to a parachute and a long line. We've done it, and to many people (including us), it *looks* more fun and thrilling than it really is and doesn't seem worth the money. If you have your heart set on it, **UFO Parasail** (325-5836) will drag you around for $75–$85 using a 800- or 1,200-foot line. You're up for 10 or 12 minutes respectively. Tandem rides available.

One tip (*especially* for guys): Don't wear any slippery shorts, or you may cinch forward in your harness creating...the longest 7 minutes of your life.

Whether you're already a certified SCUBA diver or are interested in trying it out, you've found paradise on the west side of the Big Island. Whereas the east (windward) side of the island has poorer diving due to river runoff and rough waters, the Kona side offers some of the best in the state. There are no permanent streams on the *entire* west side (from the northern tip to the southern tip), so runoff is not a problem. Kona waters are mostly shielded from winds and the ocean's prevailing northeast swell, so calmness is the norm. Fish, coral and divers appreciate the warmer water of the Big Island, the southernmost of all Hawaiian Islands. It's 75° at its coldest in February, 82° at its warmest in October. 100+ foot visibility is common.

You have your choice of boat dives or shore dives. Boats mostly leave from Kailua Pier, Honokohau Harbor and Kawaihae Harbor. Typical dives here are two tanks at two different sites. When we list a price range in the table, it refers to those who have their own gear vs. those who need to rent it.

The island has no decompression chamber. Everyone knows not to fly after a dive, but don't forget that the heights of some of our mountains simulate flying as far as your body tissues are concerned. Just the saddle *between* Mauna Loa and Mauna Kea reaches 6,600 feet. And if you decide to drive to Place of Refuge from Kona, you'll reach 1,400 feet—probably too high if you dove deep.

So you'll know our perspective when we review companies, we should tell you what we do and don't like when we go on a dive. On a bad dive, the dive master takes the group on a non-stop excursion that keeps you kicking the whole time. No time to stop and explore the nooks and crannies. Good outfits will give you a briefing, tell you about some of the endemic species here, what to look for and will point out various things on the dives, keeping it moving but not too fast. Bad outfits kick a lot. Good outfits explain the unique qualities of Hawai'i's environment. Bad dive masters may tell you what *they* saw (but *you* missed). Good companies work around your needs, wishes and desires. Bad companies keep everyone on a short leash. Good dive masters know their stuff and share it with you. Bad dive masters don't know squat but imply they know it all in order to impress you. As divers, we tend to like companies that wander toward the boat for the latter part of the dive and allow you to go up when you are near the end of your tank, as opposed to everyone going up when the heaviest breather has burned up his/ her bottle. We define bad dive shop attitude as what you experience when you walk into a shop (or onto a boat), and the crew does nothing but convey the attitude, *I'm so cool; don't you wish you were as cool as me?*

During times when we feel the diving conditions are bad (poor vis or big swells), we like to call around and ask about conditions. We appreciate the companies who admit it's bad, and we hold it against those who tell us how wonderful conditions are.

The Tops in Kona

There are lots of dive outfits on the island—some good, some bad. Four of them stand apart from the rest. Any of these three would make a good choice. If we had to pick one, it would probably be Pacific Rim Divers.

Pacific Rim Divers (334–1750) is a boat-only, husband/wife team. Their enthusiasm for diving is evident and contagious. Wife Patrice is one of the best we've seen at finding critters, and her knowledge of marine life is excellent. With their warm attitude, comfortable 26-foot boat (though it needs shade) and reasonable price, we're as happy and relaxed as can be at the end of a dive. (Their killer homemade brownies don't hurt, either.)

Big Island Divers (329–6068) is also a good company. We like how they pace the dives (not too fast, not too slow) and how they'll rinse your own gear if you like. We've noticed a certain fondness on their part for deep dives, and they have a pretty good black water dive. There's shade on the boat, though their selection of popcorn between dives deserves a rethink. They do a good manta dive, and we like how they post on their website how many rays showed the previous night. They use a 28-, 34- and a 36-foot boat carrying 7, 12 or 14 divers. Biggest gripe is that you need to check in at the shop before heading to the harbor.

Jack's Diving Locker (329–7585) is a good shop with four boats ranging from a 32-foot tin can to a 46-foot double-decker that holds 18 divers. Good ascent policy, hot shower on most, and dive masters carry slates. They do a lot of work with novices, but experienced divers will also be pleased. They are also careful with the ocean's critters. They're a *big* outfit and have had a few growing pains recently, but overall, they're still a good company.

Others in Kona

Kona Honu Divers (324–4668) has a beautiful 46-foot boat with plenty of shade for up to 18 divers. The big boat is comfortable and easy to get around on. Two dive steps into the water and two showers on board. Their guides are professional. Good briefing, pineapple and cookies between dives and a relaxed pace. Our concern, echoed by reader e-mails, is that they let their equipment get a bit long in the tooth between replacement cycles. Get it new, and you'll be happy. Otherwise, maybe not. They also do shore dives, blackwater dives and manta dives.

Sandwich Isle Divers (329–9188) has an adequate shop, and their boat is a 28-foot Force. Their attitude is good. Six divers max (which is tight). They're patient with introductory dives. Cheap snacks, and they make you wait more than an hour before they put you on the boat. (Yeah, we *know* they're not supposed to take money at the harbor, but they could tighten it up a bit.)

Manta Ray Dives (325–1687) is the same company as **Neptune Charlies** (331–2184). We've had real mixed results. Sometimes fairly good. Sometimes not. We've had good manta dives with them. We've also found them at times to be the last ones to arrive and the first ones to leave. But you should feel comforted by the fact that they know it all, have seen it all and done it all. If you don't believe us, just ask them.

Hawaiian SCUBA Shack (331–8708) had the furthest to go before we'd recommend them, but they're cheap, and it's inexpensive to rent their gear if you're looking to rent and dive on your own. A certification course is only $495, all inclusive.

In Kohala

The diving in Kohala is often richer in coral than Kona. Lush finger coral gar-

Dive Operator	Services Available	Price of 2 Tank Boat	Rent Gear Shore Dive	Camera Rental	Dive Computer	Manta Ray Night Dive	Dive Certification	Rx Masks
Big Island Divers 329-6068	Dive Shop & Boat Dives	$130-$160	$45-$60	No	$15 Extra	$120-$140 (1 or 2 tank)	$400-$750	Yes
Blue Wilderness 886-0980	Dive Shop & Boat Dives	$130-$165	$65	$40	Included	$110 (1 tank)	$400-$680	Yes
Hawaiian SCUBA Shack 331-8708	Dive Shop & Boat Dives	$149	$45	$10	$10 Extra	$149 (2 tank dusk dive)	$495	Yes
Jack's Diving Locker 329-7585	Dive Shop, Boat & Shore Dives	$140-$176	$45	$55-$85	$9 Extra	$155-$197 (Includes 1 dusk dive)	$400-$800	Yes
Kohala Divers 882-7774	Dive Shop & Boat Dives	$139-$174	$62	$45	$10 Extra	No	$395-$650	Yes
Kona Honu Divers 324-4668	Dive Shop, Boat & Shore Dives	$125-$155	$65	No	Included	$105-$135 (1 or 2 tank dusk dive)	$325-$625	Yes
Mauna Lani Sea Adven. 885-7883	Boat Dives & Shore Dives	$130-$170	No	No	None	No	$450-$800	Yes
Neptune Charlies 331-2184	Boat Dives	$125-$155	$30	No	None	$105-$130 (1 tank)	$325-$625	Yes
Ocean Sports 886-6666	Boat Dives	$147-$177	No	No	None	$119 Snorkel Only	$666	Yes
Pacific Rim Divers 334-1750	Boat Dives	$129-$168	No	$30	Included	$159 Summer	No	Yes
Sandwich Isle 329-9188	Boat Dives	$120-$140	No	No	None	No	$325-$550	Yes

dens are plentiful. It's a bit less protected than Kona and sometimes a little bumpy, especially Dec.–April (though less bumpy than most of the other Hawaiian Islands during those months). There are only a few operators there. Your best bet is **Kohala Divers** (882–7774), which has a 42-foot Radon that leaves from Kawaihae Harbor. **Ocean Sports** (886–6666) is a big outfit that does lots of stuff, so diving isn't an integral part of their DNA. SCUBA is from their 40-foot boat, up to 18 divers.

Mauna Lani Sea Adventures (885–7883) has exclusive use of a boat dock right at Mauna Lani. It's so handy and they love their dock so much that they don't stray too far from it during their boat dive and return you to it for minimal snacks between dives. Crew is good, but if they have an afternoon dive scheduled, morning dives feel a little rushed.

Last on our list is **Blue Wilderness** (886–0980). On the positive side, they usually dive the beautiful Puako Reef, and the boat ride is short. On the negative side, they seem a bit disorganized and lack focus on their customers. For instance, they might bring along snorkelers, who gobbled up the snacks while we were under. And our divemaster spent the entire trip taking photos—not of us, but for himself. The boat's on the small side. In short, you can do better.

In Hilo

Yes, they *do* dive Hilo side. Though the visibility and calmness are *much* better on the Kona side, life is abundant here and often overlooked. You may see more turtles in some spots here than Kona. There's only one dive shop, **Nautilus Dive Center** (935–6939), which sells and rents gear. They cater mostly to locals. In addition, **East Hawai'i Divers** (965–7840) gives guided 2-tank shore dives for $75. Private groups—he promises that you won't see any other divers where he takes you. He dives all over the east side. A good resource.

Manta Ray Night Dive

This dive is *so* good, we put it in the ADVENTURES chapter. If you are a diver or want to be, check out that section and make plans for the dive of a lifetime.

Blackwater Dive

If you're looking for something other than reef, consider this dive. You go out into 7,000 feet of water, and they lower you on a tether to 40 feet—*at night*. Just hang there and see what kind of exotic pelagic life wanders by. Lots of light-emitting bioluminescence, alien-like gelatinous creatures, schools of squid and perhaps even the elusive Hawaiian seahorse. **Jack's** takes small groups for $175 per person (one tank, but it's big) and had a very knowledgeable guide at press time named Matthew. **Big Island Divers** also

You could dive Puako every day of your trip, and still not see it all.

does this after their manta dive for $240. **Kona Honu** is only $145, or you can combine it with a manta dive for $235.

If You've Never Dived Before

Several companies will introduce you to SCUBA by giving instructions, then taking you down on a supervised dive. That's how we started, and we were smitten enough to get certified. **Jack's Diving Locker** does good intros. It's $55 for a one-tank shore dive, plus $40 for a pre-dive in their nifty pool with its glass wall. $195 for a two-tank boat intro. If they're full, **Sandwich Isle** is also pretty good with intros; boat dives only.

Dive Sites

Mentioning specific boat dive spots isn't particularly helpful because different companies sometimes use different names for the same spots, and you will usually go where the boat goes. As far as *shore* dive spots are concerned, here are some beauties you may want to check out on the Kona side. For Hilo side, see Nautilus Dive Center.

Puako—Virtually every dive shop and book tells you to go to the end of the road where the pavement becomes dirt. (You actually turn right *just before* the end.) They'll say go about 25 yards on the dirt, park and swim out about 50–75 yards. Turn right (north), and you should see several large vertical holes in the reef to drop through to the bottom. Exit the tunnel on the ocean side.

That's fine, but those sources don't know about the far better area. There are several public accesses along here, but the *best* is at telephone pole #120 (kitty-corner from a church 2 miles from the highway). If the PUBLIC ACCESS sign is missing, we can confirm that it *is* a public access. Park near the road, and the water is a 175-foot walk away. Entry is easy. You can see the reef edge

from the shore (polarized sunglasses really enhance it), so during the normally calm seas, kick almost straight out (slightly to the left) over the fairly shallow reef shelf so you'll end up seaward of a house with a corrugated metal roof. (Remember where you entered; other entry/exit points are harder on the diver.) Once at the reef wall (150 feet or so from shore), work your way northwest along the wall where countless chasms, arches and small caves, coupled with boundless coral, fish and the occasional turtle, create a delightful (though shallow 30–40 feet) dive. If you want to go deep (see photo on page 217), simply leave the coral behind and continue a short way farther offshore where the sand slopes relentlessly toward the abyss, broken only by vast fields of garden eels. (Approach them slowly, or they'll disappear into their holes.) If you're not too narc'd, return to the heavenly reef edge and make your way back. This is one of the few dives where you can go to 135 feet, yet still stay wet for an hour and be within your profile. Snorkelers, too, will enjoy the reef edge.

South Point—If you're a junkyard dog in search of a thrill, South Point has *lots* of fishing relics strewn about the ocean floor. Currents and surf can be unforgiving, so go only when calm. (Winter is sometimes best.) Not-so-easy entry is from rocks to the left (southeast) of the boat hoists. See page 79 for more information on this area. Stay away from the point.

Makole'a Beach—One of our personal favorites. The variety, quality and quantity of coral is exceptional. This is a *very* healthy reef, and it's unlikely you'll see it listed anywhere. We've dived it lots of times and have never seen any evidence that any other diver has been there. Unless you want to carry your gear for 15+ minutes, you'll need a 4WD vehicle to go over the lava road. This will allow you to drive right up to this black sand beach near Kona. The best diving is about 100 to 200 feet out from the right (north) side of the beach. From there, work your way south parallel to the beach. This is a fairly shallow dive (15 feet), and visibility is not the best in Kona (50–65 feet), but the quality of the dive site is hard to beat. Follow directions on page 162. Since we're sharing a heretofore unknown dive site (one where we personally take visiting guests), please make us proud by being extra sensitive to the pristine reef.

Believe it or not, they still sell disposable underwater film cameras, but we used a GoPro to snag this underwater shot out at Kealakekua Bay.

The BEACHES chapter describes nearly all the beaches around the island. Divers should read the descriptions of Kohala beaches, such as **Kapa'a Beach Park, Mahukona** and **Hapuna** (the southern end). In Kona, try the Alli Drive **Four Mile Marker** just south of **White Sands Beach** (from the cove head slightly south), **Kahalu'u Beach Park** (outside the breakwater) and **Pu'uhonua o Honaunau** (Place of Refuge).

If you've ever gazed into an aquarium and wondered what it was like to see colorful fish in their natural environment, complete with coral, lava tubes and strange ocean creatures, you've come to the right Hawaiian Island. Hawai'i features a dazzling variety of fish. Over 600 species are found in our waters. Here's our dilemma: If we blather on and on again about how good the water can be on the west side of the island, you're probably going to get sick. But we *have* to! Because this is where Kona really pays off. Usually calm, clear and teeming with fish, the Kona side offers some of the best snorkeling in the state.

We'll admit that we're snorkeling junkies and never tire of experiencing the water here. If you snorkel often, you can go right to our list below of recommended areas. But it you're completely or relatively inexperienced, you should read on.

For identifying ocean critters, the best books we've seen are *Shore Fishes of Hawai'i* by John Randall and *Hawaiian Reef Fish* by Casey Mahaney. They're what we use. You should see plenty of butterflyfish, wrasse, convict tang, Achilles tang, parrotfish, angelfish, damselfish, Moorish idol, puffer-

If you don't want to shoot photos of fish with your waterproof camera, use it to goof off, like we did with our friends here.

fish, trumpetfish, moray eel, and humuhumunukunukuapua'a, or Picasso triggerfish—a beautiful but very skittish fish. (It's as if they somehow *know* how good they look in aquariums.)

We know people who have a fear of putting on a mask and snorkel. Gives 'em the willies. For them, we recommend boogie boards with clear windows on them to observe the life below.

A Few Tips

- Use *Sea Drops* or another brand of anti–fog goop. Spread a *thin* layer on the inside of a dry mask, then do a quick rinse.

- Feeding the fish is generally not recommended since it introduces unnatural behavior to the reef, and it actually causes the variety of fish to dwindle since bolder species do well and soon crowd out meeker ones. In the past it was a common practice at Kahalu'u Beach Park, but today conservationists are making a concerted effort to dissuade fish feeding.

- Most damage to coral comes when people grab it or stand on it. Even touching the coral lightly can transfer your oils to the polyps, killing them. If your mask starts to leak or you get water in your snorkel, be careful not to stand on the coral to clear them. Find a spot where you won't damage coral or drift into it. Fish and future snorkelers (not to mention the coral) will thank you.
- Don't use your arms much, or you will spook the fish—just gentle fin motion. Any rapid motion can cause the little critters to scatter.
- If you have a mustache and have trouble with a leaking mask, try a little Vaseline. Don't get any on the glass— it can get *really* ugly.
- We prefer using divers' fins (the kind that slip over water shoes) so that we can walk easily into and out of the water without tearing up our feet. (If you wear socks or nylons under the shoes, they'll keep you from rubbing the tops of your toes raw.)
- Try to snorkel in calm areas. If you're in rougher water and a large wave comes and churns up the water with bubbles, put your arms in front of you to protect your head. You won't sense motion, and may get slammed into a rock before you know it.

Prices

You'll find the least expensive gear in Kailua-Kona. The business can be cut-throat, so look for coupons in the free magazines scattered around the island. If you're going to snorkel more than once, it's nice to rent gear for a week, leave it in the trunk, and go whenever

you have the desire. **Miller's Snorkel & Surf** (326–1771) has decent gear for $8 per day, $16 a week. The snorkel gear at **Jack's Diving Locker** (329–7585) is $9 per day, $42 per week. Divers' fins are available. **Snorkel Bob's** 329–0770 (near Huggo's restaurant on Alii Drive in Kona) has gear for $2.50–$13 per day, $9–$51 per week. Expect to get talked into the expensive stuff here. You can rent gear from a truck at Kahalu'u Beach Park for use there or at the concessionaire to the right of Kailua Pier.

You won't find inexpensive gear in Kohala, but you can try **Ocean Sports** at 886–6666, which has a shack at 'Anaeho'omalu Beach. Convenient, but they rent snorkel gear for (hold onto your wallet) $7 *per hour* or $14 per half day. They rent all kinds of other goodies there at rates that aren't *quite* as confiscatory.

Snorkel Boat Tours

These can be fun. They'll take you to a good spot, provide gear and show you how to use it, and sometimes provide lunch. OCEAN TOURS on page 210 reviews most of them and includes prices and where they take you. Our favorites are **Fair Wind II**, **Hula Kai**, **Body Glove** and **Sea Quest**.

Night Snorkeling with Manta Rays

Though not as adventurous as a night manta SCUBA (see page 229 for more), this has become a big attraction on the Big Island. Lots of companies will take you out to snorkel with the mantas. You have three ways to do this: You can swim out on your own. (From the back of Keauhou Bay it's ¼ mile each way unless you take a shortcut through the Sheraton.) You can go with a kayak company for the short paddle. We prefer **Aloha Kayak Company** (322–2868). Though pricey ($100) they leave in the dark, usually after the others are gone. You don't go in the water until they see mantas (because you get cold faster at night). And you get to roam around as much as you want. **Ocean Safaris** (326–4699) does this for $79. Way cheaper, but not as well-excecuted.

Lastly, you can take a boat out there. If you go on a SCUBA boat, you'll probably go to the airport manta site. You'll get a good briefing on mantas and get more freedom of movement, but you're a tag-along. You'll be out there for hours while the divers complete two dives. Check out the dive companies on page 216. **Big Island Divers** and **Jack's Diving Locker** does a good job for around $105. You can also take a larger snorkel boat such as **Hula Kai** (322–2788) for a 2-minute ride to the Sheraton site. The 1½-hour experience includes snacks and a cash bar for $109. **Sea Paradise** (322–5662) does this in a smaller boat for $90.

Boats going to the more reliable airport site on dedicated snorkel trips are **Blue Sea Cruises** (331–8875) from their large, comfortable boat for $101. **Ocean Encounters** (494–9150) charges $89 on their 46-foot fishing boat. And **Kamanu Charters** (329–2021) charges $95 from their 36-foot power cat.

Snorkel Sites

The chapter on BEACHES has complete descriptions of all beaches. Our usual bias toward west Hawai'i for water activities applies here. Clarity and calmness just can't compare on the Hilo side, but sea life can be just as abundant there.

On the west side, be sure to check out some of these beaches:

Kahalu'u—Easy access and lots of life.
Kealakekua Bay near Captain Cook Monument—Some of the best snorkeling in the state.
Pu'uhonua o Honaunau—Easy access, excellent area, lots of turtles and coral make it almost as good as the Captain Cook Monument.
Papawai Bay—Very interesting underwater relief.
Hapuna to Waialea Beach—Great stretch of reef.
Mahukona—Good underwater junk.
Puako—Very extensive reef.
Kiholo Bay—Strange conditions.
Kapa'a Beach Park—Interesting underwater sights.
Lapakahi State Park—Sometimes exceptional amounts of fish.

On the east side check out:
Punalu'u—Cold black sand conditions but *lots* of turtles.
Kapoho Tide-pools—Calm and unique.

Is this a misprint? Nope. Mauna Kea is 13,796 feet high, and in the winter it gets snow—sometimes a lot of it. **Ski Guides Hawai'i** (885–4188) rents gear for $50 on the off chance you somehow *forgot* to bring your own. Mauna Kea snow (called pineapple powder) is not reliable and neither is the company, so call them when you arrive to see if skiing is available. (It's usually tough to get them on the phone.) Granted, the conditions will be better at Aspen. But you can't go straight from the snow to the beach there, now can you? You'll need to take a 4WD to the observatory area where everyone but the driver can slide down the mountain on boogie boards or anything you think will do, while the driver takes the vehicle to the bottom to act as a ski lift.

If you're a little hesitant about trying SCUBA, consider SNUBA. That's where you swim below a raft with tanks and a 25-foot hose, regulator in mouth and an instructor by your side. **Big Island Watersports** at 324–1650 takes you on a shore dive near King Kamehameha Hotel in Kona for $89, or off their boat for $170. Groups of 2–6 per instructor; expect about 30–45 minutes of bottom time on the shore dives, a bit less on boat dives. They also have SCUBA available.

If you feel the need to lose yourself in the fog of a decadent overall body massage and treatment, you're in luck. The two best are the Fairmont Orchid and the Mauna Lani, both in the Kohala Resort area.

The **Fairmont Orchid** (885–2000) and their "Spa Without Walls" is the best *tropical* experience. We love their outdoor cabanas located at manmade waterfalls. Cabanas 4 and 5 are directly over the water with a small glass panel under your head to watch the koi fish during the day while you're on your stomach. Couples can enjoy an outdoor sunset massage right at the shoreline. Scrubs and facials take place inside. The only downside is that non-guests of the hotel won't have access to the fitness facilities or Jacuzzis. If that's important to you, **Mauna Lani Spa** (881–7922) is a great second choice. It's half outdoor thatched huts (not at the ocean) and half indoor treatment rooms. Their Lomi Lomi Hula massage feels like someone is doing the hula on your body with their hands. Very cool; not for the shy.

A weaker choice is the **Mandara Spa** at the **Waikoloa Beach Marriott** (886–8191). You might get good treatments, but we *consistently* have trouble with scheduling. Even when we *know* they are empty, we've been told they are "booked up."

We wish we could recommend one of the resorts in Kona. The biggest is the **Ho'ola Spa** at the **Sheraton**, and it's poorly executed. If you're looking to be pampered, go elsewhere. Facilities are limited, the only shower is in the steam room, the locker room is tiny, and they automatically charge you an extra 20% tip, even if you don't like your specific therapist.

STARGAZING

If you want to go stargazing on Mauna Kea, home to the world's finest and most coveted telescopes, **Hawai'i Forest & Trail** (331–8505) does the best job. They'll pick you up in Kohala or near Honokohau Harbor in Kona. Then they drive you to an old sheep-shearing station at the lower altitudes of Mauna Kea for a pretty good catered dinner, take you to the summit for sunset, then bring you back down to the Visitor Center for stargazing from their own telescope. While you sip hot chocolate and eat cookies, their knowledgeable guides do a good job pointing out—with lasers—the night sky. It's 7½ hours altogether for $199.

Another company, **Mauna Kea Summit Adventures** (322–2366), has a similar product, but it's not executed nearly as well. It's $204, and you get a hot meal at the Visitor Center. **Star Gaze**

Hawai'i (323–3481) will let you peek through their scopes at the Hapuna Beach Prince Hotel, Hilton Waikoloa or Fairmont Orchid for $30. Kind of hard to get excited about that one.

submarine

You won't *Run Silent, Run Deep.* There won't be the sound of sonar pinging away in the background. And it's unlikely that anyone will shoot torpedoes at you. But if you want to see the undersea world and *refuse* to get wet, *dis is da buggah.* **Atlantis Submarine** (329–6626) has a 48-passenger sub that ambles about over a very healthy reef in Kailua Bay. This is the opposite of an aquarium—this is *their* world, and *you* are the oddity. This 35-minute, $109 ride is a kick. Kids ($45) like it. Adults like it. Even certified divers like us like it. Claustrophobics will probably be too busy staring through the windows to be nervous. Photographers will want to use fast (at least 400 speed) ISO, and turn off the flash. Mornings are usually best. Wear a bright red shirt, and watch what happens to its color on the way down. Also, you have to descend (and later ascend) a ladder to get into the sub with other people standing below you. Why am I mentioning this? Let's just say that ladies should leave their skirts back at the hotel.

SURFING

Dudes, the most gnarly surfing on the west side is at **Pine Trees** just north of Kailua-Kona. (See Wawaloli on page 163 for directions.) The breaks are outstanding. In Kona, the break off the "little blue church" near **Kahalu'u** is one of the most dependable. **Banyans** on Alii Drive just south of Kona Bali Kai has excellent waves. Another great surf spot is **Old Kona Airport**, described in BEACHES. You should know that Banyans and Lyman's (just around the bend) are notorious for surfers with bad attitudes. Outsiders will be as welcome as reef rash. (By the way, a collection of surfboards is known in surfing lingo here as a *quiver.* A little kid surfer who doesn't have a job or a car yet is called a *grommet.* Double *overhead* is when the waves are huge, and if you get good enough, you might get a chance to visit the *green room.* If someone says your girlfriend is *filthy,* it's a compliment. And a *landshark* is someone who says he surfs… but doesn't.)

In Kona, **Pacific Vibrations** (329–4140) rents boards for $10–$20 per day. For lessons, **Hawai'i Lifeguard Surf Instructors** (324–0442) does an excellent job at Kahalu'u Beach Park. It's $110 for about 2 hours, though that price seems to vary *a lot.* It's usually cheaper. Also consider **Ocean Eco Tours** (324–7873) and **Kona Surf Company** (217–5329). They both charge $99 per person for a group lesson.

Stand Up Paddling, or **SUP**, is extremely popular with residents and visitors. The hardest part about learning to surf is standing up on the board while it's moving. This sport has made things easier by giving you a board big enough to dance on. SUP boards are wider, thicker and longer than the biggest longboards people commonly learn to surf on. SUP instruction focuses on keeping your balance while using a tall paddle to move you into the waves. (This provides an excellent central core workout, with your feet—of all things—hurting the most.) The sight of people standing and dipping long paddles in the water has earned SUP surfers the derogatory title "janitors" or "moppers" from traditional surfers. The size of the board, as well as the fact that you are already standing up, gives you an advantage in catching waves early. You don't have to drop in exactly where the wave is breaking. Moppers can catch waves behind the lineup, but all surfing rules apply once you've caught the wave. Traditional surfers will be more inclined to drop in on your wave since they'll feel that you didn't work as hard to get it as they did.

SUP is one area where it really pays to take a lesson to learn proper tecniques. For rates, call the surfing guys listed above. For several reasons, surfing companies seem less interested in giving SUP lessons and will make you jump through more hoops. **Hypr Hawai'i** (960–4667) in Kona does a good job. The owner is a coach at a local canoe club. It's $75 for a 3-hour rental which includes as much instruction time as you need. **Pacific Vibrations** has the cheapest rental prices. In Kohala at the Mauna Lani, **Hulakai** (896–3141) charges a little over a buck a minute for 60- or 90-minute lessons, but their SUP location isn't as good. **Mauna Lani Sea Adventures** (885–7883) has better prices and a better location at Makaiwa Bay, but the parking police won't let you in. You'll have to leave your car at Mauna Lani's public parking and walk ⅔ mile to the sand beach at the south end.

TENNIS

If you feel like a lively game of tennis (or you simply like chasing the ball), the Big Island has plenty of courts. The WHERE TO STAY chapter mentions whether each resort has courts, lighted or not (and the phone numbers for each). The nicest courts on the island are at the **Fairmont Orchid** (887–7532). This fine tennis complex even has a stadium court. (Crowds

are extra.) Rates are $30 per court for 1 hour. In Hilo, your best bet is the county **Ho'olulu Park** (961–8720). Three indoor and three outdoor courts. Indoor courts (preferred) are $2–$4 (day/night) per hour.

There are 43 *free* municipal courts scattered around the island. Rather than go into mind-numbing detail about all of them, just call the county at 961–8720 and ask for the courts nearest you.

Whale Watching

Humpback whales are common in Hawai'i between December and March or April. Humpbacks don't eat while they're here and may lose a third of their body weight during their Hawaiian vacation. (I doubt that many *human* visitors can make that same claim.) They're here to take advantage of Hawai'i's romantic atmosphere and mate in our waters (so don't stare), returning the following year to give birth. Though whales are more numerous off Maui, the Big Island is still a splendid place to see them blow and breach. From shore, you may see humpback whales causing a ruckus or just generally frolicking. But out on a boat, you can sometimes get up close and personal. Additionally, there are several other species—including giant sperm whales, pilot whales, false killer whales, beaked whales, pygmy killer whales and melon-headed whales—that reside here and require boats to see.

Captain Dan McSweeney's Whale Watch (322–0028) is our resident expert. He has spent approximately 1½ zillion hours studying whales off Kona. For $110, you and up to 32 other passengers take their 40-foot boat offshore for 3 hours of whale watching and education. Snacks provided, restrooms on board.

They "guarantee" a sighting or you can come back for free and *claim* a 90% success rate in finding whales. **Living Ocean Adventures** (325–5556) offers year-round trips for up to 6 people in their 31-foot Bertram (a fishing boat). Like Captain Dan, the owner/operator is always present. Except during humpback season, they troll two lines while they whale watch—if they get a strike, you may get to reel it in. Only bottled water provided, restroom on board. $90 for 3½-hour trip. They need four people to go out. Several other boat companies listed under OCEAN TOURS provide whale watching during humpback season, but these two companies have more experience. No credit cards.

From the shoreline, elevated vantage points are hard to come by. Near Kua Bay, **Pu'u Kuili** is a 342-foot high cinder cone that can be a good place to spot whales.

Lastly, during humpback season, we like to swim out beyond the sound of the breakers (say, 100 feet past the breakwater at Kahalu'u Beach) and listen to those soulful giants sing the blues. You certainly won't get to *see* them underwater, but their concert is often the best in town. (But I sometimes wonder if the fish all around me are thinking, "I *hate* it when the humpbacks come to town. They make such a racket when we're trying to sleep!") You can hear whales from much farther distances if your ears are a few feet underwater. (Hint: Hang upside-down.) Some years, the whale crowd is pretty raucous, constantly breaching, blowing and singing. Other years the behemoths may be strangely quiescent.

Windsurfing

Geography and winds conspire to make windsurfing and kitesurfing some-

what difficult on the Big Island. In Kona there usually isn't enough wind. And in Kohala there's usually too much of an *offshore* component to recommend kitesurfing or windsurfing unless the weather's unusual. (Offshore winds can be unsafe because they'll drag you away from the land.) At press time we couldn't find anyone consistently doing kiteboarding or windsurfing that we could recommend on the Big Island. Those passionate about it should look to the Mecca of these sports, Maui.

Zipline

Ever seen movies where military commandos don a harness, hook a pulley onto a steel cable and zip down into the action? This is similar—without the hostile fire at the end.

Ziplining has become a big business on this island, but not all zips are created equal. We zipped all the companies and found three that do a great job and two that are pretty avoidable. By the way, don't wear too-short shorts or the harness will get under your skin (so to speak). Minimum age is *usually* 10.

The most dramatic is the **Umauma Experience** (930–9477). They zip along and over the spectacularly beautiful Umauma Falls and gulch 15 miles north of Hilo. (See photo on page 228.) Zips #2 and #4 are probably the most dramatic ziplines in the state. After #4 (which had me zipping at 42 MPH over a distance of 2,000 feet) you cross a suspension bridge, then you'll have four anticlimactic zips before ending it on impressive #9 for $189. It takes 1½–3 hours, depending on the size of the group, and the van ride to the ziplines is very short. Their harnesses are good, and they'll let you go *up-*

A male humpback whale doing his best to show off to a nearby female.

side down for short periods if you like. Four of the lines are dual side-by-side. You need to be between 80 and 275 pounds. They will take kids as young as 4 years or 35 pounds, but they *may* be tethered to an instructor. For $50 extra you get to go down to the river to swim, kayak and frolic. Only ding here is they charge $45 to borrow a GoPro camera.

Skyline Eco Adventures (878-8400) north of Hilo in Honomu has seven zips. They also market it as Akaka Falls Zipline, which is misleading because you'll never see that falls. It's also unnecessary, because their final zip *is* across a beautiful waterfall, just not Akaka. The first four are fairly short, but they win the arms race with their final zip, at 3,350 feet, and it's a scream that will probably have you zipping at 40+ MPH. No pampering here, just a jacket if it rains and water refills. $170 for 2½ hours.

KapohoKine (930–2005) takes you to the Honoli'i Stream north of Hilo. Their land is on the north side, so you won't cross the stream or gulch, but some of the scenery (especially the second half) is pretty. (Try to ignore the logging roads on some of the zips.) The average length is over 1,000 feet with the final line measuring 2,217, (not the half mile they advertise). They don't let you bring any packs and only give you beverages once during the trip, along with snacks. (They'll sell you a sandwich for $15.) Safety is clearly on their minds throughout. No hanging upside down here. All lines are dual, which means you can go side by side, and there's less waiting between lines than other companies. Friendly guides and a good product overall at $179 for 3-hours. Don't step in any cow patties during the walking part, or they might threaten to make you walk back to the shop in Hilo.

Right next to Umauma Experience (but a million miles away in terms of quality) is **Zip Isle** (963–5427). To be blunt, we can't think of anything we liked about this product. Their terrain is boring (it's *not* over Umauma), groups have up to 16 people (with longer waits between zips), their harnesses feel less reassuring than others, and the first six zips average a ridiculously short 300 feet at 13 MPH. Number 7 is 1,100 feet but by that time you're getting restless. We've zipped these guys right after zipping Umauma, and the contrast is staggering. $167. At the Botanical World Adventures 15 miles north of Hilo.

Up north past Hawi is **Kohala Zipline** (331–3620). The forest and gulches are pretty, but there are downsides here. They have a self-braking system using gloves, and the tour includes two rappels, which adds to the gear you have to carry. Though they market it as a challenge course, the rappels were underwhelmingly slow, and the whole tour goes at a glacial pace. It takes 4 hours to complete the 9 zips for $169. The zips *average* less than 500 feet, and only three are longer.

Almost next door is **Big Island Eco Adventures** (889–5111), and we prefer them over Kohala Zipline. They get a mixed review. The zips start out short, but work up to a 2,600-foot beauty, *averaging* over 1,000 feet. The crew is good and forest environment is nice. About ⅔ through, they feed you snacks and drinks at their "mango hut." Eight zips and a wiggly suspension bridge for $169. Our complaint? They seem to have more slack in the zips, creating a deeper parabola. Zips end anticlimactically slow. Also, wait times

seem high here. It might take 2½ hours for your 90-minute tour. Gotta be between 90 and 250 pounds.

Their sister company in Kona is called **Kona Eco Adventures** (889–5111). Let's cut to the chase. The landscape is nowhere near as attractive as the other ziplines. It's a tree-to-tree affair, and most of the eight zips are unremarkable. (We liked the 1,000-footer, though.) The company does a good job, but overall, it's hard to justify for $150 unless proximity to Kona is key.

Finally there's **Aloha Zipline Express** (968–7529) at Pa'ani Ranch before the 13 mile marker on Hwy 11 south of Hilo. No amount of friendly service or family atmosphere (both here in abundance) can change the fact that the land here is not very suitable for ziplining. Picture zipping along a featureless, gently sloping field barely above the ground. Hard to get excited. Though marketed to people of all ages, only kids 45 pounds and over might appreciate it for $125.

If you don't scream at some point on this one, you gotta check your pulse.

The manta ray night dive is one of those few adventures that is even better with a crowd.

The adventures described below (except for the dolphin encounter) are for the serious adventurer. They can be experiences of a lifetime. We are assuming that, if you consider any of them, you are a person of sound judgment, capable of assessing risks. All adventures carry risks of one kind or another. Our descriptions below do not attempt to convey all risks associated with an activity. These activities are not for everyone. Good preparation is essential. In the end, it comes down to your own good judgment.

MANTA RAY NIGHT DIVE

This one may stay with you for the rest of your life. Imagine the following scene: You take a boat to a dark piece of shoreline, leaving just before sunset. When you arrive, perhaps another dive boat is al-

ready there. *Damn,* you think. They'll ruin it. As you slip into the water and approach what is affectionately called *the camp-fire,* numerous lights already there beckon to you, like a porch light calling to the moths. Then you see gigantic shadows blotting out the lights. *Mantas!* As you approach, one zooms over your head, missing you by an inch. There you sit, with all the other divers, mesmerized by the performance before you. One, two, maybe three stinger-less manta rays, 6–10 feet across their wings, slowly swirling, looping and soaring all about you. Like a dance performed by extraterrestrial beings, these filter-feeding leviathans are more graceful than you could possibly imagine. They seem to understand that they are on stage, and they rarely disappoint. When you think you have gotten used to their size, a goliath 14 feet across may swoop in, its enormous maw scooping up thousands of the tiny, darting shrimp that cloud the water along with the bubbles. You struggle to resist the urge to reach up and touch them—it's best to let them initiate any touching. Above the fray, a sea of needlefish gobble up what they can. Nearby, a friendly eel might slither over to give you a kiss.

It all started 30 years ago when the Kona Surf Hotel (now a Sheraton) started flooding the shoreline with light, attracting tiny brine shrimp, a form of plankton. This plankton brought large manta rays, which gobble them by the millions. Then in 2000 the resort closed (and turned off their light), and the mantas vanished. By luck they were discovered to be congregating at a spot near the Kona Airport (perplexing dive operators since there are no lights there to attract their food source). Since the resort reopened in 2005, they've returned, but there are times that they seem to take a vacation and don't show up at all. At press time, the airport location was the most manta-laden.

You will likely have plenty of air left since the dive takes place at about 35 feet, and you move very little. Diver etiquette dictates that you leave your snorkel on the boat; the protruding tube can scratch the mantas' belly. This is one of those rare dives where a crowd, as long as it's not *too* big, actually makes it better. More lights and more wide eyes. Snorkelers who try to dive down or those who use scooters can scare them off. Ask for a hood to help keep you warmer.

If you started diving because you wanted to feel like you were floating in space, night dives provide that feeling. But for this dive, weight yourself a bit heavy; it'll make it easier to stay put. (Don't assume that if the surf is up, boats won't go. Though usually calm, we see boats out there when the surf is high enough to make us grateful *we're* not there.) Some companies use 1/3–1/2 of the 50- to 60-minute dive for roaming around. Others, like **Kona Honu Divers**, spend nearly all their

The Mauna Ulu hike is an 'okole squeezer, not an average stroll.

time with the mantas. See the chart on page 216 for a list of companies doing this dive. We've had good luck with **Jack's** and **Big Island Divers**. Boats that leave from Keauhou Bay have a convenient 600-*yard* cruise out to the Sheraton site.

Lastly, if the mantas *don't* show, the night dive at the Sheraton is fairly boring. (Sorry, but it's true.) And no-shows seem more common around the full moon. (Perhaps more light everywhere makes this site less compelling to the mantas.)

If you've night dived before, *do this one!* If you've never night dived before, consider doing it now! Expect to spend about $110–$191 for this dive—the best money you will ever spend underwater, *if they show.*

If you only want to **snorkel** with the mantas, see page 221 for more.

MAUNA ULU CRATER

This short hike is not for the easily frightened or the faint at heart. Mauna Ulu erupted between 1969 and 1974. When it was all over, it left a smoldering maw 400 feet deep and 500 feet across. (That's a guess—it gets bigger all the time.) This crater is accessible via a 45-minute hike from Chain of Craters Road in Hawai'i Volcanoes National Park. See map on page 197. From there, you just walk up to Mauna Ulu Crater.

We need to stress that this is new land. The part of the hill adjacent to Pu'u Huluhulu *seems* to be the most stable, but that is a relative term. There are several areas where thin, shelly lava breaks beneath your feet. You may only drop an inch or two, but your adrenaline tells you otherwise. There may be even less stable areas around the edge. The rim of the crater is nearly straight down and crumbling all the time. If you get too close, it may break off, you may fall in, and then you're *really* out of luck. If all this doesn't dissuade you, you'll get to see a view that is beyond belief. The

crater seems raw, like an open wound on Kilauea. It usually steams from several spots. There are empty lava river banks around it where huge quantities of lava coursed their way down the mountain. There are blobs where lava spattered where it fell, large cracks with heat still escaping. This is as close as you may ever get to experiencing an erupting vent—while it's not erupting. But remember, this hike is what we call an 'okole squeezer. Permits are only required if you hike beyond Pu'u Huluhulu to Napau, so you *are* allowed to hike to Mauna Ulu without a permit or permission. That's official from the park, but some park personnel sometimes erroneously tell visitors otherwise. Morning is usually best for this hike.

MARATHON SNORKEL TO PAPAWAI BAY

Snorkeling at a beach such as Kahalu'u can be a great way to see the ocean. You can also snorkel with manta rays from a boat. But for those with an adventurous streak, the shoreline between the end of Old Airport and Papawai Bay (aka Pawai Bay) can be a real thrill.

First things first. You do this when the ocean's calm—period. If it looks even remotely like our photo, you shouldn't be anywhere near this spot. It's almost a half mile to your turnaround point. So if you can't swim a mile with fins, this ain't the time to try. Once at Papawai, you can venture into the protected cove, but the land surrounding it is private, and you are not welcome ashore. Legally, you're only allowed to stand on the sandy shoreline to the high tide mark. From a practical standpoint, you should stay in the water unless you're having some kind of emergency.

The swim features lots of cool underwater relief, fairly deep nearshore water and nice coral in the beginning. Fish life here can be exceptional. Expert snorkelers may not consider this an adventure, but the distance from the shore coupled with the narrow entry to Papawai Bay and the sometimes tricky water exit at the end all combine to make this challenging.

Park at the far end of the old runway, and you'll see a somewhat sandy cove. If you go at low tide, expect a shallow exit with plenty of urchins on all sides. We like to wear SCUBA gloves and carry a set of reef shoes tucked into the back of our board shorts to make the final water exit injury free. Enter the water from the sand and head out until you're away from any breakers. If you get beat up on the way out, the ocean's telling you to do something else that day. Because it faces south, it *tends* to get calmer seas in the winter than summer. Follow the shoreline west and notice the remarkable water clarity early on. It will come and go. The shoreline is an extended underwater cliff with lots of holes, chasms and arches. Don't get lulled into getting raked over the top of the reef by the surf. Depending in how fast you swim, Papawai Bay may come quicker than you think. You'll see some underwater debri (pipes or wiring, it looks like) at the entrance. Don't go in if you think

the surf will chew you up. The entrance is pretty narrow at the surface. The whole trip *can* be done in an hour, but will certainly take longer. Use your best judgment on how far out to sea you travel, but always roughly follow the coastline and come back to your starting point alert to the water hazards. Expect to be jostled by surge the entire way. If you're feeling halfway to tired, turn around regardless of your progress. Because there's nowhere to exit the ocean until you get all the way back to your starting point, you need to constantly assess if this whole thing feels right to you. You are committed, so don't let your excitement for adventure get ahead of your abilities.

RAIN FOREST HIKE TO PU'U 'O'O VENT

One of the few laments people voice when visiting Kilauea Volcano is that they can't readily visit Pu'u 'O'o, the origin and lava source of the current eruption. Of course, you can still see lava flowing from up close (Pele permitting) during a visit to the park, but you can't see the *actual vent* where it originates. There are places where a person can get

It's almost a half mile from Old Airport to Papawai Bay. But if the ocean looks anything like it does in this photo, don't go anywhere near the water today.

On the Pu'u 'O'o hike, the forest ends abruptly, bringing you face to face with the beating heart of the current eruption.

a glimpse of the vent from a distance (see page 121), but visiting it has been a problem. Unless, of course, you happen to know the way.

Unknown to the vast majority of island residents, the **Kahauale'a Trail** was cut by state workers in 1990 as the quickest and most direct route to Pu'u 'O'o. It just so happens that it passes through the healthiest, most beautiful and least-hiked rain forest on the entire island. Nowhere will you find a lovelier forest, no matter where you hike.

For two decades this was an awesome recreational trail. Then the state decided to close the trail to casual hikers. Mainly, we were told, because people were starting too late and getting lost, needing to be rescued. It was also closed out of concern that people would be there when winds were blowing fumes from the south over the trail. The state still allows hunters to use the trail, however. So technically, you need a hunting permit to legally hike this trail. You can get a permit online and will need a letter of exemption from a hunter education program back home. Assuming you go through that agonizing process with the Hawai'i DLNR, here's what you should expect:

First things first: *Don't hike this trail unless the weather forecast is for steady trade winds* (from the northeast or north). No exceptions. Any other winds, including light and variable winds, can bring the volcanic fumes back over the trail, which could be *very* unhealthy if sulphur dioxide levels are bad enough.

All told, it's a 4²⁄₁₀-mile hike to the edge of the forest from your car. (3²⁄₁₀ miles as the crow flies, but you ain't no crow.) The first half of the hike may as well be through the Garden of Eden. Tree ferns and 'ohi'a trees line the way, bursting with green, many covered with a velvety moss. Even if you're not up to the whole hike, a short trek through this forest is highly memorable. There are no big climbs, just lots of tiny hills and dips This is the rain forest of your dreams. The second half of the forest shows some signs of wild pigs and is not *quite* as perfect. (Only 98% perfect.) Since you're here to hunt, we're hoping you'll snag one. When you get to "the big crack" (you'll know), you're 10 minutes away.

Soon after the crack, the lush forest gives way to small clearings. The trees are looking stressed. Suddenly the forest is dying. Trees are stripped of leaves, grasses are taking over. *Something* is killing the rain forest. Then, through the trees, you see the cause—a sight as awesome as any you've ever encountered. You race to the abrupt edge of the forest and come face to face with Pu'u 'O'o a mile away. The cone, several hundred feet high and built entirely during the current eruption, angrily spews 1,500 *tons* of sulphur dioxide per day, like a snorting exhaust pipe from the center of the Earth. You are on the upslope side, and the lava should be flowing on the opposite side, so you probably won't see that. But if the wind is blowing in the right direction (which it usually is), you will have a view of the beating heart of a volcano.

Rain Forest Hike to Pu'u 'O'o

2,300' — South Glenwood Rd becomes Captain's Drive/Ala Kapena (Single lane from here.)

Kahauale'a Trail (AKA Captain's Trail)

N
W — E
S

0 _____ 1 MILE

Edge of Rain Forest

Big Crack
19°24.398'
155°06.939'

Lava flow from current eruption

2,450'
Remember where the trail exits the forest.
19°24.116'
155°06.864'

Faint Geologist Lava Trail
(Not designated for the public)

Park Boundary

Pu'u 'O'o Summit Rim
3,000'
(plus or minus; it changes all the time)

If the wind is blowing toward you (which it usually doesn't), *you shouldn't be here*. You would notice a sulphur smell. These occasional winds from the south are what's killing the forest edge. Savor this view, revel in it. But don't try to get closer. Don't try to walk up and peer into the crater floor or sometimes lava lake; the risks are unacceptable. If the wind changes, it exposes you to potentially fatal concentrated fumes. If a cloud forms, the fog would disorient you to the point that you wouldn't find your way back to the forest. Plus, you might fall from the fragile land into a lava lake—a real bummer. Best to observe it from the forest edge, soaking up the sight for your memories of tomorrow.

This hike is not for everyone. It is a fairly long day hike, and conditions are often pretty muddy. This *is* after all, a *rain* forest. (The trail received rainfall of biblical proportions during one rainstorm in 2000. A frog-strangling *32 inches* fell in one day alone.) When the trail's fairly dry, it's not too difficult; when it's real muddy, it's a tiring round trip. The center section is the muddiest.

The trail has been groomed sporadically by state workers, but hunters and other users keep it in pretty good shape. A few hunter and pig trails veer off; your path is the most worn path. You may be only a few miles from your car, but if you are off the trail, it would be the longest few miles of your life. A compass or GPS is comforting, just in case. And if you pick up our smartphone app (shameless plug here), we have the track so you'll *know* if you're on the right trail. Of course, we don't guarantee the trail's condition. In fact, we don't guarantee diddly when it comes to hiking. Nature changes quickly. A strong windstorm can return a nice trail back to jungle until workers come back to repair it. We are assuming that you will use your judgment on this. Also, guerrilla gardeners (you know...alternative farmers) sometimes tend their "crops" deep in the forest. They obviously like to stay as far from people as possible. The point is that you shouldn't stray a long distance off the trail for fear of stumbling onto their "farm" (not to mention getting lost in the rain forest).

Start *early* for this hike. You will want to be hiking by 7:30 a.m. to make *sure* you aren't on the trail when it gets dark. (Some who haven't heeded this warning, starting too late, have been caught on the trail at night and needed to be rescued.) We've run into our own readers on the trail who started at 10 or 11 a.m. and have chastised them for starting too late. Personally, we leave our home in Kona at the *indecent* hour of 4:30 a.m. in order to start hiking by 7 a.m. Time the hike to be back to your car two hours before sunset, just to be safe. It'll *probably* take 2½–4 hours each way, depending on conditions and your hiking skills. Bring plenty of water. Hiking boots (especially waterproof ones) are highly recommended, and a hiking stick (for probing mud puddles and balance) is *strongly* recommended. Most people will get their feet wet due to occasionally unavoidable puddles.

Don't like heights or falling? Not to worry; it won't last long.

Once at Pu'u 'O'o, note where the trail ends at the edge of the forest for your return. Lastly, when Pu'u 'O'o finally stops erupting, it won't be *quite* as dramatic. But you can bet it'll still be worth it. The inherent lure of this area will be here for years to come.

To get to the trailhead, take South Glenwood Road between the 19 and 20 mile markers (close to the 20) on Hwy 11 (20 miles from Hilo, 95 miles from Kona).

It's just south of the Hirano Store. The road curves to the right, then left and changes its name to Captain's Drive/Ala Kapena. From the highway it's 3½ miles *to the very end* (including the one-lane part) where you'll find the trail continuing south. Some readers have had their unattended cars broken into here, so don't leave anything valuable in yours.

JUMP OFF THE END OF THE WORLD

Cliff jumpers, rejoice. There's a place for you just past the south end of Alii Drive. (See map on page 63.) Drive to the end of the road and take the lava road by foot toward the ocean, veer left, and just before the road begins to ascend (next to a short paved section), take the trail to the right to the ocean. It's only a 5–10 minute walk altogether. There at the cliff you are confronted by a 35-foot drop to the water. You have your choices—there are several elevations above the water. And beneath you is clean, clear water up to 15 feet deep. If you *want* to hit bottom, you probably can if you do your best impression of a pencil; better to spread 'em as soon as you strike water. This is your cliff-jumping opportunity, where countless locals (who named this spot) have dared the ocean. Use your best judgment in deciding whether to jump. Judgment is what adventures are all about. The surf can rearrange the bottom, bringing in shallower boulders, so you'll have to evaluate all conditions for yourself. And there could be a critter near the surface that you could collide with. After you've jumped, do you have a nice, easy path to climb back up? No, sorry. After you hit the water in a shockingly abrupt fashion, you'll look to the left of the cave you just plummeted in front of and begin the daunting task of climbing the cliff face so you can do it all over again. Don't like those options? Then don't jump off the end of the world.

Another popular cliff-jumping place is from the boat hoist area at South Point. See page 81 for directions to that. People jump from the metal ladder area and climb up the rocks to the right (looking from the water).

CLOSE ENCOUNTER WITH A DOLPHIN

You may have heard of this one. At the Hilton Waikoloa Village there's a program called **Dolphin Quest**. They have several Atlantic bottle-nosed dolphins in their lagoon where children and adults can get in the water and interact with them. (Our own local spinner dolphins need deeper water and wouldn't successfully adapt to the program.) You stand on a shallow sandy shore with three or four other folks while the dolphins come up to you. *They* decide if they like *you*. If so, you'll be treated to an experience that you will remember for life. It's hard to express the enthusiasm people have when they get up close and personal with these ocean-going mammals. But it's undeniable that the encounter is incredibly enriching. You also can't help but notice that the dolphins seem to love their contact with humans as well.

You may be thinking, "Is this program good for the dolphins?" That's a fair question and was a concern of ours. We found out that the company used to have a similar program in French Polynesia. There, the dolphins were allowed out into the open ocean (where they could easily swim off at any time). They claimed that the dolphins always returned "home" to the program. That's a pretty good testimonial. We're not experts, but the dolphins seem pretty happy to us. (We've seen other places where we couldn't make that claim.) The water in their lagoon is replaced with fresh seawater every few hours by massive pumps, keeping it very

You didn't drive to Nanue Falls. You didn't really even hike here.
You just sort of...groped your way to this lovely waterfall.

clean for them and you. The dolphins are very active and playful, reproduce when they get to the right age (wink, wink), and the trainers seem to show them extraordinary love and affection.

If you're interested, call them at 886–2875. It's not always easy to get in on this. Kids are the most desired customer here. Personnel love to introduce kids, not only to the dolphins, but also to various issues regarding the dolphins' environment (without becoming too heavy handed). Make reservations 60 days in advance to ensure access. Cost is $220 for kids 9 and under (around 20 minutes with the dolphins, 1 hour of education camp). Adults can also schmooze with the dolphins for $210–$260. Other programs are available as well. If you don't want to pay a dime, you can watch the whole process from the nearby lawn separating the lagoon from the ocean.

If you want to see dolphins *in the wild,* your best chance on the island is in Kealakekua Bay. There are quite a few spinners that live in the bay. While kayaking across to the Captain Cook Monument, you stand a good chance of seeing them. We were once able to slip into the water here when 19 dolphins, including babies, were swimming and splashing all around us. You might also see them on a snorkel trip to the bay.

BOULDER-HOP TO A WATERFALL

If you spend any time in Hilo or along the Hamakua Coast, you'll see lots of waterfalls. But let's be honest—you didn't really *earn* them, did you? (Well, except for paying to come to Hawai'i, I guess.) But let's face it. You usually drive up to a parking area, walk over to a viewpoint and take a picture. Maybe you'll take a short trail, like Wai'ale Falls. But to see *these* falls, you're gonna have to get wet and risk falling and breaking your 'okole. Because although they're only 900 feet from your car, you can't see 'em and there is no trail. You'll have to get *in* the river and scramble upstream on big old boulders. And if you slip and fall, you probably can't even use your cell phone to call for help, so be careful.

This is not an all-day adventure (unless you drove here from Kona). It'll take most people up to an hour to struggle through the river. (Though well-balanced trail gods could probably sprint their way in 10 minutes.) Once at the falls, the beautiful, multi-tiered falls tumble into a deep pool. Take your time here, you *earned* it.

The falls are north of Hilo. Just north of the 18 mile marker, turn mauka off the highway and hang a right. The next bridge is stamped NANUE. A so-called trail on the nearside leads down to the stream. From here, head upstream as carefully as you can until there's a waterfall on your head. Flip-flops are *not* a good way to go on these rocks. Serious gear junkies would want canyoning shoes and a pair of carbide-tipped hiking sticks. Most people, however, will do fine with some local fishing tabis (available from Kmart or Wal-mart) or some hiking shoes with fairly soft rubber.

An alternative is Waikaumalo Falls farther down the same road. It's a bit farther upstream (1,250 feet). Starting at Waikaumalo Park, ignore the teaser trail behind the facilities (it only leads to frustration and despair) and instead head upstream on the nearshore bank. The boulders aren't as difficult (most of the time) as Nanue, but there's a place ⅔ of the way in where you'll have to swim across a pool to continue, and the end just before the falls is pretty clumsy. This stream doesn't seem quite as clean as Nanue, but the waterfall at the end is still rewarding.

Avoid when the streams are raging, and read up on leptospirosis, listed under HAZARDS in BASICS.

Though rare, **flash floods** can occur in any freshwater stream anywhere in the world, and it can happen when it's sunny where you are but raining up the mountain. Be alert for them.

LOSE YOURSELF IN WAIMANU VALLEY

Hawai'i is the most isolated chain of islands in the world. If that isn't enough for you, and you *really* want to get away from it all, this is the adventure for you. Waimanu Valley has all the ingredients you would expect from a pristine Hawaiian valley, such as waterfalls, feral pigs and a black sand beach. At one time it supported a large number of Hawaiians until the 1946 tsunami ruined their taro fields. These days you'll see more helicopters here than people. Hiking in takes 5–6 hours, and you may even have the valley all to yourself, if you can make the grueling 7¾ mile trek. Don't try to do this as a day hike. Stay at least two nights to really soak in the majesty of the valley.

You need to plan this adventure a few weeks in advance by calling the Division of Forestry and Wildlife (974–4221) in Hilo for a permit. We also recommend you bring sturdy shoes, a tent and water filter or purification tablets. A 4WD vehicle is required to get down into Waipi'o Valley to start the hike. If you take your rental, be sure to leave nothing in it and the doors *unlocked* to deter any would-be criminals from smashing their way into your car. (Though leaving it unlocked *may* void your rental insurance.) If you take the Waipi'o Valley Shuttle (775–7121) down into Waipi'o, you'll have to worry about looking for a ride back up after your long hike.

Park your car behind the beach near the river, but don't put your shoes on just yet. First, cross the river where it's shallow, so you can see where you're stepping. Follow the beach or the trail through the trees to the far valley wall. Here you'll find the Muliwai Trailhead.

To say it's strenuous would be an understatement. In the first mile you climb 1,200 feet of switchbacks (also known as the Z trail, see map page 132). It's by far the hardest part of the whole trip and will take an hour or longer. The trail is rough, rocky and unrelenting, and you'll be hiking in the sun unless you start before dawn. Take breaks in what little shade there is and get some pictures of Waipi'o Valley from the lookout at the end of the 4th switchback. Once on top, the trail heartbreakingly undulates up and down as it crosses 13 gulches. As you climb up most sections of the trail, take note when you see pine

You'll find crowds of wild pigs rather than crowds of hikers during your stay in Waimanu Valley.

needles on the ground. It means you're nearing the top. If there hasn't been much rain, the first fresh water you'll find is more than 6 miles in, so pack at least two liters per person.

As you enter Waimanu Valley, have your camera ready. From the trail you'll have stunning views of the black sand beach, the blanket of green on the valley floor and three gigantic waterfalls on the other side. From right to left, the falls are **Wai'ilikahi Falls** (1,080 feet), **Lahomene Falls** (1,800 feet) and **Waihilau Falls** (2,600 feet!). The last waterfall name refers to the three side-by-side falls in the back of the valley. They're only seen during heavy rains, but they're the tallest on the Big Island and third tallest in the state.

After a long descent to the valley floor, cross the river and pick a campsite. The first five sites are too close to each other; we prefer sites 6–9. Each has a fire pit, and there are two pit toilets in the area. Getting water from the river is convenient, but it tastes funky after traveling through the swamp. A spring on the opposite side of the valley has water that's infinitely better. Hike through the woods from the last campsite until you find water soaking the ground and follow it uphill to a cascading falls. At press time there was a sign saying the area was closed, possibly a long-forgotten warning from the 2006 earthquake. The trail would be very hard to follow if it wasn't marked with orange tape. Another 45 minutes along this path leads you to the base of Wai'ilikahi Falls. Its last plunge is into a verdant horseshoe valley and into a pool perfect for a refreshing swim. This will make all your hard work seem worthwhile.

We doubt you'll hike to the falls and not see any of the valley's only permanent residents. The narrow strip of land between the valley wall and the swamp is home to feral pigs. They like to drink from the

This black sand beach was created by a lava flow in 1950. It's not accessible by land and has no official name. The only way you'll ever get to it is to command your own boat.

spring, and you may hear them squealing at night. Remember, the pigs rule this valley, and we are merely their subjects. They're not usually aggressive, but it can be startling to see one face-to-face. Also, the mosquitoes are thick here, so make sure you bring your jungle juice.

Returning to Waipi'o Valley always seems to take less time. The climb out of Waimanu is also 1,200 feet in less than a mile, but the trail is smooth and in the shade most of the day. Expect to save an hour on the way back. Once in Waipi'o, we love to quickly get our shoes off and walk along the beach back to our vehicle. It's a beautiful stroll and a perfect end to one of the Big Island's most rewarding adventures.

COMMAND YOUR OWN BOAT

There are lots of charter boats plying the waters off Kona. But what if you want to do things your *own* way? At press time, only one company rented power boats. **Kona Boat Rentals** (326–9155) at Honokohau Harbor rents 21-foot, single-hull boats. They're made using an amazingly tough material/process called Roplene. With their 115-horsepower outboards, they'll cut through the water at 25+ MPH. Best of all, you *don't* need prior experience. (Though they will screen you to make sure you're not a moron.) Take it as far north as Kawaihae, as far south as Miloli'i. (Check out the otherwise-inaccessible black sand beach at N19°20.512' by W155°53.168'.) They'll outfit you with fishing or snorkel gear (SCUBA is extra). Their GPS is preprogrammed with numerous moorings, and they'll show you how to tie up to them. They'll give you some instructions, bring the boat to the harbor, and off you go.

The catch? *Price.* The half-day rental is $350; it's $475 for the day, *plus* gas. That's a big chunk of money. If you have

4 to 6 people, it's not quite as painful when you split it. Seeing the area this way is a real hoot. But nobody ever said hoots were cheap. Nevertheless, it's a great way to SCUBA, snorkel or fish *where* and *how* you want.

HONOKANE NUI HIKE

At the north end of the island where Hwy 270 ends you'll find Pololu Valley. (See page 49.) Though the trek into Pololu takes only 15–20 minutes, the more adventurous might want to venture beyond this beautiful valley to the more secluded **Honokane Nui Valley** and its accompanying stream. From the car lookout, it takes most people 90–120 minutes each way to hike into Honokane Nui. On the far side of Pololu, the trail goes up the 600-foot-high mountain, over the ridge, then drops down into Honokane. The view of Honokane Nui from the ridge top is breathtaking. Be prepared for a wet, sloppy trail going up the ridge from Pololu if it's been raining recently. (It's drier going down into Honokane.) Horseback riders occasionally take this trail and leave a few...gifts along the way. (Technically speaking, the *riders* probably aren't leaving those gifts; their *horses* are.) Usually winter is wetter.

Descending into Honokane Nui, there is a section of trail that was wiped out during the earthquake of 2006. People have put ropes in place (trust them at your own risk) to help this part that features loose dirt and rocks. Gloves are a good idea on the ropes. This is the most difficult part of the trail and one that may turn you back. Once in Honokane Nui the trail gets vague as it goes toward the beach. Don't disturb any of the rock walls here. There is a large deposit of black sand offshore, but it doesn't do *you* a lot of good. Stay out of the ocean here; it'll hurt you. On the far side of the valley is a nice stream and pool except during dry times—a perfect place to have lunch.

Although the trail continues into the next valley (Honokane Iki) it's got a number of residents (despite its remoteness), and you are less welcome there.

All in all, this is a nice hike when conditions are good. There are some ruins in the valley from days gone by when it was populated. If you are tired, you might be tempted to skirt the water's edge back to Pololu, thereby avoiding the trip up and down the ridge. If it's calm and low tide, you *might* get away with it, or you might get slammed by a rogue wave and washed out to sea, so we don't recommend it unless you're feeling lucky.

Some of the valley trail intersections can get confusing, so be observant. Bring bug juice just in case. Hiking boots are recommended. Don't cross Pololu Stream when it's raging. Leave for this hike early. Theoretically, you could walk

Pololu Valley & Honokane Nui Hike

Honokane Iki Valley

Honokane Nui Valley

Stay on this fork

440'

600'

Sloppiest part of trail

Pololu Valley

End of Road in North Kohala

400'

0

1 MILE *Pololu Beach*

270

© 2014 Wizard Publications, Inc.

S · W · E · N

all the way to Waipi'o Valley from here, but the trail disappears in spots, and only those with mountain goat in their lineage will want to try it.

HIKE TO FLOWING LAVA

This one is difficult to describe for the simple reason that we won't know where lava is flowing at the time you read this. There is an 8-mile interruption between the end of Chain of Craters road (in the park) and the end of the county road on the other side of the flow. Six miles of shoreline in the park, 2 miles on the county side. Where it will be during your visit is anyone's guess. The lava flows change location all the time, so we'll tell you how to find out where they are and how to get there. In late 2014 lava left the park and started harrassing Lower Puna in the Pahoa area.

You can call the park at 985–6000 for an eruption update. We've had mixed results with the quality of their updates. You can also look at the map posted at the park visitor center. Another source is the USGS recording at 967–8862. It's usually accurate, though they often mumble on the message.

Our website, www.hawaiirevealed.com, has an updated lava flow map on it and a link to the official USGS lava flow status, usually updated daily. Check it before you leave on your trip to Hawai'i. Western flows near Chain of Craters Road are supervised by knowledgeable park rangers, and they are pretty good about letting you get close when it's safe. Flows in the park more than a mile from Chain of Craters Road are usually *unsupervised,* and only your own common sense is there to supervise you. (And maybe your smarter spouse.) If you hike from the park, you are nearly always permitted to hike to the unsupervised flows.

What if it's flowing *outside* the park? If you look at the map on page 100, you'll see where Hwy 130 ends and a road through the lava leads toward a lava-destroyed subdivision. This lava road was cut on top of the old state road in 2014.

Until that year, lava flows were contained in the area in and around the park. But a lava tube system established itself in 2014 and Madame Pele put Lower Puna and the town of Pahoa in her sights. (See map on page 113.) If the lava is flowing in this area during your stay, it will be outside of the park's jurisdiction and into the hands of County Civil Defense.

The county is not nearly as accommodating to those wishing to get near the lava flows, and you can understand their point. The park was established around an active volcano. They have experts on staff that know what is and is not safe. The county usually takes the *keep them far away* approach because lava flows are not their specialty. Plus, instead of flowing on government property, lava in Puna might be flowing on private property. And the county doesn't want to deal with all the liability headaches associated with that. The bottom line means flows inside the park usually mean up close and personal. Lava in county or state jurisdictions usually mean bring your binoculars.

At the flows you are presented with several dangers. Lava benches form seaward of the old sea cliffs. They can collapse at any time, taking viewers with them, so *don't* go on the benches below. Collapses also can hurl rocks inland. Lava tubes travel under you. Hot water can splash on you. There may be signs where the flows enter the ocean telling you to go no farther. Heed them. There may be surface flows; watch for them.

Lava flows are *least* impressive between 10 a.m. and 2 p.m. (because the red lava is competing with the sun.) Don't hike here in the dark without flashlights.

Our preference is to hike out in the late afternoon, so we get to see lava during the daylight and at night.

There are other dangers, as well, such as bad gases that trade winds *normally* blow to the southwest, and we are counting on your own good judgment to keep you out of trouble. We are not attempting to convey all the dangers present on this hike. You'll have to evaluate some on your own. The park has a brochure about viewing lava safely that you may want to pick up. This is a thrilling hike of a lifetime, but not for the faint-hearted, and bad decisions can result in tragedy. Contrary to what you might think, *smaller* lava flows, with less steam at the ocean, are much more dramatic than large ones since they're less likely to be completely engulfed by steam.

Seeing the lava flow at night is an adventure that will stay with you for a lifetime. Walking back to your car on the undulating black lava in the dark is the price you pay.

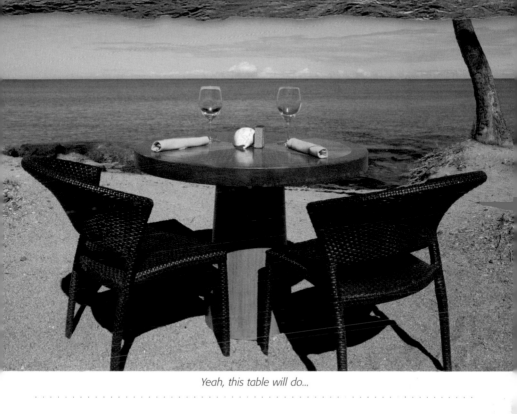

Yeah, this table will do...

By their very nature, restaurant reviews are the most subjective part of any guidebook. Nothing strains the credibility of a guidebook more. No matter what we say, if you eat at enough restaurants here, you will eventually have a dining experience directly in conflict with what this book leads you to believe. All it takes is one person to wreck what is usually a good meal. Many of us have had the experience when a friend referred us to a restaurant using reverent terms, indicating that they were about to experience dining ecstasy. And, of course, when you go there, the food is awful and the waiter is a jerk. There are many variables involved in getting a good or bad meal. Is the chef new? Was the place sold last month? Was the wait-ress just released from prison for mauling a customer? We truly hope that our reviews match your experience. If they don't, please drop us a line. We read every restaurant comment readers send, and they help us decide which restaurant to re-evaluate on a given day.

Unlike some travel writers who announce themselves to restaurants (to cop a free meal, if the truth be told), we always review *anonymously* and only expose ourselves after a meal (not literally, of course) by phone if we need additional information. By their reviews, many guidebooks lead you to believe that every meal you eat in Hawai'i will be a feast, the best food in the free world. Frankly, that's not our style. Like anywhere else, there's ample opportunity to have lousy food served with a rotten ambiance by uncaring waiters. In the interest of space, we've left out *some* of the dives. We did, however, leave in a few of these turkeys just to demonstrate that we know we live the real world. Restaurants that stand out from the others in some way are highlighted with this symbol.

For each restaurant, we list the price *per person* you can expect to pay. It ranges from the least expensive entrées alone, to the most expensive plus a beverage and usually appetizers. You can spend more if you try, but this is a good guideline. *The price excludes alcoholic beverages since this component of a meal can be so variable.* Obviously, everyone's ordering pattern is different, but we thought that it would be easier to compare various restaurants using dollar amounts than if we used different numbers of dollar signs or drawings of forks or whatever to differentiate prices between various restaurants. All take credit cards unless otherwise noted. When we mention that prices are reasonable, please take it in context. We mean reasonable *for Hawai'i.* (We *know* you pay less back home.) Food in Hawai'i is expensive, even if it's grown here. (You probably pay less for our fruit on the mainland than *we* do here.)

When we give directions to a restaurant, *mauka side* of highway means "toward the mountain" (or away from the ocean). The shopping centers we mention are on the maps to that area.

The difference between local and Hawaiian food can be difficult to classify. Basically, local food combines Hawaiian, American, Japanese, Chinese, Filipino and several other types and is (not surprisingly) eaten mainly by locals.

Most restaurants close around 9 p.m.

Lu'au, those giant outdoor Hawaiian parties, are described at the end.

When a restaurant requires **resort wear**, that means collared shirts for men (though nice shorts are *usually* okay) and dressy sportswear or dresses for women.

Below are descriptions of various island foods. Not all are Hawaiian, but this might be helpful if you encounter dishes unfamiliar to you.

ISLAND FISH & SEAFOOD

Ahi–Tuna; raw in sashimi or poke, also seared, blackened, baked or grilled; good in fish sandwiches. Try painting ahi steaks with mayonnaise, which *completely* burns off when BBQ'd but seals in the moisture. You end up tasting only the moist ocean steak. Generally most plentiful Apr.–Sept.

Kampachi–Raised just off the airport. In the wild these fish are called kahala; tasty but notoriously wormy. Farm-raised fish don't suffer from this problem.

Lobster–Hawaiian spiny lobster is quite good; also called "bugs" by lobster hunters. Maine lobster is revived on the Big Island, called Keahole Lobster.

Mahimahi–Deep ocean fish also known as a dolphinfish; served at lu'au; very common in restaurants. Sometimes tastes fishy, which can be offset in the preparation.

Marlin–Tasty when smoked, otherwise can be tough; the Pacific Blue Marlin is available almost year round.

Monchong–Excellent tasting deepwater fish, available year round. Usually served marinated and grilled.

Onaga–Also known as a ruby snapper; excellent eating in many preparations.

Ono–(Wahoo); *awesome* eating fish and can be prepared many ways; most plentiful May through October. Ono is also the Hawaiian word for delicious.

Opah–(Moonfish); excellent eating in many different preparations; generally available April through August.

'Opakapaka–(Crimson snapper); great tasting fish generally cooked several ways. Common Oct.–Feb.

'Opihi–Limpets found on ocean rocks. Eaten raw mixed with salt. Texture is similar to clams or mussels.

Poke–Fresh raw fish or octopus (tako) mixed with seaweed (limu), sesame seed and other seasonings and oil.

Shutome–Swordfish; dense meat that can be cooked several ways. Most plentiful March through July.

Walu–Also goes by other names such as butterfish and escolar. Be careful not to eat more than 6 ounces. The Hawaiian nickname for this oily fish is maku'u, which means—*ahem*, this is awkward—"uncontrollable bowel discharge." Eat too much, and you may pay more dearly than you intend.

LU'AU FOODS

Chicken lu'au–Chicken cooked in coconut milk and taro leaves.

Haupia–Coconut custard.

Kalua pig–Pig cooked in an underground oven called an imu, shredded and mixed with Hawaiian sea salt (outstanding!).

Laulau–Pork, beef or fish wrapped in taro and ti leaves and steamed. (You don't eat the ti leaf wrapping.)

Lomi salmon–Chilled salad consisting of raw, salted salmon, tomatoes and two kinds of onions.

Pipi kaula–Hawaiian beef jerky.

Poi–Steamed taro root pounded into a paste. It's a starch that will take on the taste of other foods mixed with it. Best eaten with kalua pig or fish. Visitors are encouraged to try it so they can badmouth it with authority.

OTHER ISLAND FOODS

Apple bananas–A smaller, denser, smoother texture than regular (Williams) bananas.

Barbecue sticks–Teriyaki-marinated pork, chicken or beef pieces barbecued and served on bamboo sticks.

Bento–Japanese box lunch.

Breadfruit–Melon-sized starchy fruit; served baked, deep fried, steamed, or boiled. Definitely an acquired taste.

Crackseed–Chinese-style, spicy preserved fruits and seeds. Li Hing Mui is one of the most popular flavors.

Guava–The inside is full of seeds, so it is rarely eaten raw. Used primarily for juice, jelly or jam.

Hawaiian supersweet corn–The finest corn you ever had, even raw. We'll lie, cheat, steal or maim to get it fresh.

Huli huli chicken–Hawaiian BBQ style.

Ka'u oranges–Locally grown. Usually, the uglier the orange, the better it tastes.

Kim chee–A Korean relish consisting of pickled cabbage, onions, radishes, garlic and chilies.

Kulolo–Steamed taro pudding.

Liliko'i–Passion fruit.

Loco moco–Rice, meat patty, egg and gravy. Specialty of Café 100 in Hilo.

Lychee–A reddish, woody peel that is discarded for the sweet, white fruit inside. Be careful of the pit. Small seed (or chicken-tongue) lychees are so good, they should be illegal.

Macadamia nut–A large, round nut grown primarily on the Big Island.

Malasada–Portuguese doughnut that is dipped in sugar. (Tex Drive-in is famous for them.)

Manapua–Steamed or baked bun filled with meat.

Mango–Bright orange fruit with yellow pink skin. Distinct, tasty flavor.

Manju–Cookie filled with a sweet center.

Musubi–Cold steamed rice, sometimes sliced Spam, rolled in black seaweed.

Papaya–Melon-like, pear-shaped fruit with yellow skin best eaten chilled. Good at breakfast.

Pipi Kaula–Hawaiian-style beef jerky. Excellent when dipped in poi. (Even if you don't like poi, this combo works.)

Plate lunch–An island favorite as an inexpensive, filling lunch. Consists of "two-scoop rice," a scoop of macaroni salad and some type of meat, either beef, chicken or fish. Also called a Box Lunch. Great for take-out.

Portuguese sausage–Pork sausage, highly seasoned with red pepper.

Pupu–Appetizer, finger foods or snack.

Saimin–Thin Chinese noodles cooked in a Japanese-style chicken, pork or fish broth. Word is peculiar to Hawai'i. Local Japanese say the dish comes from China. Local Chinese say it comes from Japan.

Shave ice–A block of ice is "shaved" into a ball with flavored syrup poured over the top. Best served with ice cream on the bottom. Very delicious.

Smoothie–Usually papaya, mango, frozen passion fruit and frozen banana, but almost any fruit can be used to make this milkshake-like drink. Add milk for creaminess.

Taro chips–Sliced and deep-fried taro; resembles potato chips.

KAILUA-KONA AMERICAN

Beach Tree
72-100 Kaupulehu Dr. • 325–8000

ⓞⓝⓞ North of Kona—Fantastic beachside setting at the Four Seasons at Hualalai 14 miles north of Kona. Mixed menu of pizza, sandwiches, burgers, a couple of grilled items and salads at lunch. They have a lobster burger, but at $25 we were too horrified by the price to try it. Dinner is steak, seafood and pasta. **$20–$30** for lunch, **$20–$60** for dinner. They get an ono because it's great food. But *expensive...*

Bongo Ben's Island Café
75-5819 Alii Dr. • 329–9203

Kona—Fairly broad menus with expanded offerings on the usual breakfast items, burgers, sandwiches, fresh fish, wraps and salads at lunch; add steak, pork and pasta at dinner. The atmosphere is busy and noisy from the Alii Drive traffic, but your view of the water across the street isn't obstructed by much. Breakfast is what they do best. After that, the food is pretty average, and the service can be a bit unfocused. They tend to overcharge on extras. ($3 to add avocado to your burger? Hey, avo trees are *everywhere* here.) Lots of choices from the bar, though with acceptable prices. **$9–$15** for breakfast and lunch, the top end moves to **$25** at dinner. Across from the seawall.

Bubba Gump Shrimp Co.
75-5776 Alii Dr. • 331–8442

ⓞⓝⓞ Kona—This whole restaurant is based on the 1994 movie *Forrest Gump*. You'll find most of the characters' names in the menu along with lots of shrimp dishes. The Dumb Luck Coconut Shrimp is excellent but pricey at $19. We absolutely love their hush pups (different from hush puppies). Their mango mojito is pretty darned refreshing. For dessert, try their Chocolate Chip Cookie Sundae, a sundae served in a cast iron skillet topped with caramel, chocolate, peanuts and whipped cream. Great views and a fun atmosphere make it a good experience, if you can tolerate the long wait at the door and the unusual service. If you want a server's attention, you have to flip the license plate to read "Stop Forrest Stop." On Ali'i Drive next to Waterfront Row in downtown Kona. **$13–$25** for lunch and dinner. No reservations. Railing tables all the way to the left overlook a pretty little cove.

Buns in the Sun
75-5595 Palani Rd. • 326–2774

(ONO) Kona—A bakery/sandwich joint with great food for the money. Take something as simple as a French dip, put it on their sourdough hoagies, and it becomes delicious. Tasty hot and cold sandwiches, soups and great baked goods. (Love the great sticky buns.) For breakfast they have pastries, as well as egg dishes, including kalua pig and eggs with fish and rice (a worthy choice). Avoid the biscuits and gravy; they taste like plastic. Good, flaky croissants. In the Lanihau Shopping Center off Palani Road. Breakfast is a cheap **$5–$10**; lunch is **$10–$13**. Opens at 5 a.m.

Costco
73-5600 Maiau St. • 331–4834

(ONO) Kona You'd be surprised at how many people eat at the food stand at Costco. Their pizza is surprisingly good (they use pretty good ingredients and the crust isn't bad), and it's *very* cheap. **$10** for a gigantic pizza. They also serve hot dogs, salads and a few other items. In the back of the store they have tasty whole rotisserie chickens for **$5**. You need to be a Costco member to get in. We gave them an ono because of the value—can't beat it. North Kona, see map on page 164.

Don the Beachcomber
75-5852 Alii Dr. • 329–3111

Kona—If you remember the original Don the Beachcomber restaurant, you probably also remember the end of Prohibition. This is the guy who claimed to have invented the mai tai in 1933. The theme

has been revived here at the Royal Kona Resort. The setting offers a commanding view of Kailua Bay and Alii Drive, and the torches at night give it a nice ambiance. Food, however, is unremarkable at best and definitely overpriced. And the $20 breakfast buffet is more of a glorified continental breakfast. Lunch is pizza, burgers and salads; dinner features pricey seafood but free, glorious sunsets. **$12–$19** for breakfast and lunch (the latter served at the bar), **$25–$40** for dinner. And yes, the original mai tais *are* good here. Personally, we prefer the killer bar location here for a sunset cocktail instead of the restaurant.

The Fish Hopper Seafood & Steaks
75-5683 Alii Dr. • 326–2002

Kona—The food is hit or miss here, with more misses than hits. Fish is what they do best (not surprisingly), but they also have tacos, wraps and sandwiches at lunch, and plenty of pasta and steak at dinner. Avoid the fish tacos and the bad calamari in favor of the mac nut-crusted mahi mahi. Prices are pretty high, especially at dinner ($30 for seafood pasta is hard to swallow), but the view from across the seawall is one of the better first floor views on Alii Drive. Some of their drinks, such as the Bucket of Fire, are downright amazing. **$9–$20** for breakfast, **$12–$20** for lunch, **$20–$35** for dinner. Reservations recommended. They also have gluten-free options.

Green Flash Coffee
75-6000 Alii Dr. • 329–4387

(ONO) Kona—In front of the Sea Village Condos (see map page 63), it's a convenient spot for anyone staying along Alii Drive since you won't need to drill into town and find a place to park. They make serious coffee drinks like the Earthquake with Ghirardelli chocolate and *four* shots of espresso.

It'll make your heartbeat register 7.0 on the Richter Scale. Try a breakfast sandwich served on French toast with a side of syrup. For lunch, their hot panini sandwiches are excellent. Consider the vegetable muffaletta and substitute the tapanada with pesto. Good baked goods from Mamane Bakery in Waimea. The service is friendly, but there's not much seating. A cheap **$5–$10** for breakfast and lunch. Open early every day from 6:30 a.m. So what's a green flash? Look at our description of that on page 57.

Harbor House
74-425 Kealakehe Pkwy. • 326–4166

ONO Kona—Ask anyone who frequents Harbor House why they go, and they'll give you a one-word answer—*schooners!* Located at Honokohau Harbor 2 miles north of Kona overlooking the water and boats, they serve the coldest beer on the island in ultra-thick, 18-ounce frosted schooners for around $3. (Oh, I almost forgot, they serve food, too.) This is a popular place to stop after a fishing or SCUBA excursion. The food consists of average fish and chips, fried calamari, burgers and assorted other fast food. (Good fish sandwich, though.) We didn't give 'em an ONO *because of the food;* it's just a great place to tip a cold one and watch the tranquil harbor waters while you go over your adventures of the day. If you sit near the bar, you may hear lots of watering hole talk. **$9–$15**. Head toward the harbor off Hwy 19 between the 97 and 98 mile markers and turn right at the buildings. Closes around 7 p.m.; the schooners aren't as cold near closing time.

Holuakoa Gardens & Café
76-5901 Mamalahoa Hwy • 322–2233

ONO Mauka of Kona (in Holualoa)—This is the best reason to drive up to Holualoa. Thanks to

readers for tipping us off to a place we've driven by many times without noticing. They mainly use ingredients grown nearby and clearly gush with pride over the results. The menu changes nightly based on what local farmers and fishermen supply. Beef, seafood and pasta are what they do, using incredibly creative preparations. They brag that they are a "slow food establishment," so don't be in a hurry. There's no real view and you'll hear some traffic noise over the jazz music background, but you won't care. Start things out with the very unusual pizzetas. (Fantastic use of pears and sometimes figs.) The salads are from fresh-picked local greens. (Forget the heavy dressings; just enjoy the greens.) You'll want to bring a light jacket since the elevation is 1,400 feet. This is one of those restaurants that orbits around a single dominating chef—and we hope he is happy and content to keep doing this for a long time. The desserts are stupid-good with the flourless midnight torte—when they have it—being absolute chocolate heaven. You may have to park down the road if you can't find the parking lot above the restaurant. Closed Sunday night. Reservations recommended. Brunch (**$14–$20**) isn't as good; stick with dinner, which is **$25–$40**. They also have an adjacent café for morning coffee and pastries. Almost across the street from the Kona Hotel on Hwy 180. From Hwy 11 you can cut up the mountain from Lako St. near the 119 mile marker, turn right when it dead ends, then left on Hwy 180 for less than a mile; mauka side.

Huggo's
75-5828 Kahakai Rd. • 329–1493

Kona—This is a frustrating restaurant to review. It's the best location in town, bar none. They have *gorgeous* open-air views adjacent to the ocean at Kailua Bay. They are so close to the water because they are grandfathered into the regulations restricting oceanside construction. This ocean proximity alone almost gets them an ONO. But execution is spotty. Service can be pretty bad, and for these prices, you shouldn't have to beg for water refills and wait forever for entrées. And while some recipes—such as the teri steak—are good. Others can be pretty bland. You know something's wrong when you're reaching for the empty bread tray late in the evening. Try to get a railing table where you look down onto sand, rock and water. (Preferable over the patio tables.) The adjacent lounge is a good place to enjoy a drink at sunset. Since it's so pricey and the view so important to the experience, consider them for an early dinner, because you're paying premium prices and getting a premium location but with unreliable food. **$25–$50** for dinner. Off Alii Drive, downtown Kona near Royal Kona Resort. Their next door venue is **Huggo's on the Rocks** which has a large bar and cheaper food. Burgers, fish and chips, fish tacos and a few other items. Live music nightly. A much better value than Huggo's but the table arrangements aren't as intimate with the ocean. **$15–$20**. Even though we can't give them an ONO due to unreliability, it's almost worth the gamble to give them a try for the views.

Humpy's Big Island Ale House
75-5815 Alii Dr. • 324-2337
Kona—A vast and varied menu of pub food on steroids. From pizzas to baked subs to local dishes to sandwiches and wraps, pastas and crab, burgers and more. You'd be hard pressed to walk away without something that grabs your attention. Flavors are good, but the food is pretty greasy. People watchers will like the downstairs level; ocean viewers will want the top. Both are accompanied by traffic views and sounds. The menu reflects the

Alaskan heritage of the founders with salmon and the use of halibut in the fish and chips. The garlic shrimp are potent to the point of almost overpowering. Big beer selection. **$9–$17** for breakfast (Sat. and Sun. only), **$13–$20** for lunch and dinner plus a couple pricier items. In the Coconut Grove Marketplace.

Island Lava Java
75-5799 Alii Dr. • 327-2161
ONO Kona—An awesome—and highly popular—place for breakfast. The coffee is pretty good (though sometimes not very hot), and the food is tasty and not *too* ridiculously priced for the location. (They're right across the street from the ocean with excellent views, so you ain't gonna get a bargain.) Above average baked goods and a few breakfast items like the tasty breakfast wraps. Their cinnamon rolls are obscene and utterly massive (big enough to use as a flotation device if you fall in the water), and they taste great. An easy recommendation, although the rolls don't usually come out of the oven until around 7:30 a.m. and service is sometimes attitudy. Good (though *very* pricey) fresh-squeezed pineapple juice. Get an outdoor table. Lunch is fairly well-prepared sandwiches, soups, salads and pizzas. Alii Drive in Kona in Alii Sunset Plaza. **$5–$20** for breakfast, **$10–$25** for lunch, **$15–$35** for dinner. One note: To get to the restroom you need to go through part of the kitchen, and our observations—plus reader feedback—indicate that they need to take a bit more pride in keeping up their kitchen environment.

Jackie Rey's Ohana Grill
75-5995 Kuakini Hwy • 327-0209
ONO Kona—Locals are the majority of the customers, and not just because it's not near Alii Drive. Jackie Rey's excels in every detail from

well-made drinks to decadent desserts. Choose from their respectable wine list or go for the mai tai. The dinner entrées—fish, steak, pasta and short ribs—are attractively presented, and the chef knows how to combine flavors. Finish your meal with a Triple Fudge Brownie Roll. Lunch is equally good with an array of smart salads and sandwiches, burgers and some odds and ends. **$11–$17** for lunch, **$13–$35** for dinner. No lunch on weekends. On Kuakini Hwy across from Walua Road.

Java on the Rock
75-5828 Kahakai Rd. • 329-9262
Kona—An espresso bar that serves a little bit of food. Only five items at breakfast. They cook their eggs using the cappuccino machine and put them in a tortilla. Is a breakfast burrito worth *$13?* No, and it's not particularly good. But their location is *wonderful*. It's right next to the water in an ultra-relaxing atmosphere, so you're paying for that. They're not exactly lightning fast, but with this location you're not exactly in a hurry. Around **$14** for coffee and a breakfast entree. Next door to Huggo's off Alii Drive near the Royal Kona Resort. You can't linger past 11 a.m. That's when Huggo's takes over the spot, and it becomes Huggo's on the Rocks.

Kona Canoe Club
75-5744 Alii Dr. • 331-1155
Kona—Their sign reads, FISH, BURGERS AND GROG. And although we haven't found grog on the menu, they do make a powerful mai tai, if you're in the mood. It may not be world famous like they claim, but it may make you *feel* famous after just one. Great oceanside location, especially if you get a railing seat. They seem to have slipped since our last edition. Prices went up and quality of ingredients went down. (I mean, when you pay $18 for fish and chips, frozen mahi mahi is a bit disappointing, and they have a repeating habit of overcooking it—and fries—and lots of other things.) Their mud pie, though is truly great, as you calve it like your own personal iceberg. They're fussy about substitutions, and fries are not included with entrées. **$15–$26** for lunch and dinner; more if you get the ribs. In the Kona Inn Shopping Village.

Kona Inn Restaurant
75-5744 Alii Dr. • 329-4455
(ONO) Kona—Mostly seafood with a little pasta and stir-fry. Nice ambiance—a good place for a sunset dinner. Just a strip of grass separates you from the ocean. Dinner includes many varieties of fish. Consider the *super*-rich but tasty stuffed local fresh fish. At dinner, avoid the uncomfortable antique chairs in favor of the high-back wicker chairs. **$10–$23** for lunch, **$20–$45** for dinner. The food and service are usually very good. Check out the ceiling fans—all interconnected by an old belt system. Some parents like to bring their keiki here so the munchkins can play on the grass while the grownups can dine and keep an eye on them. Things are hit or miss here. Clueless service happens a bit too often, and the ONO is marginal. Located on the ocean side of Alii Drive in downtown Kona at the Kona Inn Shopping Village. Can't miss it.

Lava Java—See *Island Lava Java*.

Quinn's Almost-by-the-Sea
75-5655 Palani Rd. • 329-3822
(ONO) Kona—Truth in advertising. You're close to the ocean but can't really see it. Lunch offers seafood, burgers and sandwiches. The fish sandwich, especially Cajun style, is excellent, as are most seafood items. (Switch

the mahi mahi sandwich for ono or ahi—it's *mo bettah*.) The clam chowder could use a little improvement. For dinner, it's the same menu plus more steak and seafood. Service is quick at lunch time. Consider the quasi-outdoor section for a nice lunch-time nautical, green ambiance. This place hasn't changed a bit over several editions. Most of the food is tastily prepared, but they do have off days. We recommend lunch over the pricey dinner. **$10–$14** for lunch, **$10–$30** for dinner. On Palani Road across from the King Kamehameha Kona Beach Hotel in Kona. Limited parking.

Sam Choy's Kai Lanai
78-6831 Alii Dr. • 333–3434

Kona—Sam Choy is a giant presence in the food industry in Hawai'i with TV shows, books and restaurants. This location sports the most commanding view in Kona, looking down from the Keauhou Shopping Center over the Kona shoreline (try to ignore the Long's roof). Sunsets from here are unbeatable. And the atmosphere effective, wide open and feels roomy. As for the food: Sam is well known for his creativeness and flavor combinations, bringing a local and Asian twist. But Sam's food seems to have gotten much healthier—undeniably at the expense of the flavor. We want to be able to recommend them, but the word "bland" keeps crossing our minds when describing the food, and dinner isn't worth the price after the view goes away. **$10–$15** for lunch, **$20–$40** for dinner. Ask for a fire pit table if you want some ambiance-setting flames nearby.

Splasher's Grill
75-5663 Palani Rd. • 326–2212

ONO Kona—Dinner prices are reasonable given the location and narrowly focused but nice views

of the Kailua Pier across the street from about half the tables. (Alii Dr. traffic noise is unavoidable here.) The menu has seafood, a number of generous pastas, steak, chicken and burgers. Lunch is a broad selection of burgers, sandwiches and wraps plus some salads. The bar is reasonably skilled and accommodating with a decent mai tai. Try the liliko'i cheesecake dipped in chocolate for dessert. Their name refers to their former location, across from the splashiest part of the seawall. Quality and portions are more than acceptable for the money and the servers hustle and care. Upstairs on the corner of Alii and Palani across from the Kailua Pier. **$10–$15** for breakfast and lunch, **$12–$20** for dinner.

• Ultimate Burger
74-5450 Makala Blvd. • 329–2326

ONO Kona—They raise lots of cattle on this island, but most burgers are made from frozen beef flown in from the mainland. Not this place. The hamburger is fresh and locally raised (which seems to have a...*beefier* flavor than standard beef). They also mix herbs into the meat, and results are wonderful. Patties are ⅓-pound, and you can get 1 to 4 of them on a bun. (For the record, we can't visualize how someone could manage to eat the 1⅓-pound TKO burger.) The quality is excellent as are the tasty (but pricey) fries. Beer is also available. A good place for tasty, guilty pleasure. In the Kona Commons on Makala north of downtown Kona. **$7–$15** for lunch and dinner.

KAILUA-KONA CHINESE

Ocean Seafood
75-5626 Kuakini Hwy • 329–3055

Kona—The food is more authentic than most Chinese restaurants, and the price is compelling. Usually well-prepared dishes, fresh ingredients and lots of attention to quality, but sometimes they drop the ball. Buffets offered most of the time—these are an *excellent* bargain. Lunch buffet for **$11**, dinner buffet **$17**. Otherwise, off the menu is **$10–$20** per person. Located in the King Kamehameha Mall in Kona. See map on page 61.

KAILUA-KONA FRENCH

La Bourgogne French Restaurant
77-6400 Nalani St. • 329–6711

ONO Kona—This *tiny* restaurant on Hwy 11 between Keauhou and Kona serves tasty and well-conceived dishes, including lamb, duck, venison, rabbit, lobster and even veal sweetbreads. Good and reasonably priced wine list. Entrée prices are in a pretty narrow range. Only dings: a bit cramped and enclosed with no view. Closed Sunday and Monday. Dinner is **$37–$47**. Reservations recommended. We haven't changed our review in a while because this place hasn't change much over time.

KAILUA-KONA ITALIAN

Bianelli's
78-6831 Alii Dr. • 322–0377

ONO Kona—Long-time visitors might remember Bianelli's. It was one of those great places that mysteriously closed. After a six-year absence, they reopened and then moved to the Keauhou Shopping Center at the south end of Alii Drive. Although it's the same owner and recipes, the food isn't quite as good as I remember. (But memory can be a funny thing, especially with food.) They have one saving grace, though. For the pizza, opt for the 12-inch deep dish crust (the reason for the ONO, but they *don't* sell it by the slice) instead of the New York. And try the killer pesto and pine nut bread. Take-out or snag an outdoor

table. **$5–$12** for lunch and dinner. No dessert, but you can go around the corner to **Moo Bettah**, which has adequate frozen yogurt and other treats.

Kona Brewing Co. & Brewpub
74-5612 Pawai Pl. • 334–2739

ONO Kona—A cool place to go for some tasty brew and a pizza or salad. Fifteen taps feature 11 or so different beers made there, as well as seasonal and guest beers. They range from the mild (Liliko'i Wheat Ale) to the not-so-mild (Fire Rock Pale Ale). We're fond of the Hefeweissen. Most of the pizzas are delicious. *Love* the Ka'u Pesto. If you normally sprinkle red peppers on your pizza, consider replacing the regular sauce with their Cajun sauce instead. In fact, they have 7 different sauces and *lots* of toppings, so the possibilities are many. As a result, we're forced to review them often so we can evaluate all the permutations. (We do it for you, only for you. Aren't we selfless?) Their Kilauea lava flow dessert is pretty criminal, and a half portion is probably enough for two. The service could use a little improvement at times, and we wish they could do something about the flies and gnats at the outside tables, but overall, this is a *great* place with good pizza and beer. They have other items, such as the tasty (and messy) pastrami on flatbread. **$14–$24** for lunch and dinner. At the end of Pawai Place off Kaiwi Street. See map on page 61. No reservations, and long waits are not uncommon.

KAILUA-KONA JAPANESE

Hayashi's You Make The Roll
75-5725 Alii Dr. • 326–1322

ONO Kona—Tasty and cheap. The sushi is made right before your eyes and tastes great. Just a few outdoor tables, but this is the place to get your sushi fix. **$5–$10.** Kona Marketplace Shopping Center off Alii Drive, *way* in the back.

Kenichi Pacific
78-6831 Alii Dr. • 322–6400

(ONO) Kona—Very well-prepared sushi in a slightly ritzy atmosphere. In addition to the sushi, they also have other entrées under the fusion genre, such as steak, seafood and lamb. In fact, their mac nut-encrusted lamb is absolutely wonderful and unexpectedly unJapanese. The attention to detail is obvious. The molten cake dessert is *ultra* rich chocolate. (Oh, yeah!) It ain't cheap here, but with good service, consistently good food and a good environment, it's *easy* to recommend. **$15–$45** for dinner. In the Keauhou Shopping Center at the south end of Alii Drive. Open nightly from 5 to 9:30 p.m. Closed Mondays.

KAILUA-KONA LOCAL

Ba-Le
74-5588 Palani Rd. • 327–1212

(ONO) Kona—OK, so it's not really local. It's part of a chain of Vietnamese noodle shops with French bread sandwiches. But the food is good for the price. Those who aren't fond of Vietnamese flavors will probably like the sandwiches, beef stew or the roast beef croissant. Lots of veggie items. **$5–$13** for lunch and dinner. In Kona Coast Shopping Center, Palani Road, Kona.

•Big Island Grill
75-5702 Kuakini Hwy • 326–1153

(ONO) Kona—Popular with local residents and a bit loud with closely spaced tables and no-nonsense service, the food is hearty local-style with items such as chicken katsu, loco moco, tempura fish (which is great) and saimin.

Portions are dependably generous, but it can take awhile to get your food. Desserts are big and deadly. (Good banana splits and excellent mud pie.) Breakfast is **$8–$18,** lunch is **$10–$22,** dinner is mostly similar with a few pricier steaks. At the corner of Henry and Kuakini.

Pine Tree Café
73-4040 Hulikoa St. • 327–1234
North Kona—Your options are limited out near the airport. This is probably your best bet. Reasonable prices and fairly good food. The menu is *huge* (except for the weak drink selection). Lots of burgers, most under $6, a good and exotic fried poke fish plate, saimin, and unusual items like the teriyaki kimchee burger. Ambiance is classic strip mall but the food is better than average. $7–$17.

KAILUA-KONA MEXICAN

Killer Tacos
74-5483 Kaiwi St. • 329–3335

(ONO) Kona—The kind of place you'd never find if someone didn't tell you about it. Tucked away in an industrial area, the name is spot on. (Well, we've never actually seen anyone drop dead here.) Killer tacos, killer burritos, killer portions and killer prices. Pretty deadly, huh? The most expensive thing is the $7 taco salad, which is…well, you know. Put kalua pig or the spicy ground beef in your burrito, or bag one of the fish tacos. The only thing that needs improving is the salsa—consider substituting it for hot sauce. See Kona map, page 61. Near the highway, on Kaiwi, near Luhia Street. $5–$9 for lunch and dinner. Closed Sunday. Cash only.

Los Habañeros
78-6831 Alii Dr. • 324–4688
Kona—We're baffled by this one. We still get e-mails from readers recommending

this place, but we have to walk away scratching our heads. Cheap Mexican eats for sure. In our last edition we said they were one step below Taco Bell. With a name like Los Habañeros you'd expect the food to be bursting with flavor. Instead, it was incredibly bland unless you showered the food with salsa. They have upped their game a bit and are now one step *above* Taco Bell. Hard to get excited, eh? In the Keauhou Shopping Center. $7–$15 for lunch and early dinner.

Pancho & Lefty's
75-5719 Alii Dr. • 326-2171
Kona—With their ultra-prominent location on Alii Drive (the view of the ocean isn't as good as you might think from the street), this place could serve really bad food and still put people in seats. (And our previous review reflected our general lack of enthusiasm.) The menu is large and varied. (Non-Mexican items are on the "Gringo Grill" section.) The nachos are hearty, the food filling, and items are more than acceptable. You won't dream about it, but it's not bad. You'd probably eat here again in a pinch…but you wouldn't tell your friends about it. Sunset sounds are filled with the squawks of flocks of mynah birds in the trees outside. Mixed drinks here are tasty and fairly potent. Overall, Pancho & Lefty's is one of those places that you can't help but notice in Kona, and is an adequate choice for a meal. $13–$30 for lunch and dinner.

Rosa's Cantina & Sunset Grill
75-5805 Alii Dr. • 326-1198
Kona—This place has the same owners as Pancho and Lefty's (but with better views from some tables if you ignore the ugly power lines). The menu is more creative with items like molcajete (too complicated to explain), punta nesta pasta, steak diablo, plus other steak, seafood and burgers. Prices ain't cheap, and if you get a table

farther from the rails, you'll feel overcharged. Like Pancho, they make a pretty good nacho, and like Lefty, other items can be lacking. In Coconut Grove Marketplace. $13–$30.

KAILUA-KONA THAI

Lotus Café
73-5617 Maiau St. • 327-3270
ono Kona—You won't drive by this place; ya gotta know it's there. It's literally part of an Asian wooden furniture store. (So no cheesy plastic tables here.) This is another example of readers tipping us off to a great place. The menu stresses Thai, but it also includes some Indian, Burmese, Indonesian, Vietnamese and Singaporean dishes. They use mostly organic ingredients from local suppliers. The variety of flavors is amazing. This is *not* a one trick pony. If you're having troubling picking, the taster's special has three small entrées—a nice way to go. Their Thai tea is pretty different than other Thai teas—real gingery. You'll either love it or hate it. You don't have go spicy to still get flavors here. But if you *do*, they also make their own dairy-free gelato to cool things off and offer various smoothies and blended drinks from it. Reasonably priced and great quality. At the back corner of Kaloko Industrial Park, top of the road past Costco at Kamanu and Maiau. See map on page 164. $10–$20 for lunch and dinner. Closed Sundays.

Kona Taeng-On Thai Food
75-5744 Alii Dr. • 329-1994
Kona—Sorry, but the food's not good enough to warrant these kind of prices. Good menu but uninspiringly prepared. Service is a little cranky. You got way better Thai choices in Kona. $13–$30. Upstairs on Alii Drive across from Kona Marketplace.

Orchid Thai Cuisine
74-5555 Kaiwi St. • 327–9437

(ono) Kona—We liked them when they had a simple, spartan atmosphere buried in the back of in an industrial area because the food was so good. Now that they've moved and have a more refined ambiance, we're as happy as can be. The food is great and very reasonably priced. *Super* good chicken satay. Good curries. The portions are on the small side, but overall this is a winner. BYOB. **$10–$20** for lunch and dinner. In Kuakini Center. Take Kuakini Hwy north, right on Kaiwi Street. Closed Sunday.

Original Thai
75-5629 Kuakini Hwy • 329–3459

(ono) Kona—We find it ironic that a place called Original Thai would plaster the definition of *original* all over their menu, claim that their food is what original Thai tastes like, then serve burgers, wraps and coleslaw as well as Thai items. What's even more strange is that they do it so well. The larb wrap is bursting with goodness, and the burgers are made with curried meat. Even the fries and coleslaw have a hint of Thai. The curries are fantastic and come in big portions. A wonderful start is a cup of coconut milk soup. It's a shame that service can be snippy. In the Ilima Court Shopping Center. **$9–$22** for lunch and dinner. Closed Monday. BYOB.

Thai Rin
75-5799 Alii Dr. • 329–2929

Kona—Nice location right across Alii Drive from the ocean. The curries are their weakest item—surprisingly bland and watery. They make a pretty good garlic eggplant and the pad Thai is tasty, but overall it's an underwhelming Thai experience. Next to Island Lava Java. **$10–$25**

(more for the lobster combo) for lunch and dinner. Lunch specials can knock the price down a couple of bucks.

KAILUA-KONA TREATS

Cuz'ns
75-5744 Alii Dr. • 326–4920

Kona—Smoothies here are real variable. Sometimes fairly good, sometimes way too thin and sweet. Pricey at **$5** each. You're better off next door at **Kona Coffee Café** (329–7131) where you can grab a cold frappe. (Don't let them twist your arm into buying their overpriced bags of Kona coffee.) At the back of the Kona Inn Shopping Village.

Hawaiian Ice Cones
75-5595 Palani Rd. • 895–8390

(ono) Kona—Probably the best shave ice in Kona. Good, fine ice and chilled syrups. (Necessary to avoid the dreaded *chunking* that happens if you don't chill 'em.) Add ice cream on the bottom, and for **$3** you have a *broke da mouf* experience. Next to Longs Drugs in Lanihau Center off Palani Road.

Kailua Candy Company
73-5612 Kauhola St. • 329–2522

(ono) Kona—Handmade chocolates are the specialty here. Expensive but delicious. Try the pricey a'a lava (dark chocolate with coconut and mac nuts) or the turtles. They also make utterly indecent cheesecake with some world-class flavor combinations sold by the slice. Near Costco off Hwy 19 at the 96 mile marker. See map on page 164. Closed Sun.

Kanaka Kava
75-5803 Alii Dr. • 327–1660

Kona—Gee, we didn't know *where* to put this one. It's a kava bar. Kava (called awa in Hawai'i) is made from a root and tastes a little like woody water. It's a mild relaxant/pain killer. Polynesians have been using it for generations, and it has cultural importance here. When you get a bowl, you're supposed to gulp it down fast; don't sip. It may make your mouth tingle. Consider it once at least for the novelty. **$6** for the kava. They also have some pupu items to wash it down. (And the owner sometimes plays a mean harmonica.) On the backside of Coconut Grove Marketplace on Alii Drive.

KLA Snacktime
73-5612 Kauhola St. • 345–6009
Kona—Their location is near Costco. It's ultra simple, but it has good shave ice—we like that they keep their syrups chilled—and it's **$5–$6**, including ice cream. They also have decent sandwiches for $5 and hot dogs for $3. Friendly folks, but don't expect much atmosphere, and if the blender's running, use a bull horn for your conversations. Extra touches here like smoothies with almond milk and ube (sweet potato) ice cream. $3 for Kona coffee. Add 25¢ for ice—there's a bit of a head scratcher for ya. No credit cards. Worth a stop.

Kona Mountain Coffee
73-4038 Hulikoa Dr. • 329–5005
North Kona—This place is filled with all kinds of treats that look great…but taste mediocre. The coffee comes straight from the coffee farm, however. Close to the airport near the 95 mile marker on Hwy 19.

Tropical Dreams Ice Cream
Various Locations
 This is the best ice cream that we've ever found in Hawai'i, and it's made on the island in Waimea. It's fairly easy to find island wide at places that serve ice cream. If you see it, snag some. It's downright wicked.

SOUTH OF KAILUA-KONA DINING

Annie's Island Fresh Burgers
79-7460 Mamalahoa Hwy • 324–6000
American—An upscale burger joint that justifies the lofty prices. Readers rave about the place and we do, too. The menu is pretty simple—burgers, chicken and fish sandwiches, a few salads and desserts. (Love the cheesecakes—especially the double chocolate, which is deadly enough for two.) When in season, the liliko'i spritzer is delicious and super refreshing. Goat cheese poppers are tasty if not particularly hot. Arrive before sunset for a nice ambiance, and check out the palm trees growing through the back of the restaurant. **$15–$20** for lunch and dinner. In the Mango Court (which has no mango trees) south of the 113 mile marker.

Big Jake's Island BBQ
83-5308 Mamalahoa Hwy • 328–1227
South of Kona—It's not that we don't like the food here, it's just that you pay restaurant prices but end up eating from plastic baskets on picnic tables outside. Food is pulled pork, ribs, brisket and other BBQ staples. **$13–$28** for lunch and early dinner. On Hwy 11 next to a fish market at the 106 mile marker.

Coffee Shack
83-5799 Mamalahoa Hwy • 328–9555
American—A good place to stop on your way to the volcano—they open at 7:30 a.m. Except when we want a *big* breakfast, this is where we often stop. *Fantastic* view down the slopes of Mt. Hualalai overlooking Kealakekua and Honaunau—try to get a railing table and check out the gigantic avocado tree and the coffee trees below you. (It's nice to sit there drinking coffee grown from those very trees.) Tables are outdoors but covered, and the place is

clean. Nice selection of coffee drinks, good homemade baked goods and breads (when fresh, which is not a certainty), a small selection of breakfast items and a decent selection of sandwiches and pizzas for lunch. Avoid the ginger bread in favor of the cinnamon rolls. Their home-grown coffee is usually tasty (occasionally off). **$13–$18** for breakfast and lunch. Service is often slow. On ocean side of highway in Captain Cook between the 109 and 108 mile markers.

Ka'aloa's Super J's
83-5409 Mamalahoa Hwy • 328–9566

(ono) Local—An unassuming pinkish house on the makai side of the highway above Kealakekua Bay. When you walk in, you might not be acknowledged. Don't take it personally, they're just relaxed. Once the grinding begins you'll be happy you discovered the local flavors here. The $8 plate lunches are a better value than the $12 combo plates. Gotta try the lau lau (just don't eat the ti leaf wrapper). The kulolo makes a decent dessert. In all, a good choice to grab local grinds. Closed Sun. South of the 107 mile marker. Cash only. 10 a.m. to 6 p.m.

Ke'ei Café
79-7511 Mamalohoa Hwy • 322–9992

(ono) American—Well, not really American, sort of a hodge-podge of items from many countries. (I guess that *is* American.) You know how you sometimes purposely get into a rut at a restaurant by ordering the same dish because you love it so much? That's how I am for the fresh fish (especially ono) on Thai curry and jasmine rice, or the (spicy) fajitas stuffed with chicken or tofu, salsa, black bean chili sauce and avocado. The decor is nicely appointed, but passing cars from the highway are too loud. Don't worry

about it, though. The flavors are unlimited. (Try the eggplant rolls with couscous inside for an appetizer or the excellent coconut shrimp rice cakes.) Also available are ribeye steak, great pork chops and a few other items. Desserts are bread pudding, a mango cobbler and more. And they make good mango martinis. Our review doesn't change much because the place is consistent. On Hwy 11 just south of Kona in Kainaliu between the 112 and 113 mile markers. **$10–$33** for dinner. Closed Sun. and Mon. No credit cards.

Mahina Café
82-6123 Mamalahoa Hwy • 323–3200

American—Readers tipped us off to their cream cheese-stuffed French toast, and we have to agree. Very good. It's like eating dessert for breakfast. In fact, that seems to be their theme. They give you a free malasada with breakfast, and other sweet items abound, including stunning pies. If you just want eggs, taters and sausage, they'll oblige. Overall, it's good, but a little shy of an ONO. **$9–$15** for breakfast. South of the 112 mile marker on the ocean side of the hwy. No view.

Manago
82-6155 Mamalahoa Hwy • 323–2642

(ono) Local—It's like eating in Grandma's kitchen. Ambiance is *so* homey, and this place never seems to change. They are famous across the island for their pork chops, which, I'm happy to say, are *not* just like Mama used to make. (Hers were always so dry.) These are moist, fatty and flavorful. (They use an ancient, cast-iron pan and cook 2,000 pounds a month.) They bring your sides at the very beginning, and you share them. They also have teri steak, butterfish, liver, etc. For dessert they feature…absolutely nothing. Pick up a Snickers bar in the lobby.

Closed Monday. South of Kona in Captain Cook off Hwy 11 at the Manago Hotel. Can't miss it. **$4–$7** for breakfast. **$10–$16** for lunch and dinner.

Mi's Italian Bistro
81-6372 Mamalahoa Hwy • 323–3880

ONO Italian—From Kona you gotta drive up the hill to get here. And from the outside, you won't be bowled over. But this is the kind of place travellers love to find. A husband/wife team serves fresh pasta, sauces from scratch and uses local ingredients combined with skill and care. The cioppino is wonderful, and you won't go wrong with the pumpkin soup or the polenta with shrimp. There's no view, but the ambiance is pleasing. Not cheap and not conveniently located just south of the 111 mile marker, but a great dining experience. **$15–$33** for dinner. Reservations recommended.

Patz Pies at Paparoni's
82-6127 Mamalahoa Hwy • 323–8100

ONO Italian—Yeah, now we're talking. An easy-to-miss pizza joint on Hwy 11 in Captain Cook that dispenses outstanding New York-style pizza for cheap prices. The owner is a genuine New York pizza-maker, and the product shows pride in workmanship. A slice is $3 and a large pizza (for two or three people) is $17–$25. That means you can expect to eat well for **$5–$12**. South of the Manago Hotel at Kamakani Street past the 110 mile marker.

Teshima's Restaurant
79-7251 Mamalahoa Hwy • 322–9140

Japanese—Clean, friendly place with simple Japanese, American and local items, such as bento, teriyaki beef and fried fish. Some items are good (such as the sashimi), though other items, such as miso, saimin and the apple pie might disappoint. This place is wildly popular with locals, but if it's Japanese flavors you're looking for, you can do better elsewhere. Also, they have a habit of bringing all the food at once. Off Hwy 11 in Honalo, just south of Kona. Lunch is **$7–$16**, dinner is **$10–$20**.

KOHALA DINING

There are a lot of ONO symbols in the Kohala dining section. That's no accident. If you're staying in Kohala, you'll find that the food choices are outstanding. That makes it difficult for us as reviewers. Normally, if we think a place is a dump, we say it's a dump. If the food or service is lousy, we say it's lousy. Unfortunately for us, most Kohala restaurants have great food and service and excellent atmosphere. This makes it hard to review without sounding like a bootlicking commercial for Kohala restaurants. The resorts go to great lengths (and expense) to feed you and keep you eating at the resort. The downside for you is that you can pay *dearly* for those ONOs. Most of the restaurants here are pricey, and you'll find that eating in Kohala will cost you more than on any other part of the island. It wasn't our intention to gush over so many restaurants in Kohala, but we can't deny the fundamental quality of their offerings at these establishments.

The restaurants at the **Four Seasons** are in the Kona dining section since they are often frequented by people staying in Kona.

If you want to cook your own meals, you'll soon learn that there are no large **grocery stores** in this area, just a small upscale market in Queens' MarketPlace. You *will* find a big store, however, a few miles up the road in Waikoloa Village.

When we mention that a restaurant has lunch only, or breakfast and dinner only, you should take this with a grain of salt. Resorts are constantly rearranging these options. Also, you'll find the resorts mentioned are shown on the maps on pages 53 and 152.

For simplicity, we are *excluding* restaurants in the northernmost part of Kohala (Hawi and Kapa'au). They are described under DINING ELSEWHERE.

KOHALA AMERICAN

The Bay Terrace
68-1400 Mauna Lani Dr. • 885-6622
(ono) Mauna Lani—At the Mauna Lani Bay Hotel, the beautiful indoor/outdoor setting and outstanding food make this a winner. The breakfast buffets (**$31**) have an excellent cross section of breakfast items and fresh fruit. Or go à la carte for $15–$25.

Blue Dragon Coastal Cuisine & Musiquarium
61-3616 Kawaihae Rd. • 882-7771
(ono) Kawaihae—A great restaurant if you can live without a view. The food is stupid good. They could make a radiator fluid martini and dirt casserole compelling. (But fortunately, they aren't on the menu.) Consider starting with the Hamakua mushroom polenta along with one of their uncommonly creative drinks, many made with fresh local tropical fruits and premium spirits. (They seem to craft their own drinks better than standard cocktails.) Then move onto any of their steak and seafood entrées. It's the kind of place where you have a hard time deciding because everything sounds so good. And their chocolate flourless whatever-itscalled dessert (with ice cream) is deadly. They tend to attract some of the better live musicians on the island, and the uncovered atmosphere, surrounded by

their building, is akin to being on the open deck of a large ship. Our only complaint is that service, while being super friendly, is not quite attentive enough for these prices. **$25–$40** or more at dinner with several cheaper items, but overall, that's the range. On the side of the Hwy in Kawaihae (Hwy 270). Call for days of operation.

Brown's Beach House
1 North Kaniku Dr. • 885-2000
(ono) Mauna Lani—Very good outdoor setting near the beach at the Fairmont Orchid. (Sometimes it gets too breezy.) Seafood is their best bet, which they do very well. They also have steak and chicken. An easy recommend. **$35–$60** for dinner.

The Canoe House
68-1400 Mauna Lani Dr. • 885-6622
(ono) Mauna Lani—The indoor/outdoor setting near the ocean at this Mauna Lani Bay Hotel restaurant, coupled with expertly prepared and presented food, make this a memorable choice for seafood plus a bit of steak and pasta. This is a great restaurant by anyone's definition and one we are happy to re-review any time we can. The sunsets from an outdoor railing table are smashing most of the year. Items change often, so we'll refrain from singling any out. It's hard to go wrong here, unless you forget your credit card. Expect **$40–$55** plus super pricey pupus. Dinner only. Reservations recommended (make them for an early dinner if you want a sunset). We've had some reader feedback complaining of bad service, but personally, we've never caught them on a bad night.

Coast Grille
62-100 Kaunaoa Dr. • 880-1111
Mauna Kea—Located at the Hapuna Beach Prince Hotel, the setting overlook-

ing Hapuna Beach is wonderful. They have indoor and outdoor tables, but it's the outdoor ones that give it the dreamy atmosphere. It's steak and seafood here, but frankly, it's not quite up to the quality it should be for these prices. The wine list is very extensive, though. Their oyster bar has several varieties of oysters and the mac nut-crusted mahi mahi is pretty good. $30–$45. Open Sundays through Thursdays only.

Hawaii Calls
69-275 Waikoloa Beach Dr.
886-6789

Waikoloa—The menu tries to do a little of everything—a little steak, seafood, pasta, ribs and chicken. Service isn't as tight as other Kohala restaurants, but we've noticed that they tend to run more specials, such as two for one or 50% off all entrées when you order a bottle of wine. The food's fairly bad for these prices with overcooked fish and embarrassingly small portions on some items. The open ambiance is a combination of tropical and modern and could use a bit more vision. There are sunset views, but it's fairly filtered through the pool area and lots of scenic palm trees. $30–$50 for dinner. At the Waikoloa Beach Marriott.

Island Fish & Chips
69-250 Waikoloa Beach Dr.
886-0005

Waikoloa—They brag about using fresh fish at this stand, but we've seen frozen mahi mahi used as the entrée. Chips along with fried fish, fried coconut shrimp, fried calamari or chicken. It's a small operation and can take a while if anyone's in front of you. The breading is tasty, but pretty thick and therefore, holds *a lot* of oil. Doesn't work for us. In the King's Shops, Waikoloa. $11–$15 for lunch and dinner.

Island Gourmet Markets
69-201 Waikoloa Beach Dr.
886-3577

ono Waikoloa—Not actually a restaurant, it's the area's grocery store with an inventory chosen specifically with resort visitors in mind. They also have a deli that has some pretty good sandwiches, a soup bar, pizza, sushi and other items for reasonable prices. (Ahh...reasonable for *Kohala*, that is.) You can also pick up fresh fruits and cookables, and some of their specials, especially on wines, can be downright reasonable. $7–$10. In the Queen's Market-Place, Waikoloa.

Kamuela Provision Company
69-425 Waikoloa Beach Dr.
886-1234

ono Waikoloa—Steak, seafood and a token veggie item at this Hilton Waikoloa Village restaurant. The views, especially from the outdoor tables, are fantastic. Inside you'll find an upscale yet casual decor. Start everything off with the tasty but *super*-pricey ($40) appetizer platter for two, which has poached shrimp, ahi poke, four oysters and king crab legs. Dinner selections seem to change often enough that we won't recommend a particular dish. The desserts are very tasty. They have one called *Sweet Note*. Order it 24 hours in advance, and it'll include a note with any message you want. (You romantic softie, you.) You may like the elevated outdoor oceanside tables for sunsets, lively indoor tables or grab a cocktail at the other outdoor tables near the top of the pool waterfall. Food and service quality are high, but they do disappoint on occasion. Wine list is acceptable. $35–$60 for dinner. Reservations recommended. Resort wear with collared shirts required, but shorts are OK.

Take the train *or boat* to the left from the lobby. In the Lagoon Tower of the resort.

Lava Lava Beach Club
69-1081 Kuualii Pl. • 769–5282

ONO Waikoloa—With such a beautiful location right on Anachoʻomalu Beach, you're happy the moment you walk through the door. The ambiance is casual, and we love their open-air seating and live music. The menu is a wide mix of items. They do fish very well, and we love their salads. $25–$55 for dinner. From the Hwy, turn on Waikoloa Beach Road, left before the Marriott, park at the lot near the end of the road. An ONO with qualifiers. Killer location and reasonably good food. But it's not the food (or the plastic glassware, since they're on a beach) you'll remember for years to come, it's the dreamy setting. That's why we chose this location for our opening chapter photo.

Manta & Pavilion Wine Bar
62-100 Mauna Kea Beach Dr.
882–5810

ONO Mauna Kea—Views from here are soothing, looking obliquely down the beach of Mauna Kea. Breakfast is a hurt-me $34 buffet, which is awesome. (As it darned well *better* be.) And if you decide to go off the menu, you're looking at items such as $16 pancakes and a $26 continental breakfast, so you might as well go for broke (literally). Dinner continues the expensive route, but you can still feel comfortable in walking shorts and a nice aloha shirt. Steak and seafood sound so tame. But we're talking about *very* skilled preparations and presentation. The goat cheese ravioli is a great way to start. They pride themselves on their incredibly vast wine selection and expertise. They also have what they call the "enomatic wine experience" that allows them to sell 48 wines by the single ounce. Service is polished. They're not perfect; we've seen them drop the ball. But overall, execution is superb. They're present when you want them, not annoying you when you don't. $40–$60 or more, especially when you start into the wine, for dinner. At the Mauna Kea Beach Hotel.

Napua
68-1292 South Kaniku Dr.
885–5910

ONO Mauna Lani—This restaurant has an unreal location right next to the beach in Makaiwa Bay. The menu is pretty small with items such as fresh fish, a couple of steaks and maybe some seared ahi using all local ingredients. This is a good place to arrive early and have a cocktail, watching the beach before dinner. Good drinks here—gotta try the wild Shave Ice Martini along with the roasted spinach dip as a pupu. The small lawn between you and the beach is a good place to park the kids while you watch 'em run around. $13–$20 for lunch, $30–$40 for dinner. While certainly not the best food on the island (they tend to overcook fish) and though pricey, it's an ONO for the cozy beachside experience.

Ocean Terrace
62-100 Kaunaoa Dr. • 880–1111

Mauna Kea—Breakfast at this Hapuna Beach Prince Hotel restaurant offers nice ocean views. Buffets ($31 with the omelette station) bring a nice variety of items. À la carte menu includes three-egg omelettes for $21, waffles for $16, and steak and eggs for $25. Kind of pricey, huh? But the quality is good. (Which you'd expect at these prices.) They tried dinner and utterly failed and scaled it back to one night a week. Avoid that night…

Orchid Court
1 North Kaniku Dr. • 885–2000

ONO Mauna Lani—Breakfast buffets are $31. They also have various "complete breakfasts" for $16–$27, but these seem overpriced. À la carte also available. For dinner (Thurs.–Mon.) they change their name to **Norio's Japanese Restaurant & Sushi Bar**, a Japanese restaurant. Overall, a nice setting and good food. In the Fairmont Orchid.

Seafood Bar
61-3642 Kawaihae Rd. • 880–9393

ONO Kawaihae—A cool tiki atmosphere featuring souped-up bar food with a local twist. For instance, they have a poke burger (pretty good), coconut shrimp sandwich, (also fairly good), ahi sashimi, etc. The beef burgers are generous, but the meat seems a bit…overprocessed. At dinner add some short ribs, fresh fish, some steak and escargot. They seem to be catering to the watering hole crowd, so expect inexpensive well drinks, margaritas and mai tais as well as beer. With the whimsical atmosphere (necessary since the view out the windows is of industrial storage tanks) and prices in line with the product for this part of the island, it's an agreeable place for lunch or dinner, and we *kinda*, *sorta* figgered we'd give 'em an ONO. **$15–$20** for lunch, **$15–$30** for dinner. On Hwy 270 before Kawaihae.

Starbucks
69-201 Waikoloa Beach Dr.
886–1888

Waikoloa—At the Queens' MarketPlace (but not in the food court). You know what to expect. We just wanted to let you know it's here.

Waikoloa Village Market
68-3916 Paniolo Ave. • 883–1088

Waikoloa *Village*—In the high-priced land of Kohala, there is some relief. This local supermarket in the Waikoloa Highlands Center has deli sandwiches, sushi, plate lunches, pastries and hot paninis, all for a good price. Plate lunches from the hot bar are popular around lunch, and most items are at their freshest during this time. Good place to stop on the go. **$4–$8**.

KOHALA CHINESE

Kirin Chinese Restaurant
69-425 Waikoloa Beach Dr.
886–1234

Waikoloa—You arrive by boat to Kirin (named after the Chinese mythical creature, not the Japanese beer) and head upstairs to the dining area, which has no view unless you get a table out on the deck (which you can reserve). Lunch includes dim sum—this can take the edge off the prices since dim sum items average around $5 each. (It's made to order, not served by cart.) Otherwise, you're looking at **$20–$50** or more for lunch and dinner. Entrées go way beyond chop suey. They have lobster served several ways, lots of seafood, duck, sizzling platters and much more. Quality is pretty good (though you're *paying* for awesome, which is why we didn't give them an ONO). At the Hilton Waikoloa Village between the Palace and Ocean Towers. Allow an extra 20 minutes to get there from your car—it's a *big* place.

Lemongrass Express
69-201 Waikoloa Beach Dr.
886–3400

ONO Waikoloa—Better to classify them as Asian rather than just Chinese. And the ONO needs to be taken in context. It's relatively cheap eats in a food court in the

Queen's MarketPlace. Not everything is good, but if you grab the right lunch special, such as the vermicelli, along with the tempura cheesecake for dessert, you'll walk away with comparatively cheap, tasty food in the land of the big wallet. Otherwise, pricier entrées would strip away the ONO. No atmosphere, so eat outside by the koi pond or the gazebo. Around **$12** for lunch, **$15–$30** for other items.

KOHALA ITALIAN

Café Pesto
61-3665 Kawaihae Rd. • 882–1071

ONO Kawaihae—Excellent selection of fine Italian food. Pizzas, pastas and some calzones. Pizza is light—feather-like crust, light sauce, light toppings. It's also delicious, and they feature several unique combinations. 9-inch pizza OK for 1 person, 12-inch for hearty, half starved appetites. Try the kalua pig-and-pineapple combination or the Oriental al Pesto with garlic, sun-dried tomatoes and Japanese eggplant. Pastas *can* be excellent but are sometimes disappointing. With that caveat, it's a great restaurant, and we recommend it wholeheartedly. In Kawaihae Center (Hwy 270 before 3-mile marker). **$13–$20** for lunch, **$15–$40** for dinner. The higher price is usually for their fresh fish special. Reservations recommended.

Romano's Macaroni Grill
69-201 Waikoloa Beach Dr.
443-5515

Waikoloa—This is part of a chain of reliable Italian comfort food, and this location is no different. The food is tasty, portions generous, and the service is good. But the prices here are a bit different than you'll find elsewhere. While eating and looking at the menu, we went to Romano's website on our phone and found that prices here are *50% higher* than locations we looked at on the mainland. We know rent at the Queen's MarketPlace must be high, but *sheesh!* Except for the confiscatory prices, they'd probably get an ONO. And when compared to others on the Kohala coast, maybe they're not that out of line. **$16–$30** for lunch and dinner.

KOHALA JAPANESE

Imari
69-425 Waikoloa Beach Dr.
886-1234

ONO Waikoloa—Elegant black-and-copper decor with wood floors and shoji doors all around, you have your choice of three types of Japanese food. Teppan-yaki style (where food is prepared in front of you by a talented, knife-wielding chef), a sushi bar (tables near there will be quieter) or washoku (where items off the menu are served tableside). The ambiance is thick with Japanese culture and music, and the quality of the food is very good. If Japanese food is not your thing, they have steak, fish and chicken. Located at the Hilton Waikoloa Village, reservations required. Dinner is **$35–$60**. Resort wear with long pants and collared shirts required.

Monstera
68-1330 Mauna Lani Dr. • 887–2711

ONO Mauna Lani—The atmosphere is nice with general seating and a sushi bar. The sushi is fresh and tasty and you get a break on the pricing if you order three pieces, making family-style eating more attractive. They also have lots of non-sushi items, including whole fish and sizzling platters. **$20–$50** for dinner. In the Shops at Mauna Lani.

KOHALA LOCAL

Hale I'a Da Fish House
61-3665 Akoni Pule Hwy.
882-1052

(ONO) Kawaihae—As you head up the hill in Kawaihae, on your right you'll pass an unassuming fish market that sells very salty shoyu poke. But their *lunch wagon* outside deserves a medal. The location isn't much (to say the least), but their $10 fish plates are excellent in quality and value. You usually get a basic choice between ahi or mahi mahi. Cash only. You'll probably want to take it to the beach because of the pesky flies. Hours 10 a.m.–3:30 p.m., closed weekends. **$7–$12**.

KOHALA MEXICAN

Boat Landing Cantina
69-425 Waikoloa Beach Dr.
886-1234

Waikoloa—In the massive Hilton Waikoloa Village, you'd never drill all the way into this property just to eat here. Their signature fish tacos $17—opt for sautéed, not fried—don't disappoint, though the $16 ceviche serving is tragically, shamefully, pitifully small. Margaritas are their specialty, but portions are small for the cost. Overall, too pricey for what you get. $20–$50 lunch and dinner.

Los Tres Mex
68-1845 Waikoloa Rd. • 989–1805

(ONO) Waikoloa Village—Their menu is small and basic, as is the location (it's more of a taco window than anything else), but the fish tacos are the real deal and the sauces plentiful. Above all else, the price is reasonable, and you can get there in a little over 15 minutes from the Hilton or Marriott. We highly recommend the mahi mahi fish tacos. **$8–$13** for lunch and dinner. Closed Sundays. Cash only. In Waikoloa Highlands Center.

KOHALA PACIFIC RIM

Roy's Waikoloa Bar & Grill
69-250 Waikoloa Beach Dr.
886-4321

(ONO) Waikoloa—Some people are born to do certain things. Roy Yamaguchi was born to run restaurants. This growing chain rarely fails to please. The food is delicious, well-conceived and nicely presented. Dishes range from dim sum appetizers, fish and beef. Specials abound and change nightly. The atmosphere is casual and somewhat noisy. The service is efficient, sometimes bordering on pestering. Prices are reasonable *for what you get*. Entrées aren't huge, so consider the delectable appetizers. Reservations strongly recommended. (Ask for a table near the glass wall overlooking the golf course pond.) Their dark chocolate soufflé is legendary. Dinner is **$30–$47**. In the Kings' Shops in the Waikoloa Resort area near Hwy 19's 76 mile marker.

KOHALA TREATS

While treats are fairly easy to come by in many of the mega resorts, if you're not staying there, you usually have to drill pretty far into them to partake. Here are some that are easier to come by.

Aloha Deli & Ice Cream
61-3642 Kawaihae Rd. • 880–1188

Kawaihae—A good place for a scoop of really good ice cream. The shakes and their other food items aren't as good. On Hwy 270 before Kawaihae.

Anuenue
61-3665 Kawaihae Rd. • 882–1109

Kawaihae—Conveniently located in Kawaihae if you're heading along the shoreline up to Hawi. The shave ice is pretty good as is the ice cream. They also have some snack food that isn't overly compelling. $3–$5.

WAIMEA DINING

Waimea is a cool place to eat—literally. Located up at the nippier 2,500-foot level, it's a nice place to eat when you're staying in the Kohala area and want to eat away from the resorts and enjoy the views along the way.

Big Island Brewhaus &
Tako Taco Taqueria
64-1066 Mamalahoa Hwy • 887-1717
Mexican—Well, these guys have the record of having the longest name. It started out as a taco place, and they expanded to brewing their own beer and even sodas. (The latter are pretty novel and kind of tasty.) The atmosphere is casual and colorful. Their Mexican selection is fairly good with mixed results. Flavors are reasonably good. The spicy beef has a nice zing to it, for instance. And the baja fish tacos on flour tortillas are great. But food is often served lukewarm. They have potential, but they need to pick it up a notch. The beer selection is about a dozen on tap, and the quality is generally good; for wine, ya got red and ya got white...that's it. $10–$17 for lunch and dinner. On the corner of Mamalahoa Highway and Kamamalu in Waimea.

Charley's Thai Cuisine
65-1158 Mamalahoa Hwy • 885-5591
Thai—With a name like Charley's, you're probably not *expecting* great Thai food. But that's what you *used* to get here. Yet something seems to have happened to this restaurant. The recipes taste different. We love Thai food be-

cause of all the flavors, yet the food now seems to be hollow. Hot, if you like, but otherwise flat. The Queen's MarketPlace location in Waikoloa has the same problem. Lunch and dinner are $12–$25. The Waikoloa location has the same menu for 25%–30% more money. In Waimea Center on Hwy 19. Avoid the lemongrass tea. It's weird and tastes kinda like...feet.

Hawaiian Style Café
65-1290 Kawaihae Rd. • 885-4295
681 Manono St. • 969-9265
ONO Local—Looks like a dive on the outside. (Then again, it looks a little like a dive on the inside.) But this is probably the best deal on the island when it comes to *quantity* and heartiness. Let me give you an example: Two eggs, your choice of meat, plus hash browns or rice. Then add either toast or two fluffy pancakes (the size of hub caps). All for $11. Now that may be obtainable back on the mainland, but it's utterly *unheard* of in Hawai'i. They're open from 7 a.m. to 1:30 p.m. daily (but close at noon on Sunday). The early lunch features thick burgers obscured by a towering mound of fries, as well as some other items. The food's not the best, but you ain't *paying* for the best. The atmosphere is laid-back with a few front tables (which probably aren't cleared or cleaned as often as they should be) and a large sit-down counter plus a few in back. This is how Mom used to cook before she found out it was bad for you. Sometimes we miss it. $7–$11. On Waimea's Restaurant Row; see map on page 135. They also have a location in Hilo.

Leilani Bakery
65-1158 Mamalahoa Hwy • 885-2772
Treats—Average baked goods served without a smile. For a place that serves

food, they have a weird habit of closing at lunch time. In Waimea Center.

Merriman's
65-1227 Opelo Rd. • 885–6822

 American—This is the best and most consistent food in Waimea. Peter Merriman is an excellent chef, and the recipes here are usually wonderful. Lunch includes spicy fish tacos, salads, fish, Chinese short ribs and sandwiches. The menu seems to change often, so we're nervous about recommending specific items. Dinner features steak and seafood, including their tasty wok-charred ahi. They have an impressive wine list, but the mark-up seems pretty extreme. And although they are fairly knowledgeable with wines, their skills are more obvious with mixed drinks. If you're in Waimea and want a great meal, this is the place to go. On Waimea's Restaurant Row; see map on page 135. Reservations recommended **$12–$20** for lunch (Mon.–Fri. only), **$35–$60** for dinner.

Pau
65-1227 Opelo Rd. • 885–6325

 Italian—A casual atmosphere with a straightforward menu of super-thin 18-inch(ish) pizzas, a few pastas (love the pesto island fish), some sandwiches and very creative salads. The pizza is outstanding. Meat lovers should consider the "whole hog." Other items are similarly pleasing. Service is friendly and accommodating. Desserts are their weak point. Prices in line with quality. **$12–$18** for lunch and dinner. In Waimea's Opelo Plaza.

Red Water Café
65-1299 Kawaihae Rd. • 885–9299

 American—We don't really know how to categorize them. Creative entrées from different regions. Japan (sushi), America (steak),

Hawai'i (banana wrapped fish) and more. The food and music seem to simply reflect the owner's interests, which fortunately seem to coincide with ours. Ambiance is woody and eclectic. Portions are ample. The yellow curry dish rocks. There's live music some nights. Don't let them seat you in the back area, if you can avoid it. **$20–$34** (or more, if you go nuts on the sushi) for dinner. In Restaurant Row.

The Fish & The Hog
64-957 Mamalahoa Hwy • 885–6268
American—Also known as Huli Sue's, they have a comfortable down-home atmosphere, but many of the items could use some work. In short, stick with the fish but ditch the hog, other than the pulled pork, which is good. The gumbo is bursting with flavor, and they have a tasty fish sandwich. Avoid the tame Greek salad, the tough brisket and the mediocre ribs. They talk up their cold pressed juices, which we were aching to try, but were then told that they don't offer them without pre-ordering. Some readers have told us that this is their favorite Waimea restaurant, and we understand the argument, but we honestly think you have better choices in the area. **$13–$30**. Avoid the liliko'i cheesecake dessert unless you like it real sour. Just across from the 56 mile marker on Hwy 19.

Underground Pizza
64-974 Mamalahoa Hwy • 885–7888
Italian—Some things should be better left buried. $18 for a very large, very avoidable pizza. Across from Fish and Hog near Hwy 19's 56 mile marker.

Village Burger
67-1185 Mamalahoa Hwy • 885–7319
 American—Gourmet ⅓ pound burgers made from

locally raised beef, plus veal burgers, veggie mushroom burgers, ahi and taro. Quality is top notch, and you can take your food to one of the food court tables or one of the few outdoor tables. Fries are extra, and the Parmesan fries are *outrageously* good. They also make expensive but wicked shakes. $9–$15 for lunch and dinner. In Park er Ranch Center.

Waimea Coffee Co.
65-1279 Kawaihae Rd. • 885–8915
American—Waimea's best coffee shop with a limited breakfast selection. (The breakfast sandwich is good—consider it on the Parmesan bagel—but it can take awhile.) For lunch they have some paninis and several salads. The coffee is good and service...it can be one of those places where you feel invisible. You walk up to the counter, stand there for perhaps five minutes while you are never acknowledged by several employees. You finally ask about ordering, and they tell you to go to the other end of the counter where you are again ignored. Finally you place the order, and they are as friendly as can be. It's nice to be visible again. This has happened on multiple occasions. Indoor and outdoor seating, free Wi-Fi and a drive-thru window. They also have reasonably tasty baked goods, including their almond sticky bun. In Parker Square in Waimea. $5–$12 for breakfast and lunch.

Yong's Kalbi
65-1158 Mamalahoa Hwy • 885–8440
Korean—Korean food with a local twist. Good fried mandoo (Korean dumplings). Be brave when picking some of the odder items (but avoid the chicken katsu). $8–$14 for lunch and dinner. Closed Sunday. In Waimea Center.

HILO AMERICAN

Fast Food
Hilo's fast food joints are mostly clustered around Puainako Town Center up Hwy 11 from town.

Hilo Burger Joint
776 Kilauea Ave. • 935–8880
A likable place with a great selection of burgers using lots of unusual combinations, such as the nacho burger (nacho cheese, black beans, jalapenos, tortillas and sour cream on top), wasabi burgers, Greek burgers, etc. All served on $1/3$-pound patties from a local ranch. Don't go for just the typical burger, get creative here. They also a have a full bar and 23 beers on tap for around $6 each. The atmosphere is a cross between a bar and a restaurant. Service is friendly. Just south of Pauahi St. in Hilo. Parking can be a problem; check the side streets. $10–$16 for lunch and dinner. Live music most nights.

Island Naturals Market Deli
1221 Kilauea Ave. • 935–5533
A health food store with a small cafe. Menu changes daily but stresses vegan sandwiches and salads as well as smoothies for relatively cheap prices. At Kekuanaoa and Kilauea at the Hilo Center Shopping. (No, we didn't get those last two words mixed up. Someone *else* did.) $5–$10.

Just Cruisin Coffee
835 Kilauea Ave. • 934–7444
Aptly named, because just cruisin' also describes the service, which is *sloooow*. On the busy corner or Aupuni and Kilauea, this is a convenient spot for morning joe on the go. Limited assortment of breakfast bagels, muffins. Also lots of smoothies and blended coffee drinks. Hit the drive-thru or sit at one of the few ta-

bles scattered about and use the free Wi-Fi. They also have a limited food menu for lunch with cold sandwiches and salads. Coffee and a tasty sausage, egg and cheese bagel is about **$8**.

Ken's House of Pancakes
1730 Kamehameha Ave. • 935–8711

ONO A Hilo staple, they offer a vast menu that's hard to absorb. The whole menu is available 24 hours a day—unusual for a Big Island restaurant. Service is sometimes unresponsive because the place can get crowded, but if you eat breakfast at the counter, it's fast and efficient. (Just when I need it, because I'm grumpy before my coffee.) Their corned beef hash loco moco is a delicious heart attack in a bowl. You ain't paying for gourmet here, and you won't get it. You're paying for dependably large portions of acceptable food at reasonable prices. That's why they eked out an ONO from us in a moment of weakness, and it's for breakfast and lunch *only*. Breakfast is **$8–$15**, lunch is **$10–$15**, dinner is **$13–$25**. On Hwy 11 near Hwy 19. Open 24 hours. Things can get boisterous after midnight, when the bars close.

Le Magic Pan
64 Keawe St. • 935–7777

ONO An artsy, Frenchy kind of atmosphere with a menu that focuses primarily on crêpes at pretty reasonable prices. (We didn't put them under FRENCH, because, well, they're not *really* French.) Each crêpe is based on a different place. The Parisian is ham, mushroom and cheese on a crêpe. The Polish is sausage, tomatoes, mushrooms, olives, spinach and cheese. Then ya got Greek, Alaskan, Russian, etc. They also have salads and great dessert crêpes. Lunch and dinner are

$11–$15. Service is friendly but can be *unapologetically* slow and would cost them their ONO if good food wasn't so hard to get in Hilo. Near the corner of Waianuenue in Hilo.

Queen's Court
71 Banyan Dr. • 969–6470

This is the main restaurant in the Hilo Hawaiian Hotel. With giant windows overlooking Coconut Island, this should be a great restaurant...but it ain't. Try not to laugh when they put a tiny, stale roll in front of you at the beginning. (It's not much bigger than the pat of butter.) Although the menu has an appealing selection of seafood, some pasta and kalbi ribs, the preparation is consistently lacking. Lastly, their bartending skills are non-existent. We're not trying to beat them up, but they could do *way* better with their great location. **$15–$28** for dinner, it's **$44** for their thrice weekly seafood buffets. Breakfast buffets are **$22**. The adjacent **Wai'oli** Lounge often has live music.

Seaside Restaurant
1790 Kalanianaole Ave. • 935–8825

They built their reputation on freshwater fish raised right there in a large, serene pond, but they have mostly gravitated more toward ocean fish because, we're told, "It's less work." If you want the mullet, you have to order in advance because they need to go catch it, and odds are they'll simply say it's "not the right season." If they didn't have the view of the pond, the atmosphere would be merely adequate and a bit loud. Service is friendly. The freshwater fish that they buy from others like aholehole (we're not making that up) is served head and all. Avoid the lobster. Overall, the food's reasonable (love the butterfish, but you gotta be careful not to eat too much) but overpriced. Some tables include a show called *count how many skeeters the geckos can eat*. **$18–$35**. In east Hilo past Banyan Drive 2½ miles east of Hwy 11. Reservations recommended. Closed Monday.

HILO ITALIAN

Café Concerto
808 Kilauea Ave. • 934–0312

(ONO) It's so hot inside you'll feel like a baked ziti if you don't grab an outdoor table. The menu is authentic, as is the owner. He'll probably come around to talk; ask him about his "homemade digestive." The flavors are there and the prices are right, but don't expect anything fancy. Good ravioli. Dinner is **$8–$15**. BYOB, no corkage fee. Open from 5:30 to 9 p.m. Closed Sunday and Monday. At Apuni St. and Kilauea Avenue in Hilo. Additional parking around back. Only dings are relatively small portions and annoyingly wobbly tables outside.

Café Pesto
308 Kamehameha Ave. • 969 6640

(ONO) Similar to (but not as good as) the Café Pesto mentioned in Kawaihae on page 265. On Kamehameha between Mamo and Furneaux in Hilo.

HILO JAPANESE

Ocean Sushi
235 Keawe St. • 961–6625

(ONO) *Ah*, Sushi lovers, rejoice. You've found a sushi place that serves killer sushi for cheap, cheap. Not much of an ambiance; just close your eyes and revel in the variety and quality. Rolls are anywhere from $2–$5, and they have platters and boxes with all kinds of selections. Service is fast and efficient. If the wasabi is still stinging, try one of their ice cream pies to put out the fire. Figure around **$10–$15** for lunch or dinner. On Keawe near Haili St. Closed Sunday.

HILO LOCAL

Café 100
969 Kilauea Ave. • 935–8683

(ONO) Possibly Hilo's most popular eating establishment. This is the most successful local restaurant on the island. For nearly 70 years they've served cheap, tasty, artery-clogging food and are legendary for their loco mocos. (These consist of fried eggs over rice and Spam or a similar meat—if there *is* a similar meat—all smothered with brown gravy.) They have nearly a dozen varieties of loco moco, along with burgers, chili, stew, sandwiches and specials for as little as $2. We gave them an ONO because this is quintessential local food. But if you're watching your cholesterol or fat intake, it'll rock your Richter Scale like no other place. Grab your food at the window and eat at one of the outdoor tables. Less than $5 for breakfast, **$3–$8** for lunch and dinner. On Kilauea near Mohouli in Hilo. Closed Sunday.

Puka Puka Kitchen
270 Kamehameha Ave. • 933–2121

Tasty entrees and stuffed pitas set in a tiny hole in the wall. (*Puka* is Hawaiian for hole.) Food's good and the prices cheap. Even though the menu is short, it's hard to choose between the sautéed ahi, the locally raised lamb or the seafood platter. We're partial to the lamb, but they often run out. Their ahi Don is also pretty good. Get there early to increase your chances. Open 11 a.m. to 2:30 p.m. for lunch. Dinner served Tues.–Sat. Closed Sundays. **$8–$14**. On the corner of Kamehameha and Furneaux in Hilo.

HILO MEDITERRANEAN

Oasis Café
211 Kilauea Ave. • 990–1961

ONO We didn't know how else to classify them. The menu sounds like a cruise around the Med Sea. Falafel, shwarma, babaganoush, pitas, kale pizza and Greek wraps. Everything is made fresh and the flavors are exotic. This is a hole in the wall, so don't expect much ambiance. Just a nice dining change of pace. Price is very reasonable at **$8–$12** for lunch. On the corner of Ponahawai and Kilauea. Closed Sun.–Tues.

HILO THAI

New Chiang Mai Thai Cuisine
110 Kalakaua St. • 969–3777

The curries and pad thai are flavorful, but the heat index of the dishes can be erratic, and the service, though *sometimes* nice, can also be comically indifferent. (A fun game can be to *bet* on how many visits to the table it takes before your server utters a single word to you.) The non-Thai entrées aren't bad, but overall, the food is mediocre. That said, it's not too often we single out a Thai restaurant for dessert, but their honey banana (with ice cream) is excellent. Lunch and dinner, both cost **$10–$20**. Dinner only on Sunday. Between Keawe and Kinoole streets in Hilo.

Sombat's Fresh Thai Cuisine
88 Kanoelehua Ave. • 969–9336

ONO *Very* good flavors and a real treat considering the prices. Don't neglect the wonderful green curry chicken—exceptionally good and complex flavors. Or the vegetables with oyster sauce. The heat level isn't overly high, so prod them if you want them to wound you. It's BYOB, and they'll even give you a nice beer glass if you bring your own. Good quality and an obvious attempt to keep things healthy, growing most of their own herbs and buying produce from local farmers. It's **$10–$23** for lunch and dinner. Next to Ken's House of Pancakes near the corner of Kamehameha and Hwy 11 in Hilo. Park around back. No lunch on Saturday. Closed Sunday.

HILO TREATS

Big Island Candies
585 Hinano St. • 935–8890

Tasty but amazingly overpriced chocolates, cakes, nuts and candies. You can also look through the glass and watch the whole process. It's a tour bus magnet, so it's either packed inside or dead, depending on your timing. On Hinano Street off Kekuanaoa, east Hilo.

Two Ladies Kitchen
274 Kilauea Ave. • 961–4766

ONO These two ladies quit their days jobs to invest all their time into making mochi. It's a smooth, doughy dessert made from rice flour and traditionally stuffed with red bean paste. Here you'll find mochi stuffed with peanut butter, brownies, sweet potato or some confectionary morsel. Their best is the strawberry mochi, which cost **$2.75** each. *(Well worth it.)* You can get assortment packs of eight for **$7–$8**. On Kilauea near Ponahawai in Hilo. Closed Sun.–Tues.

DINING IN PAHOA

Pahoa is the main place to eat when you're in lower Puna (meaning Kapoho to Kalapana). All the restaurants are on the main (and only) road going *through* town (not on the bypass). Most maps call it Government Main Road, some call it Pahoa Village Road. Once in town you can't miss 'em.

Black Rock Café
15-2872 Government Main Rd.
965-1177

American—A giant menu with burgers and subs at the low end, steak, seafood and frozen lobster tails at the high end with pizza in the middle, all in a diner-like atmosphere. Overall, the food is mostly fine, sometimes even good. Their biscuits and gravy is the best in Pahoa. (Of course, that's akin to having the greatest Mongolian food in all Ecuador.) The draft beer is embarrassingly cheap, and it's possible that fact colored our judgment; we almost gave 'em an ONO. (But when the beer wore off, we got ahold of our senses.) The Bananas Foster is their best dessert. Service can be *slooow*. $6–$10 for breakfast, $7–$20 (more for lobster) for lunch and dinner.

Boogie Woogie Pizza
15-2937 Government Main Rd.
965-5575

(ONO) Italian—New York style pizza with a bit of New York-style attitude. The pizza's pretty good and tastes even better if you call it in and arrive 10–15 minutes late. They'll keep it in the oven on a pan and the crust gets a tad crispy. By the slice and a side is around $3. They also have spaghetti and some sandwiches. BYOB. $3–$10 for lunch and dinner. In short, an inexpensive pizza fix that is reliable. On main road in Pahoa. Don't confuse them with the nearby **New York Pizzeria**, which is *very, very, very* avoidable. 'Nuff said.

Kaleo's Bar & Grill
15-2969 Government Main Rd.
965-5600

(ONO) American—In terms of ambiance and food, it's the nicest restaurant in Pahoa. The menu is all

over the place, but we haven't found anything that wasn't good. From the black blue burger to coconut chicken curry to seafood dynamite to fresh fish, preparation and ingredients are top. It can get loud inside, but overall, you'll enjoy this place. Good wine list. On main road in Pahoa. $17–$30 for dinner.

Luquin's Mexican Restaurant
15-2942 Government Main Rd.
965-9990

Mexican—This decidedly unkempt place has traditionally been the busiest, most bustling restaurant in Pahoa with (consistently bad) live music on one side and lots of loud chatter on the other. Standard Mexican food, plus a few specials like tofu enchiladas and tacos, potato tacos, fish tacos (very popular) and taquitos, fish and shrimp. The food is on the bland side, but the bottle of Tapatío on the table can rectify that. They also have some American items. Prices have crept up—they aren't that cheap anymore. The service is friendly (but can be *oh-so-slow*), and the portions are large. You're likely, especially at dinner, to spend your evening dining with Pahoa's upper crust—complete with stinky dreadlocks and clothing that hasn't been washed since tie-dye was king. A pitcher of *high octane* margaritas is $15, and beer is cheap. Desserts are reasonable but unpredictable—stick with the flan. Breakfast is $8–$13, lunch and dinner are $13–$24.

Ning's Thai Cuisine
15-2955 Government Main Rd.
965-7611

(ONO) Thai—Good Thai offerings here. The food is flavorful, and they're willing to give it heat if you ask. If you want to hurt, ask for "Thai hot." $10–$20 for lunch. Sundays is dinner only. In downtown Pahoa; can't miss it.

DINING NEAR HAWI

Bamboo Restaurant

55-3415 Akoni Pule Hwy • 889–5555
American—Located in an old, quaint dry goods building in Hawi with a quirky, tropical ambiance, they have an eclectic menu with uniquely prepared foods. We've given them ONOs in the past, but the quality has declined in the last couple years. You can still get a great meal here, but you can get disappointed more often than we'd like. Lunch is fresh fish, BBQ pork sandwich (which is good), stir fry, burgers and sandwiches. At night add more steak, seafood and money. Prices, especially at dinner, are pretty high. I mean, $38 for a rack of ribs? Phew—pretty steep, we'd say. Our reader e-mails seem to have tracked our own observations and have turned more negative than positive. They have a gallery inside the building offering all kinds of nice, locally carved wood and other products. Lunch is **$12–$22**, dinner is **$17–$45** per person. Closed Sunday nights and Mondays.

Gill's Lanai

54-3866 Akoni Pule Hwy • 315–1542
American—A small shack with a few outdoor tables. Menu is fish tacos (avoid the "naked" preparation), hot dogs (reasonably priced and includes fries), fresh fish and chips and Hawaiian poke. Food's not stellar, but it's pretty cheap. **$8–$12** for lunch. On the mauka side of the Hwy on your way into Kapa'au.

King's View Café

54-3897 Akoni Pule Hwy • 889–0099
ONO **American**—On the makai side of the highway in Kapa'au, they have 6-, 12- and 16-inch pizzas, hot and cold sandwiches and some pretty big salads made from local greens along with cheap-tasting Roselani ice cream. The personal pizzas come with a *small* salad for around $10. The food's pretty good, the pizza flavorful, and they use nice, fresh greens for the sandwiches and salads. Service can be slow, even if no one is ahead of you. **$10–$15** for lunch and dinner. Across from the King Kamehameha statue.

Kohala Coffee Mill / Kava Kafe

55-3412 Akoni Pule Hwy • 889–5577
ONO **Treats**—This place and the Kava Kafe to the right have the same owner. Though they have regular (and somewhat reasonably priced) entrées such as burgers, some good wraps and sandwiches, what sets these two places apart are their vices. Killer Tropical Dreams ice cream, lots of varieties of fudge next door, and after 5 p.m. they break out the kava for $3 per shell. (They also have some flavored kava, though purists would turn up their noses. See Kanaka Kava review for more on kava.) Live music some nights. **$5–$10** for the food, **$3–$8** for the vices. Across the street from Bamboo Restaurant in Hawi.

Sushi Rock

55-3435 Akoni Pule Hwy • 889–5900
Japanese—In the last building in Hawi inside a store called **Without Boundaries** before heading toward Kapa'au, this small operation (we're talking six *tiny* tables and some bar stools) has very fresh and nicely conceived non-traditional sushi for reasonable prices. Their Valrhona Dark Chocolate Cake comes with an unfortunate green tea glaze that ruins it. What we liked better was their homemade vodka fusions, which they use to make a mean liliko'i martini. **$12–$30** for lunch or dinner. Avoid the drink specials in favor of another piece of sushi. Service can be agonizingly slow.

DINING NEAR 'AKAKA FALLS

Hilo Shark's Coffee
28-1672 Old Mamalahoa Hwy
963–6706
American—There's not much to eat between Hilo and Honoka'a. In Honomu on the way to 'Akaka Falls on Hwy 220, this place has coffees, teas, smoothies, shakes, breakfast sandwiches, waffles, wraps, melts and more. Great interior layout with a couple of booths, big couches and a cool, shaded back porch with a few more tables. **$5–13**. Open 8 a.m. to 6 p.m., except Sunday when they close at 4 p.m. Good food, but no ONO because service can be nasty and dismissive, depending on who ya get.

Woodshop Gallery Café
28-1692 Old Government Rd.
963–6363
ONO American—Also in Honomu town on the way to Akaka Falls, this small café has a good ahi sandwich, a taro and a garden burger, and other sandwiches. Food's not quite as good as **Hilo Sharks Coffee**, but the overall experience is better. **$5–$10**. Otherwise, **Mr. Ed's Bakery** (963–5000) has a big selection of surprisingly *tasteless* baked goods. (Of course, of course.)

What's Shakin'
27-999 Old Mamalahoa Hwy
964–3080
ONO American—On the 4-mile Scenic Drive (between the 7 and 11 mile marker on Hwy 19). This is a fantastic place to get outrageous smoothies as well as a small lunch menu of dependably tasty items, such as chicken wraps, roast beef sandwich, chicken nachos and *super* fresh salads. The smoothies, their signature items, often start with frozen bananas (instead of ice) and most, such as the peanut bradduh, are wonderful. They also sell Tropical Dreams ice cream and some fruit such as papaya and pineapple. **$7–$12**.

DINING IN LAUPAHOEHOE

Laupahoehoe is the tiny town north of Hilo and 'Akaka Falls before you get to Honoka'a.

Back to the '50s Highway Fountain
35-2074 Old Mamalahoa Hwy
962–0808
ONO American—This place has come a *long* way since our last edition. A '50s-style diner with old-fashioned service and good, hand-formed local burgers, loco moco, Tater Tots, roast beef and chicken. With their thick, retro atmosphere, much improved food and friendly service, this place shines. Enter the town of Laupahoehoe from the road that parallels the highway mauka of Hwy 19 on either side of the 25 mile marker. **$6–$12**. Closed Monday and Tuesday.

DINING IN HONOKA'A

Café Il Mondo
45-3626 Mamane St. • 775–7711
Italian—Pizza, calzone, lasagna, salads and hot sandwiches. Lots of different coffee drinks. The pizza is pretty good (not great) with crunchy crust. Calzones are large and tasty. Fairly good meatball sandwich. Service is slow at times. One thing that rubs us the wrong way: They don't serve alcohol and encourage you to BYOB. Then they quietly charge you $2–$5.75, depending on how many are in your party, for corkage. Tacky. And oddly, medium and large pizzas are *only* available to go. Can't eat 'em at the café. On 240 in

Honoka'a, ocean side. $10–$15 for lunch and dinner. Closed Sunday. No credit cards.

Simply Natural
45-3625 Mamane St. • 775–0119
American—A health food restaurant that serves eggs and pancakes for breakfast (try the taro banana pancakes), sandwiches, soups and salads for lunch. The taste isn't compelling, but it's not bad. $5–$10 for breakfast (coffee is pretty weak), $8–$12 for lunch. On Hwy 240 in Honoka'a.

Tex Drive-In & Restaurant
45-690 Pakalana St. • 775–0598
(ono) Local—Every good restaurant does at least one thing well, and Tex is a perfect example. Most of the food is merely adequate fast food, such as burgers, teriyaki chicken, 12-inch pizzas, etc., for lunch; cheap (and it tastes that way) breakfasts. But Tex *excels* at making the best malasadas (a Portuguese doughnut dipped in sugar) on the island, served fresh and warm throughout the day. The plain ones are delicious, but they also have them filled with Bavarian chocolate, tropical fruits, etc. We *never* hesitate to stop by when we're in the neighborhood. Located on Hwy 19 near Honoka'a and the 43 mile marker. Sometimes the wait (even if nobody is ahead of you) can be long. Don't overlook the drive-in window. $7–$12 for breakfast, lunch and dinner (cheaper for the malasadas).

DINING AT KILAUEA VOLCANO

Café 'Ohi'a
19-4005 Haunani Rd. • 985–8587
American—A simple, tiny place with a simple, tiny menu and the tiniest side salads we've ever seen. Basic sandwiches, chili and the occasional special while they last (such as lasagna or the roast

pork.) The chili's not bad (no spice, though). They have some pretty scrumptious pies for dessert. The few outdoor tables are pretty basic. (They don't need to clean them off—the birds seem to do it for them.) But the price is cheap. $7–$12 for lunch and early dinner. On Haunani Rd.

Kilauea Lodge & Restaurant
19-3948 Old Volcano Rd. • 967–7366
(ono) American—This cozy restaurant in the sometimes chilly village of Volcano serves delicious food in a warm atmosphere. The owner/chef was a make-up artist on *Magnum P.I.* when he bought this place. He went to Europe to learn how to cook and has excelled nicely. Dinner items, such as fresh fish, steak, venison, antelope, rabbit, chicken and sometimes ostrich, are all expertly prepared and presented. Though I love fresh fish, this is the place I like to go for a good *red meat* experience. Expensive, but *very* good food and *very* good service. One of the best restaurants on the island. We like to get a table near the "International Fireplace." $10–$15 for breakfast and lunch, dinner is $25–$40.

Lava Rock Café
19-3972 Old Volcano Rd. • 967–8526
American—Admirable selection of hearty burgers, sandwiches, chili, salads (try the liliko'i dressing), chicken, fajitas (which you can avoid), fresh-tasting taco salad, stir fry and more. Many items are veggie and most cost about $8–$10 with generous portions. (Good milkshakes.) Breakfast items include some clever omelettes and French toast with 'ohelo berry. Lunch and dinner are pretty hit or miss—like great club sandwiches and utterly horrible French dip. Service is so-so. An amazingly variable restaurant. You may get a good experience, or you may get ticked off.

Feeling lucky? **$7–$11** for breakfast, **$9–$13** for lunch, **$12–$22** for dinner. Right in Volcano Village. No dinner on Sunday and Monday.

The Rim at Volcano House
Hawaii Volcanoes National Park
756–9625

(ono) You won't be overwhelmed with dining selections *inside* Hawai'i Volcanoes National Park—this is it. And if you've visited this place in the past (before their closure between 2010 and 2013), boy are you in for a surprise. The food is great here. Breakfast is an **$18** buffet stressing local ingredients as do the other meals. Lunch brings a limited selection served pupu style. Expect steak and seafood for dinner, with some great fish offerings. The view here is as delicious as anything on the menu. It overlooks all of Kilauea Crater. (Though we've occasionally seen people sitting at the window by themselves, with their backs to the window—*go figure!*) Lunch may be a zoo with buses dropping people off by the dozens at noon. At dinner, hotel guests and area residents create a quieter time. Though the crater view disappears with the sun, you may see a nice glow in Halema'uma'u Crater. About **$20** for lunch, **$25–$45** for dinner. (Reservations recommended for dinner.) In the same building is **Uncle George's**—a bar that sports a similar view, a lunch-time alternative with some killer pupus. Try the BBQ prawns or the awesome sliders. **$13–$20**. By the way, after 7 p.m. the entrance to the park is probably unstaffed, so you won't need to pay to get in.

Thai Thai
19-4084 Old Volcano Rd. • 967-7969

(ono) Thai—Excellent menu of curries, soups, stir fry, noodle dishes and vegetarian items. It's probably safe to say they're overpriced, but the quality is top notch, so consider it a splurge. They have good Pad Thai. Curries are unusual, and curry lovers (like us) will either like the novelty (we do) or dislike the flavor. (Avoid the red.) Good (and generous) summer rolls. If you like heat, they'll wound you here. Thai hot *means* Thai hot, so go milder unless you've got an asbestos-lined tongue. Our only concern is the service can be uneven. Rushed at times, slow at others. If you catch 'em at the right pace, you'll like the place. Desserts are sparse—get the tapioca pudding. Decoration is beautiful and calming. **$15–$30** for lunch and dinner. In Volcano Village. Closed for one full month—sometimes longer—each year when owners go back to Thailand.

DINING NEAR SOUTH POINT

Ocean View Pizzeria
525 Lotus Blossom Ln. • 929-9677

(ono) Italian—Pizza, sandwiches, some baked goods and ice cream. The pizza is just OK, but their hot deli sandwiches are good and the reason for the ONO. (Your choices are meager around here unless you want to hit the grocery store.) In fact, the Italian sausage Parmesan with marinara on garlic bread is delicious. In the big shopping center on the mauka side before the 77 mile marker. **$5–$10**.

DINING IN NA'ALEHU

Hana Hou Restaurant
95-1148 Spur Rd. • 929-9717

(ono) American—Na'alehu is a pretty remote place on your way to the volcano, and it's surprising and gratifying to have great food in the middle of nowhere. We've seen them have off days, but not often. Breakfast includes different kinds of hash browns and corned beef hash, homefries with salsa, sour cream and eggs, etc. Lunch and dinner include plate lunches, sandwiches (including a surprisingly good grilled cheese) and specials. Consider their tasty liliko'i lemonade. And lastly, it's *mandatory* that you try their homemade pies. Better than your own grandmother's. $7–$10 for breakfast, $10–$20 for lunch and dinner. Look for a sign on the ocean side shoulder of the road in Na'alehu.

Punalu'u Bake Shop
95-5642 Mamalohoa Hwy • 929-7343

(ONO) **American**—Though their namesake sweetbread doesn't really work for us, most of their other baked goods sure do, such as the delicious the liliko'i-glazed Portuguese malasadas and the wonderful apple turnovers. They also have hot and cold sandwiches. On the highway, can't miss it. $5–$10.

ISLAND NIGHTLIFE

Not in the same league as what you'll find in Honolulu or any other big city, but on the Big Island we don't exactly spend *all* our evenings watching old reruns of *Gilligan's Island*. (Well... maybe Fridays.) There *is* life after sunset here.

Kona—Kona has the liveliest nightlife. Every Friday, the Entertainment section of the local newspaper, *West Hawai'i Today,* lists everything that's happening for the week ahead. Very handy. Much of the action takes place on Alii Drive. It's easy to walk downtown and check out what's shakin'. Directions to these places are in their reviews. For cocktails, the **Billfish Bar** at the Courtyard King Kamehameha Hotel is famed for their cheap drinks. **Don's Mai Tai Bar** at the Royal Kona Resort has a great happy hour. Most of their mai tais are excellent, especially the Original, Pele's Volcanic and the Don Jito. (That's just our hard work ethic shining through.) Service can be thin, but the location works. **Huggo's** can be very romantic, and they often have live music. Jazz on the left side and a local guitarist on the right at **Huggo's on the Rocks**. **Kona Brewing Co. & Brewpub** (334–2739) on Kuakini and Palani behind Kona Business Center is a good place for a cold, locally made beer. A dozen or so different brews and some wines. (No mixed drinks.)

The **Aloha Theatre** south of Kona up in Kainaliu often has fun local plays. Call 322–9924 for more information.

Big Island Comedy Company (329–4368) is a roving comedy act (find them mostly at restaurants and hotels around Kailua-Kona). Call for locations and dates.

Moviegoers will want to call **Keauhou Cinemas** (324–0172) or the **Makalapua Cinemas** (327–0444) in Kona to see what's playing.

Kohala—Nightlife is a resort affair (so to speak). Many of the mega-resorts have lounges. Good places to have a drink include **Kamuela Provision Company** at the Hilton Waikoloa Village, **Brown's Beach House, Lava Lava Beach Club, Kahakai Bar** and **Luana Lounge** at the Fairmont Orchid, and the **Beach Tree** at the Four Seasons (325–8000).

Outside the resorts in Kawaihae, check out **Blue Dragon** (882–7771) for their consistently excellent live music along with their awesome food. (Pricey, though.) Call for days of operation.

Hilo—The **Hilo Burger Joint** (935–8880) at 776 Kilauea Ave. has some very good live music most nights, and their bartending skills tend to be pretty high. (Great burgers, too.) **Cronies Bar & Grill** (935–5158) at 11 Waianuenue is a pretty good sports bar with good beers, bar games and a young, lively atmosphere. Food is adequate.

LU'AU

We've all seen them in movies. People sit at a table with a mai tai in one hand and a plate of kalua pig in another. There's always a show where a fire dancer twirls a torch lit at both ends and hula dancers bend and sway to the beat of the music. To be honest, that's not far from the truth. Lu'au can be a blast, and, if your time allows for one, they are highly recommended. The pig is *usually* baked all day in an underground pit called an imu, creating absolutely delicious results. Shows are usually exciting and fast-paced. Although lu'au on O'ahu can make you feel like cattle being led to slaughter, the lu'au on the Big Island are smaller, more intimate affairs of usually 100–200 people. Most lu'au include all you can eat and drink (including alcohol) for a set fee (except where noted below). If the punch they are serving doesn't satisfy you, they usually have an open bar to fill your needs.

Different resorts hold their lu'au on different nights. These change with the whims of the managers, so verify the days we list before making plans. Many lu'au advertise that they are rated number one. By whom? At any rate, this is what we thought of them. We noticed that for this edition, some lu'au have taken a *dramatic* turn for the worse, especially in Kona. We've never seen such a downturn in quality and can only chalk it up to cutbacks and changing attitudes. But there is one bright spot.

In Kona, the most dramatic turnaround we've ever seen in a lu'au is at the Sheraton Kona Resort (326-4969). Their previous effort was called Firenesia and was probably the worst lu'au in the state, complete with lip syncing on stage (which felt like a bad Godzilla movie), a stupid story line and bad food. And they would close the bar early (just when you needed it the most.) Well, somebody in management must have finally seen the show because boy, did they turn it around. This lu'au, called **Haleo**, now has one of the best shows on the island. The show is what you would want from a good lu'au, including a great MC. The stage is very visible and large enough to give the dancers wiggle room. The show is the right length, it flows well, and the performers are talented. Other aspects of the lu'au aren't as good. Though they tell you to arrive at a certain time, ask what time they actually allow people in. The food is adequate—not bad, not great. The free but limited bar closes when the show starts. There's no imu ceremony. And don't get too attached to that lei they give you before you have your photo is taken, 'cause they're gonna take it—along with the sweat from the last guy—right back. (**$95**) Don't bother with the Ali'i upgrade for $15. Mondays only.

The second best in Kona is the **Royal Kona Resort** (329-3111). The food isn't very exciting, but it's not bad. The show is presided over by a Hawaiian lounge lizard. (But they do it pretty well.) The free bar closes around 7 p.m., and it's so poor that many people end up walking over to the poolside bar to *pay* for better drinks. The imu ceremony, when they unearth the pig, is good but it's hard to see through the crowd. When you see the torch lighters, follow them to the pit right away and stand there so you can get a better view. The location is the real star here—*right* next to the water. Like the King Kam (below), they erect a safety net for the fire knife dancer. Tables on the north (right) side are usually served last. Mondays–Wednesdays and Fridays—**$88**.

King Kamehameha's Kona Beach Hotel (326–4969). This *was* a lousy lu'au. Then they came in and improved it. Now they've cut back on the things that made it good and seem intent on charging for extras that used to be free. (Holy cow! They're acting like the *airlines*...) The food is average, and free bar closes at 7 p.m. The "imu ceremony" is just two hotel cooks picking up the pig. Their show is average. Tuesdays, Thursdays and Sundays—**$88**. Preferred seating is an extra $19, bringing you closer to the stage.

In Kohala, the best is also the one that only does it on Tuesdays, the **Mauna Kea Beach Hotel** (882–5810). They have a good imu ceremony outside the grounds, where they pull the pig from the ground. They handle serving the food well, and the quality is very good. As soon as you're seated, you're free to head to the buffet, and getting seconds is easy. The bar is better than most, and you can get table service, but drinks are extra. (It's still open during the show, but they discourage you from ordering during that time.) The first half of the show is very strong and very Hawaiian, though the second half stalls a bit. Unfortunately, the stage is a bit low, so those in back won't see as much. (And it can be pretty *loud* for those up front.) Overall, a pretty classy lu'au. **$106**. *Usually* Tuesday & Friday nights, sometimes they cancel one night.

The next would be **Fairmont Orchid's Gathering of the Kings** (326–4969). If you're looking for a traditional, old fashioned lu'au...this *ain't* it. It's a Vegas-style lu'au with modern interpretive dance and lip-syncing. Production value is very high, and they work hard, but it feels out of place. They play a recording complete with commentary that the performers follow. They try to get *everyone* in the audience on stage at the beginning, which can be awkward. The food is *excellent*. Drinks are included, beer, wine and mai tais. It's **$109**. Gathering of the Kings works if you discard your notions of what a lu'au show should be, and you can accept a decidedly non-Polynesian experience. Saturdays only.

Waikoloa Beach Marriott (886–6789) has mediocre food and a good show. They ask you to show up at 5 p.m., then make you wait an hour for no discernable reason before eating, with no entertainment provided during that time. If you don't have a food ticket in your hand, you *have* to go to the towel desk first. Although drinks are free, you may have 3 bartenders for 300 people, so expect long lines. And they don't have an imu ceremony. Located adjacent to the fishponds at 'Anaeho'omalu. Saturdays and Wednesdays—**$102**.

Legends of Hawai'i (886–1234, ext. 54) Polynesian show is at the Hilton Waikoloa Village on Tuesdays, Fridays and Sundays. But there's no view and they charge you **$115** and an additional $26 for valet parking and front row seats. A bit less compelling.

And finally, this isn't really a lu'au, but we didn't know where else to put it. Called **An Evening at Kahua Ranch** (882–7954), this takes place on an 8,500-acre cattle ranch located at the 3,200-foot level of Kohala Mountain Road (250) with sweeping ocean sunset views. Instead of Polynesians dancing the hula, you'll hear a performer playing Charlie Daniels or Vince Gill, perhaps off-key, but he plays a mean fiddle. You'll also get a bit of line dancing, some stargazing, roping, branding of wood and fireside s'mores. The food is good and hearty—they do meat and 'taters well here. Drinks are beer, wine and soft drinks—no mixed drinks. But they're generous. You won't leave hungry or thirsty. It cools off more here after sunset than it does at the shoreline, so a light jacket may help. And you are a long bus ride from Kona. Some may find the entertainment hokey, but this 3-hour event is family-run and done in earnest. **$129** which includes transportation. Wednesdays only.

DINNER CRUISES

A couple of companies in Kona offer two wildly different experiences.

Body Glove (326–7122) does it right. Their "Historical Dinner Cruise" is a 3-hour boat ride from Kailua Pier that heads to Kealakekua Bay. Along the way their impressively researched narration keeps things interesting. The food is very good, and their mai tais are better than we expected. (Only one free drink; then it's a cash bar.) You'll want to snag a table on the lower deck as soon as you board. (Preferable to the upper deck.) This is a well-oiled machine and one of the best dinner cruises we've seen. **$118.**

The other company is **Spirit of Kona**, aka **Blue Sea Cruises** (331–8875). They use a glass bottom boat, which can afford cool views when they turn the lights on at night. (Though we've noticed that staring at the glass panes below seems to trigger nausea in some people.) The food's reasonably good and the staff is laid back, but they aren't as smooth as Body Glove (literally and figuratively). Customers seem more anxious for their 2-hour cruise to be over than Body Glove's 3-hour trip. It's **$110** and unlimited drinks are included. No kids under 8.

In Kohala, **Ocean Sports** (886–6666) has a 65-foot catamaran called **Alala** (they use the smaller **Sea Smoke** if they don't have enough customers) for dinner cruises out of Kawaihae Harbor. The cruise is relaxing, and the friendly crew is always asking if you want anything. They motorsail much of the time, and you can chill out on the trampolines if you like. (Outdoors is preferable because their old, hazy cabin windows make the interior less desirable.) The food is acceptable—nothing more—and they start serving the simple buffet as soon as they leave port. Since serving-tray food doesn't improve with time, you feel a bit pressed to start eating, even if you want to relax with the unlimited drinks or champagne first. This nitpicking aside, this is a good 2-hour cruise for **$129.**

ISLAND DINING BEST BETS

Best Pizza—Kona Brewing Co.
Best Malasadas—Tex Drive-In
Best Use of a Pound of Sugar—One Cinnamon Roll at Island Lava Java
Best Meal Away from it All—Holuakoa Café & Gardens in Kona or Blue Dragon in Kawaihae
Best Meal by a Fireplace—Kilauea Lodge
Best Burger—Annie's Island Fresh Burgers
Best Bargain for Food *Volume*— Hawaiian Style Café
Best Mexican Food—Killer Taco
Best Cheap Local Plate Lunch—Hale I'a
Best Dinner Cruise—Body Glove
Best Use of Glassware—Schooners at Harbor House
Best Thai Fix—Lotus Café
Best Way to Eat Your Fruit—Strawberry Mochi at Two Ladies Kitchen
Best Place to Take Your Food to Go— Sunset at Pu'uhonua o Honaunau
Best Lu'au—Sheraton Kona Resort
Best Sunset Cocktail—Don's Mai Tai Bar at the Royal Kona Resort

Hotels shown in this color. Condominiums shown in this color.

Rental Agents

Abbey Vacation Rentals...........................(866) 456–4252 or (808) 331–8878
Classic Resorts ....(800) 642–6284 or (808) 885–5022
Elite Property Management, LLC ....(877) 336–6751 or (808) 327–6751
Hawaii Island Bed & Breakfast Association ....www.stayhawaii.com
Hawaii Resort Mgmt./Kona Hawaii Vacation Rentals ..(800) 244–4752 or (808) 329–3333
Keauhou Property Management, Inc. ....(800) 745–5662 or (808) 326–9075
Kona Coast Vacations ....(877) 322–2407 or (808) 329–2140
Mauna Kea Resort Luxury Vacation Rentals ....(808) 880–3490
South Kohala Management *(no cleaning fees)* ....(800) 822–4252 or (808) 883–8500
SunQuest Vacations ....(800) 367–5168 or (808) 329–6438
Waikoloa Vacation Rentals *(no cleaning fees)* ....(808) 987–4519
West Hawaii Property Services, Inc...................(800) 799–5662 or (808) 334–1199

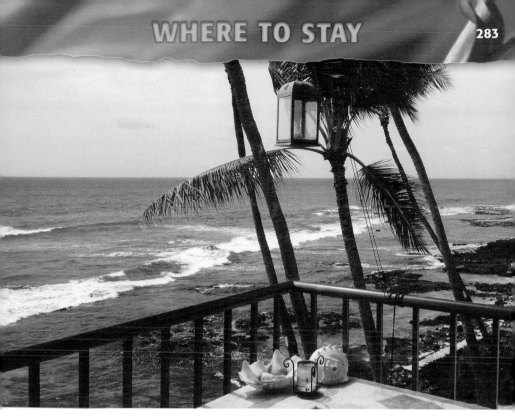

Room with a view...

Your selection of where to stay is one of the more important decisions you'll make in planning your Big Island vacation. To some, it's just a place to sleep, and rather meaningless. To others, it's the difference between a good vacation and a bad one.

There are four main types of lodging on the island: hotels, condominiums, bed and breakfasts, and single family homes. The vast majority of visitors stay in one of the first two types. But B&Bs and single family homes are often overlooked and can be very good values. If your group or family is large, you should strongly consider renting a house for privacy, roominess and plain ol' value. There is a list of rental agents in the index at left, each willing and happy to send you a list of homes they represent. We also have a B&B referral service there.

Hotels usually offer more services, but smaller spaces and no kitchens. **Condominiums** usually have full kitchens, but you won't get the kind of attention you would from a hotel, including daily housekeeping service. There are exceptions, of course, and we will point them out when they come up. You can find their locations on the various maps throughout this book.

All prices given are RACK rates, meaning *without any discounts*. Tour wholesalers and travel agents can often get better rates. Most resorts offer discounts for stays of a week or more, and some will negotiate price with you. Some won't budge at all, while others told us *no one* pays RACK rates. Also, these prices are subject to taxes of around 13.5%.

See all Web reviews at: www.hawaiirevealed.com

These are *subjective* reviews. If we say that rooms are small, we mean that we've been in them, and they feel small or cramped to us. If we say that maintenance is poor, we mean that the paint might be peeling or the carpets are dingy, or it otherwise felt worn to us.

The gold bar indicates that the property is exceptionally well priced for **SOLID GOLD VALUE** what you get.

The gem means that this hotel or condominium offers something *particularly* special, not *necessarily* related to the price.

A REAL GEM

HOTELS

All hotel rooms described **(shown in this color)** have air conditioning, an activity or travel desk, telephones, lanais (verandas), cable TV, and have cribs available upon request. None have room service unless otherwise noted. If you are a smoker, call about smoking policies because most hotel rooms in Hawai'i are designated non-smoking.

CONDOS

One of the confusing aspects to renting a condo **(shown in this color)**, especially in Kona, is the fragmented nature of the market. Each unit usually has a different owner, they all use different rental agencies to manage them, and it changes all the time. (Spreadsheets, blinding headaches and blurred vision are all necessary to figure it out.) Therefore, when *we* review them, we may look at 10 units and get 10 winners. *You* may rent one and get a dump because the owner is using furniture from a landfill and carpet from the finish line at the Ironman Triathlon. You never truly know what you're going to get

because condominium owners usually have complete autonomy in how they furnish their individual units. (Notice how we neatly cover our 'okoles, so that if you get a less-than-charming condo in a resort we recommend, we can always say you got one of the few duds there.)

Also remember that most (not *all*) condos have cleaning fees—especially in Kona. We don't list the fees because they will vary for each unit, rental agent or owner. Expect to pay $80–$250. And beware that cleaning standards in Kona condos aren't as good as other areas around the state. You may also pay a cleaning fee in some Kohala condos rented from agents, so be sure and ask.

When we describe a particular resort, we will often give the names or phone numbers of one or two companies that dominate the rental pool. But realize that this does not always do justice to the *entire* property. When we describe rates and units, they are for the rental agents we list. Different agents have different policies for the same complex.

Once you have decided where you want to stay, you can contact the resort. You may also want to contact some of the **rental agents** on page 282 to determine if they represent any units from the property you have chosen.

Many condos have minimum stays—usually three nights. We don't always list this because it changes with different rental companies. More and more rental agents are also requiring you to pay *all* of your condo rental costs before you arrive. It may make you nervous, but you might not have a choice if you're intent on staying at a particular place.

Three bedroom/two bath units are described as 3/2; two bedroom/one bath units are described as 2/1, etc. Differentiation between half baths and full baths is not made. The price spread for rooms of

See all Web reviews at: www.hawaiirevealed.com

a given size is due to different views, different locations within the resort and seasonal fluctuations. So when you see that a 2/2 unit rents for $140–$180, you should figure that $180 units have a better view or are closer to the water. Also note that, unlike some other Hawai'i locations, Kona condo RACK rates seem more negotiable. The terms Oceanfront, Ocean View and Garden View are used rather capriciously in Hawai'i, so you should be skeptical of them.

Unless otherwise noted, all condos come with telephones, complete kitchens, coffee makers, lanais (verandas), cable TV, ceiling fans, coin-op laundry rooms, free local calls and have cribs available upon request. Housekeeping is done only when you check out, and units won't have air conditioning or elevators unless otherwise noted. If you are a smoker, you will want to check policies before you book. Condos don't allow smoking in the units, and some even restrict you from smoking on the lanai and property, too.

BED & BREAKFASTS

Rather than describe the countless B&Bs scattered about the island, you're better off using the **Hawaii Island Bed & Breakfast Association**. Their B&B members are permitted and inspected. You can find them through their website www.stayhawaii.com. We also have lots of links to B&Bs on our website, but it's not practical to personally review them the way we do other accommodations.

WHERE SHOULD I STAY?

Throughout the book we talk about the positives associated with the various areas. In deciding where to stay, here are three negatives for each major location worth considering:

Kohala: Food will cost you more and so will places to stay. You are far from the town of Kailua-Kona and its available resources. You are far from the volcano.

Kailua-Kona: Vog will be more of a nuisance in Kona. Traffic, while not *nearly* as bad as the mainland, can be troublesome at commute time. There's more noise along Alii Drive.

Hilo: Activities are less numerous. The ocean is less pleasant. Rain will probably be a companion. There are no mega-resorts on this side of the island; choices are fewer and of lesser quality in general.

Kohala

Kohala is famous for its **mega-resorts**. These destination resort hotels have tons to see and do on the premises, pricey restaurants offering superb atmosphere and cuisine, and almost unending sunny weather. The developers have created oases in the lava desert where lava once stretched uninterrupted for miles.

You will notice that accommodation prices are high in Kohala. These snazzy resorts don't come cheap. We leave it up to you to decide if it's in your budget. A lot of them have REAL GEM icons next to them. We like to think of ourselves as stingy with these, but facts are facts— these *are* gems. But like the genuine article, these gems come at a price.

Picking the best mega-resort in Kohala is not a straightforward process. All of them have radically different personalities, so *your* personality is key to which one you'll like best. Most of these resorts do a great job at creating an atmosphere. The question is, is it *your* atmosphere? In our view, the Mauna Lani Bay Hotel has the best exotic tropical feel. The Fairmont Orchid has the richest, most luxurious feel. The Hilton Waikoloa Village has the most jaw-dropping elaborate, yet family-oriented feel. And 10 miles south of the main

See all Web reviews at: www.hawaiirevealed.com

Kohala resort area, The Four Seasons has some of both Mauna Lani's and the Fairmont Orchid's assets—rich and luxurious, yet also a great tropical feel. Most of these resorts are world class, and we don't say that lightly. Choosing one just depends on what you want.

If it's a cheap **condo** you're looking for, go elsewhere. Kohala only has upscale condos for rent.

Kailua-Kona

The resorts in Kailua-Kona and the surrounding area aren't of the same caliber as the glitzy mega-resorts of Kohala, but neither are the prices. You'll find that you can stay and eat in Kona a lot cheaper than Kohala. Condos are far more numerous here than hotels. Some condos are a downright bargain, while others can only be recommended to in-laws.

Most accommodations in Kailua-Kona are along Alii Drive. This road fronts the shoreline, offering splendid ocean locations and sunsets. The penalty for staying on Alii Drive is auto noise. Cars and motorcycles scoot by, sometimes creating unpleasant reminders in *some* condos that you are still in the real world. (Other condos keep their rooms far enough from the road to keep them blissfully quiet.)

The high season in Kona is December through March, and most condos charge more at that time. Also, most condos have a minimum stay.

If you're looking for a good deal and have a little time before your trip, the Internet is the place to find individual vacation rentals. Try VRBO.com for deals from individual owners of small vacation rentals, B&Bs and houses. We have links to some of them from our website at **www.hawaiirevealed.com**. From the web you can also search for individual condo owners. If you're not a web person, from the mainland, you can buy an individual newspaper or get a short-term subscription from *West Hawai'i Today* newspaper (329–9311) on the west side, or *Hawai'i Tribune-Herald* (935–6621) on the east side. It'll cost you a few dollars, but you may save hundreds or even thousands of dollars on your accommodations. Just remember that you won't have the security of working with an established rental agent or company.

Hilo

Your choices in Hilo are much more limited than on the western side of the island. The number of overnight visitors here is a fraction of what the Kona side gets. The hotels are older here, and Hilo's economic woes mean once-grand hotels often have closed wings and shuttered restaurants and spas. But you shouldn't expect Kohala prices either. Hotels can be had quite cheap in Hilo, so even if you are staying on the western side, you should strongly consider staying at least a night here when you are exploring this side or visiting the volcano. That'll keep Hilo from becoming a blur during an around-the-island driving frenzy.

Most of the hotels are located along Banyan Drive. Many have outstanding views of Hilo Bay. There are also a few lovely inns and decent hostels around town, too.

Volcano Village

The town of Volcano Village has a limited number of places to stay, but many of the choices you *do* have are superb. If you are spending a week on the Big Island, at least one night should be spent here. This is the most convenient place to stay when you explore the volcano. You can take your time and do the volcano justice. Remember, it gets chilly here at 4,000 feet, so bring something warm and waterproof. There are lots of B&Bs in

See all Web reviews at: www.hawaiirevealed.com

Volcano Village, so check out the service listed on page 282 or check our website.

Other Places to Stay

Out of the main areas, accommodations are few and literally far between. **Waimea** is cool and sometimes chilly at 2,500 feet. There are lots of restaurants to choose from. The northern tip at **Hawi** has a few simple hotels and a nice inn, but your dining choices are fewer. Down at the **southern tip** you'll find an often-forgotten resort but even fewer dining options to choose from. Finally, in **Honoka'a** near Waipi'o Valley is a cheap hotel that also has hostel beds.

WHERE ARE THE REST?

You'll notice that some of the resorts listed here don't have full reviews. That's because we reviewed more places than we have room for.

Also, we wanted to include aerial photos of the resorts. After all, a picture speaks a thousand words (and a thousand words take too long to read, anyway).

So we had a choice. Give you less info on *all* of them or do detailed reviews on only a *portion* of them. Neither choice seemed palatable.

So we came up with a *third* way: List minimal info on all (including if they are GEMS or SOLID GOLD VALUES), print full detailed reviews on *most,* and post full reviews of *all* on our website at **www.hawaiirevealed.com**. After all, most people use this section before they come to the islands. And with the web (which has infinite space), we could do more, like post larger aerial photos of the resorts with specific buildings labeled when appropriate, provide constant updates when necessary, and put links to the various rental agents or hotels right in the review, allowing you to go to their sites

and get more photos of the rooms. You should remember, however, that resorts post photos to lure you in, and some aren't above posting modified or overly flattering shots when they were new and sparkling. Our aerials don't lie and are designed to give you a feel for their ocean proximity (does oceanfront *really* mean oceanfront?), so you'll know what kind of view to expect from a given location within the resort. Resorts whose reviews are only on our website are identified with **WEB REVIEW**.

Please remember that all these reviews are *relative to each other*. This is important. Even staying at a dump right on the ocean is still a *golly gee!* experience. In other words, *Hey, you're on the ocean on the Big Island!* So if we sound whiny or picky when critiquing a resort, it's only because their next door neighbor might offer such a better experience. It doesn't mean you'll be miserable; it just means that *compared to another resort, you can do better*.

KOHALA

Fairmont Orchid, Hawai'i
(800) 845–9905 or (808) 885–2000
1 North Kaniku Dr.

540 rooms, pool and spa, 5 shops, 5 restaurants, 17 conference rooms, business center, 10 tennis courts (7 lighted and one stadium court), 2 golf courses, empty fridge, free room safes, wi-fi throughout, hi-speed Internet access in rooms ($15 per day), Keurig coffee mak-

A REAL GEM

See all Web reviews at: www.hawaiirevealed.com

ers in rooms with free coffee daily, room service, day spa, free use of sauna and steam rooms, beauty salon, free 24-hour fitness room, valet parking, children's program ($85 per day), lu'au, wedding coordinator.

We try not to blather on about a resort—it hurts our credibility. But when it's right, it's right. The Fairmont Orchid has an intoxicating richness that permeates everything. The lush grounds have a very sculpted and precise feel. Nothing is out of place. The inside is just as flawless. The lobby, halls and rooms (updated in 2013) are all richly furnished with lots of wood and fine carpets—even the elevators are paneled in koa with crystal chandeliers. The overall effect of the resort's rooms and common areas is European-Hawaiian elegance. The entire staff seems obsessed with pleasing you. Restaurants are what you'd expect, on the higher end with delicious results. They have their own garden on property and use items they grow for their recipes. The manmade beach is usually calm and protected. Lots of activities are available. The tennis complex is the best on the island, and the two Mauna Lani golf courses are humbling and world-renowned. You can get a massage next to the ocean at the "Spa Without Walls," where the sound of the surf helps you relax (as if you'll need any help) or by their waterfall with windows in the floors to watch the fish.

They have an optional $75 per adult ($65 per child) per stay activity package that'll cover snorkel gear, surfing and snorkel lessons, a kayak, etc. Parking is $17 and valet parking is $22. Local calls are free. Laundry is valet only. Casabella chairs (2 chairs with a retractable cover) by the pool are $45 and $60 by the ocean and include fruit, water and dry snacks. Umbrellas by the pool are free.

The Fairmont Orchid is exceptional in many ways. It has become popular with business travelers, and if you're looking to be pampered, consider it. Rooms (522 sq. ft.) are $399–$579. Some of the partial ocean views will require imagination to see the ocean. RACK rates are high—this ain't for the budget traveler—but they often have specials to ease the pain a bit. They also have a gold floor (for more money), which has more personalized services and its own lounge. Suites (which are *very* nice) are $859–$3,900 and are 1,050–2,752 sq. ft.

Fairway Villas
(800) 688–7444 or (808) 886–0036
(800) 822–4252 or (808) 883–8500
69-200 Pohakulana Pl.
WEB REVIEW

The Fairways at Mauna Lani
(800) 822–4252 or (808) 883–8500
(866) 456–4252 or (808) 331–8878
68-1125 N. Kaniku Dr.
WEB REVIEW

Four Seasons Resort Hualalai
(888) 340–5662 or (808) 325–8000
72-100 Ka'upulehu Dr.

243 rooms, 5 pools, keiki (kid) pool, lava snorkel pool, 4 spas, 3 restaurants, 42-inch HDTVs, empty fridge, coffee makers in rooms with free coffee daily, wi-fi in

A REAL GEM lobby, rooms and some other

See all Web reviews at: www.hawaiirevealed.com

areas, day spa, 8 tennis courts (4 lighted), 5 conference rooms, 24-hour business center, free laundry room, free local calls, 24-hour room service, valet parking, free children's program, *private* golf course. This resort *shines*, even among its superb competitors. 37 one- and two-story bungalows in several semi-circles with 6–8 rooms per building, including a few golf course buildings. They used a lot of local materials, giving the resort a very Hawaiian feel. All units (even golf course units) have nice ocean views. (Building 25 is closest to the water.) Second-floor rooms have better ocean views, but first-floor rooms have a pleasant garden on the other side of the bathroom glass with a second private *outdoor lava shower* ensconced in the garden where water gurgles over a short lava ledge. What a great place to have your morning shower! (A handful of first floor rooms *don't* have the lava shower—so be sure and ask.) This makes the first floor a better value than the higher-priced second-floor rooms. Overall, rooms are of average size, nicely furnished with cool slate floors and understated but tasteful furnishings.

One feature we've never seen anywhere else is a large, lava anchialine pond with 1.8 million gallons of fresh and salt water. Connected to the ocean, its level rises and falls each day with the tide. Inside are 40 species of fish, including a spotted eagle ray. You won't find a safer place to snorkel in the state. It's great to be there when they feed the fish.

If you bring your keiki, you'll find a free licensed children's program for young'uns 5–12. They also have a free teen center with game consoles. Their sand-lined kid's pool even has kid-size lounge chairs and free beach toys. The resort is the only one with a *truly* private golf course. Only guests and residents of the development are allowed to play, so tee times are spaced farther apart. It's a very nice, player-friendly, Jack Nicklaus course for about $250. The same goes for the day spa, which offers enough luxuriating decadence to melt your toenails. The resort fronts a beach, but the swimming is poor due to a lava shelf. They do have a manmade quasi tidepool at the shore for wading. However, just a short stroll south is Kuki'o Beach with somewhat better swimming.

Services here are extraordinary, even for a Kohala resort. (Examples: chilled towels at the pool, Evian spritz service, sunglass cleaning, fresh fruit kabobs, sunscreen—but you have to apply it yourself. How's that for pampering?) The swimming pools are scattered around the resort. The adults-only Palm Grove pool has a swim-up bar and serves "adult" shave ice flavors, like mai tai. Most resort items, like self-parking, room safes and cabana chairs are free. Valet (overnight) parking is $21 (free during the day). Their restaurants are excellent. No surprise there. If you have kids, the Seashell is the semi-circle you want; honeymooners (or those who want the quietest region) should choose the Palm Grove. Rooms of 635 sq. ft. are $695–$1,475. Suites (1,050–4,900 sq. ft.) are $1,600–$12,000!

Hali'i Kai
(800) 367–5004 or (808) 886–4307
(808) 987–4519
69-1029 Nawahine Pl.
WEB REVIEW

Hapuna Beach Prince Hotel
(866) 774–6236 or (808) 880–1111
62-100 Kauna'oa Dr.
WEB REVIEW

See all Web reviews at: www.hawaiirevealed.com

Hilton Waikoloa Village
(800) 221–2424 or (808) 886–1234
69-425 Waikoloa Beach Dr.

1,241 rooms, 3 pools, 3 spas, empty fridge, free room safes, hi-speed and wi-fi Internet access in room, wi-fi in some common areas, **SOLID GOLD VALUE** 42-inch HDTVs, room service, coffee maker with free coffee daily, 9 restaurants, 8 lounges, valet parking, fitness room, day spa, beauty salon, 8 tennis courts, two golf courses, 24 conference rooms, business center, coin-op laundry, tons of shops, tram and a boat service, lu'au, wedding coordinator.

Where do we start? How about *wow!* This is the one you've probably heard about. This resort, built in the late '80s and spread over 62 acres, is the most elaborate of them all. (By the way, despite its name, it is not located in or next to the town of Waikoloa Village.) Three separate towers are joined by a tram and boat network right out of Disneyland. A swimming pool has a pounding waterfall and an Indiana Jones-type swinging bridge overhead. There is a dolphin pool where lucky guests can get in the water with dolphins. The whole experience is described in ADVENTURES on page 236. More than $7 million worth of artwork is spread all over the resort. Parrots and exotic birds are also scattered about. There are multiple concierge desks around to assist in booking activities, making reservations or pointing the way to a particular part of the resort. Large groups will find the meeting facilities superb—from their 24 conference rooms to the ballroom the size of Waikiki to their business services area. The restaurants here are excellent.

The one thing the Hilton doesn't have is a great beach. (They have a manmade inland lagoon beach instead.) But 'Anaeho'omalu Beach is a half-mile walk or drive south. There's a large ocean-fed lagoon where guests float around in kayaks, paddle boats and rafts. In terms of amenities, the Hilton Waikoloa is an excellent place for families. Kids will *never* get bored here. There's a shallow swimming pool with a sandy beach at one end, a water slide and enough activities to wear out any teen or crumb-cruncher. Their kid's camp (Club Keiki) is $90 per day (for the first child, less for second or more), and there is also a night camp. (Non-guests can also enjoy the kid's camp for a higher fee.) Consider a ground floor cabana room in the Lagoon Tower in front of the dolphin pool where kids can frolic on the grass. There is also a "Splash & Relax" program, which gets you a room and use of pool for the *day* (10 a.m.–6 p.m.) for $160 per day for up to 4 guests.

The resort might seem overwhelming at first. It cost over a third of a *billion* dollars back in the '80s to construct, and a staggering 900 employees are needed to run it all. You won't see all of them running around, however. That's because they go from here to there via an extensive underground tunnel network. When you're down there, you're likely to run into your chef in uniform cruising along on a three-wheeled bike. You may wish *you* had one to get around the enormous property.

The entire resort is oriented inward, resulting in a destination that is self-contained. Some people who visit the Hilton Waikoloa snort that it's not real. Frankly, they miss the point. It's not *supposed* to represent reality. It's fantasy, escape, a leap into Never-Never Land. You wouldn't

See all Web reviews at: www.hawaiirevealed.com

sniff that Disneyland is phony, would you? The designers of the Hilton Waikoloa Village did a great job of achieving their objective—making an out-of-this-world playground/fantasyland for adults and kids. If that's what you are looking for, you will find it here in abundance. If you want to experience a calm piece of authentic old Hawai'i, you've come to the wrong place.

The Lagoon Tower rooms went through complete renovations in 2012 with great results. Avoid connecting rooms, unless you need them, as your neighbor can easily be heard through the closed doors—especially in the Ocean Tower. You may feel your pocketbook being emptied at every turn with extra charges—self-parking is $17 (but motorcycles are free, as if you care), valet parking is $22 (but complimentary for hybrid cars—which ain't real easy to rent), cabana chairs are $50 per day by the pool (but casabella—2 chairs with a retractable cover, are free by the lagoon), and the fitness room is $20 per day. They do have a *mandatory* resort charge of $25 per day—which covers Internet access, local calls, cultural activities, DVD rentals and some other discounts. Rates are *very* reasonable for Kohala (but the spread is huge). Rooms of 530 sq. ft. are $174–$799. The 56 suites (1,060–3,000 sq. ft.) range from $450–$2,600.

Islands at Mauna Lani
(800) 642–6284 or (808) 885–5022
68-1375 Pauoa Rd.

Kolea
(808) 987–4519
(866) 456–4252 or (808) 331–8878
69-1000 Kolea Kai
126 units, a/c, pool, keiki pool, spa, BBQ on the lanai, free wi-fi, free fitness room,

washer/dryer in unit, private elevators in many. It's hard to imagine being unhappy here. These are some of the most impressively appointed condos we've seen, and it's **A REAL GEM** the only condo complex in Waikoloa that's next to a beach. Rooms are richly furnished with high-end appliances, African mahogany trim and high ceilings throughout, travertine floors, granite countertops, a wall of glass that'll fold away from the 430 sq. ft. lanai (and its separate kitchen), making it part of the living space, and so much more. Even the closets light up automatically when you walk in. Although decor varies from unit to unit, we didn't see any that weren't outstanding. They have a sand bottom children's pool with its own waterfall, but it can get crowded during busy seasons. (The first agent listed has an agreement with Hilton Waikoloa Village that guests may use the pools there—which are *much* bigger but probably just as busy.) First-floor units are the least expensive because views might be encroached upon by a home in front of you. (Third-floor units have best views, especially buildings 4–8, 10 and 12.) An easy place to love. 2/2 units (1,270–1,554 sq. ft.) are $275–$450. 3/3 or 3/4 units (1,716–2,147 sq. ft.) are $375–$700. 5-night minimum but no cleaning fee. Second agent has some higher prices and a 3-night minimum.

Mauna Kea Beach Hotel
(866) 977–4589 or (808) 882–7222
62-100 Mauna Kea Beach Dr.

See all Web reviews at: www.hawaiirevealed.com

Mauna Lani Bay Hotel & Bungalows
(800) 367–2323 or (808) 885–6622
68-1400 Mauna Lani Dr.
WEB REVIEW ◆

Mauna Lani Point
(800) 642–6284 or (808) 885–5022
68-1050 Mauna Lani Point Dr.

116 units, a/c, pool, BBQ, spa, washer/dryer in unit, sauna, free wi-fi, daily housekeeping service. The interiors have nice furnishings, huge master bathrooms, pleasing layouts, good location and relaxing views across the golf course. Many of the units have been nicely updated, so ask for one. Some have very good ocean views. They have done a lot building maintenance recently, and the property was looking sharp on our last visit. 1/2 units (1,100 sq. ft.) are $415–$550, 2/3 units (1,700 sq. ft.) are $560–$790. 3-night minimum. Basic grocery package available for an extra fee.

Mauna Lani Terrace
(800) 822–4252 or (808) 883–8500
68-1399 Mauna Lani Dr.

80 units, a/c, pool, spa, sauna, keiki pool, washer/dryer in unit, free hi-speed Internet access, BBQ, twice weekly housekeeping. Most units overlook the ancient fishponds, creating an amazingly tranquil setting. Some units have ocean views as well. Buildings J, K and L often have nice sunset views. Many units have higher-end furnishings and some have been updated. 2- and 3-bedroom units are better. Most units have stairs leading to them—either up or down. There are two units available without stairs—one in building F and the other in building G. Master bathrooms are large. The complex is right next to the Mauna Lani Bay Hotel. Grounds are nicely groomed and mature. Even though this is an older property, it has been very well-cared for, and we still like it. 1/2 units (1,058–1,150 sq. ft.) are $299–$575, 2/3 (1,407–1,481 sq. ft.) units are $399–$875. 3-night minimum.

A REAL GEM

Shores at Waikoloa
(877) 997–6667 or (808) 886–5001
69-1035 Keana Pl.
WEB REVIEW

Villages at Mauna Lani
(800) 822–4252 or (808) 883–8500
68-1025 N. Kaniku Dr.
WEB REVIEW ◆

Villas at Mauna Kea
(808) 880–3490
Kamahoi Pl.
WEB REVIEW ◆

Vista Waikoloa
(800) 822–4252 or (808) 883–8500
(866) 456–4252 or (808) 331–8878
69-1010 Keana Pl.
122 units, a/c, pool and 2 spas, free fitness room, business center, washer/dryer

See all Web reviews at: www.hawaiirevealed.com

in unit, elevator, free hi-speed Internet access in some units, BBQ. Considering the caliber and the fact that it's in Kohala, this is a very good deal. Units are large and nicely furnished, the layout is pleasing, grounds are well-groomed, the bathrooms have nice, deep tubs. Ocean views aren't overwhelming—most are blocked by the Kolea resort or trees. But if you want a condo in Kohala, this is as close as you'll come to inexpensive yet pleasant. Buildings E & F are the best, A & B *feel* the closest to the road. 2/2 units (1,262–1,406 sq. ft. plus huge lanais) are $169 $240. 3-night minimum.

SOLID GOLD VALUE

Waikoloa Beach Marriott
(800) 922–5533 or (808) 886–6789
69-275 Waikoloa Beach Dr.
WEB REVIEW

Waikoloa Beach Villas
(800) 688–7444 or (808) 886–0036
69-180 Waikoloa Beach Dr.
WEB REVIEW

Waikoloa Colony Villas
(877) 997–6667 or (808) 886–8899
(800) 822–4252 or (808) 883–8500
69-555 Waikoloa Beach Dr.
WEB REVIEW

Wai'ula'ula at Mauna Kea
(808) 880–3490
(800) 822–4252 or (808) 883–8500
62-3600 Amaui Pl.
WEB REVIEW ♦

KAILUA-KONA

Alii Villas
(800) 799–5662 or (808) 334–1199
75-6016 Alii Dr.

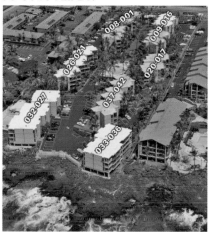

125 units, pool, washer/dryer in unit, BBQs, free wi-fi in most from top set of numbers. Units are fairly small, but with prices at $75–$125 for 1/1 units (620 sq. ft.). The pool is away from the ocean in the middle of the complex. Shop around with different rental agents. This ain't the greatest place to stay; it's pretty institutional-feeling, and the views feel the same from most units, but the location and price are fairly decent. 3-night minimum.

SOLID GOLD VALUE

Banyan Tree
(800) 367–5168 or (808) 329–6438
76-6268 Alii Dr.
WEB REVIEW

See all Web reviews at: www.hawaiirevealed.com

Casa de Emdeko
(800) 367–5168 or (808) 329–6438
(877) 322–2407 or (808) 329–2140
75-6082 Alii Dr.

WEB REVIEW

Country Club Villas
(800) 367–5168 or (808) 329–6438
78-6920 Alii Dr.

WEB REVIEW

Courtyard King Kamehameha's Kona Beach Hotel
(800) 367–2111 or (808) 329–2911
75-5660 Palani Rd.

452 rooms, pool and spa, 2 restaurants, 10 conference rooms, 2 lighted tennis courts, 7 shops, free 24-hour business center, free wi-fi or hi-speed Internet access in **A REAL GEM** the rooms, coin-op laundry, empty fridge, free laptop room safes, coffee maker in room with free coffee daily, free 24-hour fitness room, day spa, wedding coordinator, lu'au. Built in the mid '70s, the King Kam (as it's known locally) is a Kona fixture. Located next to the Kailua Pier, the hotel is fronted by the tiny but calm Kamakahonu Beach. The 'Ahu'ena Heiau shown on page 59 is also on the grounds. This area was the home of King Kamehameha during his later years, and his legacy has been adopted by the hotel in paintings and artwork (they give tours).

It's amazing what $35 million and a great design team have done for this aging hotel. The new owners renovated in 2010 and the lobby *again* soon after that when a tsunami flooded it. The results are remarkable and why it earned a REAL GEM rating. Rooms can be described as modern and fresh. The design is rooted heavily in Hawaiian nature patterns and is reflected in everything from the coffee bean fabric on the chairs to lava pattern on the hallway carpets. This design works for us and it has modern touches we like, such as hand-held shower heads and MP3 adapters. Microwaves may be rented for $10/day. Rooms either have two queen beds or one king. The renovation did away with connecting rooms. The staff is really proud of the currect look and shows it with *a lot* of aloha toward guests. The infinity pool is very inviting, but we wish they had a few more umbrellas around it. More retail space was planned at press time. Parking is $12; local calls and toll free calls are $1.

King Kam is the center of the universe every October when the Ironman Triathlon takes place. Most of the athletes stay here, as do many from the television crews, and rooms are hard to get then. Rooms (348–380 sq. ft.) are $369–$534, suites (837 sq. ft.) are $919. Discounts are easy to get. When booking rooms, some can be had for $149 and up. At that price this would also be a SOLID GOLD VALUE.

Hale Kona Kai
(800) 421–3696 or (808) 329–2155
75-5870 Kahakai Rd.
39 units, pool, a/c, elevator, free wi-fi in rooms and by pool, BBQ, free calls to U.S. mainland and Canada. Broken into two wings **SOLID GOLD VALUE** (the short wing and the long wing) with no grounds. Rooms are

See all Web reviews at: www.hawaiirevealed.com

pleasant and clean, and the living rooms and bedrooms both look out on the water from ocean-facing units. In ocean-facing units in the long wing, you will not get tired of watching the turtles in the tide-pools below. Many units have been updated. The pool's so close to the ocean you'll get sprayed on big surf days. Rooms ending with 07 and 08 have bedrooms that face each other, affording less privacy. The SOLID GOLD VALUE is because of their stellar ocean proximity. Definitely get an ocean-facing room here. 1/1s (648–696 sq. ft.) are $150–$195. (Around $30 extra gets you a pretty nice wraparound lanai.) Lots of repeat guests here. 3-night minimum.

Holualoa Inn
(800) 392–1812 or (808) 324–1121
76-5932 Mamalahoa Hwy, Holualoa
WEB REVIEW 💎

Kahalu'u Bay Villas
(800) 367–5168 or (808) 329–6438
78-6715 Alii Dr.
WEB REVIEW

Kahalu'u Beach Villas
(866) 456–4252 or (808) 331–8878
78-6721 Alii Dr.
WEB REVIEW

Kanaloa at Kona
(800) 688–7444 or (808) 322–9625
(800) 745–5662 or (808) 326–9075
78-261 Manukai St.
WEB REVIEW 💎

Keauhou Akahi
(800) 367–5168 or (808) 329–6438
(800) 799–5662 or (808) 334–1199
78-7030 Alii Dr.

48 units, pool, washer/dryer in unit, BBQ. Fairly quiet, small and tidy. The grounds are particularly fragrant—kudos to the gardeners. 1/2s (750 sq. ft.) are $99–$127. If you see any units referred to as 2/2s, they're just 1/2s with alcoves converted to a second bedroom. 3-night minimum.

Keauhou Kona Surf & Racquet Club
(800) 799–5662 or (808) 334–1199
(866) 456–4252 or (808) 331–8878
78-6800 Alii Dr.
WEB REVIEW

Keauhou Palena
(800) 799–5662 or (808) 334–1199
78-7054 Kamehameha III Rd.
WEB REVIEW

Keauhou Punahele
(800) 367–5168 or (808) 329–6438
78-7070 Alii Dr.
WEB REVIEW

Keauhou Resort
(800) 367–5168 or (808) 329–6438
78-7039 Kamehameha III Rd.
WEB REVIEW

See all Web reviews at: www.hawaiirevealed.com

Kona Alii
(877) 336–6751 or (808) 327–6751
(800) 367–5168 or (808) 329–6438
75-5782 Kuakini Hwy.
WEB REVIEW

Kona Bali Kai
(800) 367–5004 or (808) 329–9381
(800) 367–5168 or (808) 329–6438
76-6246 Alii Dr.
WEB REVIEW

Kona By The Sea
(877) 997–6667 or (808) 327–2300
75-6106 Alii Dr.
WEB REVIEW

Kona Coast Resort
(800) 799–5662 or (808) 334–1199
78-6842 Alii Dr.
WEB REVIEW

Kona Hotel
(808) 324–1155
76-5908 Mamalahoa Hwy, Holualoa
WEB REVIEW

Kona Islander Inn
(800) 244–4752 or (808) 329–3333
75-5776 Kuakini Hwy
WEB REVIEW

Kona Isle
(800) 367–5168 or (808) 329–6438
75-6100 Alii Dr.
WEB REVIEW

Kona Magic Sands
(800) 244–4752 or (808) 329–3333
(800) 367–5168 or (808) 329–6438
77-6452 Alii Dr.
37 rooms, pool, a/c in *some*, BBQ. You can see and hear the ocean right from your bed. Units are *very* small (450 sq. ft.)—a studio with a kitchenette. The bed area is converted from the lanai in

some rooms, so you may just have a railing outside your sliding glass door. Upper floors have better views. Units ending 01–04 have **SOLID GOLD VALUE** extra large 250 sq. ft. lanais, but may get noise if the restaurant below is open. Units ending in 01 can see (and hear) the people on the beach next door, and *they* can see *you*. Rooms can vary a lot, so ask for a remodeled unit. The prices have gone up and down like the stock market and are currently $115–$160—a good deal. The second agent listed has some even *cheaper* prices. 3-night minimum.

Kona Makai
(800) 367–5168 or (808) 329–6438
(877) 336–6751 or (808) 327–6751
75-6026 Alii Dr.
WEB REVIEW

Kona Nalu
(800) 367–5168 or (808) 329–6438
76-6212 Alii Dr.
WEB REVIEW ◆

Kona Pacific
(877) 336–6751 or (808) 327–6751
(800) 244–4752 or (808) 329–3333
75-5865 Walua Rd.
WEB REVIEW

Kona Reef
(800) 367–5004 or (808) 329–2959
(800) 367–5168 or (808) 329–6438
75-5888 Alii Dr.
130 units, a/c, pool, spa, elevator, wash-

See all Web reviews at: www.hawaiirevealed.com

er/dryer in unit, free wi-fi in rooms and by pool, computer kisok in office, BBQs. Buildings A and D are fairly quiet (except for the sound of the ocean), but units next to Alii Drive get a lot of road noise. The rooms are not bad, not great. If you're gonna stay here, try to get a corner unit—especially building in A. Although there's a/c in most, it's not in the bedroom, and it may get hot in there (and not the way you intend). If you need a room that's elevator-accessible, you want Building F. That's because in the other buildings, during a fit of design goofiness, the elevator only stops *between* floors, and there are a lot stairs here. Your other option is a ground floor unit in Building A or D for access without stairs. 1/1s (611–651 sq. ft.) are $119–$330. 2/2 units (905–1,120 sq. ft.) are $249–$525. Those RACK rates feel high, but few pay them since discounts are as easy to get as a sunburn. 2-night minimum. The second set of phone numbers has overall cheaper prices and a 3-night minimum.

Kona Seaside Hotel
(800) 367–7000 or (808) 329–2455
75-5646 Palani Rd.
WEB REVIEW

Kona Seaspray
(808) 322–2403
78-6665 Alii Dr.
WEB REVIEW

Kona Tiki Hotel
(808) 329–1425
75-5968 Alii Dr.
WEB REVIEW

Makolea
(800) 367–5168 or (808) 329–6438
78-216 Makolea St.
WEB REVIEW

Manago Hotel
(808) 323–2642
82-6155 Mamalahoa Hwy, Capt. Cook
WEB REVIEW

Na Hale O'Keauhou
(800) 367–5168 or (808) 329–6438
78-6833 Alii Dr.
WEB REVIEW

Pineapple Park Kona
(877) 800–3800 or (808) 323–2224
81-6363 Mamalahoa Hwy, Kealakekua
WEB REVIEW

Royal Kona Resort
(800) 222–5642 or (808) 329–3111
75-5852 Alii Dr.
WEB REVIEW

Royal Sea-Cliff Resort
(800) 688–7444 or (808) 329–8021
75-6040 Alii Dr.

See all Web reviews at: www.hawaiirevealed.com

154 units, tennis court, a/c, free room safe, 2 pools, spa, washer/dryer in unit, free wi-fi in rooms and by pools, business center, daily housekeeping service upon request for an extra fee, BBQs, local calls are $.75. The resort is run similarly to a hotel, though units are individually owned and half are timeshare. Condos are fairly large. Note from the aerial photo that the middle rooms, though many are called "Partial Ocean View," have poor ocean views. (Think of the resort as a tree and try to get a room on a branch, not the trunk.) Also, since the floors are stair-stepped, upper-floor units look down on the lanais of the floors beneath them. So behave yourself on the lanais, unless you're at the top. Some of the rooms could use some updating, others have been updated, but none were in poor condition and all were very clean. Be sure to bring your sunglasses as the reflection off the white paint on the buildings can be blinding. They have lots of packages available, so you shouldn't end up paying RACK rates. There is an Aloha Party once a week with pupus. Studios (600–650 sq. ft.) are $239–$259, 1/1 units (850–925 sq. ft.) are $269–$409, 2/2 units (1,100–1,300 sq. ft.) are $309–$449. 2-night minimum.

Sea Village
(800) 367–5168 or (808) 329–6438
(877) 322–2407 or (808) 329–2140
75-6002 Alii Dr.

WEB REVIEW

Sheraton Kona Resort & Spa
(888) 488–3535 or (808) 930–4900
78-128 Ehukai St.
509 rooms, pool, 2 spas, 3 lighted tennis courts, free 24-hour fitness room, room service, valet parking, 4 restaurants, 3 lounges, empty fridge, 2 shops, 8 conference rooms, free 24-hour business center, wi-fi throughout resort, coin-op laundry room, coffee makers in room with free coffee daily, free laptop room safes, wedding coordinator, wedding chapel, day spa, lu'au. It's best described as sophisticated, understated, islandy, and a bit stark with *lots* of concrete, but it embraces its oceanside location. (But there is no sand beach here, and they could use more plants in the interior areas.) They cater to families here, and it's reflected in their multi-level water feature with 200-foot waterslide, waterfall and pool that meanders into the atrium of the hotel. The fitness room (for those who can't bear to be on vacation without working out) is state of the art with a killer view of the ocean. The teen center gets very busy and has foosball, air hockey, ping-pong, widescreen TVs, game consoles and more. They have a lot of cultural activities on site. They have a good wedding infrastructure, including an oceanfront chapel and licensing on site. Couples can get a private ocean view massage and Jacuzzi in the day spa. It also has a "salt room," which we've *never* seen before. It's just a room where they blow microscopic Himalayan salt on you (or you *could* just sit next to the ocean).

There is a *mandatory* resort fee of $30 that covers self-parking (valet is $7 extra), Internet, local calls and 30-minute international calls, a trolley that runs guests all the way into Kona Town and some other items. They had a REAL GEM rating in our last edition, but we felt the staff was not attentive enough on this

See all Web reviews at: www.hawaiirevealed.com

visit, and our readers agreed. Room updates completed in 2012 are fresh but not remarkable and included carpets, "Sweet Sleeper" beds, painting, bath tiles and fixtures. Rooms (450 sq. ft.) are $199–$279, suites (925–3,000 sq. ft.) are $950–$2,550. Their partial ocean view category is worth the upgrade from mountain view.

Uncle Billy's Kona Bay Hotel
(800) 367–5102 or (808) 329–1393
75-5739 Alii Dr.
WEB REVIEW

White Sands Village
(800) 367–5168 or (808) 329–6438
77-6469 Alii Dr.
WEB REVIEW

HILO AREA

Arnott's Lodge
(808) 969–7097
98 Apapane Rd.
WEB REVIEW

Country Club Hawai'i Condo Hotel
(866) 935–7171 or (808) 935–7171
121 Banyan Dr.

147 rooms, free wi-fi in some rooms on lobby side or in lobby, lanais on most (except room numbers ending in 9, 17, 10 and 22), microwave and empty fridge, coffee maker (free coffee in lobby), washer/dryer in some others use coin-op laundry, daily **SOLID GOLD VALUE** housekeeping only if you pay the daily rate, and local calls are an extra 52¢. So what are they—a hotel or a condo? They're a condotel with rooms owned by individuals, so expect wide variations among the rooms. There are also many long-term renters/owners here. Their lease on the land expires in 2015, so things may change. Some rooms have been updated and are acceptable, but *not all*, so keep looking until you find one with surroundings you like. The day staff has improved here and shows more aloha than in the past. Rooms (around 300 sq. ft.) are $74–$94, kitchenettes (add a hot plate) are also $74. Cheaper weekly rates available, without housekeeping service, make oceanfront rooms $75. We're giving it a SOLID GOLD VALUE for this edition based on getting a decent room and view for your money.

Dolphin Bay Hotel
(877) 935–1466 or (808) 935–1466
333 Iliahi St.
WEB REVIEW

Hilo Bay Hostel
(808) 933–2771
101 Waianuenue Ave.
WEB REVIEW

Hilo Hawaiian Hotel
(800) 367–5004 or (808) 935–9361
71 Banyan Dr.
WEB REVIEW

Hilo Naniloa Hotel
(866) 940–2782 or (808) 969–3333
93 Banyan Dr.
WEB REVIEW

See all Web reviews at: www.hawaiirevealed.com

Hilo Seaside Hotel
(800) 560–5557 or (808) 935–0821
126 Banyan Way

135 rooms, restaurant, pool, coin-op laundry, no elevator, empty fridge, wi-fi or use kiosk in lobby, coffee maker with free coffee daily, lanais on deluxe rooms overlooking koi pond, free safety deposit boxes at front desk, coin-op laundry. Very clean, simple (but *very* dated) rooms across from the Ice Pond. Very warm staff, well-maintained building and grounds with the only pool in Hilo that felt desirable to us and *included* lounge chairs. Rooms facing that pool (interior side of property—#16–29) are preferable since they're away from the street noise on this busy corner. As a second choice, get a room facing the koi pond. Rooms (around 350 sq. ft.) are $130–$150 and include a full breakfast. You will usually get a discount, and if you get a room for $119, it's a SOLID GOLD VALUE.

Hilo Tropical Gardens
(808) 217–9650
1477 Kalanianaole Ave.
WEB REVIEW

The Inn at Kulaniapia Falls
(866) 935–6789 or (808) 935–6789
100 Kulaniapia Dr.
WEB REVIEW ◆

The Palms Cliff House Inn
(866) 963–6076 or (808) 963–6076
28-3514 Mamalahoa Hwy, Honomu
WEB REVIEW ◆

Shipman House B&B Inn
(800) 627–8447 or (808) 934–8002
131 Kaiulani St.
WEB REVIEW ◆

Uncle Billy's Hilo Bay Hotel
(800) 367–5102 or (808) 935–0861
87 Banyan Dr.

144 rooms, pool, restaurant, free wi-fi in lobby and rooms, or you can use lobby kiosk for a fee, coin-op laundry, empty fridge, coffee makers with free coffee daily in superior and oceanview rooms, free safety deposit boxes at front desk. Owned by the same family as the Kona Bay Hotel and built in 1964 with wings added until the 1970s. Rooms are decent-sized but looked old, dated and worn on our last visit. This may be due to their land lease expiring in 2015, so things could change. The grounds and common areas were also in need of care—especially the pool deck, which has no lounge chairs. Free "light" continental breakfast (toast, store-bought muffins, papaya and coffee) is included. The kitchenette wing has no elevator for some reason. Avoid standard rooms. If you go oceanfront, get a wrap-around lanai. Rooms (approx. 550–600 sq. ft.) are $117–$144, kitchenettes (approx. 600 sq. ft.) are $139. Discounts are usually available.

See all Web reviews at: www.hawaiirevealed.com

Wild Ginger Inn & Hostel
(800) 882–1887 or (808) 935–5556
100 Puueo St.

WEB REVIEW

VOLCANO VILLAGE

Please visit our website where we include aerial photos of Volcano Village accommodations.

Chalet Kilauea Collection
(800) 937–7786 or (808) 967–7786
19-4178 Wright Rd.
6 rooms, shared lanais on some, free wi-fi and computers, hot tub, daily housekeeping. Built in 1942, this inn is part of a larger collection

SOLID GOLD VALUE of properties that have been through lots of changes over the years, sometimes good and sometimes not so good. For this edition we found current management really putting in the effort with *some* pleasing results, others not so much. The Continental Suite is a very romantic bridal suite with double shower in the bathroom. The Treehouse Suite is two-story; a wooden spiral staircase leads to the bedroom with its dreamy view. The bathroom has a Jacuzzi bathtub and a *fireplace*! The bungalow is the most private. Though they have toned down some of the extra touches, they still offer an optional *continental* breakfast for around $6 and afternoon tea in the common area. The grounds are lush with a large koi pond. Low ceilings in the main house make rooms feel smaller, but helps keep them warmer on cold nights (which happens at this altitude). All rooms have TVs and DVD players (rentals in lobby), some rooms have LED fireplace "artwork," which feels a *bit* out of place—just for mood, really. Rooms (275–500 sq. ft.) are $110–$185. Prices have come down *a lot* since our last review and are more in keeping with room decor which varies considerably.

They also have other properties off-site. Volcano Hale has 6 *small* simple rooms with TVs, free wi-fi and computers, shared remodeled baths, shared kitchen and living area, and housekeeping service every third day for $45–$60 (a very good deal for those on a budget). The 5-room Lokahi Lodge is also a good deal at $95–$130 and has larger rooms (most were updated, so ask for one) with baths, microwave, fridge, hot tub, free wi-fi and computers in common area, housekeeping every third day. All renters may enjoy facilities at the Chalet, like the afternoon tea and breakfast. These two off-site properties earn them a SOLID GOLD VALUE for this edition.

Holo Holo In
(808) 967–7950
19-4036 Kalani Honua Rd.
2 private rooms (with bath), 2 semi-private rooms (shared bath), 12 dorm beds, shared baths and kitchen, TV room, pay-per-load laundry, free wi-fi and a computer, no phones, heated rooms. This was built back in the mid-1980s and is still owned by the same family. The property is not as lush as others in area and feels more utilitarian and a bit run-down. They close daily from 11 a.m. to 4:30 p.m. to clean and ask guests to leave unless the weather is terrible outside. The hostel provides sheets and bedding, but BYOT (bring your own towel or rent one for a buck). There is no place to lock up valuables. The dorms and semi-private rooms are old, but the private rooms are fairly new and clean. Unless your budget puts you in the dorms, you'll get more for your money elsewhere. Private rooms are $75 per couple, semi-private rooms are $60 per couple. Some of those accommodate up to 5 family members for an $18 extra per person

See all Web reviews at: www.hawaiirevealed.com

charge. Dorm beds are $24 (there are no co-ed dorms).

Kilauea Lodge
(808) 967–7366
19-3948 Old Volcano Rd.

12 rooms, coffee makers with free coffee daily, free wi-fi, no TV or phones (except

in off-site properties), lanai on one, restaurant, centrally heated, fireplaces in some, hot tub **A REAL GEM** (available to guests at any of their properties). Opened in 1938 as a YMCA youth camp, this quaint lodge was converted in 1986 by Albert and Lorna Jeyte. (He was a make-up artist on *Magnum P.I.*) The whole thing is very well done and lovingly maintained. There are different styles of rooms, such as the Honeymoon Deluxe (very romantic), Hale Maluna building (snug rooms with fireplaces and incredible skylights in the bathrooms), Hale Aloha building with larger rooms and a common sitting room. They also have four off-site homes—three 2-bedroom units and one 1-bedroom unit that all have full kitchens. Our favorite off-site house was the 2-bedroom Ola'a Plantation, which was *utterly* charming but only has one bathroom. All the grounds are lush and well-tended. The staff is top-notch. Full breakfast is included in the price of all rooms/houses. Rooms (225–325 sq. ft.) are $190–$205. 1/1 cottage without kitchen (400 sq. ft.) is $205–$245. Homes (750–1,700 sq. ft.) are $220–$295.

Volcano House
(866) 536–7972 or (808) 756–9625
Hawai'i Volcanoes National Park

33 rooms, restaurant, bar, daily housekeeping, lanais on ground floor units (annex building only), 2 shops, free laptop room safes, coffee maker with free coffee daily, free local calls, heated rooms (some also have electric fireplace), free wi-fi resort-wide, connecting rooms

available. This hotel is located on the rim of Kilauea Caldera inside Hawai'i Volcanoes **A REAL GEM** National Park. It was closed in 2010 while they waited for the best concession bidder and reopened in 2013. Before that closure it was the longest "continually running" hotel in the state. Volcano House opened across the street in 1846 (which pre-dates the national park) as just a 12x18-foot hut without anyone hosting it. Over the years more buildings were added, eventually totaling 100 rooms. Sadly, the hotel burned to the ground in 1940 (except the 1877 building, which now houses Volcano Art Center) and was rebuilt only a *year* later on its current land. (We need to find out the name of *that* contractor.) The new building was supposed to be temporary, but the park decided it was good enough, and so it stands today. The hotel is a protected park concessionaire and though our expectations were low in the past, we're pleased to say that this hotel, like the park itself, is well-run. The 2013 renovations restored it to the style it had in the 1940s (but with updated amenities, of course). The rooms all have new bathrooms with showers only. They are bright and clean. They have phones and radios, but no TVs. At night most people either head down to the lava flows (Pele permitting), relax at the bar or just curl up by the fire in the lobby fireplace. Some of the rooms (especially 29 and 33) have excellent crater views. The restaurant gets unbelievably busy at lunch but quiets down more at night. The food is very good; see our review in ISLAND DINING. Rooms (200 sq. ft.) are $285, deluxe rooms (300 sq. ft.) are $385. No minimum stay. They also operate 10 cabins for $55 at Namakani Paio.

See all Web reviews at: www.hawaiirevealed.com

Volcano Inn
(800) 628–3876 or (808) 967–7773
19-3820 Old Volcano Rd.
16 rooms (9 are off-site but nearby), 3 hot tubs, shared lanai, TVs, free wi-fi, hot breakfast available for extra, common room with **SOLID GOLD VALUE** fridge, microwave, free coffee/tea (all day in main building) and computer, no daily housekeeping if you book at a discounted rate. Started in 1989, this is an excellent choice in Volcano. Don't confuse this with other properties with *similar* names. The grounds are lush. The rooms are not overly Hawaiian in decor or updated, but they are *very* clean. Though the rooms vary greatly in size and amenities at the different sites, we didn't see any we would *not* stay in from the smallest budget room to the largest family room. All have dehumidifiers, and family rooms have gas fireplaces. The family rooms and corner window rooms (off-site) also have kitchenettes. You can enjoy their hot tubs 24 hours a day in cozy areas of the gardens surrounded by ferns, lights and Hawaiian music CDs. Great staff. Rooms (100–960 sq. ft.) are $99–$149. Discounts on longer stays. What a deal!

Volcano Village Lodge
(808) 985–9500
19-4183 Road E
5 rooms, hot tub, free wi-fi and computer in lobby, coffee makers with free coffee daily, breakfast included, empty fridge, microwave, TVs (only for DVD viewing from **A REAL GEM** their free library), iPod docks, courtesy phone in lobby (your cell may not work), daily housekeeping. What a find! This property is small, just over 1 acre, and was originally built as an artist's workshop, but converted in 2006 with buildings added over time. The stand-alone rooms are set amid a very lush,

dense tropical forest of native plantings. Each feels very private and intimate. All are lavishly furnished in different themes with expensive bedding and fireplaces. Fresh flowers, bathrobes, slippers, flashlights, beach mats and even flip-flops are supplied. Breakfast is placed in your room the previous afternoon, so you may enjoy it at your leisure and usually includes a hot dish that may be warmed in your microwave along with the usual fruit, coffee, bagels, etc. They have a masseuse on call. Great staff. Perfect for a romantic getaway. Rooms (300–600 sq. ft.) are $280–$375. 2-night minimum.

WAIMEA

Please visit our website where we include aerial photos of all Waimea accommodations. Things get chilly up here at 2,500 feet.

The **Jacaranda Inn** (808) 885–8813 at 65-1444 Kawaihae Rd. Built in 1897 as a Parker Ranch manager's house, it's been converted into a charming inn. Think of it as **A REAL GEM** the kind of inn that Mark Twain would have stayed at a century ago in a beautiful setting. There are 8 different rooms and a cottage that backs up to a stream, each with its own theme in purple (the color of jacaranda trees) and quaintly furnished, with free wi-fi in main house. Some rooms have TVs, but none has a phone—one is available in main house. No guest laundry. Each has a private bath and entrance. Most bathrooms have double Jacuzzi tubs—*very* romantic. Rooms (454–665 sq. ft.) are $129–$199, 3/3 cottage with kitchen (1,695 sq. ft.) is $250–$450 for 2 up to 6 people. A restaurant on site was planned at press time. Best choice in Waimea.

There's also the 30-room **Kamuela Inn** (800) 555–8968 or (808) 885–4243

See all Web reviews at: www.hawaiirevealed.com

at 65-1300 Kawaihae Road. This is a quaint inn that needs updating, but new managers are slowly making changes—fresh paint, some new furnishings, free wi-fi throughout and a coin-op laundry. The setting is well-groomed, the staff is very helpful, but the small rooms (*slightly* larger in newer wing) are *real* variable in terms of quality. If they are not full, keep asking to look at rooms until you find one that suits you. Lanais on some, TVs, connecting rooms available, no phones (pay phone available) and continental breakfast included. Rooms (135–319 sq. ft.) are $69–$94, kitchenettes (362 sq. ft.) are $109, suites (362–969 sq. ft.) for $119–$189.

Lastly, **Waimea Country Lodge** (800) 367–5004 or (808) 885–4100 at 65-1210 Lindsey Road. 21 good-sized rooms, hi-speed Internet access ($10). It was looking *very* tired and smelled moldy on our visit. One good feature; newer granite kitchens in kitchenette rooms. Rooms (309–422 sq. ft.) are $79–$205, kitchenettes (376–422 sq. ft.) are $98–$165. No guest laundry. The hotel was sold at press time, so things *may* change—we hope.

NORTHERN TIP OF THE ISLAND

Please visit our website to view the aerial photos of all accommodations on the northern tip of the island.

In Hawi, the **Kohala Village Inn** (808) 889–0404 at 55-514 Hawi Road is an excellent value. It's a quaint, simple, old 19-room inn with TVs and no a/c, free wi-fi in lobby, daily housekeeping upon request, some rooms have a fridge, no place to secure your valuables. No phones, but they'll take messages. Rooms are small and basic but *very* clean. It's likely that if you have noisy neighbors, you'll hear 'em. If you

need a desk, ask for a room with a table. Back building rooms are quietest. Rooms (200–400 sq. ft.) are $75–$95. Suites (420 sq. ft.) are $120–$140.

In Kapa'au, the **Kohala Club Hotel** (808) 889–6793 at 54-3793 Akoni Pule Hwy was built in the late 1800s as an English gentleman's club. Left in disrepair, it has been restored by its present owners (who are very nice). Consider this a historic experience, *not* a lavish one. 8 rooms with TVs, DVD players, no a/c or phones, but you can use the lobby phone, BBQ and lots of outdoor space to wander. Small rooms (110–143 sq. ft.) are $52–$81 for the cottage for up to 4 people. Tony, the small poi dog, will greet you. Cash only.

Also in Kapa'au is **Hawaii Island Retreat at Ahu Pohaku Ho'omaluhia** (808) 889–6336 at 54-250 Lokahi Rd. This place was lovingly finished by the owners in 2010 as a luxury **A REAL GEM** retreat for those wishing to get away from it all and find themselves. Built on 50 acres high on a cliff overlooking the ocean, it houses 10 rooms, 7 yurts, saline pool, spa, health spa, fitness room, infrared sauna, 4 meeting rooms, 24-hour room service, light meal available (great for late check-ins), valet-only laundry, free wi-fi, no a/c. The inn was started by the same woman who opened the Spa Without Walls at the Fairmont Orchid. Even some of the antiques from that hotel adorn the lobby and rooms. They grow and manage practically everything they serve at their restaurant—from herbs to vegetables to chicken eggs to goat's cheese (which is *yummy,* by the way). They pride themselves on being organic, green and sustainable, from the solar panels to composting to the windmill. A unique and hearty breakfast is included. They will also do lunch and din-

See all Web reviews at: www.hawaiirevealed.com

ner, if arranged in advance. Fabulous, helpful staff. You can really tell they enjoy making guests feel happy and welcome. Basically, they are there for *your* needs—if you want to be left alone, so be it. If you want a historic tour of the grounds, facial and massage, they'll arrange that, too. The pool is a tranquil infinity edge with a nearby private massage hut. The antique-filled rooms have all the modern amenities you want, like a deep soaking tub, separate shower (some double showers) and expensive bedding, but no phones or TVs. (They do have CD players with iPod docks.) The yurts (round tent structures) have 2 beds, toilet, and sink, but showers are at the nearby showerhouse, which is private and nicer than many bathrooms we have seen elsewhere. (Think of the yurts as upscale camping.) Overall, this is a tranquil, peaceful place and a great choice for a family reunion, wedding or small group retreat. You may not want to leave; we never do. Rooms (375–450 sq. ft.) are $425–$500, yurts (200 sq. ft.) are $195.

SOUTHEAST PART OF THE ISLAND

Located near Punalu'u Beach is **Colony One at SeaMountain** (800) 444–6633 or (808) 928–6200 at 95-788 Ninole Loop Rd. This property on the south side of the island is a *long* way from other towns. Please visit our website for an aerial photo. 76 units, pool, spa, free wi-fi in rooms, BBQ, washer/dryer in most or coin-op laundry. The condo complex is mostly timeshares (though you won't find any salesmen around) in the heart of SeaMountain, a very remote region in the southern part of the island. The grounds are pleasant and units, though not remarkable, are clean and consistent in decor through the above agent. Think of this as an alterna-

tive place to stay if you want to explore Hawai'i Volcanoes National Park (28 miles away) but still want to stay near the shoreline where it's more tropical (though the units are not beachside). It's quiet and peaceful. Lots of stairs at this property, mostly in the units themselves. The prices used to be very good, but the local management office closed and now the prices feel high to us. You may find owners renting units at better prices, but the decor/quality will vary. Closest (not *cheapest*) grocery shopping is in HOVE. Studios (475 sq. ft.) are $93–$142, 1/1 units (700 sq. ft.) are $113–$171, 2/2s (1,000 sq. ft.) are $122–$213. Prices include tax. 2- or 3-night minimum avoids cleaning fee.

HONOKA'A

About 8 miles from Waipi'o Valley is **Hotel Honoka'a Club** (800) 808–0678 or (808) 775–0678 at 45-3480 Mamane St. 18 rooms (upstairs rooms are best with TVs and ocean views—no phones), free wi-fi. This place is more than 100 years old and some common areas look like not much has changed since then or in the many years we have been reviewing them. Rooms are also feeling worn. They have new low-flow toilets, but the showers need replacing. This is *not* a party place and you *probably* will hear your neighbor. No laundry facilities. For the hostel part, no lockers, but they provide sheets and towels. The breakfast is *very* basic, so skip it and head up the road. Rooms (approx. 150 sq. ft.) are $70–$119; suites (approx. 250 sq. ft.) are $135–$145. On the hostel side: Beds are $25 per person, small private room with single bed is $35. Taxes included in rates. Please visit our website for an aerial photo.

INDEX

Dining Index on page 244, Where to Stay Index on page 282.

INDEX

Dining Index on page 244, Where to Stay Index on page 282.

INDEX 309

Dining Index on page 244, Where to Stay Index on page 282.

INDEX

Dining Index on page 244, Where to Stay Index on page 282.

INDEX

311

Dining Index on page 244, Where to Stay Index on page 282.

Your Vacation from **Start** to *Amazing!*

Brutally honest, anonymous reviews. No paid advertisements accepted—ever.

Start with our **best-selling guidebooks & eBooks.**
*Trusted for over **20 years** by millions of travelers.*

Companion website with hundreds of free unbiased reviews.
Easy online resort bookings with great rates.

User-friendly apps know where you're at, even when you don't.
Find all the hidden gems even without a cellular signal.
GPS locations, roads and hiking trails all personally verified.

"A must for any serious visitor."
—The New York Times

"The best guidebook. Every nook and cranny is explored by long-time residents."
—Conde Nast Traveler

"...the authors are continually updating the content with new gems, taking into account reader feedback."
—The Discovery Channel

Look for our books, eBooks and apps in your favorite bookstore or online.
Visit our website for recent updates, aerial photos and unbiased reviews, booking information, local events, weather information and so much more to plan and have your best vacation—*ever!*

www.hawaiirevealed.com • aloha@wizardpub.com
Follow us on Facebook & Twitter @hawaiirevealed

WIZARD PUBLICATIONS INC *Believable Guides for Unbelievable Vacations*®